Jesse Livermore Boy Plunger

The Myrtle Press
London

TOM RUBYTHON

Jesse Livermore Boy Plunger

The Man Who Sold America Short in 1929

FOREWORD BY PAUL TUDOR JONES

also by Tom Rubython

Life of O'Reilly
- the biography of Tony O'Reilly

The Rich 500
- the 500 Richest people in Britain

The Life of Senna
- the biography of Ayrton Senna

Dog Story - An Anthology
- the life and death of our best friends

Shunt
- the biography of James Hunt

And God Created Burton
- the biography of Richard Burton

In the Name of Glory
- the greatest ever sporting duel

For John Rubython,
the master of his own game
for over 50 years

First published in the USA and Canada in 2015
by The Myrtle Press

1 3 5 7 9 10 8 6 4 2

Library of Congress Cataloguing-in-Publication Data

ISBN: 978 - 0 - 9906199 - 1 - 8

Typset in ITC Garamond by: CBA Harlestone
Reproduction by: Fresh Vision, London

Printed and bound in England by
CPI Group (UK) Ltd, Croydon
CR0 4YY
United Kingdom

Published by:
The Myrtle Press
4 North Street
Bere Regis
Dorset, BH20 7LA
United Kingdom
www.themyrtlepress.com

Distributed in the USA and Canada by:
National Book Network
4501 Forbes Boulevard, Suite 200, Lanham, MD 20706
Tel: 001 301-459-3366
www.nbnbooks.com

Contents

ACKNOWLEDGEMENTS   xi
Tom Rubython

PREFACE   xiii
Tom Rubython

FOREWORD   xv
Paul Tudor Jones

PROLOGUE   xvii
Jesse Livermore

CHAPTER 1: Death by His Own Hand   1
The final meltdown

CHAPTER 2: The Story Begins   9
An unpromising childhood

CHAPTER 3: The First Trade   15
Paine Webber in Boston

CHAPTER 4: Bucket Shop Heaven   29
Makes first fortune

CHAPTER 5: The Bucket Shop Phenomenon   39
Gambling on shares transfixes America

CHAPTER 6: Marriage and Move to New York   47
The boy becomes a man

CHAPTER 7: Down and Out   57
Back to the bucket shops

CHAPTER 8: Do or Die: Back to Wall Street   67
A re-learning process

CHAPTER 9: San Francisco Earthquake   77
$250,000 profit in a few days

CHAPTER 10: A Period of Self Analysis   83
Fundamental change in outlook

CHAPTER 11: Prelude to a Profit   89
A bearish state of mind

CHAPTER 12: Stock Market Meltdown   103
Credit crisis threatens America

Contents

CHAPTER 13: Enter Morgan   109
Livermore makes $1 million in a day

CHAPTER 14: The Corn Trade Experiment   131
First serious trades in commodities

CHAPTER 15: The Life of Riley   137
Buys yacht - luxury lifestyle begins

CHAPTER 16: Newspaper Notoriety   143
Lady Luck rescues 'Cotton King'

CHAPTER 17: Under the Influence: Cotton Fiasco   149
Seduced by Teddy Price

CHAPTER 18: Ultimate Betrayal   159
The treachery of Teddy Price

CHAPTER 19: Six Lean Years   165
Going slowly nowhere - The lost period

CHAPTER 20: Official Bankruptcy   173
The ultimate humiliation

CHAPTER 21: Dramatic Return to Form   181
Makes $5 million, pays off debts

CHAPTER 22: War and a Coffee Scam   193
Roasters outwit Livermore

CHAPTER 23: The Great Escape   201
Margin and short selling under threat

CHAPTER 24: Divorce, Marriage, Family   207
Dottie steals his heart

CHAPTER 25: The Effortless Millions   215
Deals galore as he makes $15 million

CHAPTER 26: Respectability is Bought   229
Great Neck house purchase

CHAPTER 27: The Piggly Wiggly Affair   235
Another day, another controversy

CHAPTER 28: Legendary Status is Conferred   245
Publication of fictional biography

Contents

CHAPTER 29: Big Offices, Big Staff & Big Money   251
Move into the big time of Wall Street

CHAPTER 30: Ups and Downs   265
Battle for supremacy with Arthur Cutten

CHAPTER 31: Manipulating a Profit   271
A fortune from Freeport Texas

CHAPTER 32: Good Times at Great Neck   277
The halcyon years

CHAPTER 33: Shenanigans at Great Neck   285
The bad times start

CHAPTER 34: Prelude to a National Disaster   295
America binges on shares

CHAPTER 35: Seven Incredible Days   307
Livermore makes $100 million in a week

CHAPTER 36: Personal Disaster   321
Home life falls apart

CHAPTER 37: Official Bankruptcy No.2   333
$100 million seemingly disappears

CHAPTER 38: Personal Tragedy   339
Ex-wife shoots eldest son

CHAPTER 39: Partial Recovery   347
The good times are over

CHAPTER 40: Reflections in a Book   351
Understanding the good times

CHAPTER 41: Reflections on a Life   357
Jesse Livermore's final reckoning

CHAPTER 42: Postscript   365
Chaos is left behind

"Livermore is the best man on the
stock market tape the speculative
world has ever known"

Jack Morgan
October 1929

Acknowledgements

*B*oy *Plunger* has been in the works for more than 18 years, ever since I first learned of the existence of Jesse Livermore. But, before attempting it, it was necessary to wait patiently until Livermore's fictional biography *Reminiscences of a Stock Operator* came out of copyright at the end of 2013. *Reminiscences* is a remarkable book by a remarkable journalist, Edwin Lefèvre. And in 2010 it was made even more remarkable by Jon Markman with an annotated edition that sought to explain the background to Livermore's stories, something Markman did remarkably well – thanks Jon.

The aim of this biography was simply to recreate an accurate account of the life of Jesse Livermore. Now a confession – it's only about 90 per cent accurate. It's best to be honest and, when recreating events that are 130 years old, that is about the most that can be expected of any biographer. I have done my best to check and recheck the truth of events that happened so long ago but people remember things in many different ways and, more often than not, people misremember. And these misrememberances, once committed to print, can be repeated many, many times.

There is no great army of people behind this book, just a small bunch of talented professionals, most of whom I have worked with for many more years than I care to remember.

I have to thank David Peett for the inspiration. We are both disciples of Livermore. David is a man who spends his life poring over statistics in the British Library in London and trying to predict the rises and falls of the stock market: something he does remarkably accurately but, as he will only too readily admit, that is only just a small part of the game of being a consistently successful investor.

Ania Grzesik is responsible for the design and the layout of this book. Laying out and being in charge of a book's production is a particular challenge. So many books are simply thrown together any-old-how, and I hope you will agree that this is not one of them.

And thanks to Kiran Toor who has sub edited most of my books. That is also not always an easy task, and Kiran copes better than most. Also to Jez Douglas for lovingly tending to the old black and white photographs that appear in and enhance this book.

Paul Tudor Jones, a man who really understands money – how to make it and what to usefully do with it when it has been made – generously agreed to

ACKNOWLEDGEMENTS

write the foreword. Nobody is better qualified to do so.

An author needs a researcher and a typist to collate it all, and Erin Hynes fulfilled that task admirably. And for the final manuscript reading, I thank Ian and Rose Gibbins, Ian Dexter, Ed Maxwell and Christopher Rubython.

And someone has to sell the book and organize the inevitable book tour, which this time takes me to London, Edinburgh and Manchester, New York, San Francisco and Chicago. Thanks to Mary Hynes for that. Also to our printers at CPI, Ian Booth and Justin Manley, who as always have coped with endless page changes even when the presses were primed and ready to roll.

I regard photographs as very important to my books. Photography was nowhere near as sophisticated and developed a process as it is now and obtaining the right photos was incredibly difficult. So my thanks to Nigel Oxley at Corbis, Lucy Kelly at Getty Images and Laura Wagg at Associated Press for delving into the past to find what we wanted. Zach Dixon at the Baltimore Sun was also very helpful in telling us where to go.

My ability in being able to write so knowledgeably about Jesse Livermore's extensive nautical adventures was all down to Louisa Watrous at Mystic Seaport, Connecticut's nautical museum. She scoured the museum's archives to get me what I wanted, including the superb photograph of the Athero II.

Oh and commiserations to my lawyer, Marvin Simons. As all the characters in this book had departed, the libel reading and subsequent advice and changes usually demanded were not necessary and neither was his invoice.

Thanks also to Eddie Broughton, my accountant of 29 years, who made it possible for me to take eight months away from earning a proper living and kept me on the financial straight and narrow.

I would also like to thank the New York Times for allowing me full access to its digital library. Of all the newspapers in the world, the NYT has made the best job of digitizing its back catalogue and making it easy for someone like me to access it.

And finally thanks to my wife, Beverley, who thinks that what I do is so effortlessly easy that it is not real work at all. In truth, she may have a point although it doesn't feel like that at the time – only afterwards.

There are also numerous others who play much smaller parts, but I am grateful for all your efforts on this book and thank you all.

Having said all that, as always, the words that follow and any errors or omissions are naturally my responsibility alone.

Preface

The chaos within him

By Tom Rubython

Jesse Livermore was always well aware of his own limitations, which the writer Eddy Elfenbein later described as the "chaos within him". The same writer also said the whole of Livermore's life was spent chasing a dream, "the great, illusory dream of gamblers everywhere: to impose form and coherence on chance itself." No one would probably argue against that definition of a man whose career nickname was 'Boy Plunger'.

He took steps early in his business life to safeguard himself against himself. He invested $900,000 in annuities for his wife and children, save he was not able to provide for them himself. He confessed, perhaps foretelling events to come, that "I knew a trading man would spend anything he can lay his hands on. By doing what I did, my wife and child are safe from me." The only condition of the annuity was that he himself could never touch it or its content. Remarkable as that is, it is true.

But his life was never defined by his personal affairs. The life of Jesse Livermore was defined by his business life. If ever there was a stock market god, then Jesse Livermore was it. 85 years after his principal success, shorting shares and possibly even causing the 1929 crash, briefly becoming one of the top ten richest people in the world, he is still spoken of in revered terms. The 1929 crash has come to define him more than anything else and has overshadowed the other remarkable achievements of his life, which have defined four generations of investors since.

Modern day stock market operators name him as the man from whom they have learned most. Many hedge fund bosses hand out copies of his fictionalized biography *Reminiscences of a Stock Operator*, a book published 90 years ago, to every new employee. The rules of the game according to Jesse Livermore make *Reminiscences* the must-read book for people who work in the hedge fund business. It is as relevant to successful share trading now as it was then.

One of Jesse Livermore's most famous quotations is: "There is only one side to the stock market; and it's not the bull side or the bear side, but the right side." It really doesn't get much simpler than that, but Livermore often repeated that it took him longer and cost him more money to learn that truism than any other lesson in life. He was adamant that until that general principle became stuck in a traders' mind, consistent moneymaking would be all but impossible. And it took him a long time, as he put it, to "get it lodged in his head." But Livermore found out early on that it took a long time for him to learn all the lessons of all his mistakes.

It was those basic principles that governed his trading and ultimately made him a legend. Livermore's key strength was his ability to learn from losses and turn that learning into successful trading. He often said: "My losses have taught me that I must not begin to advance until I am sure I shall not have to retreat. But if I cannot advance, I do not move at all. I do not mean by this that a man should not limit his losses when he is wrong. He should. But that should not breed indecision. All my life I have made mistakes, but in losing money I have gained experience and accumulated a lot of valuable don'ts. I have been flat broke several times, but my loss has never been a total loss. Otherwise, I wouldn't be here now. I always knew I would have another chance and that I would not make the same mistake a second time. I believed in myself."

Indeed, he did believe in himself and that belief stood him in good stead until 1932 when he lost his mojo and never recovered it. Sad to say, the last ten per cent of his life was not a happy time and it is clear from his suicide note that, in the end, Jesse Livermore considered that his extraordinary life had been a failure. The inability to hold on to his wives or to the respect of his children or his money had finally driven him to his death by his own hand.

In the end, he lost sight of his own identity and didn't know whether he was a highly talented stock speculator or just a lucky gambler who happened to be in the right place at the right time.

That brutally honest self-analysis haunted him in his final years and ultimately would define his legacy.

Tom Rubython
Bere Regis,
Dorset, England
September 30th 2014

Foreword

The legacy of Jesse Livermore

By Paul Tudor Jones

J esse Livermore was a larger-than-life, full-blooded character who happened to embody every great trading maxim of the time. As Livermore frequently said: "There is nothing new under the sun in the art of speculation" and that maxim applies as much to the markets of today as it did then. And my guess is that it will hold true for time eternal as long as man's basic emotions – fear, greed, happiness, sorrow, elation, dejection, excitement and apathy – remain intact.

The best lessons I learned from Jesse Livermore were his repeated failures and how he dealt with them. He lost his entire fortune four or five times, and I did the same thing although I was fortunate enough to do it all in my twenties on very small stakes of capital. I lost $10,000 when I was 22 and $50,000 when I was 25. At the time, it was all I had to my name and it felt like a fortune.

It was then that my father flew up from Memphis and sat me down in my tiny New York apartment and began lecturing me as lawyers do: "Leave the gambling den behind. Come home and get a real job in a safe profession like real estate." Of course I did not, and the rest is history. And real estate in the past six years has been about as safe as shooting craps to pay the rent, so I was twice blessed. If I'd taken my father's advice, I might have lost all my money again these past few years in my fifties.

I think it's no coincidence that our greatest champions, our greatest artists, our greatest leaders, our greatest everything all seem to have experienced some kind of gut-wrenching loss. I think their greatness, in part, was fashioned on the crucible of defeat.

Two years before Abraham Lincoln was elected, as perhaps our finest ever president, he lost that monumental senate race to Stephen Douglas. To a certain extent, I think that holds true in my field as well. I am leery of traders who have never lost it all. I think that intense feeling of desperation that accompanies such a horrifically deflating experience indelibly cauterizes great risk management reflexes into a trader's very being.

There are two unpleasant experiences that every trader will face in his lifetime at least once and, most likely, multiple times. First, there will come a

FOREWORD

day after a devastatingly brutal and agonizingly long stretch of losing trades and you'll wonder if you will ever make a winning trade again. And second, there will come a point you begin to ask yourself why it is you make money, and if this is truly sustainable. The first experience tests an individual's grit; does he have the stamina, courage, guts and smarts to get up and engage the battle again? The second moment of enlightenment is the one that it is actually scarier because it acknowledges a certain lack of control over anything. I think I was 38 years old when, one day, in a moment of frightening enlightenment in 1993, I knew that I really did not know exactly how and why I had made all the money that I had over the prior 17 years. That threw my confidence for a jolt. It sent me down on to a path of self-discovery that even today is a work in progress.

Many of us are blind to key psychological elements of ourselves; that's why people go to therapists or get outside help for any number of problems. That was what happened to me in 1993. Then, a combination of people helped me discover that my trading style had incorporated some inimitable traits, completely unbeknownst to me. These bad habits were responsible for the worst year of my career, and the only one that came close to being negative for my trading accounts.

It's easier for someone on the outside to understand why people do what they do than it is for people to figure it out for themselves. Individually, each of us probably thinks we are just about perfect, which of course is why marriage was invented - to kill off that delusion.

The point is that it is in many ways easier for readers of this book and Edwin Lefèvre, the author of Livermore's fictional biography, to figure out the psychology of Jesse Livermore's trading than it was for Jesse himself. It's not so easy to see yourself, and it's even harder to clearly describe what you might see in yourself. From reading this and Lefèvre's book, we can probably see more of what was unique about Livermore than Livermore could ever have seen for himself.

Paul Tudor Jones
Connecticut
United States of America
October 1st 2014

Prologue

A man must believe in himself

By Jesse Livermore

A man must believe in himself and his judgement if he expects to make a living at this game. I know from experience, and it took me five years to learn to play the game intelligently enough to make big money when I was right.

My task was very simple: To look at speculation from another angle. But I didn't know that there was much more to the game than I could possibly learn in the bucket shops. There I thought I was beating the game when in reality I was only beating the shop. At the same time, the tape-reading ability that trading in bucket shops developed in me and the training of my memory have been extremely valuable. Both of these things came easy to me. I owe my early success as a trader to them and not to brains or knowledge, because my mind was untrained and my ignorance was colossal. The game taught me the game. And it didn't spare the rod while teaching.

I didn't have as many interesting experiences as you might imagine, and the process of learning how to speculate does not seem very dramatic at this distance. I went broke several times, and that is never pleasant, but the way I lost money is the way everybody loses money who loses money in Wall Street. Speculation is a hard and trying business, and a speculator must be on the job all the time or he'll soon have no job to be on.

When I am wrong, only one thing convinces me of it, and that is to lose money. And I am only right when I make money.

That is speculating.

Jesse Livermore
New York City
United States of America
April 1923

CHAPTER 1

Death By His Own Hand

The final meltdown

1940

O n the evening of Wednesday November 27th 1940, in the exclusive Cub Room at New York's fashionable Stork Club, Don Arden, a society photographer, stopped off at Jesse Livermore's table where he was eating supper with his third wife Harriet.

It was very noisy as the photographer asked Livermore if he minded having his photo taken. "Not at all," replied Livermore, adding: "But it's the last picture you'll take because tomorrow I'm going away for a long, long time." No one took any notice, however. The flash bulb went off and Arden got his shot. With that, Livermore's wife, whom he affectionately called Nina, and who, in return, always called him Laurie, got up to dance with her friends and left her husband brooding at his table alone. He had no need of company that evening as he was in the middle of taking the biggest decision of his life: whether to end it all.

The resulting photograph was haunting; by the time it left the darkroom, the subject would already be dead. The youthful Boy Plunger looked youthful no more. Whereas he had always seemed 10 years younger than his real age, as he entered his fifties the process had reversed and he now looked 10 years older. Although only 63, he had the look and gait of a man in his late seventies.

The following morning, on Thursday November 28th, he left his triplex apartment at 1100 Park Avenue and walked to his office at the top of the Squibb Building at 745 Fifth Avenue, overlooking Central Park. But nothing much was happening at the office. These days, he passed his time as a stock market consultant trading shares, not very successfully, for others. The rules of the stock market, and what constituted acceptable behavior, had changed with the advent of Franklin Roosevelt's Securities & Exchange Commission in 1934, which made life very difficult for the old breed of traders like Livermore. The new SEC laws had gradually worn him down. Now, almost every method

1

he had used to amass four large fortunes, which briefly had made him one of the richest men in the world, were outlawed and illegal. As he sat in his office each morning, all he could do was think about the glory days, long since passed, and how to wile away the hours until lunch.

At lunchtime, he ventured out to the nearby Sherry-Netherland Hotel. The hotel enjoyed fine views of Central Park, situated at the junction of Fifth Avenue and East 59th Street. It had been open for barely 13 years and occupied a very small part of what was then the largest single block of residential apartments in the world. Built of limestone, the brown edifice was one of the most elegant buildings of the period and the public rooms were styled in a mixture of all of the best of the renaissance period. The bar where he often ate lunch was small and intimate and had been designed for the prohibition era. But it suited Livermore and over the years became his favorite place in the whole of Manhattan. It was a place where he could lose himself in his own thoughts as he gazed out across Central Park.

In the old days, he had even kept a suite of rooms at the Sherry-Netherland as his Manhattan base. When the stock market closed, he would leave the office early and enjoy regular liaisons with young showgirls introduced to him by his friend, the impresario, Florenz Ziegfeld Jr. He later recalled those times as the "happiest days of my life." He had only finally vacated his rooms in 1936, when he and his wife bought a permanent apartment in Park Avenue.

For that reason, and for the memories it held, Livermore's choice for the location of his death was probably no accident. It had also been his lunch venue since 1927 and he regularly stopped-by for a cocktail after work, often to share a drink again with old girlfriends, most of whom, by that time, were married with children.

But the mood of the man who walked into the Sherry-Netherland that lunchtime was not that of the most successful investor Wall Street had ever seen. Instead, it was the mood of a has-been who believed his life had ultimately been for nothing. His multi-million dollar fortune was long gone and he relied for his income on a modest annuity and the generosity of his wife. She was wealthy in her own right from her four previous marriages, all of which had ended in widowhood.

In his mind, Livermore had been a complete failure – a failure in business and a failure in his personal life. He was well aware of the cause of his failures, as he had analyzed them many times over. His problems could be summed up all too easily in one word, "consistency". Although he was arguably second only to John Pierpont Morgan in Wall Street folklore, he had veered throughout his life from being America's richest man to America's poorest man – once achieving both distinctions inside a five-year time frame. He was also much married, and his personal life over the years had been as controversial as one man's could be. By his own estimate, in between making millions on the stock market, he had bedded hundreds of women, most of them whilst he was married and many of them not yet turned 21.

That Thursday, Livermore was seated at a table by himself, enjoying a chicken salad with a glass of white wine and scribbling in a notebook that was attached to his wallet. He then got up and left for the walk back to his office. According to those whom he acknowledged along the way, he appeared to be finalizing in his mind events that would transpire later. It would be typical of Livermore to plan his own death just like he planned every stock market move he ever made.

But when he returned to the Sherry-Netherland three hours later, at around half past four in the afternoon, there was nothing at all for anyone to be suspicious about. Carl Fischer, the barman who had served him at lunchtime, mixed the first of two tumblers of a cocktail known as an 'Old Fashioned', a strong mixture of whisky and bitters. It appeared to be the Dutch courage Livermore needed to get the deed done.

He sat at a small table in the bar for a half an hour, speaking to no one, sipping his drink and writing in his pocket notebook. Every so often he looked up, deep in thought. Fischer later recalled him acting more "fidgety" and "nervously" than normal, but nothing out of the ordinary.

Then he gestured to Fischer and ordered a second Old Fashioned. Half an hour later, Carl Fischer, the last person ever to speak to him, asked him if he wanted his drink refreshing a third time. He didn't and simply said "that will be all" as he reached for his money clip to settle his final tab. At 5:25pm, the 63-year-old got up and walked into the Sherry-Netherland's lobby and right across to the men's cloakroom without stopping. His eyes met those of Eugene Voit, the hotel manager, but no words were exchanged. Voit was the last man to see him alive and later said: "There was nothing unusual about Mr Livermore's appearance, he looked normal and cheerful enough to me."

Livermore had difficulty finding his coat but finally retrieved it from behind a pile of others. Folding it neatly, he sat down on a chair in the corner of the cloakroom and placed the book in the left hand pocket of his jacket. Then he unbuttoned his shirt and took a Colt .32 automatic revolver from his right hand coat pocket. He was left-handed and, calmly and coolly, he raised the gun to the left side of his head and pulled the trigger. He fell back into the chair. There was very little blood and indeed no sign that anything untoward had occurred. Anyone observing the man in the chair would have thought he had just fallen asleep. Surprisingly, the small cloakroom seemed to have contained the noise of the shot and no one heard a thing. Livermore was a marksman and an expert on guns. He would have known precisely what to do to kill himself cleanly and with no fuss.

At 5:35pm, the attendant Patrick Murray, making his hourly rounds, entered the cloakroom and saw Livermore slumped on the chair. Murray, believing Livermore had collapsed and was ill, immediately called Vincent Murphy, the hotel's assistant manager. Murphy recognized Livermore and tried to rouse him. He then saw blood trickling from the bullet's exit wound behind his right ear. It was a remarkably clean shot. Murphy spotted the gun on the floor and instantly realized what had happened in the cloakroom. He told Murray to wait by the door and not to let anyone in as he rushed for a phone at reception. He dialled the East 67th precinct of the New York Police Department and briefly explained the situation. The duty officer, who had no idea who Livermore was, said he would dispatch a crew and an ambulance. Next, Murphy dialled the office of Eugene Voit.

When Voit arrived downstairs, the two men went into the cloakroom and stood silently around Livermore's body, unconsciously protecting his privacy until the police arrived. The policeman immediately realized Livermore was dead. The ambulance arrived from Metropolitan Hospital and waited outside on the kerb. Inside was Dr Villeminia, a surgeon who specialized in head injuries, but there was nothing he could do other than pronounce Livermore dead and call the Medical Examiner's office.

An Inspector Patrick Kenny arrived to take charge of the police operation. By then a swarm of New York paparazzi had assembled outside tipped off by hotel staff.

Once Kenny had assessed the situation, he walked to 1100 Park Avenue with Eugene Voit to break the news to Livermore's wife, Harriet. She immediately became hysterical and Kenny put a call out to her doctor. The men stayed until the doctor arrived and put her to bed with a strong sedative. From the apartment, Kenny called Livermore's son Jesse Jr and was forced to relay the news of his father's death to him over the telephone, something he didn't like doing. He asked him to come to the Sherry-Netherland immediately and formally identify his father's body. A stunned Livermore agreed. He went to his bedroom and put on a chequered suit, smart overcoat and a trilby. He walked down to the street to find a cab. Oblivious to all else, he left behind his keys and wallet. It was 6:45pm by the time he arrived at the hotel. As he stepped out of the cab, seemingly in a daze, cigarette dangling from his lips, a sea of flashbulbs went off. He stared directly at the cameras and walked inside the hotel lobby without paying the cabbie. The bellboy, realizing what had happened, paid off the fare.

Jesse Jr was in a terrible state and stood in the hotel lobby shaken to the core uncertain what to do. Voit and Kenny grabbed him and took him straight to the cloakroom for the formal identification. Hotel staff had closed off a small dining room next to the cloakroom and he was ushered inside. A telephone was brought in and young Livermore was told he could stay and use the room as long as he needed. Within an hour, news had circulated downtown and journalists thronged the hotel lobby. A police incident van had arrived outside the hotel and police cars were parked haphazardly with the lights flashing. Despite that, business carried on in the hotel remarkably unaffected and the majority of guests in the lobby remained indifferent to the fact that the great Jesse Livermore had just died a few feet from where they stood.

By this time, the general manager of Livermore's office, Walter McNerney, had arrived. He attempted to comfort Jesse Jr, and when he had calmed down, they broached the subject of how to tell his younger brother, 17-year-old Paul who was at boarding school in Lakeville, Connecticut, at the famous Hotchkiss School. Schools didn't come more prestigious or expensive than Hotchkiss. It was a feeder school to Yale and past pupils had included Henry Luce, Henry Ford II, Forrest and John Mars, Harold Stanley and Tom Werner.

McNerney told Jesse he would take care of making that call. With that, Jesse put on his coat and walked through the streets to his father's apartment.

With a very heavy heart, McNerney got the number of the school from reception and picked up the receiver to dial the headmaster, George van Santvoord. The receptionist of the 600-pupil school was reluctant to put him through until he told her the nature of the call. When she realized what had happened, she didn't hesitate. Van Santvoord had been headmaster for 14 years and this was not the first phone call like this he had received. He had driven ambulances at the front in France during the First World War, and he was used to delivering bad news. McNerney informed him that Livermore's chauffeur was already on his way to pick up Paul.

Paul Livermore was in a room studying at just before eight o'clock when a friend knocked on the door to tell him he was wanted in the headmaster's office. For any boy of 17, that was almost always bad news.

When he arrived, Van Santvoord knew there could be no preamble, so he simply told him his father had shot himself and was dead. After a few seconds taking in the news, Paul fainted into the headmaster's arms. Van Santvoord lay him down and called for water. Paul remained in the headmaster's office clutching his glass of water until the chauffeur arrived to drive him to his father's apartment in Park Avenue where his stepmother, who had regained her composure, was waiting for him at around 10 o'clock.

Meanwhile, New York's assistant Medical Examiner, Raymond Miles, had arrived at the Sherry-Netherland at 9:45pm and was greeted by McNerney, who had taken charge of the situation. Miles took just 20 minutes to examine the body and complete his paperwork. He informed McNerney that an autopsy would not be necessary as the cause of death was readily apparent. Afterwards, he spoke to reporters in the lobby to confirm the bare details that Livermore was dead, but he refused to comment on the cause of death. The Medical Examiner released the body to the family and McNerney took care of the arrangements for collection of the body with the Campbell Funeral Church at 81st Street and Madison Avenue. McNerney waited until the ambulance arrived from the funeral home and had taken Livermore's body away.

Inspector Kenny remained, completed his paperwork and wrote up the official report, which he had been ordered to deliver to the home of the Police Commissioner that night.

Kenny's report stated that there was no doubt about what had happened. Death had come by Livermore's own hand. The gun was found by his feet and a suicide note in his pocket. The note was scribbled in longhand over eight-pages of his notebook and addressed to his now five-times widowed wife. Kenny laboriously wrote the exact contents of the suicide note in his report before he handed it to McNerney who delivered it to Jesse Jr at the Livermore apartment.

Whilst there was nothing strange about Livermore's suicide, there was certainly something strange about his wife. It was later revealed in the newspapers that her previous four late husbands had also committed suicide, and Livermore had made it a fifth. It was a remarkable series of coincidences that were never properly explained. But what wasn't in doubt was that Livermore had taken his own life whilst in a depressed state.

In modern times, Livermore would have been described as clinically depressed in the final years of his life. Later, he was labelled autistic and bi-polar. Ironically, a few years earlier, he had written that the job of a Wall Street investor was not for people of "inferior emotional balance." The irony was lost on no one that day.

Livermore had been a very popular regular at the Sherry-Netherland ever since it had opened and had always tipped extremely well – the tears flowed even amongst the staff that evening. That night, the manager gathered all the staff in his office and commanded a few moments silence in honour of a favored patron.

When the news of his death filtered out, all of New York was agog for more details. But there was nothing forthcoming from the hotel. The New York Police Commissioner decided to hold a press conference the next day; such was the clamor from the press for more details. At the hastily scheduled conference, Inspector Kenny read out passages from his suicide note. It revealed that Livermore had repeated himself throughout with the same words: "This is the only way out... I am tired of fighting... I am unworthy of your love... I am a failure." It reflected his state of mind, and the final sentence read: "My dear Nina, can't help it, things have been bad with me, can't carry on any longer, I am truly sorry, but this is the only way out for me – Love Laurie." Kenny said that the note was "coherent but repetitious." The Commissioner stated that Livermore had obviously been under "great emotional stress" when he wrote it.

Afterwards, friends said they did not recognize the man who was portrayed in the following days' newspapers. They blamed his third wife for his suicide especially when they heard the fate of her four previous husbands. They told reporters that until he met Nina, he was not the clinically depressive man he became. They were clear that her personality had somehow changed her husband's view of life. One friend said: "To lose two husbands to suicide may have been coincidence, but to lose five speaks of something else." Exactly what, the friend did not choose to define.

The obituaries in the days that followed were long and generous. They focused on Livermore's activities during the 1929 crash and the period of his life between 1929 and 1934. During those years, he had managed to amass a fortune said to be as much as $100 million, but by the end of it he had turned it into minus $5 million.

In truth, this period defined him and explained more than anything else the events that follow.

JESSE LIVERMORE - BOY PLUNGER

CHAPTER 2

The Story Begins

An unpromising childhood

1877 - 1890

America's Civil War had been over for barely 12 years and its hero, Ulysses Grant, was the 18th President of the United States when Jesse Livermore was born in the little hamlet of Shrewsbury, Massachusetts. Shrewsbury was part of Acton, an industrial town where 2,000 generally prosperous citizens lived in mostly timber houses. The district of Acton was a lucky place – it was on the winning side in the Civil War and had contributed the first troops to Abraham Lincoln's call to arms on April 15th 1861. It came to pass into legend that following the call, by half past seven the following morning, 52 Actonians had shipped out by train and reported for duty in Washington less than 18 hours later. The politicians in Washington never forgot and treated the district of Acton favorably forever after.

The area had first been shown the way to prosperity by the arrival of the first railroad in 1843. Initially the Fitchburg line, as it was known, served the mills with a freight-only service, later expanded to a passenger service with plush coaches. The branch line grew and became more sophisticated and eventually was like a spider's web flowing through Acton and the outlying area.

Acton was most famous as a manufacturing center for wooden barrels, which were then of huge importance in American commerce. There was never any unemployment in Acton because of the industriousness and entrepreneurship of its citizens, and no skilled man or woman went without a job.

The vast number of wooden barrels churned out every day meant hundreds of jobs in the four giant wood mills that dominated the town. Acton also had mills grinding corn, processing wool and manufacturing gunpowder, all lucrative trades. In fact, the town had been at the forefront of advancing the manufacturing techniques for all three industries, and Acton became one of the first large-scale manufacturers of wool cloth in America. The town also had factories engaged in pencil manufacturing, cigar rolling and a huge production line making basic furniture.

With America booming and so much business available, the railway lines expanded rapidly and linked all the Acton mills to the vast markets that existed in Chicago and Boston.

The growth of the railways and the building of more mills became a virtuous circle as factories sprang up alongside the track. New townships arose from the dirt as settlers flocked to the town. One of the first department stores in America, called Tuttle's, opened its doors and the Exchange Hall, said to be America's first shopping center, was built from the huge taxes being generated from expanding local businesses.

The only blip on the horizon was the stock market panic of 1873 and the recession that followed, but in truth it barely dented the lives of the newly wealthy citizens of Acton. It was the unskilled men who didn't fare so well and they were left to till the land, barely eking out a living.

In that category fell Jesse Livermore's parents, Hiram and Laura Livermore. Hiram and Laura had married in 1862 and almost immediately began a family. Their daughter, Mabel, was born in 1864 and Elliot 18 months later. They were dirt farmers and fully paid up members of the poor. He was a farmhand, and his job came with a small cottage. Hiram was a typical rough-hewn, strong type, hindered by the inescapable fact that he was not a very good farmer. So much so that, in 1876, he was thrown out of work and put out of his tied farm cottage by bailiffs. 36-year-old Hiram and 31-year-old Laura were forced to move to his parents' house at nearby Paxton where his widowed father, Jason, 70, had a small holding.

But moving in with his father was no free ride, and Hiram had to work hard to pay for his family's board and lodging. The work mainly consisted of ploughing fields from five in the morning to ten o'clock at night, seven days a week. The fields around Paxton consisted of dust and dirt strewn with hard rocks. It made ploughing the land very difficult, if not impossible. But Hiram had no choice but to knuckle down and work like a dog in return for his father's support and the wellbeing of his wife and two children.

So it was not greeted as the best of news when, on October 19th 1876, Laura announced to the family that she was pregnant with their third child. Hiram and his father, Jason, were horrified but in those days there was little that could be done and they all made the best of it. On July 26th of the following year, a new baby boy was born to the Livermores. They named him Jesse Lauriston Livermore.

Young Jesse was doted on by his siblings, Mabel, then 13, and Elliot, 11. His mother believed him to be a miracle although Hiram was indifferent to his new son, seeing him just as another mouth to feed.

No one expected anything of him and it was assumed that in due course he would work the land just like his father, brother and grandfather before him. But they hadn't figured on Laura Livermore, who proved a natural and confident mother. This time, she was determined to enjoy bringing up her youngest son with the help of his brother and sister. Despite very limited resources, she was a homemaker and smothered her new son with love and affection. It went some way to compensating for the fact that Hiram showed little emotion towards his new son. He just assumed Jesse would grow up like him, a big, strong boy whom he could put to work on the land as quickly as possible, alongside his brother. But that was the last thing Laura had in mind for her new son, and as soon as he could understand, she steered young Jesse towards the finer things in life.

It was just as well, as Jesse proved a frail young boy, often ill and with next to no strength in his bones. He eschewed the outdoor life. But despite his frailties, it was clear early on he was a gifted child with a strong intelligence. He learned to read and write by the age of three and a half, and by the time he was five he was devouring every piece of written word he could get his hands on. Old newspapers from nearby Boston were brought into the house especially for him and, early on, he became interested in the numbers on the financial pages – he found they made sense to him. As quickly as his mother collected books from neighbors, he read them all.

It was no surprise that he excelled at school, and in his first report his teachers described him as "imaginative and intelligent." Naturally he was top of his class in mathematics. His math teacher wrote in his report that he used "deductive reasoning to arrive at logical conclusions." He found he could easily solve complicated equations in his head and had no need for pen or paper. The teachers had never seen anything like Jesse Livermore and, writing in his second school report, the math teacher described him as a "prodigy," a word she said she had never used to describe a pupil before. She went on to write that very complex calculations just came "easily to him." She admitted that by the time he was 10 years old he was already much cleverer than his teachers in most subjects. So much so that his first biographer, Richard Smitten, described his brain as "computerlike." Everyone was impressed with young Jesse, except, of course, his father, Hiram.

Except for physical strength, Jesse proved superior to his father in every way. On July 26th 1890, he turned 13. He was 13 going on 17, a fine figure of a man, tall and slender with flashing blue eyes and perfect white teeth. He was the image of his mother and possessed huge self-confidence for his age. He had nothing in common with his father at all.

But Hiram saw his son only as an extra pair of hands to be put to work. On that day, he took Jesse to one side and told him his school days were over and it was time to start work alongside his 24-year-old brother, Elliot. By then, the now 80-year-old Jason had been forced to retire and he had passed the smallholding to Hiram. His father told him he believed an education was "unnecessary" for the life of a simple farmer, which he assumed his son would become, and he had to join the family business tilling the land.

But young Jesse resisted, and the law was on his side. He had the presence of mind to tell his father he was staying in school, which the law allowed him to do. And that was that as there was little Hiram could do until the boy was older. So a mightily relieved Jesse happily went back to school believing he had won the right to finish his school days and attend higher education. But little did he know that his father was merely biding his time.

A year later, there were no more niceties from his father, and Hiram simply terminated his son's schooling unilaterally. Now the law was on his father's side and it clearly stated that a parent could take a child out of school any time after their birthday, and there was nothing Laura, or anyone else, could do about it.

It was an act of unspeakable cruelty. The father handed his talented son a set of farm overalls, telling him his school days were over and that he was now one of the family's breadwinners.

Laura was absolutely appalled by her husband's treatment of Jesse and, for the next few years, husband and wife hardly spoke to each other.

But what to do? Jesse told Laura he would not work on the farm and decided to leave, even though he was only 14. Laura was horrified at the thought of losing her son. But she quickly realized that she couldn't persuade him away from his chosen course of action, merely counselling caution and promising her full support for whatever he decided. She told him his departure should be planned so as to give him the best possible start in the world.

And so began an amazing conspiracy between mother and son as they planned Jesse's departure. He needed money, something that was in short supply in the Livermore household. It would take a few months of his mother saving up before there was enough.

They devised a plan that saw Jesse uncomplainingly going to work with his father and brother every day whilst his mother secretly saved up every spare cent from her allowance, which she kept secret from Hiram. When the sum reached six dollars, Laura knew it was enough and that it was time for Jesse to depart.

The following morning, Jesse splashed water over his face and feigned illness and lay still in his bed when his father came to rouse him. His mother declared he had a temperature of 103 and could not work that day. Hiram wanted to turf his weedy son out of bed but Laura came between father and son and physically prevented it.

Hiram thought better of it and quickly backed off, grabbed his overalls and left for the fields. As soon as he was gone, Jesse dressed while his mother packed his few belongings into the only travel bag the family owned. With that, they walked to the main road, keeping their heads down to avoid the gaze of Hiram working in the fields. When they came to the road, Laura waved down a horse-drawn goods wagon and asked the driver where he was headed. When he said Boston, Laura negotiated a five cents fare and handed it over. The driver agreed to take Jesse to a house in Boston, where Laura had arranged for her son to stay. With that, mother and son embraced, unsure whether they would ever see each other again.

Tears streamed down Laura's face as her son climbed aboard the wagon. But Jesse was strangely composed. He knew his new life was just beginning, and he determined to put his old one out of his mind. And so Jesse Livermore jumped up and sat beside the driver, waved his mother and Acton goodbye and motioned to the driver to proceed. He was headed for Boston town and a completely new life on his own at the age of barely 14.

JESSE LIVERMORE - BOY PLUNGER

CHAPTER 3

The First Trade

Paine Webber in Boston

1891 - 1894

Jesse Livermore may have only been 14, but he looked and behaved like someone at least six years older. Everything came so easily and so naturally to him. Almost as soon as the wagon driver had moved off, Jesse told him to forget the address his mother had given him and asked the reluctant driver to drop him off at the Milk Street branch of Paine Webber, the Boston stockbroker. "But I promised your mother," cried the driver. But Livermore flashed a persuasive smile, and the driver did his bidding without further argument.

Years of reading the financial pages of old newspapers inspired his judgement that the Milk Street branch of Paine Webber was where he might be most favorably received and most likely to be offered employment. It was also conveniently the nearest brokerage to his prospective lodgings.

As Livermore alighted on a Boston pavement in July of 1891, all he had was the suit of clothes on his back, a few belongings packed in his travel bag, five dollars and a seemingly inexhaustible supply of self-confidence. He knew exactly what he wanted and that was a job at Paine Webber – any job he could find in that building. He couldn't wait to get started and the cart had barely stopped moving before he jumped down, grabbed his bag from the rack and thanked the driver for a comfortable ride.

But then he paused and stood on the pavement for at least five minutes contemplating his next move. He subconsciously thanked his mother for dressing him in what passed for a smart business suit, sensing it would make all the difference to what happened in the next few minutes.

Paine Webber had been founded 21 years earlier by Billy Paine and Wally Webber. Headquartered in Boston's financial district in Congress Street, it was already the biggest stockbroker outside of New York. The advent of the telegraph had seen it spread its tentacles throughout Boston, opening multiple branches and dominating share dealing in the city.

Livermore stood and watched Paine Webber's well-heeled customers coming and going before he summoned up the courage to walk through the front door himself. He finally took a deep breath and entered a world he had read so much about but never dreamed he would be a part of.

He couldn't quite believe the difference between the life he had been living barely 10 hours earlier and where he found himself now. He felt like Peter Pan.

His first impression was the glorious noise of the ticker machines that he had often read about but never experienced, and then the hubbub of the latest share prices being shouted out and the frenzied conversation of investors. To his ears, they made the most magical sound.

The ticker tape machines fascinated him most and he went straight over to where they stood and got his first look. There was a row of them clattering away, spewing out long strips of white paper. Hunched over the machines were groups of smartly dressed men looking out for the latest share prices. They were continually interrupted by boys, some younger than him, tearing off the ticker print out in two-foot strips, the boys handed the strips of paper to other boys called runners who took the strips to a giant blackboard where more (older) boys stood on a platform chalking up the latest prices of all of the stocks traded on Wall Street in New York. Once on the tape, these were generally the prices at which deals were struck until the next price arrived some 15 minutes later. At busy times, the boys, and sometimes even customers, stood by the ticker machines shouting out the prices to the blackboard boys as the tape fell into a wicker basket below in a continual unbroken strip. The tickers themselves were covered by a glass globe to prevent tampering. At busy times, the glass globes actually got warm.

Many customers sat in the gallery and the rest sat or stood in front of the blackboard watching the prices and often making spur of the moment decisions to buy or sell, depending on what the tapes delivered.

The stock ticker had been introduced 20 years before and had revolutionized share trading. Earlier, prices had only been made twice a day on the floor of the stock exchange in Wall Street and were then fixed for up to four hours at a time. The arrival of the ticker meant that prices were continuously updated and could change as many as 100 times a day. To facilitate fast trading, all the companies quoted were given an official abbreviation of three letters, which was printed on the tape followed by the latest price. It was an incredibly simple system and its introduction had meant that the number of share owning

Americans had grown from a few million to over ten million.

The main advantage of the ticker was that shares could be traded anywhere, not just in the major stock exchanges. It had meant regional brokers like Paine Webber expanded very quickly, and it established branches as fast as premises could be acquired.

By the turn of the century there were 5,000 ticker machines installed across America, linked by ever improving telegraph services. Eventually, there came the ability to have multiple tickers working off the same telegraph line, which meant prices flowed even more quickly to brokers' offices. Paine Webber found that the faster the quotes changed, the more shares changed hands.

Livermore stood there, starry eyed, physically transfixed to the spot, mentally taking it all in. It was exactly as he had imagined it would be and all he had hoped for. He had already formulated a plan in his head of what to do, and there was no time to waste. He knew that confidence was the key and any hesitation would be instantly noted and punished. So, mustering every ounce of self-confidence he possessed, he marched up to the main counter. There were half dozen clerks standing behind the counter. As soon as he had identified which one was the manager, he asked one of the customers standing in line his name: "Jack Hemmings" came the reply.

Armed with a name he knew what he had to do. He looked around for the person whom he considered to be the most prosperous customer on the premises. His eyes alighted on a clean-shaven, greying, 60-plus year old sitting steely-eyed in front of the blackboard silently with his arms folded.

Without hesitating, Livermore went and sat down next to him and introduced himself. "Jesse Livermore newly arrived from Acton", he announced. "And whom might I be speaking to?" The man look around and saw a boy he guessed to be 19, or thereabouts, with blonde hair and blue eyes. Jesse Livermore cut a very good first impression. "Michael Hennessy" he replied. It was such a favorable and open response that Livermore forgot the pre-amble he had planned and decided that honesty was his best policy. He replied: "I'm here for a job on the blackboards and wondered whether I might use your name for an introduction to Mr Hemmings. I know no one in Boston and you would be doing a young man a great favor. A favor, one day, I would be glad to return." Hennessy was no fool and immediately asked Livermore his school pass rate in Math. Livermore, having anticipated the question, told him and then added: "I am particularly good at mental arithmetic."

Satisfied with the grades and the answer, Hennessy fired some numbers at him. Livermore responded perfectly. A very impressed Hennessy looked at him again and said: "Mr Livermore, we have a deal, but don't think I won't want the favor repaid someday." Livermore flashed the toothy smile for the second time that day and grabbed for his hand to seal the agreement. He then turned and marched off to the counter watched by a bemused Hennessy and asked Jack Hemmings for a job armed with his impeccable reference.

Michael Hennessy has spotted something that he liked instantly about Jesse Livermore in those few seconds, and it was a scenario that would be repeated again and again throughout Livermore's life. People immediately trusted him and, what's more, Jesse Livermore always repaid that trust.

Hemmings automatically glanced over to where Hennessy was sitting and received what he described many years later as a "confirmatory smile." With that, Hemmings didn't waste words and told Livermore he was hired for a trial, as a board boy, for $5 a week. There was no point in any preamble. If Hennessy recommended him, then he was worth a trial and if it didn't work out what did it matter? Paine Webber desperately needed smart board boys; the profits of the whole business actually depended on it.

Livermore was amazed at the pay on offer – he had expected at the most two dollars a week plus tips. Back in Acton, $5 was a small fortune. In Boston, it was just a week's work. A boy could not have been happier that grey afternoon as he strolled out of Paine Webber. Straightaway, he asked directions to his mother's friend's lodgings and looked forward to writing to his mother to tell her he had already secured a job and would not be a burden.

An hour later, Jesse was standing outside the house of Carmel Clancy, a lady about the same age as his mother. Clancy took in gentlemen lodgers for $3 a week. He knocked on the door and a few seconds later she opened it up and immediately gave him a hug. At that moment, he realized he couldn't have landed better on his feet if he had tried.

He breathlessly told Carmel he already had a job and would be able to pay her the $2 a week special rate his mother had mentioned. She waved her hands and said it didn't matter – she was delighted to have her old friend's son in her house.

Carmel Clancy was a childless widow in her mid-forties and it would be an understatement to say she had been delighted to receive Laura's letter asking if her son could board with her. Carmel had written back straightaway and, ever since, had been looking forward to the knock on the door.

That night, as he blew out the candle by his bedside, Jesse simply could not believe his luck. His room in the attic space at the top of the house was everything he could have wished for. That night, he wrote to his mother telling her of his good fortune.

The following day, Carmel made him breakfast at five o'clock and prepared him a small packed lunch. He left the house half an hour later for the 45-minute walk to Milk Street. He then had to wait outside for another three quarters of an hour until the cleaners opened up at seven o'clock. The two Irish cleaners were dubious about letting him in but relented when they heard his story and were treated to the smile. His early entrance gave him a whole hour and a half to explore the offices before Jack Hemmings arrived as the clock struck half past eight. Hemmings was surprised to see Livermore sitting in front of the counter and briefly couldn't remember who he was. But once he had established his identity, he handed him a tunic made of alpaca, the standard office uniform, and told him to wipe the blackboards clean. The other board boys came in one after the other, and Livermore made sure he introduced himself to them all.

Trading started at 10 o'clock and initially he was given the job of tearing off the white tape from the six tickers and passing it on to the boys that worked the blackboards. It sounded simple but it was non-stop and backbreaking. When the markets were open the tickers were going flat-out recording the prices of not only stocks but also commodities, such as cotton and wheat. It was even more confusing as trading heated up an hour after opening, and he and the customers took to shouting out prices straight off the ticker. But none of it fazed him.

Livermore immediately became popular with the customers. He talked to them, even offered them advice from the little knowledge he picked up. He was brilliant with the numbers, and the customers soon started to use him as a human calculator. Hemmings loved having him around, as he made for a happy shop. He was quickly put on the boards at lunch times and mastered it faster than anyone had before. He discovered he had what was later called a photographic memory for numbers, and he only ever needed to be told a price once. His recall of the numbers was 100 per cent perfect and, as quickly as the prices were shouted out from the ticker, he could get them down on the board and confirm them from memory. As he said: "They couldn't come too fast for me. I always remembered numbers, no trouble at all."

At the end of a week, Hemmings enrolled him on the permanent staff and he was given a raise to six dollars a week. In those days, the market was also open for two hours on a Saturday morning but with reduced activity. There was no extra pay for working Saturday mornings, but Livermore volunteered straightaway, making him very popular. Together with another boy called Jake and a single teller, they more or less ran the whole operation on a Saturday morning. After the first week, Jesse found he was picking up tips from the customers, and many of them slipped him a dollar on the Friday afternoon and thanked him for his help.

At the end of that first week, he had 20 dollars in his pocket with only the rent to pay. The friendship with Hennessy proved to be a fruitful one and Jesse started offering him opinions on stocks – opinions that the older man liked and actually found he could earn money from, although he didn't tell his new young friend that.

With his new source of independent wealth, Livermore found he could now afford to buy all the newspapers on the day they were published. He also discovered that the newspaper's stock tipsters were very average and he could do far better from just reading the tape. Reading the tape became Livermore's fascination, and he soon found he could predict the correct upward and downward motion of prices at least 70 per cent of the time. He passed on all his hunches to Hennessy, whose end of week tips to Livermore gradually rose from a dollar to five dollars and then ten dollars by the end of the year.

Livermore soon learned that he had a real talent for what he called "reading the tape". As he described it later: "A battle goes on in the stock market and the tape is your telescope. You could depend upon it seven out of ten cases."

He also became fascinated with the actual numbers as much as the names of the stocks, and he committed what he could to memory and the rest to his notebook. As he described 25 years later: "I'd jot down the figures I wanted and would study the changes, always looking for repetitions and parallelisms of behavior – learning to read the tape, although I was not aware of it at the time. The fluctuations were from the first associated in my mind with upward and downward movements. Of course, there is always a reason for fluctuations, but the tape does not concern itself with the why and wherefore. It doesn't go into explanations. I didn't ask the tape 'why' when I was fourteen, and I don't ask it today at forty. The reason for what a certain stock does today may not be known for two or three days, or weeks, or months. But what the Dickens does that matter? Your business with the tape is now – not tomorrow. The reason can wait. But you must act instantly or be left. Time and again, I see this happen. You'll remember that Hollow Tube went down three points the other day while the rest of the market rallied sharply. That was the fact. On the following Monday, you saw that the directors passed the dividend. That was the reason. They knew what they were going to do, and even if they did not sell the stock themselves, they at least didn't buy it. There was no one inside buying; no reason why it shouldn't break."

At night, when he read the day's newspapers, he often found the reason for a rise and fall – but after it had already taken place. It made him realize that the tape was always first and the explanation often a distant second. That realization gave him a huge edge.

He was learning so much that he would have worked happily at Paine Webber for nothing. And as every month went by, his knowledge of the markets increased. He mixed and chatted to all the customers easily and so found he knew as much, or more, as many of them. He thought that perhaps only Michael Hennessy knew more.

Livermore may have been popular with the customers but increasingly not with his fellow board boys, who found him rather aloof. He just didn't, for whatever reason, mix easily with his fellow workers. He always told them he was too busy to socialize, as he said: "If the market was active it kept me too busy to let me do too much talking. I didn't care for it anyway during business hours."

By the second month, Livermore found himself keeping a proper journal, continually observing and noting down the stock patterns. His small notebook was constantly in and out of his pocket, and he transferred the data to his journal at night. He started to believe that the market moved mechanically and that, once a stock started rising, it stayed rising for a period. As he explained: "I noticed that in advances as well as declines, stocks were apt to show certain habits, so to speak. There were no end of parallel cases and these made precedents to guide me."

He quickly cottoned on to the art of what is known today as 'trend following' and what are called 'moving averages.' He worked for almost a year on what he called a "defined moving average" - the most precise way of measuring it he could find. He settled first on a 10-week period and produced charts for a host of stocks in which he was interested. It became the heart of his trading system and rarely let him down. He remembered how he forecast the direction of the market: "I got so interested in my game and so anxious to anticipate advances and declines in all the active stocks that I got a little book. I put down my observations into it. It was not a record of imaginary transactions such as so many people keep merely to make or lose millions of dollars without getting the swelled head or going to the poorhouse. It was a sort of record of my hits and misses, and next to the determination of probable movements, I was most interested in whether I had observed accurately: in other words, whether I was right.

"Say that after studying every fluctuation of the day in an active stock, I would conclude that it was behaving as it always did before it broke eight or ten points. Well, I would jot down the stock and the price on Monday and, remembering past performances, I would write down what it ought to do on Tuesday or Wednesday. Later, I would check up with transactions from the tape."

He also learned that there was nothing new in the stock market and that everything that happened had happened before. And what had happened before would happen again at some point in the future. Therefore, the present could be foretold often by looking at the immediate past. As he said: "Speculation is as old as the hills. Whatever happened in the stock market today has happened before and will happen again."

He was rigorous in his application and day by day, week by week, month by month, tested the methodology of hundreds of systems every night in his room at the lodgings: "After I had taken down hundreds of observations in my mind, I found myself testing their accuracy, comparing the behavior of stocks today with other days."

His journals grew in number and there was nothing random about his research and observations.

Very quickly, he formed his basic philosophy of trading by numbers. He wasn't interested in the companies or what they did, he was only interested in the price. He learned that he was only interested in the change of price of a stock, as he said: "Why did they change? I didn't know. I didn't care. I didn't think about that. I simply saw that they had changed. That was all I had to think about: that they were always changing."

He simply saw little value in questioning the reason for a change in price. He quickly learned that rational analysis was almost a waste of time despite the amount of time the brokerage's customers seemed to spend doing it. "That is how I came to be interested in the behavior of prices. I had a good memory for figures and I could remember in detail how prices had acted on the previous day just before they went up or down."

Repeating patterns often made his hair stand on end, as he could see what the next move was. He called them "numerical patterns." As he explained: "It was not long before I was anticipating movements in prices in my mind. I looked for stock prices to run on form. I had 'clocked' them. You could spot where the buying was only a trifle better than the selling."

He began trading a phantom book every day, and he found it performed very well. But he also understood the emotion of trading and how different it could be when real money was on the line.

He also noticed that as many as a half of Paine Webber's customers appeared to lose money on a consistent basis. Only the established regular customers such as Hennessy seemed to come out regularly ahead, and they showed similar consistent patterns of trading: never in a hurry to trade. Weeks would sometimes go by before Hennessy put on a trade and, when he did, Livermore noticed he rarely lost. In the end, Livermore saw that the losing clients had one thing in common; they took their profits quickly but let their losses run. It was a formula for disaster, and the successful traders worked out that losses had to be taken as quickly as profits. It was a mistake that Jesse Livermore swore never to make. But he failed to take enough heed of Hennessy's patience: something that would bite him time and time again later in life.

When he thought he had mastered the basic numbers of the market, Livermore turned his attention to what he called "the emotional equation." He split it into two and decided that "greed" and "fear" were the two most dangerous facets of a stock trader's make-up. He watched the customers be consumed by them and lose money as a result. He knew if he could eliminate both from his own emotional make-up, he had a better chance of succeeding. He also knew it was easier said than done.

Eventually, there came the time for the theory to stop and the action to start. After 18 months of intense work and his 16th birthday still a few months away, he decided it was time for him to buy his first share. But he had no intention of trading at Paine Webber even if that were possible. He also had less than $200 to invest: peanuts in the world of Wall Street, even then.

So he was forced to turn to the bucket shops for his first action. Bucket shops were an American phenomenon of the time made possible by the arrival of the stock ticker tape machine. The term 'bucket' had originated in England and transferred across the Atlantic, and the first bucket shop in America opened in 1877. The bucket indicated an activity at the bottom of a market, and effectively bucket shops were for amateur investors and the latter day equivalent of horse racing betting shops – the difference being that instead of horses racing, the prices of stocks and shares were the running. They were a forum for investors who traded with limited resources and did not have enough cash to open a brokerage account at a bone fide stockbroker. The difference was that a stockbroker treated a customer as a client to be nurtured. In a bucket shop, the customer was an adversary to be profited from.

The bucket shops did not buy and sell shares but effectively took bets whether a share would rise or fall. A punter could sell or buy a share effectively making a simple bet on a price change. It was almost the same thing as buying a share, but not quite. The prices at which shares were traded were based entirely on the ticker tape and sometimes, in times of heavy volume, these were very different to the actual prices on the floor of the stock exchange.

The system worked whereby a customer put up the equivalent of 10 per cent of the value of shares being bought or sold. Anyone could bet on a share straightaway and a betting shop-type slip was issued. It could be cashed in at any time as well. The bet was good whilst the margin held. If a share bought fell more than 10 per cent, the bet was wiped out and the house won the money. The house tended to win more than 50 per cent of the time, hence the profit.

The bucket shops varied in standard from carpeted salons to sawdust on the floor shacks. Most bucket shops had a single ticker but the better ones had rows of tickers and fast changing pricing – as good as any top brokerage. The prices were transferred to blackboards almost immediately, just like a proper broker.

Many of the bucket shops in the United States, especially the rougher establishments, were owned by a cast of shady characters, including the infamous Abraham Rothstein. The New York-based Rothstein, later more famous as the father of Arnold Rothstein, a major league mobster, was a pioneer of bucket shops and early on saw the shops as another extension of the rackets he ran elsewhere. Abraham Rothstein set up the original system of share betting, which all his competitors copied. Boston had nearly a dozen bucket shops, half of which were owned by Rothstein and effectively run from New York.

The bucket shops thrived because they turned away successful punters. Anyone who won consistently was banned, leaving a rump of losers who enjoyed the pure gambling element and fast turnover. The typical punter wanted to have a thrill and be entertained. Winning came second. Consequently, bucket shops were very profitable in bear markets but the owners often struggled in strong bull markets.

At first, the authorities viewed bucket shops as a good thing, bringing the opportunity for share owning to the working classes. Historian Charles Taylor called them "a democratized exchange where the common people could speculate." It was a good description.

They grew like Topsy to the extent that by the turn of the century bucket shops were trading the equivalent of more than one million shares a day, seven times the volume of the official stock exchange. When the tail started to wag the dog, however, the problems started. And when successful punters were turned away, the authorities turned against them and the bucket shop phenomenon was all over by 1923. But for Jesse Livermore, they were his start, and he made the most of it.

But even the great Jesse Livermore was frightened of making his first trade with real money. In fact, he was downright scared. But he got a break one day when one of his fellow Paine Webber board boys approached him as he was eating his lunch. The boy, who was a lot older than Jesse, leaned over and whispered: "Have you got any money?" Livermore asked him why he wanted to know, and so it began. The older boy wanted to make a bet that the Burlington railway stock was about to rise. But he didn't have enough money on his own to get a reasonable bet together.

Burlington was the pet name for the Chicago, Burlington and Quincy Railroad, which had been public since 1862 and consistently paid an annual dividend for 30 years. It was what was known as a bellwether stock. The older boy said to him: "Well I've got a dandy tip on Burlington. I'm going to play it if I can get somebody to go in it with me." Livermore replied: "How do you mean, play it?"

It was a genuine question at the time. Livermore seemed unaware of the bucket shop phenomenon. But he also knew neither he nor the other boy had enough cash to open an account at a proper stockbroker.

The boy retorted: "That's what I mean – play it. How much you got?" Livermore said instinctively: "How much do you need?" The boy said: "'Well, I can trade in five shares by putting up $5, and I am going to buy all the Burlington the bucket shop will let me carry with the money I give him for the margin. It's going up I'm sure. It's like picking up money. We'll double ours in a jiffy."

Livermore was intrigued. By then, $5 was nothing to him. That night he pulled out his journal, which held all his stats, and consulted his notes on

Burlington. He remembered: "I wasn't interested in doubling my money but in his saying that Burlington was going up. If it was, my notebook ought to show it. I looked. Sure enough, Burlington, according to my figuring, was acting as it usually did before it went up. I had never bought anything in my life, and I never gambled with the other boys. But all I could see was a grand chance to test the accuracy of my work, of my hobby. It struck me at once that if my dope didn't work in practice, there was nothing in the theory to interest anybody. So I gave him all I had, and with our pooled resources he went to one of the nearby bucket shops and bought some Burlington. Two days later we cashed in. I made a profit of $3.12."

In the intervening period between placing the bet and cashing in his winnings, Livermore learned everything there was to know about bucket shops and how they worked. He was soon ready to go: "After that first trade, I got into speculating on my own hook in bucket shops. I'd go in during my lunch hour and buy or sell – it never made any difference to me." In fact, the whole focus of his life changed. He was impressed with himself as he stuck rigidly to the system he had developed in his journal: "I was playing a system and not a favorite stock or backing options. All I knew was the arithmetic of it. As a matter of fact, mine was the ideal way to operate in a bucket shop, where all the trader does is bet on fluctuations as they are printed by the ticker on the tape."

It took a matter of weeks before Livermore's earnings exceeded what he was earning at Paine Webber, including his tips from customers. As he admitted later: "I did mighty well on my own hook. I was taking much more money out of the bucket shops than I was pulling down from my job."

The decision to leave his job at Paine Webber was more difficult than it appeared, and it took him at least a year to make up his mind and then another year after that to actually leave. He was making over $50 a week in the bucket shops at lunchtimes and evenings. It was very easy money and he wanted to focus on it full time. But Paine Webber was a knowledge factory where he picked up intelligence. He was also the star employee and felt a certain loyalty to Jack Hemmings and to Michael Hennessy, who was now a good friend and who also had come to rely on the young Jesse. For Livermore to stay or go was a life changing decision and, for once, he was indecisive. So he sought the advice of his mother, Laura.

He made a trip back to Acton for the weekend. As he expected, his mother was dead against it. When he explained why he wanted to leave, Laura said she had no idea what her son was talking about. He quickly realized that he did not want advice but affirmation. When he could see he was getting nowhere, he laid out $1,200 on his mother's kitchen table. It was all the money he had earned in the bucket shops. As he explained: "I laid the cash in front of my mother – all made in the bucket shops in a few months, besides what I had taken home."

Laura had never seen that much money before and any objections she had to her son's plans vanished almost immediately. She had no idea how her son, who was not yet 18, had earned so much money. But she didn't disapprove either. As Livermore said: "My folks objected, but they couldn't say much when they saw what I was making. I was only a kid, and office boy wages were not very high."

But it was not all plain sailing with his mother. She begged him to put the money into a bank or into a special savings account. When he told her he intended to risk it on more share trades, she was incandescent. Laura felt he had been lucky and it was time to stop riding his luck. As Livermore recalled: "My mother carried on something awful. She wanted me to put it away in the savings bank out of reach of temptation. She said it was more money than she ever heard any boy of fifteen had made starting with nothing. She didn't quite believe it was real money. She used to worry and fret about it. But I didn't think anything except that I could keep proving my figuring was right. That's all the fun there is – being right by using your head."

Even though he wanted to deploy more capital, Livermore split his money into two and handed $500 to Laura for safekeeping. He also repaid her original $6 loan with interest. There was one condition attached; she was not to tell her husband Hiram she had the money. Laura readily agreed.

So Jesse Livermore returned to Boston with $700 of capital, determined to gamble everything to test his skills. As he said: "If I was right when I tested my convictions with ten shares, I would be ten times more right if I had traded in a hundred shares. That is all having more margin meant to me – I was right more empathetically. More courage? No! No difference! If all I have is ten dollars and I risk it, I am much braver than when I risk a million if I have another million salted away."

By the end of that weekend, he had finally decided that he had to leave Paine Webber to pursue his dreams. And what big dreams they were to become.

CHAPTER 4

Bucket Shop Heaven

Makes first fortune

1894 - 1899

Jesse Livermore's decision to leave Paine Webber to pursue his dreams was a real wrench even for the fast maturing 16-year-old. It proved so for both him and the customers of the Milk Street office. Livermore finally made the decision on the eve of his 17th birthday, after more than two and half happy years at the firm. He dreaded telling Jack Hemmings and his friend Michael Hennessy the most.

Hemmings, with whom Livermore had formed a real bond, was shocked and surprised and spent hours trying to talk his star employee out of it. He told Livermore that a big career was waiting for him at Paine Webber and offered him a big uplift in pay. But Livermore had made up his mind and was determined to leave no matter what blandishments were put in front of him. Only when Hemmings suggested a near trebling of his basic pay, did he falter and tell him he would think about it. But, ultimately, he didn't care to change his mind.

It was perhaps worst for Michael Hennessy, who was on the verge of tears the day his young protégé finally walked out. Over the past three years, the old man and the youngster had formed a close relationship born out of the mutual trust they felt for each other. The trust matured into a strong personal bond that had been forged almost from the first minute they met. Livermore knew he owed Hennessy everything, and Hennessy had become the affectionate father figure he never had. For Hennessy, the young boy had uncovered emotions he never thought existed within him and Jesse essentially became the son he had always wanted.

Finally realizing he wouldn't change his mind, Hennessy got the regular customers together and held a collection. Not one regular failed to contribute to the pot, and $108 was the final total. Hennessy chipped in a further $100, which gave Livermore $208 to take on his travels. The sum amazed Livermore, and it was his turn to get misty-eyed when he opened the two envelopes.

Livermore had told no one why he was leaving, and the Paine Webber regulars assumed he had simply outgrown Boston and was headed to New York to seek his fortune. The explanation suited Livermore perfectly, and he didn't try to dissuade anyone that that was his intention. He kept his plans to himself as he didn't want the hailstorm of disapproval he knew would come his way if people knew he was leaving the established brokerage firm of Paine Webber for a career in the bucket shops. In the end, he said his farewells, walked out the door and refused to look back – it was the only way he could handle the emotion.

Livermore did not waste any time and the following Monday he got started in his new career by familiarizing himself with all 15 of Boston's bucket shops. There was quite a variety in Boston at the end of the 19th century. He had a choice of the cheap sawdust on the floor establishments or the posher salons. Despite the contrast in images, the shops had one thing in common; they were all fundamentally dishonest enterprises where the dice was dramatically loaded in favor of the house.

The cheaper establishments were the domain of Abraham Rothstein, and the management of them was gradually being taken over by Rothstein's 18-year-old son Arnie, a genius at mathematics. The Rothsteins were the kings of the bucket shops all along the East Coast. Young Arnold was a teenage prodigy where organized crime was concerned. Better known as 'the great brain' by his friends, he was already regarded as a financial genius at 15 years of age. Like Livermore, he had started young, gambling in public houses when he was barely 14. He had been phenomenally successful and would gradually take over from his father, becoming the king of New York's underworld. Rothstein Jr would become immensely rich from his criminal enterprises, making his father look like a relative pauper.

The other option for Livermore was the posher shops that preferred to call themselves salons. They were plush refined places with couches where customers were plied with fresh coffee and delicious French pastries. The salons were run by an outfit called Haight & Freese, a thinly veiled criminal concern that attempted to disguise the upmarket bucket shops by making them look like genuine brokerage houses.

Haight & Freese, headquartered in Boston, gradually built up a small chain of bucket shops in New York and Philadelphia but expanded until it had 70 branches up and down the east coast. Haight & Freese's subterfuge extended to pretending that it was placing orders at the stock exchange to match the tickets it contracted for. In reality, it was trading with its own head office and was entirely ticker based with no regard to actual prices on the floor of the exchange.

But Livermore wasn't interested in the coffee or the pastries, just the money he could extract from outwitting the bosses at Haight & Freese. But that was for later. Initially, he concentrated on Rothstein's cheaper shops.

Once he found his feet, he established a routine that was always the same. He went into a shop as soon as it opened in the morning, already knowing what he wanted to buy having "doped up" on his statistics the previous evening. His trading style never changed; he checked the ticker to make sure the price of his chosen stock was still behaving the way it had previously and almost straightaway handed his cash to the clerk and said whether he wanted to buy or sell. He went short as often as he went long – it was all about the price. The clerk took the latest price from the board and grabbed a chitty, writing down the stock bought and how many, the amount of cash put down, and then time and date stamped the transaction.

Livermore simply paid over his money, picked up his chit and waited for the right time to cash it out. But if the price didn't behave as he had predicted, he got out straight away. If not, he stayed with it as long as it felt right. And that was the secret of his success: he cut his losses as quickly as he took his profits. It was an unfailing recipe for success.

When he was ready to get out, he always timed his exit to perfection, slapping his ticket down on the clerk's desk at precisely the right moment – usually when the ticker price was fresh. If it wasn't, the clerk usually waited for the next price to come through on the ticker or took the prevailing one. No one could play the ticker like Livermore played it – it was a big part of his skill.

The clerk always wrote the closing price on the ticket and time and date stamped it again. Livermore then took it to the cashier and got his money. If the bet had been a losing one and the margin wiped out, the ticket just lapsed. A customer could never lose more than the margin he had put down. His 70 per cent success rate continued, and he also found he was very lucky. Soon, he was effortlessly earning money, sometimes over $200 a week. As he said: "At seventeen, I was making a good living out of the stock market."

Although he tried not to attract any attention to himself, his trading style was so precise and so confident that he could not help but get noticed. Not many traders took money out of the bucket shops, and the ones that were successful did not go unnoticed.

He always followed his own standard practice so as to minimize any attention. He found he fared better in the bigger posher shops where he could lay down bigger bets. But he spread his bets over all the shops in Boston, always with the intention of not attracting too much attention.

Even so, Livermore was not as aware as he perhaps should have been of the bucket shops' attitude towards winning customers. So it came as quite a surprise when he was told at one of the shops controlled by Arnie Rothstein that he was not welcome and that his business was no longer required. The rejection shocked him to the core; he thought he was a model customer. And it was then he realized why the bucket shops had so few winning customers – they had all been warned off.

He was soon made aware of the fact that successful punters eventually became *persona non grata*. Most of the bucket shop proprietors expected to win most of the time, and when they found Livermore winning 70 per cent of the time, they had a simple solution – they just banned him. But with Livermore, it was more than losing money. They actually feared his presence in their shops. An aura of mystery surrounded him. The proprietors became paranoid that he was planning a big sting that could ruin them. But the truth was somewhat different. Livermore was happy with his $200 a week, spread over a dozen or so shops, and he expected the bucket shops to play the game fairly and believed that winning customers like him were actually good for business.

That might have been the case had Livermore taken a more flamboyant approach to his trading.

But that was just not his style, as he explained: "I kept my business to myself. It was a one-man business. It was my head, wasn't it? I couldn't see where I needed to tell my business to anybody else. My business has always been the same – a one-man affair. That is why I have always played a lone hand."

He preferred his one-man status and he wanted to live or die solely by his own decisions, and as long as he could keep getting his bets accepted at the bucket shops, they would in turn have to honor them.

For Livermore, naturally, the integrity of the payout was vitally important. He wasn't about to risk any money on a one-way bet. As he said: "Bucket shops in those days seldom lay down on their customers. They didn't have to. There were other ways of parting customers from their money, even when they guessed right. The business was tremendously profitable when it was conducted legitimately – I mean straight." He added: "No welsher could ever get back in the game."

It was about the only thing bucket shops did honestly and otherwise they seemed to have every other trick up their sleeve in order to fleece customers of their cash.

Maybe if he had been more voluble in his trading, the bucket shops would have tolerated him for longer, but he saw no reason to be: "Prices either were going the way I doped them out, without any help from friends or partners, or they were going the other way, and nobody could stop them out of kindness to me." It was a philosophy he adopted throughout his life; he rose or fell on his own decisions. He wasn't interested in other people's opinions.

But gradually, one by one, the inevitable happened and he was banned from virtually all the bucket shops in Boston. As he explained: "It didn't take long for the bucket shops to get sore on me for beating them. I'd walk in and plank down my margin, but they'd look at it without making a move to grab it. They'd tell me there was nothing doing." It became a familiar scenario.

It was in this period, when he was flicking from shop to shop desperate to get some bets down, that he was nicknamed 'The Boy Plunger.' The first part of the nickname was easy to understand, as he was still under 18. The second related to his quick decisions to put down very big stakes.

He became a gadfly flicking between shops: "I had to be changing brokers all the time, going from one bucket shop to another. It got so that I had to give a fictitious name." He changed his trading style and even began deliberately losing to create a false impression. As he said: "I'd begin light, only fifteen or twenty shares. At times, when they got suspicious, I'd lose on purpose at first and then sting them proper." But it would only work for so long before the shop owners worked out who he was and sent him packing. As he admitted: "After a while they'd find me too expensive and they'd tell me to take myself and business elsewhere and not interfere with the owners' dividends."

But before he left, he decided to have one last try: "I made up my mind to take a little more of their money away from them." Livermore decided to try the hotel lobbies, where bucket shops had kiosks with tickers: "I went to one of the hotel branches and asked the manager a few questions and finally got to trading." It went well and Livermore was up $700. But, as he remembered: "The manager began to get messages from the head office asking who it was that was operating. The manager told me what they had asked him, so I told him my name was Edward Robinson of Cambridge. He telephoned the glad news to the big chief. But the other end wanted to know what I looked like.

When the manager told me that, I said to him: 'Tell him I am a short fat man with dark hair and a bushy beard!' But he described me instead, and then he listened, and his face got red, and he hung up and told me to beat it.

'What did they say to you?' I asked him politely. 'They said: "You blankety-blank fool, didn't we tell you to take no business from Jesse Livermore? And you deliberately let him trim us out of $700."' He didn't say what else they told him."

The game was almost up, as he admitted: "I tried the other branches one after another, but they all got to know me, and my money wasn't any good in any of their offices. I couldn't even go in to look at the quotations without some of the clerks making cracks at me. I tried to get them to let me trade at long intervals by dividing my visits among them all. But that didn't work."

He was eventually forced out of the Rothstein and other smaller shops into the arms of Haight & Freese, which had no problem taking his bets. Livermore remembered: "It was the richest bucket shop in New England, and as a rule they put no limit on a trade. I think I was the heaviest individual trader they had – that is, of the steady everyday customers. They had a fine office and the largest and completest quotation board I have ever seen anywhere. It ran along the whole length of the big room, and every imaginable thing was quoted. I mean stocks dealt in on the New York and Boston Stock Exchanges, cotton, wheat, provisions, metals – everything that was bought and sold in New York, Chicago, Boston and Liverpool. It was the finest in New England. It had thousands of patrons, and I really think I was the only man they were afraid of."

Haight & Freese were reluctant to ban Livermore outright, especially as his reputation now went before him and everyone knew who the Boy Plunger was; he had become a minor celebrity.

But eventually even Haight & Freese grew tired of consistently losing and banned him. It was the last place he was welcome, and he realized that his time in Boston was nearly up.

But Livermore determined to go for a last big hit before he left Boston and the bucket shops behind. Haight & Freese had branches in every manufacturing town in New England. Livermore figured he could go in under the radar and even adopted disguises, including false facial hair. The disguises worked. As he remembered: "They took my trading all right, and I bought and sold stocks and made and lost money for months."

Eventually, the Haight & Freese managers began to realize what was going on and tried a new tack to combat Livermore's success. It changed the terms of its trading for certain customers. Effectively, it made Livermore put up more margin and widened the spread on business it did with him. First it was half a point, then a full point and finally one and a half points. The increase in margin severely restricted his trading, as he had less capital available. The increase in the spreads also vastly increased his risk. It was a double whammy calculated to lose him his edge. As he bluntly admitted: "They didn't refuse my business point blank because they knew it would give them a black eye to publish the news that they wouldn't take a fellow's business just because that fellow happened to make a little money. But they did the next worse thing – that is, they made me put up a three point margin and compelled me to pay a premium at first of a half point, then a point, and finally, a point and a half."

Livermore gave an example of what he was faced with: "Suppose a share was selling at 90 and you bought it. Your ticket read, normally, 'Bought ten shares at 90 1/8.' If you put up a point margin, it meant that if it broke 89 ¼ you were wiped out automatically. When Haight & Freese tacked on that premium, they were hitting below the belt. It meant that if the price was 90 when I bought, instead of making my ticket 'Bought at 90 1/8,' it read: "Bought at 91 1/8". Why, that stock could advance a point and a quarter after I bought it, and I'd still be losing money if I closed the trade. And by also insisting that I put up a three-point margin at the very start, they reduced my trading capacity by two thirds. Still, that was the only bucket shop that would take my business at all, and I had to accept their terms or quit trading."

Livermore still managed to come out ahead although his profits were severely restricted. He just put on bigger and bigger bets using all his capital. As he described: "Neither the killing premium nor the three-point margin they made me put up reduced my trading much. I kept on buying and selling as much as they'd let me. I sometimes had a line of 5,000 shares."

Finally, there was a showdown over his commodities trading and a sugar contract. As Livermore remembered: "The Haight & Freese people were not satisfied with the awful handicap they had tacked on me, which should have been enough to beat anybody. They tried to double-cross me. They didn't get me and I escaped because of one of my hunches."

Livermore was short 3,500 shares of sugar, split into seven tickets for 500 shares each. He recalled: "Haight & Freese used big slips with a blank space on them where they could write down additional margin. Of course, the bucket shops never ask for more margin. The thinner the shoestring, the better for them because their profits lie in your being wiped. Well, this day, I remember, I had up over $10,000 in margin.

"I had put out my 3,500 shares of Sugar at 105 1/4. There was another fellow in the room who was short 2,500 shares. I used to sit by the ticker and call out the quotations to the board boy. The price behaved as I thought it would. It promptly went down a couple of points and paused a little to get its breath before taking another dip. The general market was pretty soft and everything looked promising. Then, all of a sudden, I didn't like the way Sugar was doing its hesitating. I began to feel uncomfortable. I thought I ought to get out of the market. Then it sold at 103 – that was the low for the day – but instead of feeling more confident I felt more uncertain. I knew something was wrong somewhere, but I couldn't spot it exactly. But something was coming and I didn't know where from. I couldn't be on my guard against it. That being the case, I'd better be out of the market.

"You know, I don't do things blindly. I don't like to. I never did. Even as a kid I had to know why I should do certain things. But this time I had no definite reason to give to myself, and yet I was so uncomfortable I couldn't stand it. I called to a fellow I knew and said to him: 'You take my place here. I want you to do something for me. Wait a little before you call out the next price of Sugar, will you?'

"He said he would, and I got up and gave him my place by the ticker so he could call out the prices for the boy. I took my seven Sugar tickets out of my pocket and walked over to the counter, to where the clerk was who marked the tickets when you closed your trades. But I didn't really know why I should get out of the market, so I just stood there, leaning against the counter, my tickets in my hand so that the clerk could not see them. Pretty soon, I heard the clicking of the telegraph instrument and I saw Tom Burnham, the clerk, turn his head quickly and listen. Then I felt something crooked was hatching, and I decided not to wait any longer. Just then, Dave Wyman, by the ticker, began: 'Su—' and quick as a flash I slapped my tickets on the counter in front of the clerk and yelled, 'Close Sugar!' before Dave finished calling the price. So, of course, the house had to close my sugar at the last quotation. What Dave called turned out to be 103 again.

According to my dope, Sugar should have broken 103 by now. The engine wasn't hitting right. I had the feeling that there was a trap in the neighborhood. At all the events, the telegraph instrument was going like mad and the clerk had left my tickets unmarked where I left them and was listening to the clicking as if he was waiting for something. So I yelled at him: 'Hey, what in the hell are you waiting for? Mark the price on these tickets – 103! Get a gait on!'

Everybody in the room heard me and began to look toward us and ask what was the trouble. For, you see, while Haight & Freese had never laid down, there was no telling, and a run on a bucket shop can start like a run on a bank. If one customer gets suspicious, the others follow suit. So Tom looked sulky but came over and marked my tickets 'Closed at 103' and shoved the seven of them toward me. He sure had a sour face.

"Say the distance to the cashier's cage wasn't over eight feet, but I hadn't got to the cashier to get my money and the man by the ticker yelled excitedly: 'Gosh! Sugar 108!' But it was too late. So I laughed and called over to Tom: 'It didn't work that time, did it, old boy?'

"Of course, it was a put up job. Together, we were short six thousand shares of Sugar. That bucket shop had my margin and Henry's, and there may have been a lot of other Sugar shorts in the office; possibly eight or ten thousand shares in all. Suppose they had $20,000 in Sugar margins. That was enough to pay the shop to thimblerig the market on the New York Stock Exchange and wipe us out. In the old days, whenever a bucket shop found itself loaded with too many bulls on a certain stock, it was common practice to get some broker to wash down the price of that particular stock far enough to wipe out all the customers that were long of it. This seldom cost the bucket shop more than a couple of points on a few hundred shares, and they made a thousand dollars.

"That was what the Haight & Freese did to get me and the other Sugar shorts. Their brokers in New York ran up the price to 108. Of course it fell right back, but a lot of others were wiped out. Whenever there was an unexplained sharp drop which was followed by an instant recovery, the newspapers in those days used to call it a bucket-shop drive."

The Sugar trade was Livermore's swan song in Boston's bucket shops for the time being. He had outstayed his welcome but was leaving with $10,000 to his name, a considerable fortune at the turn of the century, especially for a teenager.

It was also arguably the heyday of the bucket shops. They survived for another ten years, but it was all downhill as they were intermittently hit by some sophisticated stings.

An unnamed New Yorker took Haight & Freese for $70,000 in one hit with a carefully constructed sting. He was a member of the New York Stock Exchange and figured out that there would be no comeback or complaints if he launched a sting against the bucket shops.

He assembled a team of 35 men to pose as customers and go into 35 different bucket shops on the same day. They kept to the larger offices and, at virtually the same time, bought the same share to the maximum possible amount on the day.

The unnamed New Yorker then flooded the market with buy tips and bid up the price. He had picked a stock with some bull following, and the trick drove the price up quickly. There were few obstacles to putting up the price over four points. The 35 men cashed in their tickets together and made an average of $2,000 each, exactly as planned.

The bucket shops were badly hurt that day but considered it a blip. The New Yorker repeated the same trick three times in the following 18 months making over $250,000 in all.

The most audacious trick he pulled was to go long and then switch short in the same day on Western Union shares, with the sting being operated twice by the same team.

All in all, Livermore managed more than four years before all the bucket shops refused point-blank to let him into their establishments. Despite spending well over $1,000 a year on living expenses, he left Boston with $10,000 to his name, clocking up average earnings of over $4,000, some eight times the average wage of the time. He remembered: "I was only twenty when I first accumulated ten thousand dollars in cash."

Between leaving Boston and arriving in New York, he spent some time at home in Acton with his mother. When he told her he had $10,000, she urged him to stop trading and see sense: "You ought to have heard my mother. You'd have thought that ten thousand dollars in cash was more than anybody carried around…She used to tell me to be satisfied and go into some regular business. I had a hard time convincing her that I was not gambling, but making money by figuring. But all she could see was that ten thousand dollars was a lot of money, and all I could see was more margin."

CHAPTER 5

The Bucket Shop Phenomenon

Gambling on shares transfixes America

1880 - 1910

Ever since the first one opened in 1880, bucket shops were controversial in the minds of America's legislators, enforcement agencies and the general public. At its core, the debate was about the widespread confusion between the real meaning and intent of speculating and that of gambling. It became almost a national debate in America. At the time, seemingly everyone had an opinion. Psychologists didn't help much and declared that the same acquisitive drive and addictive thrill lay behind both gambling and speculation.

People who really knew what they were talking about understood there was little if any difference and that speculating was no different from gambling. The math is the same and the mind-set required for success in each is the same. Perhaps the only difference between the two was the public policy response to each. One financier of the time said share-trading skills were exactly the same as for playing poker.

It was a generally held view that speculation was acceptable and lawful but that gambling was generally unacceptable and illegal. It became a serious grey area in the law, and that confusion and ongoing debate allowed bucket shops to operate semi-legally for more than 30 years. They were able to flourish and become a huge multi-million dollar business and provide a gambling opportunity to ordinary citizens in an era where any kind of gambling was largely taboo.

The guttural human instincts of speculating and gambling may have been the same, but it was the confusion and lack of clarification by lawmakers that meant the police could not intervene. Without police intervention, a bucket shop could remain open indefinitely provided it had access to a reliable supply of official exchange quotes for shares and commodities. And they did have that – supplied by the telegraph companies. The telegraph companies provided that ingredient and bucket shops depended upon the supply of continuous share quotations from major exchanges, which also gave them the appearance of respectability: something they didn't deserve.

When they first opened for business in the late 1870s, bucket shops were small, independent store-front operations, typically located in the poor and less salubrious districts of large towns and cities. It had all started in 1868 when an American called Edward Calahan invented the ticker machine, so called because of the noise it made. The ticker was effectively a printing telegraph that listed the latest share prices from the stock exchange on a paper tape. The first ones were unreliable and ineffective. But then they were worked on by no less an engineer than Thomas Edison. By 1875 Edison had perfected the process. Then, as was his wont, Edison took it further and invented a new process that allowed four ticker machines to work off one telegraph line. Edison called his invention the 'quadruplex'. The quadruplex patent was licensed first by the Western Union telegraph company and ruthlessly marketed to the financial markets, stockbrokers and bucket shops.

Western Union exploited to the hilt the growing demand for real-time financial information. Soon it was not only supplying the telegraph lines but started buying the ticker machines as well, leasing a package deal to the bucket shops for a lucrative monthly payment. By 1880, Western Union was leasing thousands of ticker machines to bucket shops, and it became its most profitable division. At the height, it serviced 5,000 accounts with multiple machines and earned untold profits.

For the first ten years, bucket shops were ignored but they came to the notice of stock exchange officials in early 1880 when officials of the Chicago Board of Trade (CBOT) suddenly recognized them publicly as a growing threat from which they were earning no revenues at all. By the summer of 1880, CBOT asked telegraph companies transmitting market quotations to cease supplying a ticker service to bucket shops. It asked them to only supply recognized brokers. But the request was fruitless without any legislation to back it up and telegraph companies, such as Western Union, simply ignored the requests.

By 1890 bucket shops had become a huge business, some say dwarfing the official turnover of the exchanges themselves. *The New York Times* reported that a syndicate had been formed known as the 'big four' which controlled all the bucket shops in New York and had offices in every major city. The newspaper reported that the big four were very well capitalized and highly profitable. But also that none of them were run by characters that could in any way be described as "respectable". Recognition by *The New York Times* gave the big four a huge boost, and they gradually moved out from their traditional suburban sites into downtown areas. The shops they opened downtown were indistinguishable from retail offices run by firms such as JP Morgan. In fact, the shops were decorated to look like a traditional stockbroker's office. No one could tell the difference.

Haight & Freese, one of the big four, operated 70 branches up and down the east coast of America. The Coe Commission Company of Minneapolis, specializing in commodities, operated 100 offices across the northern states. M. J. Sage Company of New York, also specializing in commodities, owned and controlled 200 branches in the south.

It was then that the bosses of the major exchanges in New York and Chicago woke up. They came to believe that bucket shop offered serious competition to regular stockbrokers on the basis that they charged lower fees, offered smaller margins and traded in smaller lots of shares. They seemed unaware that a trade in a bucket shop was not a trade at all.

It took a long time for people to become aware that there was one crucial difference between buying a share, or a commodities contract, in a bucket shop as opposed to a stockbrokers: all trades were fictitious. When a punter bought a share he was betting against the house, and it was not a genuine transaction. No shares changed hands: just money and a promise.

By 1890, anti-gambling reformers estimated that some 5,000 bucket shops existed throughout the country, including 200 in New York, over 100 in Chicago, and at least one in each town with a population of 10,000. One reformer claimed in 1887 that bucket shops had so penetrated American commerce that they accounted for 90 per cent of activity in commodities.

The next pressure point came when ticker machines began to be installed in saloons and bars. Punters were drinking and watching the prices and then nipping into a nearby bucket shop to place a bet on whether a share price would go up or down or a commodity such as sugar or wheat would rise or fall. When this started happening, the authorities became seriously worried.

Stockbrokers as well as commodity traders started to feel serious competition from bucket shops. One prominent broker on the New York Stock Exchange complained in 1889 that the "indiscriminate distribution of stock quotations to every liquor-saloon and other places has done much to interfere with business. Any person could step in a saloon and see the quotations." Indeed, by 1889 competition from bucket shops had depressed the value of a seat on the New

York Stock Exchange by nearly half, from $34,000 to $18,000, and a seat on the Chicago Board of Trade by over two-thirds, from $2,500 to $800.

The trouble really started with the powerful farming lobby which was effectively the nation's food producers. The farmers believed that the fevered trading in cotton and wheat in bucket shops was driving prices down. They had a point, with hardly any genuine trading in cotton or wheat, prices naturally drifted downwards. The farmers saw little difference between speculation in futures contracts and outright gambling. The editor of a leading farming journal of the day stated that trading the future price of agricultural commodities was pure gambling and therefore illegal. He said: "The principle of gambling demands the same condemnation and the same treatment by authorities."

Eventually the police were goaded by the constant pressure and the New York Police Department announced a crackdown to arrest bucket shop proprietors on the charge of running illegal gambling houses. But they were stopped in their tracks by an editorial in *The New York Times* which stated: "Suppose some zealous citizen should come along and want to press the same sort of charge against the New York Stock Exchange?" The crackdown suddenly died a death as the Police Commissioner and the head of the NYSE digested the newspaper's words and their implications.

They weren't helped when so-called experts seemed to come out in favor of the bucket shop argument. Ben Hutchinson, a well-known trader with a seat at the Chicago Board of Trade, publicly declared that speculators (like him) served no useful economic function. He admitted: "We're gamblers". Henry Crosby Emery, an economics professor at Columbia University, confessed that "the gaming instinct" was integral to speculation. However, he continued: "That speculation is not mere gambling, and whether it is better or worse than gambling is a question on which opinions will long differ."

In 1882, the Chicago Board of Trade renegotiated its contracts with the telegraph companies and insisted upon a provision giving them the right to deny applications for its ticker service, which it made clear would not be granted to bucket shop operators. It had effectively cut off the oxygen to the bucket shops.

The big four bucket shop owners simply went to court and were very successful at securing court injunctions prohibiting Western Union from removing their tickers. In a series of rulings at the state and federal levels between 1883 and 1903, the courts continually upheld the right of bucket shops to obtain market quotations. The judges ruled that bucket shops had as much right to the quotations as brokers.

But the rulings didn't stop Western Union coming under serious pressure to discontinue the service to bucket shops and to restrict its service only to genuine stockbrokers. But it was reluctant to abandon the highly profitable market. When Western Union did take action, it did so half-heartedly and only when it came under pressure from the major exchanges, state and federal courts, which were in turn pressured by anti-gambling reformers. Western Union merely went through the motions, and any machines that were removed were re-installed a few weeks later.

So it was left to private citizens and organizations to act. In 1887, eight years after the first bucket shop opened, the president of the Chicago Board of Trade, a ferocious man called Abner Wright, evicted the Baltimore Postal Telegraph Company and the Baltimore & Ohio Telegraph Company from the floor of the Chicago Exchange. He ordered his security staff to rip out their telegraph equipment and toss it onto the pavement. Wright believed that bucket shops were really gambling dens and betting parlors, with share prices substituting for horses and dogs. Without the price feed, Wright believed they would wither and die.

The trouble for Wright was that there was more than one outlet for share and commodity prices, and not everyone shared his strong puritanical views. After four months, with the bucket shops still getting their prices, he took an axe to some suspicious cables leading out of the basement believing that they were telegraph lines. They were in fact the exchange's regular telegraph lines, linking it to police and fire departments. When that didn't stop the bucket shops, he gave up.

In 1890, Western Union's president Norvin Green was hauled in front of the US Congress and admitted that just under half of his company's message traffic was of a "purely speculative" nature, including share trading, commodity trading and horse racing.

In a 1903 case in federal appellate court, a panel of three judges ruled that the vast majority of transactions on the Board of Trade were "in all essentials gambling transactions." It was a devastating ruling for the stock markets.

The beginning of the end for bucket shops came in 1906 when a relatively obscure journalist called Merrill Teague wrote an exposé, syndicated across America, on the bucket shops. Teague wrote that $100 million of bets were being placed on shares and commodities every year. He estimated that the bucket shops were making real combined annual profits of $35 million. Another huge slice of the $100 million was going to the telegraph companies whom Teague accused of being "accomplices". The balance was going to organized crime. It was a wake up call for the authorities, and genuine attempts at crackdown began for the first time.

The big four quickly responded and repositioned themselves as bone fide competitors to the NYSE. They defended bucket shop commodity trades to real ones at the Chicago futures market. They cited figures showing that only about one per cent of wheat trades on the Chicago Board of Trade resulted in delivery of actual grain. It concluded that 99 per cent of transactions were settled on the basis of price differences, exactly as bucket shops settled accounts with their customers. They accused the major stock exchanges of being monopolists seeking "to crush the independents." A big breakthrough came when the journalist at the centre of it, Merrill Teague, now a well-known figure, had to admit that as far as commodities were concerned, the big four were right in their conclusions.

However, the seeds of the bucket shops' demise had already been sown a year earlier, in 1905. The exchanges searched for solutions amongst civil law statutes and finally came across the copyright laws. If they could prove the prices it quoted were also copyright, it could deny bucket shops the use of them. In May that year, after nail biting hearings, the United States Supreme Court finally ruled that the Chicago Board of Trade owned its quotations and could provide or deny them to anyone it wished. Armed with this decision, CBOT and the major exchanges spent the next several years getting injunctions and gradually closing the bucket shops down. Five years later, the bucket shops had ceased to exist – finally defeated by the copyright laws.

In 1909, almost after the event, the Governor of New York, Charles Evans Hughes, formed a committee to investigate abuses in organized speculation. The committee took its time but eventually reported that "speculation exhibits most of the pecuniary and immoral effects of gambling on a large scale." But the committee also heavily criticized the NYSE, finding little difference between it and bucket shops. It said: "Only a small part of the transactions upon the Exchange is of an investment character. A substantial part may be characterized as virtually gambling."

But after thirty years of investigation, expensive litigation, a sustained public relations campaign, and protracted negotiations with the major telegraph companies, nothing had succeeded in closing down the bucket shops. Wright's headstrong actions in 1887 had clearly demonstrated the frustration and futility many exchange officials felt in their attempts to cut off the bucket shops. In the end, it was a relatively impecunious civil law that forced the bucket shops to close. By then, Jesse Livermore was well gone. He was a legitimate share trader on the American stock exchange. But he never forgot his start in the now defunct bucket shops.

CHAPTER 6

Marriage and Move to New York
The boy becomes a man

1900 - 1901

Jesse Livermore's four years in Boston's bucket shops had been tremendously educational. In his best week, he earned more than he had in the whole of his two and a half years at Paine Webber. When he finally came to leave Boston, he had $10,000 in his account at his bank: considerably less than his peak fortune of $25,000 but an overall return of 1,000 per cent in three years of trading.

The heavy losses at the very end were regrettable, but after the initial shock of seeing a big chunk of his capital disappear so quickly, he soon came to regard it as educational.

He readily admitted: "The tape reading ability that trading in bucket shops developed in me and the training of my memory have been extremely valuable. Both of these things came easy to me. I owe my early success as a trader to them and not to brains or knowledge because my mind was untrained and my ignorance was colossal. The game taught me the game. And it didn't spare the rod while teaching."

It led Jesse Livermore to learn some really important things about himself and his psyche. The losses occurred because something happened in his head – something that he did not understand or even realize was happening until it was way too late.

The realization that his time in Boston was over had appeared to trigger a small chemical change in his brain. Almost immediately, he had started trading differently and ultimately far less successfully. It was then that he first realized how different mindsets could affect his trading in a substantial way. As he later recalled: "I let my craving for excitement get the better of my judgment."

Apart from that, he was also continually worried and hassled by the lengths to which he had to go to get his trades on at all. All of the bucket shop owners had got wise to him, including Arnie Rothstein, who seemed to take a personal interest in the young man he called the boy plunger. During that period, Livermore had to wear endless disguises and used multiple false names to get any action at the bucket shops. The disguises worked for a time, but eventually Rothstein's men saw through them.

With all his troubles and the end in Boston near, he found his mindset was completely askew. Another problem, he realized later, was that he was trading with far too much cash; he was overtrading by a factor of three.

By the end, he found himself continually playing the big hand – in effect he was trying to clean out the bucket shops before he was finally banned. Predictably, it couldn't work and it didn't work. Although in reality he had little choice but to stop as he was banned from virtually every shop.

He was eventually left with only Haight & Freese to trade with, which gradually changed the rules and reduced his margin. His edge had gone and he started losing heavily. And by the time Haight & Freese had finished adjusting the trading rules, he could no longer beat them. But he had enough sense to stop before he lost everything, which looked likely at one point. $10,000 was still a vast sum of money, and with it he figured he could be a player in New York.

But a week later, he found he couldn't stop as easily as he thought and soon lost another $7,500. As he said: "After years of practice at beating them, I let the bucket shops take away most of my winnings."

One day, he just upped and left Boston on the train with his belongings packed in two small suitcases. This time he had enough cash to stay in hotels until he got himself established. He quickly settled in New York and found the hotel life very agreeable. In those days, half of the rooms in top New York hotels were reserved for what were called 'permanent residents' and Livermore effortlessly became one of those. He felt as though he had come home, and in a sense he had.

Initially, his plan was to trade in New York's bucket shops. He assumed that New York would be just as full of bucket shops as Boston had been. But he was dead wrong. The Haight & Freese $70,000 sugar sting had put some of the New York bucket shops out of business for good. And when variations of the sting were repeated three times in the following 18 months, the New York shops simply closed their doors. The bucket shop bonanza in New York was well and truly over for everyone just as Livermore arrived. Even if the stings hadn't driven them out of business, the New York Stock Exchange and the police would have done. The shops prospered for another three years in Boston and other big conurbations, but they never reappeared in New York.

For Livermore, it was a shock, and he realized he would have to become a legitimate investor and start trading at a proper stockbroker just as everyone else did.

But he was in no hurry, and his first few weeks in New York were used for getting his head straight and analyzing what had really happened in the last few weeks in Boston.

The losses bothered him more than he cared to admit to himself, even in his more candid moments of self-examination. But in a pattern that was to continue for the rest of his life, he decided that there was no one to blame but himself. The market was not wrong and could never be wrong in his eyes, and he was determined not to become the gambler who blamed the pack of cards for his losses.

The first stage of his self-analysis was to go through each losing trade and analyze exactly where he had gone wrong. He discovered it all came down to one issue – timing.

He came to an astonishingly self-evident conclusion, and it was a lesson he would find himself re-learning throughout his life. He concluded that he could not be trading all the time. There was a time when he should be in the market and a time when he shouldn't. His recent losses were a classic case of over-trading.

His self-analysis concluded that he profited from seven out of ten of his deals, but in the three that he lost out on, his losses were in excess of the ones in which he profited. But he also concluded that when he was absolutely sure he was right, he was always right. His dud trades came on the deals he was not sure about. The introspection and his realizations heartened him immensely, and he made the decision to carry on and to make the transition from bucket trader to Wall Street trader. Now he had to find a broker that also met his ambitions and aspirations. It didn't take him long to find the right one as serendipity was on his side once again.

On September 14th 1900, the very day he arrived in New York, the 23-year-old walked into the offices of a brokerage called Harris, Hutton & Company, run by 25-year-old Edward Hutton. The New York office was a new branch of Edward Hutton's uncle's stock broking firm, based in Cincinnati. Edward had joined the firm when he was 15 years old and become a partner five years later. The 25-year-old nephew had convinced his uncle to open a New York branch just a few months before.

Livermore had read about the new firm in the Boston newspapers and liked what he read. Somehow, he saw compatibility between him and Edward Hutton. The two similarly aged and similarly ambitious men took to each other as soon as they were introduced. Both were destined to become phenomenally successful financiers, passing into Wall Street legend. Their negotiations couldn't have gone better, and Ed Hutton took Livermore's $2,500 and deposited it into his first brokerage account. He told him that he was good enough for another $22,500 of credit so Livermore could put out a line of $25,000. As Livermore remembered: "I arrived in this city in the morning, and before one o'clock that same day I had opened an account with the firm and I was ready to trade."

It was heady stuff but no more than he had been used to in Boston at the height of his fortunes. There was also a raging bull market starting to develop on Wall Street. Livermore's arrival in New York was perfect timing in that respect but it also provided a false situation as he began to trade on the big board. Effectively, any long trade made in that period was almost certain to be successful although Livermore didn't quite realize that at the time. As he recalled: "How natural it was for me to trade there exactly as I had done in the bucket shops, where all I did was to bet on fluctuations and catch small but sure changes in prices."

But the favorable conditions completely masked the underlying difficulties, as he admitted later: "Nobody offered to point out the essential differences or set me right. If somebody had told me my method would not work, I nevertheless would have tried it out to make sure for myself, for when I am wrong only one thing convinces me of it, and that is, to lose money. And I am only right when I make money. That is speculating."

Ironically, that first day's trading in New York proved singularly unsuccessful. Although his first day was a losing day, it felt good to him. As he explained: "I watched the board and saw something that looked good to me. It was behaving right. I bought a hundred at 84. I got out at 85 in less than half an hour. Then I saw something else I liked, and I did the same thing; took three quarters of a point net within a very short time. I began well, didn't I? Now mark this: On that, my first day as a customer of a reputable Stock Exchange house, and only two hours of it at that, I traded in eleven hundred dollars minus for the day. It didn't worry me, because I couldn't see where there was anything wrong with me. My moves, also, were right enough, and if I had been trading in the old Cosmopolitan shop, I'd have broken better than even. That the machine wasn't as it ought to be, my eleven hundred vanished dollars plainly told me. But as long as the machinist was all right, there was no need to stew. Ignorance at 22 years old isn't a structural defect."

On day two he started winning, and Livermore quickly became the new brokerage's most active trader, sometimes racking up thousands of dollars every week in commission and interest charges for the brokerage. And he was very successful doubling his capital and credit line within the first three months.

By early 1901, it was clear to anyone that the bull market was in full flow. Up to then, 250,000 had been the record number of shares traded in a day. By the end of that year, the record was smashed by a factor of 12, and three million shares were traded in a single day. And Livermore was riding the boom as hard as he could. As he recalled: "I remember my very first day in New York. The bucket shops, by refusing to take my business, drove me to seek a reputable commission house. They were having some pretty lively times those days, and the market was very active. That always cheers up a fellow. I felt at home right away. There was the old familiar quotation board in front of me, talking a language that I had learned before I was fifteen years old. There was a boy doing exactly the same thing as I used to do in the first office I ever worked in. There were the customers – same old bunch – looking at the board or standing by the ticker calling out the prices and talking about the market. The machinery was to all appearances the same machinery that I was used to. The atmosphere was the atmosphere I had breathed since I had made my first stock market money. The same kind of ticker and the same kind of traders: therefore, the same kind of game. And, remember, I was only 22. I suppose I thought I knew the game from A – Z. Why Shouldn't I?"

He was making money effortlessly, which was far more to do with the boom than his own talents. Everything was going up, and he was continually long. On one memorable Monday, he bought $90,000 worth of Northern Pacific Railroad stock, and by Friday he had made $50,000 - in less than a week. He had used only $10,000 of his own money and the rest was margin. In effect, he had turned $10,000 into $50,000 in five days

Unsurprisingly, Livermore became a very good customer of Harris, Hutton & Company, and Ed Hutton and he became extremely good friends. Less than a month after meeting, Livermore attended Hutton's wedding to Blanche Horton on October 9th 1900 in St Louis.

The wedding was to be fateful for Livermore in more ways than one because, whilst there, he met a girl called Nettie Jordan whose family lived in

Indianapolis. Nettie was attending the wedding on her own, and she was as struck with him and he was with her. It was love, or rather lust, at first sight and the two had consumed far too much liquor at the wedding breakfast and spent their first night together a few hours later. Neither were virgins, but Livermore had never been with a woman like her. He found the experience in bed very different to anything he had known before. As for Nettie, she believed she had found her prince charming and was determined to hold on to him. He was wealthy, good looking and charming in a quiet, reserved way. She was very pretty, very slim and very outgoing. She followed him back to New York.

Within a matter of weeks, Jesse and Nettie were married at a small ceremony in the presence of just Ed and Blanche Hutton. The following week, Nettie took Jesse home to meet her parents in Indianapolis and, the week after that, they went to meet Hiram and Laura in Bridgeport.

Livermore was starting to live his dream, and the Livermores and Huttons became an inseparable foursome, socializing at every possible opportunity.

The newly married couple could afford to move straight into a serviced apartment nearby the burned out Windsor Hotel on Fifth Avenue, at the corner of East 47th Street. So much money was coming in that, as soon as they were settled, they began looking for a weekend residence in the country. Livermore had always been drawn to the sea and quickly found a cottage in the seaside town of Long Branch in New Jersey. The cottage was right on the beach and the couple enjoyed an idyllic lifestyle by the standards of the time.

Livermore also took his first proper vacation on a cruise liner from New York to Southampton, England. They had the best cabin and enjoyed the four-day crossing in some style. As soon as they alighted in Southampton, Livermore rented a private train carriage, and they toured Europe in the spring of 1901. By all accounts Nettie returned across the Atlantic with $12,000 worth of diamonds in her handbag that her new husband had bought for her.

The diamonds caused quite a sensation when the Livermores returned to America and disembarked from their steamship in New York harbor. When Nettie Livermore was asked to open her handbag for inspection, she willingly and somewhat naïvely told a customs officer her generous husband had bought her the diamonds in Paris. The officer called for help and, soon, Mr and Mrs Livermore were in a side office answering questions and wondering whether they would be arrested. Customs officials wanted to know about the duty that needed to be paid and what arrangements Livermore had made.

Livermore genuinely believed he had bought the jewels with the duty already paid and he was stunned the Parisian jeweller had failed to mention it.

The customs officials soon put him right. Unable and unwilling to immediately pay the $7,200 import duty, the diamonds were seized, much to the upset of Mrs Livermore. The following day, Livermore got up early and collected a banker's check from National City Bank and hurried down to the port to retrieve his wife's jewels.

Although no one had any idea who he was, the New York Times duly reported the story the following day. As Livermore later recalled: "The first time I ever got in print was when my wife came back from Europe in 1901 with $12,000 of jewels in her handbag."

The bad news did not end there, and the good times Livermore had enjoyed from his very first day in New York were about to crash. Livermore was about to learn a very sharp and expensive lesson – not to confuse luck with ability. Belatedly, he discovered that there was a fundamental difference between trading for real on the stock market and trading in bucket shops. And it came down to a very simple fact that Livermore had inexplicably failed to notice.

In a bucket shop, the ticker price was the price at which shares were bought and sold. But it was not the actual price on the stock exchange floor. The world of the bucket shop revolved around the ticker price rather than the reality of the floor price. On the real stock exchange, the ticker was only the communication medium, and the real price being quoted on the floor of the exchange could be very different.

Livermore soon realized that the ticker was actually 30 or 40 minutes behind the market at the best of times, and when the market was moving really quickly, the ticker could be as much as two hours behind. Unfortunately, he didn't take on board what he could clearly see with his own eyes.

And that lesson was learned in the most painful way when he went short and gambled on a correction he saw coming in May 1901. It was more difficult for Livermore to operate in a bull market, as he was a natural bear who always saw trouble just around the corner. And he knew full well that shorting shares in a rising market was a risky proposition at the best of times and extremely risky in a raging bull market.

But his bearish instincts overwhelmed him, and he thought he saw a window to make some quick easy money. One day in May 1901, before the market opened, he put in an order at Harris Hutton to sell $100,000 shares of U.S. Steel short, a thousand shares at $100 as Livermore later remembered. And then he sold another 1,000 shares of Santa Fe Railroad short at $80 using up his entire capital and leveraging it 4 to 1. Both shares were stock market staples that had risen sharply in the boom and were overbought. There was nothing wrong with Livermore's logic or his judgement – both stocks were due a correction. There was huge volume in the shares and the prices were very volatile.

Livermore was spot on with his instincts and, sure enough, when the market opened the following day both shares fell like a stone. The problem was that his order could not be filled at the opening price and by the time it could, the prices had fallen to $85 and $65 respectively. His orders were filled at those levels and they were the prices at which he had planned to buy back in. Livermore immediately realized that although he was right, he was also wrong and he quickly attempted to get out. But that was easier said than done as the market turned quickly under the weight of an extraordinary volume of trading.

Instinctively, he knew he was in trouble and that the whole market would pile back in to buy at the new lower prices. So he ordered his position covered but was too late, and the price rocketed as demand for the shares soared. It was every trader's worst nightmare and he waited anxiously to find out what price he would have to pay to buy back the shares. It turned out to be at a 10 per cent premium to the overnight price, and that meant a 25 per cent loss on both shares. As he was leveraged 400 per cent, his loss was magnified four times and he lost a total of $50,000 inside a few hours.

Suddenly, he was a busted flush and it wiped out all his capital – all because the ticker was overwhelmed by the volume and was two hours behind the real prices. He was ruined, and all his cash was gone in an instant.

He stood in the public lobby at Harris Hutton's offices thinking that yesterday he had been worth $50,000 and full of self-confidence, and today he was worth nothing with his confidence, his reputation and his self-esteem shattered. He was devastated and shaken to the core of his being.

He didn't feel any better when it was pointed out to him that his thinking had been right, and if he had been able to execute his trades at the prevailing ticker price, he would have made $50,000 instead of losing $50,000. He ruefully recalled many years later: "The tape always spoke ancient history to me as far as my system of trading went, and I didn't realize it."

It was a very naïve mistake to make, but then Livermore was only 23 and his only real experience of trading stocks short was in bucket shops, which he belatedly realized played to very different rules. It was not lost on him that the same trade in a bucket shop, even under his old restricted terms, would have yielded him a profit of at least $30,000.

He was also surprised how his own trades had moved the price so quickly even before they had been placed. As he explained: "My order was fairly big [and] my own sale would tend further to depress the price. In the bucket shop I didn't have to figure on the effect of my own trading. I lost in New York because the game was altogether different."

That night, he sat down in the dark of his apartment and tried to work it all out. The loss gnawed away at the whole fabric of his being and, most of all, at his own self-belief.

He also realized that his undoubted tape-reading skills were of no benefit in New York as the tape was so behind. He was completely at sea, flaying around with no solution in sight: "It was not that I was not playing it legitimately that made me lose, but that I was playing it ignorantly. I have been told that I am a good reader of the tape. But reading the tape like an expert did not save me. I might have made out a great deal better if I had been on the floor myself, a room trader. In a particular crowd, perhaps I might have adapted my system to the conditions immediately before me. But, of course, if I had got to operating on such a scale as I do now, for instance, the system would equally have failed me on account of the effect of my own trading on prices. In short, I did not know the game of stock speculation. I knew a part of it, a rather important part, which had been valuable to me at all times. But with all I had lost, what chance does the green outsider have of winning, or rather, of cashing in? It didn't take me long to realize that there was something wrong with my play, but I couldn't spot the exact trouble. There were times when my system worked beautifully, and then, all of a sudden, nothing but one swat after another. I was only twenty-two, remember; not that I was stuck on myself that I didn't want to know just where I was at fault, but at that age nobody knows much of anything."

His financial demise had an immediate effect on his marriage. The following day, Nettie decided she had not married the financial wunderkind she thought she had eight months earlier. The final straw for her came when Livermore asked her to get out all the jewelry he had bought her. He told her he intended going down to the pawn shop and getting what he could for it to give him some new capital. Even though he had bought it all for a total of $30,000, he would only be able to get 10 per cent of that but he desperately needed the $3,000 the jewelry would fetch.

But Nettie had other ideas. She refused outright to have anything to do with it and walked out, taking her jewelry box with her and getting on a train to Indianapolis to her parents. When she arrived, she deposited the jewels in her father's safe. That was effectively the end of the marriage, and Nettie commuted back and forth between Indianapolis and New York to collect her things until Livermore departed for Boston four weeks later. They didn't see each other again for six months. Not for the last time, Livermore had shown that his judgment of women was not in the same class as his judgment of the stock market.

It was time for another intense few months of soul searching. With no capital to trade and no wife to bother him, Livermore had plenty of time to think. He realized that he was a man free from ego and from any sense of entitlement. He realized that he was a man who had no illusions as to his ability. He remembered those hard times and days of introspection much later: "My task was very simple – to look at speculation from another angle. I didn't know that there was much more to the game than I could possibly learn in the bucket shops. There, I thought I was beating the game when in reality I was only beating the shop."

And that was the nub of his dilemma. He finally realized he had never beaten the market but merely bucked the bucket shop system that was designed to rip off its customers. Livermore had proved too smart to be ripped off, but in the process he had confused himself as to his abilities. What was really difficult came easily to him, but the less onerous task of actually dealing in physical stocks and shares proved to be much more difficult for his brain patterns to work out.

CHAPTER 7

Down and Out

Back to the bucket shops

1901

With Nettie gone and his personal and business life in ruins, there was nothing left to hold Jesse Livermore in New York. There were no money making opportunities available to him, nor was there any money left in his pot to take advantage of any opportunities that did come along.

For the first time in his life, he didn't know what to do. He was not only broke but actually in a minus situation in his brokerage account at Harris Hutton. Livermore knew that pawning Nettie's jewels was his last hope of staying in the game. Without any access to cash, there was absolutely no way back for him in the stock market.

His solution was temporarily to withdraw from life. He shut himself in, closed the curtains and spent two weeks alone in his apartment mourning the departure of his wife and his money – unsure which he missed the most. In truth, it was the money that troubled him most deeply and he dreaded returning to Harris Hutton to face the music. After the second week, he pulled himself together and summoned up the courage to return to the office, wholly unsure of what his reception would be.

Livermore fully expected there to be plenty of trouble awaiting him upon his return. At worst, his brokerage account would be closed and burly men would come for his furniture and take his pocket watch, the last things of value he owned. At best, they would give him time to pay – but that, he thought, was a longshot.

But what he expected and what he actually found turned out to be very different things.

To his amazement, as soon as he walked through the door, it was almost like business as usual. People behaved as though he had just returned from a two-week vacation. Despite owing the firm $500, there was absolutely no sense of recrimination. Harris Hutton was co-owned by a Canadian called Jim Harris, a man who almost regarded failure as a virtue – not necessarily to be rewarded but not to be treated with scorn either. So Livermore found himself being treated just as he had before his disaster. In fact, he noted a strong sense of sympathy for his predicament.

But it was Livermore's luck that, as it so happened, Jim Harris was in New York when he returned to the office. And Harris was very eager to meet Livermore, as he had heard so much about him over the past months. As soon as Livermore walked in, Harris strode out to meet him and shook his hand firmly. Harris greeted him with the immortal words: "Jesse Livermore, I presume." Many years later, when Livermore became famous, Harris recalled he had no idea where the words had come from but that they had just seemed appropriate.

Harris expected his customers to pick themselves up from adversity and was always ready to help them do it – provided they were willing to help themselves. He thought Livermore was a man who would help himself.

Harris asked if he could sit in on the meeting as Hutton and Livermore discussed what had happened and what to do about the outstanding debt of $500. Ed Hutton was certainly well aware of his situation, as the two men had discussed the vagaries of the delayed ticker many times in the past. Livermore offered to pay off the $500 at $50 a month until it was cleared and told his friend he expected his account to be suspended until the debt was paid.

But that, he found, was not at all what Hutton had in mind.

Livermore listened intently and was amazed as Hutton told him that he was prepared to lend him money to get started again. Hutton offered to credit his brokerage account with $1,000 cash, leaving him $500 to trade. Livermore sat back and thought long and hard as to how he might respond. But then it was Hutton's turn to be amazed. Livermore turned him down flat. He told Hutton that extending credit to him was no good to him and that if he took up his offer he feared he would only lose it all again. Jim Harris was equally stunned by Livermore's absolute honesty and realistic grasp of the limits of his own abilities. It was not what he was used to hearing from customers who fell into debt.

Livermore told Hutton that he had only one option and that was to go back to the bucket shops to rebuild his fortunes. He said: "I'm not sure yet that I can beat the game in this office, but I am sure I can take money out of the bucket shops. I know that game and I only have a notion I know what went wrong here."

Then Livermore took a gamble and cheekily asked if he could have the $1,000 as a cashier's check to take away and trade elsewhere. Hutton looked him straight in the eye across the desk and wondered what he should do. At that moment, Jim Harris tapped Hutton on the arm and they adjourned outside to the corridor to discuss it.

Livermore was on tenterhooks and knew exactly what was being discussed outside. He also knew that his whole future depended on the outcome.

After a minute or two, Harris and Hutton returned to the room and this time Harris did the talking. He told him he was not going to give him $1,000 but $2,000 and that he could take it away until he was ready to come back and trade with the firm again.

Hutton called in the chief cashier and ordered him to issue a cashier's check for $2,000 made out to Livermore for cash. Harris also told him not to chase the $500 debt on Livermore's brokerage account. The chief cashier raised his eyebrows and asked if he could speak to both men privately. For the second time, they adjourned to the corridor. Livermore's previous relief turned to renewed panic. He knew that neither Harris nor Hutton would overrule their chief cashier if he was against the loan. But he needn't have worried. A smiling Ed Hutton returned to the room alone and they chatted about their families as they waited for the check to be prepared. When the chief cashier returned, Hutton signed it with a flourish, placed it in an envelope, handed it to Livermore and wished him well. There was nothing to sign and no pledges to give. It was a remarkable act of trust and generosity by Harris and Hutton – one that Jesse Livermore would not easily forget.

But in truth, getting his hands on the $2,000 stake money proved to be the easy part. Livermore had nowhere to go to invest it. He certainly wasn't welcome at any bucket shop back in Boston and there were none left open in New York. He recalled: "After some thinking, I decided to go to St Louis."

It was a wise choice as there were two major chains of bucket shops based in St Louis: C.C.Christie and the Coe Commission Company. They were known as being reliable and, by the standards of the industry, respectable. They were also very big and very profitable, with multiple branches spreading out from St Louis. There was no danger of them welching on winning bets.

Livermore vacated his rooms in New York and sold off his furniture. When he had pared back his possessions to a single suitcase, he took the first train to St Louis.

As soon as he got to St Louis Union Station, he booked into the Station

Hotel adjacent to the railway and, after a quick lunch, set out to inspect the bucket shops in the city. He went to the Coe Commission Company first. Coe's flagship St Louis shop was one of the biggest in America. It leased its ticker machines and lines from Western Union. It had so many machines that it was Western Union's biggest customer in St Louis and at one point accounted for half of its revenues in the city. Coe was run by two brothers, Louis and Angelo Coe. The huge shop regularly attracted over 300 customers at any one time and they spent most of the day gathered around the rows of ticker machines.

When Livermore arrived, business was in full swing. This was just what he wanted, and he felt he would be able to trade in anonymity for at least a week before he was spotted and identified as Boston's notorious boy plunger. He had no doubt at all that he could earn significant money. As he said: "I knew I could beat them. I was going to play dead safe – carefully and conservatively."

His only concern was not being banned, and he lived in constant fear of being exposed as the notorious plunger: "My one fear was that somebody might recognize me and give me away because bucket shops all over the country had heard of the boy plunger." He was in absolutely no doubt he would be straight out of the door once he was identified. He also knew that once one shop exposed him, the word would get out around St Louis, and he would no longer be welcome to trade anywhere.

So Livermore made himself as inconspicuous as he could and mingled with the crowd for at least two hours, surveying the setup carefully before he put his money down. As he remembered years later: "In such a crowd, I stood a better chance of being unnoticed. I stood and watched the board carefully until I picked out the stock for my initial play." His fear of being recognized was very real. Although he was now 23 and had matured mentally, physically he still looked 18. It made him very easy to spot.

Livermore found he was as nervous as when he had made his first trade six years earlier: "I looked around and saw the order clerk at the window where you put your money down and get your ticket. He was looking at me, so I walked up to him and asked: 'Is this where you trade cotton and wheat?'"

The desk clerk replied: "Yes sonny."

Livermore pretended naïveté: "Can I buy stocks too?" The clerk replied: "You can if you have the cash." A relieved Livermore told him in his most boastful voice: "Oh I got that all right." The clerk was skeptical: "You have, have you?" But he smiled when he said it.

Livermore asked: "How much stock can I buy for one hundred dollars?" to which the clerk replied: "One hundred if you got the hundred." Livermore shot back, testing the clerk's willingness to do business with him: "I got the hundred. Yes, and two hundred too!"

According to Livermore's recollections, the clerk replied: "Oh my."

With that, in the best commanding manner he could muster, he said: "Just you buy me two hundred shares." It was all an act, of course, as Livermore had not told him the share he wished to buy and the clerk said: "Two hundred what?"

Livermore looked at the board pretending to have no idea what he wanted to buy: "Two hundred Omaha", he finally shouted out as if he had decided at random. Livermore recalled: "He took my money, counted it and wrote out the ticket." Livermore, who gave his name as Horace Kent, had chosen wisely; Omaha was short for the Chicago, St Paul, Minneapolis and Omaha Railway Company, one of the popular speculative stocks of the day.

After he took hold of his stamped chit, Livermore was very pleased with himself. He sat down and hid himself amongst the other customers and, as he put it, "waited for the roll to grow."

But Livermore's arrival had been noted by co-owner Louis Coe, who called the desk clerk into his office to enquire about Mr Kent. When Coe told the clerk he thought he was a ringer, the clerk, so taken in by Livermore, replied: "He's no ringer boss, his name is Horace Kent and he's a rah-rah boy playing at being used to long pants." Coe, against his own better judgment, took the clerk at his word.

After he finally got his money down, Livermore grew more and more confident. He had planned his return most carefully and could only see upward movement in Omaha. He was duly rewarded with a handsome profit a few hours later. After that, he was in and out, trading up to half a dozen times a day. But after a few days, he knew it could not last once Coe's head office got wind of one customer relieving them of substantial amounts of cash. As soon as that happened, it was only a matter of time before they guessed who Horace Kent really was. He remembered: "In two days, I made $2,800, and I was hoping they'd let me finish the week out. At the rate I was going, that wouldn't be so bad. Then I'd tackle the other shop and, if I had similar luck there, I'd go back to New York with a wad I could do something with."

But, predictably, it was not to last and on the morning of the third day, as he attempted to buy 500 more shares, the clerk said to him: "Mr Kent, the boss wants to see you." Livermore knew straightaway what that meant, but he went along with it just in case: "I knew the game was up. But I asked him: 'What does he was to see me about?' 'I don't know.' 'Where is he?' 'In his private office. Go in that way.'" The clerk pointed to a door. Livermore went in, and Louis Coe sat waiting behind a desk. Coe said simply and without ceremony: "Sit down, Livermore" and pointed to a chair. He said: "Listen, kid. I ain't got nothing against you. Nothing at all, see." When Livermore feigned not to understand, Coe stood up and proved to be a very large man. A frisson of fright coursed though Livermore's veins as he wondered what was coming next. Coe continued: "I know all about you. I make my money coppering suckers." Gesturing towards the door, he said: "Just come over here, Livermore, will you?" As he opened the door, he pointed to customers in the big room: "Do you see those guys? Take a look at them, kid. There's 300 of them. 300 suckers. Then you come in, and in two days you cop more than I get out of the 300 in two weeks. This isn't business kid – not for me. I ain't got nothing against you. You are welcome to what you've got. But you don't get any more. There isn't any more here for you." With that, he showed Livermore to the front door of the shop and saw him onto the pavement.

As far as the Coe Commission Company was concerned, Livermore's trading was over.

Livermore then went straight to the nearby shop of C.C. Christie, one of a chain run by the Christie brothers, which was in the same block as Coe. The Christies were extremely rich and had started off running pool tables in public houses and later built up a chain of dedicated pool clubs. When Western Union brought the ticker to St Louis, they quickly latched on to the potential profit to be made in bucket shops and soon were operating a small chain. The Christie shop was smaller than Coe's but it had an upmarket image and a much better class of customer. But there were also fewer of them, and it was a lot less easy to hide than it had been at Coe. Unfortunately for Livermore, a newcomer was all too easily spotted.

The manager of the Christie shop, Jamie Davis, a fiery red-haired man, was known as one of the canniest managers in St Louis, and very little got past him. And so it proved as Davis spotted Livermore almost immediately he entered the shop.

Unaware, Livermore approached the desk clerk and asked to buy 1,500 shares of the Brooklyn Rapid Transport Company. It was not an unusual request, as Brooklyn was a bull stock and a favorite of speculators. It ran all the rail lines east of New York. The clerk, who had already been warned that Livermore was in town, pressed a bell button hidden under the counter to alert Davis, who then looked out of his office window.

Although he had been warned to look out for Livermore, the clerk had not been told not to trade with him and so, with no instructions to the contrary, he accepted the order. But before Livermore could pay over his money and have his ticket stamped, Davis pounced out as if from nowhere. He seized the ticket and pushed Livermore away from the counter to halt the transaction.

Livermore coolly told him that the clerk had accepted his order and the transaction was valid. At that, the manager said: "Livermore, you go back to Coe. We don't want your business. Livermore simply demanded the ticket confirming his transaction. The manager said: "You get no ticket here. Don't ever come back here to trade; we don't take your business." It was said in a loud voice in front of all the other customers as though Livermore was a common criminal. Livermore was totally humiliated and turned on his heel, intent on returning to his hotel. A group of unpleasant looking men had lined up behind Davis, and Livermore suddenly felt very uncomfortable. He was in no mood to hang around and it was immediately clear that it was not only time to get out of the shop, but out of St Louis altogether.

Livermore was livid at the manner in which his trade had been rejected. If Davis had been more discreet, he figured he might have had a chance of trading elsewhere in St Louis. But such was the commotion that he knew it would be circulating everywhere within hours that the notorious boy plunger was in town, and every desk clerk of every bucket shop in St Louis would be on the lookout for him.

He realized the game was up and checked out of the Station Hotel and caught the first train back to New York.

When he got there, he went straight to Harris Hutton and paid off the $500 debt and the $2,000 loan, leaving him around $2,000 to trade with. He was careful to make sure that his credit was re-established. Ed Hutton was delighted to have him back and immediately sent a telegram to Jim Harris with the good news.

He booked into a cheap hotel to save money and resumed his New York bachelor life very much as before. But his luck was no better and, although he lost no more money, he didn't make any either. He spent his days struggling to keep his head above water; not losing became his mantra, and he grew so cautious that a profit seemed unattainable anytime soon.

But then he got a lucky break. An old-timer came in and started talking about a new office Christies had opened up in Hoboken, a coastal resort in New Jersey. It was the closest they could open to Manhattan while staying within the law. To encourage business, Christies was offering low margins and welcoming all. That is, unless his name was Jesse Livermore. But Livermore guessed he might not be recognized in a brand new shop with new staff, especially if his first trading day was a Saturday.

The following Saturday, Livermore chased over to Hoboken and, sure enough, the clerk on the desk did not recognize him. It was also clear that, this Saturday, the clerk was running the shop on his own with no manager present and just a few board boys for company. Livermore chatted to the clerk for a while, careful to give the impression that he knew nothing about shares or trading. The trick worked and Livermore found himself being "sold" by the clerk who was desperate to take some money off him.

Livermore was aware that the market had been rising all week and he figured it was due a correction and that that correction would happen before the market finally closed down for the week. In those days, the end of the trading week was Saturday lunchtime. At 11:15am Livermore, against the market direction, started shorting stocks heavily. The clerk was very glad to take his money, and Livermore placed bigger and bigger bets until he had parted with $2,000. As he took Livermore's money, the clerk, with only a hint of irony, said to him: "I hope you make a lot of money." Almost as soon as he had said it, the market suddenly turned as traders started taking profits. 40 minutes later, Livermore covered all his positions as the market began to rally in the last five minutes of trading, just as it usually did as traders balanced their books before the end of the week. It had been a fantastic run and, altogether, Livermore had made $5,100 from a $2,000 stake. The clerk could hardly believe his eyes; nothing like this had ever happened to him before. He added up Livermore's profits and checked it again and again. But the result was the same: Livermore had made a 150 per cent profit in 45 minutes.

The clerk quickly realized that it was more cash than he had on the premises. But Livermore wanted his money. The clerk was in a dilemma as 20 or so other punters had followed Livermore's lead, and he had over $1,000 to pay out on top of the $5,100. The clerk begged Livermore to let him pay out the smaller punters first and see what was left. At the end, the clerk only had enough to repay Livermore his stake plus $800. He had no choice but to wait until Monday morning for his money. Livermore was confident he would get his money and agreed to wait. He was back at Christies by midday on Monday.

When he got there, he found Jamie Davis, the manager of the St Louis office waiting for him. Davis had come over specially to see who it was had taken the shop for over $5,000 in less than an hour. He secretly suspected it might be Livermore and wanted to see for himself. He recognized Livermore straightaway, and a minor verbal fracas ensued after Davis reminded him that he had told him he was not welcome anymore at Christies.

This time, Livermore was unworried and not at all intimidated. He knew he was in the right and that there was no question he would not be paid – especially with customers in earshot.

This time, the boot was on the other foot and Davis was anxious for them not to be overheard. Sensing an advantage, Livermore told Davis he would come and trade when he liked and they had better honor his bets. Because the office had been set up to attract New York high rollers and had been advertised as being open to everyone and anyone, Davis was in a quandary and did not want customers getting wind of what was going on. He changed tack and begged Livermore to lower his voice. He sold Livermore a hard luck story, stressing the need to look after his employees and feed his wife and children. He begged Livermore not to return. Livermore was in no real mood to argue and he knew it would be fruitless anyway as Davis would simply increase the margins and the spread and render his trading unprofitable just as Haight & Freese had done a few years earlier.

When Livermore demanded his money, Davis paid him out the full $4,300 in cash that he was owed without argument. Having been paid, Livermore grudgingly agreed not to come back and took his leave. He had already surmised a better plan in his head to relieve Christies of some more cash. He was still angry about having been humiliated by Davis in St Louis.

Instead of returning himself, he sent in a ringer who gambled small amounts and lost before finally returning to sting the shop. Livermore eventually managed to win another $2,800 with the ringer following his instructions and shorting shares at the precise moment for maximum leverage.

After that, Christies' New Jersey shop seemed doomed to failure. Sophisticated New York punters piled in as a fevered bull market began. It was the bucket shop's worst nightmare as losses mounted and the bulls gave the shop a daily beating. Christies was forced to close the office, and Davis paid for the failure with his job. Altogether, the Christie brothers had lost over $85,000 on the venture – and they were not used to losing.

It also proved to be the last trade Livermore would ever do in a bucket shop.

He returned to focus on Wall Street, still looking for an edge but determined to keep his losses small as he gained an education. He knew he would eventually work out how to trade profitably, although at that stage he didn't know how. He could read the tape perfectly, but if the tape was delayed and prices were decided by what was actually happening on the floor, his systems didn't work.

He cut his trading right back and only made a move when he felt 100 per confident of a result. It was the most frustrating but, ultimately, the most rewarding period of his life.

CHAPTER 8

Do or Die: Back to Wall Street

A re-learning process

1902 - 1905

After his experiences in St Louis, Jesse Livermore finally realized that his days trading in bucket shops was definitely over. Not because he was too easily recognized or that it got too difficult to trade, but because of a visit he received one day at his New York hotel. The visitor did not give his full name or his address or really say very much at all. But his very presence sent a message that no sensible man would ignore. The dark haired visitor, distinguished by a broken nose, was tall and lean, extremely well built and in his middle fifties with a Brooklyn accent.

Despite his appearance, his overall manner was quietly charming and in different circumstances Livermore could have sat down with him and enjoyed a pleasant hour together discussing the vagaries of life in New York.

The man, who introduced himself only as 'John', sat down alongside Livermore on one of the sofas in the hotel lobby. The choice of venue for their 'chat' was no accident; Livermore felt a lot safer being highly visible in a very public place. But there was no scene and no drama although Livermore was under no illusion that he was expected to sit down and just listen.

'John' opened the conversation: "Look Jesse, may I call you Jesse? The boss doesn't like what you have been up to of late and has asked me to come and have a few words." Livermore feigned mock ignorance and momentarily looked away. 'John' raised his voice an octave and said simply: "*Compris?*" This time Livermore nodded and didn't let his attention wander again. He had heard that word used before in New York and knew the undertone.

He told Livermore that he worked for certain interests who controlled a chain of commission houses. He explained that as "grateful" as his principals were for Mr Livermore's custom in the past they would prefer it if he now did not honor them with any more of his "custom." The way that 'John' explained it left no part of the message in doubt. Livermore told him that the message was being received "loud and clear" and that, in future, he would confine his "custom" to the brokerage houses in New York.

With the purpose of the meeting concluded, Livermore and 'John' did indeed enjoy a few minutes of what might be termed pleasant conversation. Once the unpleasant part of the day was over, 'John' explained that he managed and trained boxers for a living and recommended to Livermore that if he ever wanted a good night out, then one of his promoted matches was unbeatable for entertainment value. In fact, he offered him tickets for an upcoming fight he was helping promote. Livermore thanked him and explained he was currently single and unattached but said he would certainly take him up on such an offer in the future. They exchanged contact information and, with that, the man shook Livermore's hand and left. The two had got on very well together. Just as he left, 'John' turned round and acknowledged that if a return visit proved necessary he would find it difficult. But it was all part of the act, and Livermore knew instinctively he must never give cause for there to be a return visit. Livermore was in no doubt that he must never set foot in a bucket shop again, and if he did he might come to serious harm. 'John' was an expert at delivering such messages, and Livermore knew enough about life to heed them. He also guessed that the pleasant 'John' was only the messenger, and the people who came next would not be so pleasant or accommodating. Although, by nature, Livermore didn't like being told what to do, this was one message he would heed.

Livermore had no idea who had sent 'John' to see him. He suspected it might be Arnie Rothstein but it equally could have been the Coe brothers. But he didn't really care to find out.

So Livermore returned to Harris Hutton. He immediately paid the $8,000 spoils of his plundering in St Louis into his brokerage account. His $2,500 debt was already repaid and, after withdrawing enough cash for a month's living expenses, he had $5,000 to trade with, meaning a leveraged pot of between $20,000 and $50,000. It was enough to do some serious damage if he could identify some good stocks to buy and sell.

Livermore also suddenly felt more comfortable upon his return to Wall Street. After his experiences with Ed Hutton and Jim Harris, he felt like an insider rather than an outsider, and this made him feel much more confident with what he was doing. He now knew his future was trading the markets and knew he was going to have to learn how to trade legitimately and make money.

With time on his hands, Livermore analyzed to death the differences between trading in real time and trading in what he called "ticker time". Secretly, deep inside, he was glad that the bucket shop avenue had been closed off to him. He knew he had to move on and once and for all learn how to play in Wall Street. He readily admitted: "If it hadn't been for them refusing to take my business, I never would have stopped trading in them. And then I never would have learned that there was much more to the game of stock speculation than to play for fluctuations of a few points."

But the chasm of his understanding frightened him, and he realized that the game had changed for him. He also gradually realized that the automatic stop loss, a by-product of bucket shop trading, was one of the keys to his trading style. As he explained: "Trading in the old fashioned bucket shop had some decided advantages over speculating in a reputable broker's office. For one thing, the automatic closing out of your trade when the margin reached the exhaustion point was the best kind of stop loss order. You couldn't get stung for more than you put up, and there was no danger of rotten execution of orders, and so on."

He began to gradually work out that bucket shop trading was the market equivalent of shadow trading, simulated trading or paper trading as it is more commonly known. Paper trading is when investors test systems on paper and simulate trades. But Livermore thought that simulated trading was a waste of time as he said often: "I have heard of people who amuse themselves conducting imaginary operations in the stock market to prove with imaginary dollars how right they are. Sometimes these ghost gamblers make millions. It is very easy to be a plunger that way. It is like the old story of the man who was going to fight a duel the next day. His second asked him: 'Are you a good shot?' 'Well,' said the duelist, 'I can snap the stem of a wineglass at 20 paces.' 'That's all very well', said the unimpressed second. 'But can you snap the stem of a wineglass while the wineglass is pointing a loaded pistol straight at your heart?' With me, I must back my opinions with my money."

Although Livermore was only in his mid-twenties, the learning curve he had been through made him a man much wiser than his years, as he was fond of saying: "It takes a man a long time to learn all the lessons of all his mistakes. They said there are two sides to everything. But there is only one side to the stock market; and it's not the bull side or the bear side, but the right side. It took me longer to get that general principle fixed firmly in my mind than it did most of the more technical phases of the game of stock speculation. "

"My losses have taught me that I must not begin to advance until I am sure I shall not have to retreat. But if I cannot advance, I do not move at all. I do not mean by this that a man should not limit his losses when he is wrong. He should. But that should not breed indecision: All my life I have made mistakes, but in losing money I have gained experience and accumulated a lot of valuable 'Don'ts'. I have been flat broke several times, but my loss has never been a total loss. Otherwise, I wouldn't be here now. I always knew I would have another chance and that I would not make the same mistake a second time. I believed in myself.

"A man must believe in himself and his judgement if he expects to make a living at this game. That is why I don't believe in tips. If I buy stocks on Smith's tip. I must sell those stocks on Smith's tip. I am depending on him. Suppose Smith is away on holiday when the selling time comes around? No, sir, nobody can make big money on what someone else tells him to do. I know from experience that nobody can give me a tip or a series of tips that will make more money for me than my own judgement. It took five years for me to learn to play the game intelligently enough to make big money when I was right.

"I didn't have as many interesting experiences as you might imagine. I mean the process of learning how to speculate does not seem very dramatic at this distance. I went broke several times, and that is never pleasant, but the way I lost money is the way everybody loses money who loses money in Wall Street. Speculation is a hard and trying business, and a speculator must be on the job all the time or he'll soon have no job to be on."

All of those thoughts were revolving around Livermore's head as he tried to settle down and trade properly and respectably on Wall Street. Luckily for him, a gigantic boom was building on the street. As Richard Smitten, an earlier Livermore biographer, put it: "The market was starting to boil." Well over three million shares a day were being regularly traded. It seemed that everyone in America was trading shares from industrialist millionaires to boot shine boys. He remembered it well years later: "In previous flush times I had heard, Wall Street used to brag of 250,000 share days, when securities of a par value of $25 million changed hands. But in 1901, we had a three million-share day. Everybody was making money. The steel crowd came to town, a horde of millionaires with no more regard for money than drunken sailors."

Livermore was a minnow trading alongside some Wall Street greats: names like John Gates, Loyal Smith, Hetty Green and John Drake. Hetty Green was an heiress and the first serious woman investor on Wall Street. She had inherited

$6 million and set it to work.

Whilst they played with millions, Livermore played with his thousands.

One thing he was sure of was that America was in a bull market. He was continually long, and with the market the way it was, a monkey could have made money – something he understood very well: "I played more carefully and did better for a while. Then we ran into the big boom of 1901 and I made a great deal of money. That is, for a boy. You remember those times? The prosperity of the country was unprecedented. We not only ran into an era of industrial consolidations and combinations of capital that beat anything we have had up to that time, but the public went stock mad."

He was also enjoying himself as a single, good-looking young man in New York with money in his pocket seemingly to burn. His fair hair and complexion and clear light blue eyes were an attraction to the opposite sex. He was also unusual in not having any facial hair, almost *de rigueur* in America in the early 20th century. It wasn't a choice; it simply didn't grow easily on his face. As he readily admitted: "As soon as I was in easy circumstances, I began to live pretty well. I made friends and had a good time. I was not quite 25, remember; all alone in New York with easy money in my pockets."

He readily admits that having that good time was just as important to him as his career as an investor when he was in his twenties: "The game of beating the market exclusively interested me from 10am to 3pm every day and, after 3, the game of living my life."

But as good a time as he was having, he did not forget his primary purpose, which was to learn how to trade on the big board with the vagaries of the delayed ticker and to make money. As he told, Edwin Lefèvre, author of Livermore's fictional biography, years later: "Don't misunderstand me. I never allowed pleasure to interfere with business. When I lost, it was because I was wrong and not because I was suffering from dissipation or excesses. I could not afford anything that kept me from feeling physically and mentally fit. As a young man, I never kept late hours because I could not do business properly on insufficient sleep."

During those four years, his expectations were very low and this could have had a psychological effect on his performance. As he admitted: "I didn't expect to do as well as I did in the bucket shops but I thought, after a while, I would do much better because I would be able to swing a much heavier line." During that period, he continually sought to defend his performance: "I was doing better than break even, and that is why I didn't think there was any need to deprive myself of the good things in life. I was acquiring the confidence that comes to a man from a professionally dispassionate attitude to his own method of providing bread and butter for himself." It was all part of his constant self-analysis. In his early years, Livermore was continually assessing himself and seemingly pacing himself for life.

By then, he had had seven years of studying the ticker tape, he realized he had a natural aptitude for it. But he also realized that he had not perfected the art and was only being successful because the market movement was one way. As he said: "I was making allowances for the actual execution of my orders on the floor of the Exchange and moving more cautiously. But I was still sticking to the tape – that is, I was still ignoring general principles; and as long as I did that, I could not spot the exact trouble with my game." He was making less than a hundred dollars a week and in his predicament he recalled the stock market career of Russell Sage, an investor from the previous generation: "Some men like old Russell Sage have the money making and the money hoarding instincts equally well developed and, of course, they die disgustingly rich."

Livermore believed his lack of real success was an inability to grasp that fundamental difference between a gambler and a speculator. He realized he was still in the bucket shop mind-set and was a million miles away from the techniques of men like Sage.

Eventually, after a couple of years, Livermore did believe he had worked out the changes he needed to make in his trading style and to define whether he was a speculator or a gambler.

In his own mind, he defined that the gambling instinct was what he called "betting on fluctuations" and genuine speculating was "anticipating advances and declines". It had taken him over ten years to work out that relatively simple lesson of life. But it made a huge difference to him from that point on. Now he just needed to put it into practice, and that would take time as well. He was mightily relieved and vowed he would never forget what he had learned and become a gambler again: "Before I can solve a problem, I found I must state it to myself. When I think I have found the solution, I must prove I am right. I know of only one way to prove it and that is with my own money."

He was continually looking for an edge, a break in the upward trend where he could go short, then long, and make a killing. He constantly researched the burgeoning railways sector and read all the trade reports he could find. His chance came again with the big railway stocks. By then, he had $10,000 capital, which he could leverage up to $50,000, and maybe double that with the permission of the house. He saw a break and then reversed himself and made $50,000 profit in less than a week. But then he managed to lose almost exactly the same amount when he tried something similar. This continued for many months as he gradually accumulated capital, but it was an agonisingly slow process.

It made him hungry for more. He knew that the market never went up in a straight line but in steps. So he waited for a short-term reversal and then the rally he was sure would come.

This style of trading continued throughout the boom, and sometimes he won and sometimes he lost. He literally trod water in New York for four years, holidaying and enjoying himself as much as he worked whilst he tried to establish that elusive trading technique by which he could consistently make money.

Livermore never dreamed it would take as long as four years, but it did. As he ruminated to Edwin Lefevre: "Slow as my progress seems now, I suppose I learned as fast as I could, considering that I was making money on balance." He was also, by his own admission, over cautious and too anxious. He admitted being obsessed with "curbing his youthful impetuousness."

But a bull market was raging and impetuousness in those conditions was a real asset. However, he ruefully conceded: "I made my mind up to be wise and play carefully and conservatively. Everyone knew that the way to do it was to take profits and buy back your stocks on reactions. And this is precisely what I did, or rather what I tried to do. I often took profits and waited for a reaction that never came. As I saw my stock go kiting up ten points or more, I was sitting there with my four-point profit safe in my conservative pocket. They say you never go poor taking profits but neither do you grow rich taking a four-point profit in a bull market. When I should have made $20,000 I made $2,000, and that is what my conservatism did for me."

Livermore cursed himself when that happened and rued the days when he frequently cashed out of winning positions prematurely in a bull market because he was determined not to lose his roll. As he told Lefevre 10 years afterwards: "It was never my thinking that made big money for me; it was always my sitting. Got that? My sitting tight. It is no trick at all to be right on the market. Men who can be both right and sit tight are uncommon. I found it one of the hardest things to learn. But it is only after a stock operator has grasped this, can he make big money.

"The reason is that a man may see straight and clearly and yet become impatient or doubtful when the market takes its time about doing as he figured it must do. That is why so many men in Wall Street lose money. The market does not beat them; they beat themselves...because they cannot sit tight.

"Especially in a bull market when shares were really only going one way; in a bull market, your game is to buy and hold until you believe that the bull market is near its end."

Livermore was brutally honest about his out-of-character behavior for four years between 1902 and 1906, when it seemed he continually sold out long before a market move was finished. He broke all his own rules continually in the name of conservatism. He admitted that he was drifting and the lack of success or failure lulled his senses: "If I had lost oftener perhaps it might have spurred me to more continuous study. Studying my winning ways I discovered that, although I was often 100 per cent right on the market, that is, my diagnosis of conditions and general trend, I was not making as much money as my market "rightness" entitled me to. Why wasn't I?"

The question gnawed at his mind for close on four years. But life was easy and the living was good, and finding out never seemed to be a priority. He spent most of his summers in Palm Beach, Florida, a town he enjoyed immensely and in which he quickly made friends.

Meanwhile, Ed Hutton was enjoying his own success and, in 1904, had split from his uncle to form his own firm of stock brokers, named E. F. Hutton & Co. This time, his partner was his brother Franklyn Hutton. Naturally, Livermore moved his account to follow his friend, who quickly opened sub branches in Palm Beach, Saratoga and San Francisco. Livermore made sure he only holidayed in one of these places so he was close to a Hutton office at all times.

Despite his sluggishness, by 1906, after four years, Livermore had accumulated capital of his own of around $100,000. For him, it was chickenfeed but by the standards of the time he was a very wealthy man. He could have carried on earning $20,000 a year for the rest of his life and lived a very good life, indeed. But that was not his destiny, and he knew it. He either had to get on or get out. By then he was 28 years old and, although he was enjoying himself as a young man about New York, he was very unsure as to whether he had a long-term future trading stocks. As quickly as he got to the top of a hill, he seemed to fall right back down again.

So in April, he decided to sell everything he had open and go on a month's vacation to Palm Beach, partly to consider his next move. But he quickly got bored sitting in the sunshine, and after three days of the vacation, on impulse, he wandered into the Palm Beach office of E. F. Hutton with his close friend Jake Peters. Peters also dabbled in the stock market and, at the time, rather more successfully than Livermore. The bull market was still raging and traders like Peters had never known it any other way. He was yet to experience his first bear market and sometimes Livermore thought that he did not even understand the concept that shares could go down as well as up. When he bought a loser, he just held onto it for a few weeks until it reversed itself and he trousered an easy profit. To him, that was the stock market. Livermore feared for him but enjoyed his company.

As they stood in front of the tape machine, Peters was keen for some action, but Livermore demurred. As he described his feelings: "I had no interest in the market one way or another and was enjoying my rest." But Peters continually encouraged him to live up to his reputation and plunge in. Eventually, Livermore told Peters to "shut up" and his stunned friend pulled back and sat down on one of Hutton's comfortable brown leather sofas to read the *Palm Beach Daily News*, affectionately known as 'The Shiny Sheet' because of its high quality newsprint. Peters hid behind its large pages. It was rare for his friend to be rude, and he knew when to back off.

Livermore just stood very still and quiet. He could feel something happening inside his head, a sensation he had not experienced before. As was to happen many times in the future, Livermore was struck by a sudden impulse to do something based on nothing at all. Richard Smitten described it as "some kind of psychic urge." But psychic 'surge' was probably a more accurate description. Livermore had often had these urges in the past and, more often than not, disregarded them. But he eventually realized that almost every time he did so, he was wrong. As he recalled: "I was looking over the quotation board, noting the changes, and they were mostly advances – until I came to Union Pacific and I got a feeling that I ought to sell it. I can't tell you anymore. I just felt like selling it. I asked myself why I should feel like that and I couldn't find any reason at all for going short of United Pacific."

He went up to the desk identified himself as an account holder, not that the clerk didn't recognize him, and said: "Sell 1,000 Union Pacific." The clerk was surprised but he knew what to do as Livermore signed the order slip. Not so Jake Peters who literally jumped up from the chesterfield sofa, dropped his newspaper on the floor and literally tried to stop the transaction before it was too late. But Livermore just took his copy of the order slip and calmly waited for his order to be confirmed.

This time he had no fears about any delays as he knew the stock was headed upwards, and the longer it took the better the price. Peters soon calmed down and became convinced that Livermore had some inside information, after all only a maniac would have done what he did if he hadn't.

Peters tried to extract from his friend what he knew, as he himself was bullish on Union Pacific and was actually holding a small parcel of shares himself. But Livermore brushed him aside and told him he was acting only on his own instincts, which Peters simply didn't believe. The two men argued right in Hutton's inner lobby as Livermore thought hard to himself about selling some more: "If I was right in selling the first thousand, I ought to have a little more." So after five minutes more thought, Livermore went back to the clerk's desk and sold another 1,000 shares of Union Pacific. Peters accused him of losing it and believed he might have suffered sunstroke. He begged his friend to leave and tried to steer him out of the Hutton office and back to his hotel room to take a nap.

Peters later recalled that he did believe that his friend was having some sort of mental breakdown, so contrary were his actions to the mood of the market and common sense. At that moment, Livermore returned to the clerk's desk for a third time saying to Peters: "I don't know why I want to sell it, I only know I want to." Now he had sold 3,000 shares of Union Pacific and by the end of the day was already into a significant loss of around $7,500.

He slept surprisingly easily that night, even though he had ended the day $7,500 worse off as he recalled: "I went out of the office 3,000 short in a rising market and I wasn't worried a bit."

The next morning, as soon as the office opened, he was back without his friend and sold another 2,000 shares.

It was April 17th 1906. With 5,000 shares sold short, Livermore decided that he needed to return to New York to oversee the investment. He said: "Suddenly it was no time to be on vacation." He caught the train back that night: "There was no telling what might happen and I thought I'd better be Johnny-on-the-spot and, there, I could move quickly if I had to." The shares had carried on rising but as the market neared its closed, the ride turned slightly and Union Pacific declined for the first time. But Livermore was still $12,000 light on his total investment.

As he lay asleep in his New York hotel room, things started happening in San Francisco that were to have the most extraordinary effect on his life.

CHAPTER 9

San Francisco Earthquake

$250,000 profit in a few days

1906

A t eight o'clock on the morning of Wednesday April 18th 1906, Jesse Livermore was sound asleep in his New York hotel room after arriving back late from Palm Beach the previous evening.

3,000 miles away, across the country in California, it was five o'clock in the morning and the city of San Francisco slept contentedly. Barely two minutes later, the earth shook and all 410,000 citizens were awoken as the San Andreas Fault suddenly ruptured. There were two quakes. The initial quake was hardly noticeable but, 20 seconds later, the earth tremored for 42 seconds at force eight, just about as bad as it gets. It shattered the surface of the earth for a length of 296 miles across California. At its epicentre, the ground moved 28 feet.

Initially, around a quarter of the city's buildings collapsed, 375 people were reported killed and thousands injured. Over 100,000 people were estimated to be immediately homeless. It was a major disaster, as San Francisco was the largest city in California and the ninth largest in the United States of America. But initial reports emanating from San Francisco underplayed the bad news; it was a crisis that could be contained and the word was that the city could speedily be rebuilt. Many of its buildings were constructed from wood, and timber was plentiful and cheap. But it was wishful thinking, and that became the problem itself when fractured gas mains caught fire. The fires spread to the wooden buildings very quickly and, within 12 hours, it seemed that the whole city was ablaze. The damage from the fires quickly exceeded any damage done by the earthquake.

The San Francisco Fire Department, paralyzed by a leadership vacuum, seemed frozen and unable to respond. By sheer bad luck, the San Francisco fire chief, Dennis Sullivan, had been badly injured in the initial quake and was in a coma. As a result, no one knew what to do and there was little leadership.

There was also no water as the mains had been destroyed. What might have been a containable situation rapidly spiralled out of control as inexperienced fire crews started dynamiting strips of land to create firebreaks, which just served to set off more fires.

And then, just as things couldn't get any worse, homeowners started setting fire to their own properties. Their reasoning was simple. Household insurance didn't cover earthquake damage, but fire related damage was fully covered. Two thirds of San Francisco was effectively burnt out before the fires began to subside 48 hours later. In total, an estimated 277,000 people were made homeless inside the first week.

The whole of the city was quickly relocated in temporary buildings and tents as aid began to flood in from the rest of the country and the army took charge. The beaches were filled with families under canvas.

That morning, at around midday, the first reports filtered through to New York City about what had happened. By then, Livermore was at the offices of E. F. Hutton watching and waiting for any action on Union Pacific. Everyone was surprised to see him back from his vacation three weeks early and, soon, the whole office was buzzing about his contrary behavior and wondering whether they should follow him. But all thoughts of that faded away when the news from San Francisco and the enormity of the disaster began to resonate. The evening paper's headline read 'Earthquake disaster in San Francisco'.

At first, the relatively good news meant that the stock market shrugged off the disaster and it barely fell at all. It gave everyone a false sense of confidence.

On Thursday, news of the fires was received in New York but still the market held up. But Livermore was becoming increasingly sure of his ground. He went in to the office of Ed Hutton and closed the door. He told him: "Ed, this is a lot worse than the newspapers are making out. I need cover to sell another 5,000 of Union Pacific." Hutton was surprised and delighted by his friend's newfound enthusiasm after four years of doing nothing. He also agreed with Livermore's analysis of the situation in San Francisco. Since the breaking of the news of the earthquake, Hutton had been unable to raise anyone at the firm's San Francisco office and feared the worst.

He signed off on the extra credit, and Livermore immediately sold another 5,000 of Union Pacific, bringing his short holding to 10,000 shares.

Later that afternoon, Hutton called Livermore back into his office. His face was ashen as he told him he had just heard that the Hutton San Francisco office had burnt down, and he did not know the fate of his staff there. Both men were baffled by the relative strength of the stock market in the wake of such a catastrophe. Livermore advised Hutton to go short on his personal portfolio. It was very timely advice.

But it was not completely risk-free and a sure thing. Privately, Livermore was completely bemused by Wall Street's relative strength, and he just couldn't understand it. As he said: "It was exasperating to see the blindness of the street." And whispering in his ear all the time was his vacation friend Jake Peters, who also had returned from Palm Beach. He told Livermore he was plain wrong, and the bull market would continue as strong as ever despite what was happening in California. As he whispered: "Your skin will be where all the other bear hides are stretched out in the sun, drying." It was remarkable bravado, but Livermore was certain that Peters' confidence was misplaced. So much so that he decided to go for broke.

That evening, Livermore went to see Ed Hutton again to ask for more credit, this time to sell another 10,000 Union Pacific shares. Again, Hutton signed it off and now Livermore was 20,000 shares short. He was nearly $3.5 million worth of shares short, an extraordinary investment for the time. And it had all begun on a simple hunch. But since the earthquake, it had become much more than that. One thing of which Livermore was certain was that Union Pacific could not go up, and that made his investment, in his mind, risk-free.

The following morning, Friday April 20th, the market finally cracked. By the afternoon, it had virtually collapsed after waves of bad news from San Francisco. Union Pacific held up better than most, but still went down with the trend.

Livermore soon cashed out and bought the 20,000 shares back, and by Saturday morning he had covered all his positions and bagged a $250,000 profit. It could have been much more, but he decided not to push his luck. He banked the cash to bring his net worth up to $350,000. Then he reverted back to cautious mode, determined not to lose his profits and become poor again.

But, once again, he rued his caution as the stock market continued to fall.

The damage to the US economy was immense as San Francisco's port was an important trade hub. A few days later, newspapers were carrying the first estimates of the insurance loss from the earthquake and fires. It was $400 million, a sum of money few people could even imagine. Although the loss would be spread over at least a dozen of the big re-insurers, it panicked the market afresh and, on April 25th, the collapse reached its zenith and the market fell 10 per cent in the space of a few days, wiping out over $1 billion of market value. But Livermore sat on his hands as the market tanked and lost millions of dollars that he could have made in profits from being short.

He kept out of the market, fearful of himself and of a rebound in stocks that could wipe him out again.

Two months later, he resumed his summer vacation but this time took the train to Saratoga Springs, a spa resort, north of New York. It was the time of the big racing festival and it seemed that all of New York society was in Saratoga. Saratoga was famous for its mineral springs and, with a raft of fine hotels and casinos, it was a favorite vacation spot for wealthy New Yorkers. The attraction for Livermore was that it contained an E. F. Hutton branch office.

But instead of a calming and relaxing vacation, Livermore found Saratoga a town full of people discussing the stock market and when it might recover. Everyone had a stock market tip for him, but he closed his ears. It seemed that word hadn't got around that Jesse Livermore never listened to market tips. But, after a week, the fevered atmosphere finally got to him and he popped into the E. F. Hutton office to study the tape.

He immediately noticed that Union Pacific was on the rise and it looked to him as though a big buyer was accumulating the stock. Without any thought, he bought 500 shares and kept buying 500 blocks until he held just under 4,000 shares at around 160 each, $600,000 worth. His buying pushed the price up on its own, and he was quickly showing a good profit. The office was abuzz and many Hutton customers followed him in.

Amidst the buzz of the office, the manager called him over and told him his boss was on the phone and needed to speak urgently. Livermore was surprised as the long distance telephone call was still a rarity in 1906, and only two per cent of American households actually owned a telephone. Livermore's immediate thought was that Ed Hutton had withdrawn his credit line and he would have to sell-off half his line. But as soon as the manager handed over the receiver, Livermore heard Hutton screaming down the long distance line: "What the devil's the matter with you – are you crazy?"

Hutton told Livermore that insiders, with knowledge of Union Pacific's affairs, were running up the stock and had been for days. They were feeding him big quantities of overpriced stock and he was sucking it all up. He called the perpetrators of the scheme "highbinders" Hutton told Livermore he was being taken for a sucker: "You can't expect a miracle every time you plunge in that stock. Get out while you've still got a chance." When Livermore argued the opposite, Hutton told him: "Don't be a sucker, get out right away. It's liable to bust wide open any minute." He added: "I've done my duty. Goodbye" and slammed down the receiver.

Livermore was seriously taken aback by Hutton's manner. He had never acted that way before and he concluded, against his better judgement, that there must be very good reason: "I knew he was in a position to hear things."

But still Livermore was not convinced. He knew he could read the tape, and what was happening felt like the opposite of what Ed Hutton was telling him: "Ed was a very clever chap, unusually well informed and a real friend, disinterested and kind hearted. All I had to go by in my purchase of Union Pacific was my years of studying the behavior of stocks and my perception that certain symptoms which experience had taught me usually accompanied a substantial rise."

But Livermore did what he never did: listened to external advice and reversed himself. Throwing his own judgement to the wind and going totally against his own instincts, he sold out of a stock the tape told him was going up.

Worse than that, with total confidence in Ed Hutton's judgement, he also sold four thousand Union Pacific shares short at 162. It was to prove a disastrous move.

The very next day, the directors of Union Pacific suddenly declared a 10 per cent dividend, a dangerous position for any investor who was short the stock. To add to Livermore's discomfort, many of the people like Jake Peters, who he thought were amateurs, were actually holding substantial long positions and suddenly found themselves with huge gains.

Livermore recalled that one man he described as "dull-witted," who had actually made a mistake buying the stock, made $350,000 overnight and was able to instantly retire and become a gentleman farmer.

Livermore said years later: "I got what I deserved for disregarding the voice of experience and listening to the voice of a tipster. I had set aside my own convictions for the suspicions of a friend, simply because he was disinterested and as a rule knew what he was doing...I had been a ninny to let Ed Hutton shake my own resolution."

In truth, that dividend was a one-off event that no one could have foretold. The news caused a sensation on Wall Street, especially amongst financial journalists who initially suspected multifarious practice on the part of the Union Pacific directors. They couldn't believe the board was being so generous with the railroad's money. The truth was that financial pundits had failed to spot how well Union Pacific had been doing and that its huge cash-generating activity was burning a hole in its corporate pockets.

The dividend announcement reverberated around the markets for at least a week. There was no prior precedent for what had happened. The *New York Times* called it a "mad scene."

The instant he heard the news, Livermore knew he had to get out before Wall Street fully absorbed what had happened and the stock skyrocketed, as it surely would.

Livermore got a tiny sliver of good luck. The dividend increase had actually been paid out just before he had shorted his shares, so he was not liable for the dividend – he had dodged that bullet. But still, the rise in the share price had the potential to ruin him if he didn't move quickly. Because the actual payment date of the increased dividend was uncertain, the speculators in the stock froze until they had clarity. By acting very quickly, Livermore managed to buy in 4,000 shares at prices between 165 and 174 whilst the uncertainty reigned.

So shorting the stock cost him a relatively modest loss of $40,000. But of course, his profit, had he held on to his original position, would have been as much as $200,000. But Livermore was mightily relieved to have got out, calling it: "A low price for a man to pay for not having the courage of his own convictions – it was a cheap lesson." In reality, it was a remarkable escape but Livermore never gave himself any credit for that. He believed he just got lucky.

Having got out, Livermore could see the price was going a lot higher and he immediately bought 4,000 shares and held them overnight and then got out again, making $55,000 and thereby realizing a small profit on the whole affair. Then his caution kicked back in, and he was grateful to exit with his fortune intact.

But the incident had a long-running effect. It finally gave Livermore back his old confidence in himself. He had been precisely right and his experienced friend, Ed Hutton, precisely wrong. As he revealed: "I gained confidence in myself, and I was finally able to shake off the old method of trading. It was my last haphazard, hit-or-miss operation. From then on, I began to think of basic conditions instead of individual stocks. I promoted myself to a higher grade in the hard school of speculation."

The ship was set fair for the greatest opportunity of his life so far.

CHAPTER 10

A period of self-analysis

Fundamental change in outlook

1906

At the end of his vacation in Saratoga, Livermore went on to Palm Beach. He had no intention of rushing back into the market. After years of being relatively poor, he was enjoying his healthy bank account that now contained nearly $400,000.

He also determined to help his parents and siblings. He bought his mother and father, now in their seventies, a splendid house in Bridgeport, Connecticut. He also helped out his sister, 43-year-old Mabel, and her husband, Arthur. His brother Elliot, now 41 and married to Carrie with two children, was starting to do really well for himself developing houses in the boom state of Florida.

The desire to enjoy himself also coincided with the return of his confidence. Although the incident with Ed Hutton had been, on the face of it, disastrous and lost him several hundreds of thousands of dollars, it had served to rejuvenate his mind and had completely restored his confidence in himself. Not only had he been 100 per cent right, but a market expert – a man who rarely made a wrong move – had been 100 per cent wrong. It inspired him no end, and now he was mentally refreshed, totally confident in his own abilities again and ready for action wherever it appeared.

He spent much of his time in Saratoga in self-examination mode. After the Hutton fiasco, he believed he was now completely free from the mind-set he called "speculative prejudice." It was all part of his learning process even though he was amazed, in hindsight, at how long it had taken him to learn some pretty basic lessons of the stock market.

He also promised himself that he was finished with trying to make small gains from tape reading. Up to now, most of his focus had been speculating on individual shares and how they would perform in the short term. Now, he was determined to rely on what he called "major market movements" to make his money. He also decided that he would only play for what he called the "big swing." Henceforth, he would study the market and simply wait and wait for a significant market change rather than being in and out all the time.

And he didn't care if the swings were up or they were down. He resolved that from now on he would only trade long in bull markets, short in bear markets and not at all when the market was moving sideways. In truth, he had discovered what is today called 'trend following' and coined it long before the term would become fashionable.

His new thinking would require him to completely change his style. He admitted he found it rather difficult to focus all his thought and his considerable analytical and mathematical powers on the direction of the market rather than the direction of individual stocks. As he said: "I wasn't lazy but I found it easier to think of individual stocks than of the general market. I had to change that, and I did." He added: "Obviously, the thing to do was to be bullish in a bull market and bearish in a bear market. I had to grasp that general principle firmly before I saw that to put it into practice really meant to anticipate probabilities. It took me a long time to learn to trade on those lines."

He found he had to wean himself off following individual stocks and his tape reading methods, but the realization that it was vitally important stiffened his resolve. As he explained: "The moment I ceased to be satisfied with merely studying the tape, I ceased to concern myself exclusively with the daily fluctuations in specific stocks."

He also stopped taking any notice of opinions he read in the press. He still read them but did not act upon them. For a short while, he even considered ceasing to read the daily and weekly newspapers and cut himself off from the media altogether. But eventually he realized that was a step too far.

After Hutton, he believed he had proved that his obsession with making his own decision and not being influenced by others had been proved correct. He also became more certain of his theory on prejudices.

Speculative prejudices were an issue that had long bothered him. Livermore believed that stock market decisions all came back to prejudices and that investors were prejudiced about all sorts of things. One of the hardest prejudices he found he had to overcome was investors who were optimistic and bullish simply because they owned shares. He just couldn't understand that mindset at all and was determined not to be infected by it, as he explained: "You find many people, reputed to be intelligent, who are bullish because they have stocks. I do not allow my possessions – or my pre-possessions either – to do my thinking for me."

He also managed to rid himself of another problem that often affected his trading for the worse. He was obsessed with what he called "making my daily bread out of the market." As a full-time trader, he felt that he had to get a salary out of the market and often traded to achieve that, and for no other reason. He realized that this was a mistake and that his daily, weekly or monthly income was totally irrelevant to his long-term prosperity.

But the thought that overwhelmed him and the problem he was most aware and concerned about was his personal solvency and the lack of consistency. He was very conscious that he had been effectively broke three times in his short career. He euphemistically described it as a "money management" problem. Whether that was the correct description or not, he knew exactly what the problem was but was still unsure how to handle it and to prevent it from happening again. Although he had recovered his financial status all three times, the stress and anxiety he went through in those periods affected his whole well-being.

He boiled down the problem to its essence, which he defined as having enough cash to maintain his positions in the market until they came to fruition.

The problem was leverage – he was always highly leveraged, sometimes as much as 20 times depending how generous his brokers were. If he was fully extended on a position he believed in, then it needed only a five per cent adverse movement to wipe him out. As ever, his problem was simple and it was a problem that dogged him throughout his career and would cause him much heartache time and time again. He wanted answers, or a system, on how he could maintain a position until it did what he predicted it would do. For the moment, the solution evaded him but it dominated his thinking.

For all his faults and problems, he was encouraged by the fact that he was right about a stock's performance almost 100 per cent of the time, but it was always the timing of his investment that he got wrong. With poor timing and trading on margin, it was very easy to go bust even when he was right.

The revelations kept on coming. As well as resolving never ever to have his judgement affected by tips or external advice, he also resolved never to be swayed by the relative price or value of a share. He came to believe that a share was never too high a price that it couldn't be bought or conversely a share was never too low that it couldn't be sold short.

Having decided that he was no longer a short-term opportunity seeker or, to put it more crudely, a bottom fisher, he was now a trend follower tracing what he called "following the path of least resistance."

During the Saratoga vacation, he believed that his mind-set changed fundamentally. As he explained: "I began to see more clearly, or perhaps I should say more maturely."

There was one other problem Livermore had to solve; one that was entirely of his own making, came with success and was common to many other investors. It was the temptation to close a trade early, seeking out a small but guaranteed profit, when a bigger gain was just around the corner.

Livermore had always firmly believed in taking losses early and profits late. He believed the greatest fault in any investor's behavior lay in these two conundrums. But it was easier said than done; something he all too clearly realized. Taking his losses early was an easy mathematical problem for him to solve. He had always had 10 per cent as his limit for getting out. But there was no easy mathematical equation for the other direction. That would always be down to his own money management skills, and he was in no doubt it was his Achilles' heel.

After Saratoga, Livermore believed he solved many of the problems he referred to as "his baggage". As he explained: "For years, I had been the victim of an unfortunate combination of inexperience, youth and insufficient capital."

But he also knew that he still had many negatives to overcome. The self-analysis itself had revealed many potential personal faults he had not yet experienced but knew that he soon might. But perhaps his best attribute had also been exposed during the days of introspection in Saratoga. He was imbued with the fear that he did not know everything and that he was vulnerable. It was a fear he had never felt in his teens. As he explained: "I still had much to learn, but I knew what to do. No more floundering, no more half-right methods. Tape reading was an important part of the game; so was beginning at the right time; so was sticking to your position. But my greatest discovery was that a man must study general conditions, to size them so as to be able to anticipate probabilities. In short, I had learned that I had to work for my money. I was no longer betting blindly or concerned with mastering the technique of the game, but with earning my successes by hard study and clear thinking. I also had found out that nobody was immune from the danger of making sucker plays. And for a sucker play, a man gets sucker pay; for the paymaster is on the job and never loses the pay envelope that is coming to you."

In time, he came to view Saratoga as a "self-help conference with himself as the only attendee." He had gone a long way down the road of solving those in-built problems. Now all he had to do was put his new strategies and tactics into action to make the profits he always knew that he could.

When he returned to New York at the end of the season, he was a new man. And everyone, it seemed, noticed the change. The new, mature Livermore found attitudes towards him had changed: "My brokers ceased to think of me as a sporadically lucky boy plunger. They now regarded me as a star asset of the brokerage."

With much of his baggage disposed of, he could now fully concentrate on the market. But as 1906 rolled on, he found himself in a bearish state of mind.

JESSE LIVERMORE - BOY PLUNGER

CHAPTER 11

Prelude to a Profit
A bearish state of mind

1906 - 1907

B ack in New York, Jesse Livermore found that he was just about the only
man on Wall Street who was bearish. The raging bull market continued
in full swing regardless of what had happened in San Francisco and
regardless of a tightening of credit around the world. Bulls were everywhere
driving up shares higher and higher every day.

The effects of the San Francisco earthquake had not yet become apparent
even though it was now clear that the cost of rebuilding the city was $400
million, which would all be paid for by insurance companies, with the money
ultimately drawn down from the stock market.

But the bigger problem was the loss of GDP to the whole American economy.
The cost of that in one year would be more than twice the insurance losses.
The cost of the gradual loss of confidence in the American economy was
something else altogether.

There were also other problems globally. The Boer War had ended in 1902,
but not before Britain and its empire allies had spent nearly $1 billion, making
it the most expensive war in history up to that point. The war had eaten into
Britain's reserves and, much worse, retaining the hard-won peace was also
proving very expensive with thousands of British soldiers now permanently
stationed in South Africa.

Much of the San Francisco earthquake losses had been insured at Lloyds of
London, adding to Europe's financial woes. Taken together, San Francisco and
the war had sucked money out of the world's economies on a scale that had
never before been seen. Livermore noted: "It was good hard cash that went
up in cannon smoke in the Boer War."

Livermore was an insatiable reader of newspapers and, as a result, he
was more aware of the world's economic problems than most people. As
he recalled: "Much actual wealth the world over had been destroyed, and

everybody sooner or later must feel the pinch. And therefore nobody would be in a position to help anybody."

In the past, whenever America had money supply problems, gold had been shipped from Europe to help ease the burden. But now there was no gold to ship, and what little there was went to San Francisco in insurance payouts, as Livermore could see all too clearly: "Millions were being spent feeding non-producing soldiers in South Africa." He was thought to be referring to the vast amounts of money Britain was spending on the peace in South Africa. It was, in modern parlance, a "double whammy" for the economies of the world.

The earthquake in San Francisco was gradually starting to touch every American, regardless of where they lived. Livermore explained: "The disaster touched everybody – manufacturers, farmers, merchants, laborers and multi-millionaires. I figured that nothing could stave off one peach of a smash and, such being the case, there was but one thing to do: sell stocks."

Livermore came to the irrefutable conclusion that change in the market's direction was at hand, and he forecast a bear market imminently. But there was just one problem with the prognosis – the bull market was still roaring and it was obvious to no one else that the bear was in waiting. In fact, the general impression was precisely the opposite. Once again, Livermore's friend and trading buddy Jake Peters, flush from his success in Union Pacific, couldn't have been more bullish and was not afraid to tell Livermore his views at every opportunity.

But Livermore wouldn't be shaken from his opinion and, despite what was going on around him his conviction remained absolute. For all that, he did not know exactly when the market would permanently turn, he just knew it would.

For all those reasons, Livermore could only be bearish. But it was to take almost a year for him to be proved right. As Livermore recalled much later: "I thought that the money outlook was particularly serious." But at that moment, few other people seemed to.

Eventually he realized that there was no hurry and, instead of plunging in, he sat on his money for the first half of 1906. He had plenty of time to think about what was going to happen next.

In the end, after months of waiting, he could contain himself no longer. He freely admitted later that, despite all his rationalizing, he was unaware of the extreme dangers of getting his timing wrong: "I did not notice that there was another lock on the door – a time lock. It was a perfectly natural oversight and

I had to pay the usual tuition: a good whack per each step forward."

The whacks were gradual.

Then, when all the signs were good in late July of 1906, he plunged and said: "Since we undoubtedly were entering upon a genuine bear market, I was sure I should make the biggest killing of my career."

His first foray in the summer, trying to find the bottom, veered wildly off course. He was initially right and, in line with his new thinking, did not take his profits. But then, the market rallied and began a steady advance that showed no signs of flagging. Livermore's losses grew, and he was not alone in his suffering: "One day it looked as if not a bear would be left to tell the tale of the strictly genuine bear market." In the end, he was worn down, and he sold out at a substantial loss. As he recalled: "I couldn't stand the gaff. I covered and it was just as well. If I hadn't, 1 wouldn't have had enough left to buy a post card. I had lost most of my fur, but it was better to live to fight another day."

Livermore was almost thrown back into another period of self-analysis: "I had made a mistake. But where? I was bearish in a bear market. That was wise, and I had sold stocks short. That was proper. But I had sold them too soon, and that was costly. My position was right, but my play was wrong." It was a familiar refrain.

Livermore had lost half of his net worth in that play and realized that he could have lost it all.

With $200,000 remaining, he tried again in September. He went through exactly the same process, and a day after he had invested his full amount, the market went up again. Half his money was lost.

Now he was down to $100,000 but, equally, he appeared remarkably sanguine about his losses. As he put it: "Another bite out of yours truly."

So he waited and then again went through the same process and plunged in, believing the market was about to break again. But exactly the same thing happened, and he found himself with just $50,000 left in his pot.

At this point, Livermore admitted he thought about abandoning his newly-found principles to go back to tape reading and speculating on single shares, but he persisted: "I figured I must win if I held out."

Around this time Livermore realized he still was missing part of the picture. There must, he thought, be a way of mitigating his losses whilst he tried to find the market turn. It was to occupy much of his thoughts as he watched his fortune diminish for no good reason at all. His self-analysis during the crisis was inconclusive. He knew he was right, but he was wrong. He also knew he was in a battle against the market, and he might not win. He just hoped he could hold on. But, amidst all this confusion, one thing remained clear in his head. Never at any time was he in any doubt that he was right. He attempted to rationalize what had happened: "I had observed certain facts but had not learned to co-ordinate them. My incomplete observation not only did not help but actually hindered."

One mistake he discovered was that he had stopped reading the tape without really noticing. Although he was no longer interested in short term single share gains, he realized that tape reading was still an essential for reading momentary market movements. He swore not to make that error again.

But now, he was faced with three losing forays and a near 90 per cent loss of his money. Again, he tried to rationalize it: "I was 29 years old, and I had been at the game for 14 years. But the first time I traded, because of a crisis that was still to come, I found that I had been using a telescope. Between my first glimpse of the storm cloud and the time for cashing in on the big break, the stretch was evidently so much greater than I had thought that I began to wonder whether I really saw what I thought I saw so clearly...Was I fundamentally wrong in being bearish or merely temporarily wrong in having begun to sell short too soon?"

Livermore was never in any real doubt. It led him to his fourth foray into the market as the market looked as though it had begun a sell-off. In early November, he plunged in again leveraging his remaining $50,000 as far as he could. Then the market inexplicably rallied again, and within a week he was out.

This time Livermore had exhausted all his liquid funds and lost his remaining $50,000. As he recalled: "There I was right and busted." It was clear he had moved too soon. As he said: "I should have walked and not sprinted."

This time round, Livermore found the lack of money much less of a problem than in the past. Possibly Ed Hutton felt guilty about the advice he had given him, which he knew had cost him as much as $200,000 in lost profits.

Hutton agreed to extend him credit even though his capital was exhausted. As Livermore said: "The firm had confidence in me and relations were of the pleasantest. I think they felt I was bound to be right again very shortly, and they knew that with my habit of pushing my luck, all I needed was a start and I'd more than recover what I had lost. They had made a great deal of money out of my trading, and they would make more."

But the psychological damage was as great as the financial damage. Four substantial rounds of losses affected Livermore, and his personality underwent a change. As he described it: "I was no longer aggressively cocksure." But in reality, he was not behaving like a man who had lost $400,000 in a few months. Despite the losses, his confidence was sky high and he just knew he was right. As he explained: "If a man didn't make mistakes, he'd own the world in a month. But if he didn't profit by his mistakes he wouldn't own a blessed thing. I have always found it profitable to study my mistakes."

Amazingly, Livermore showed no hesitation when he believed the time had come for his fifth plunge into the bear market of 1906. By then, it was December and the market was winding down for the holiday, but he was undeterred: "One fine morning, I came downtown feeling cocksure once more."

The reason for his enthusiasm came from an advert announcing new share offerings from two railroad companies, Northern Pacific and Great Northern. Both the companies were controlled by the leading railways entrepreneur of the time, 68-year-old James Hill. Hill controlled a multitude of rail companies across the US and Canada. His ambition was to build a transcontinental railroad that linked all parts of the United States. All his companies were expanding fast and were highly leveraged. Like Livermore, Hill knew that capital was drying up and that, unless he raised some soon, he would run out of cash to fund expansion commitments he had already made.

Hill was an innovator, so he decided to innovate. He invented the partially-paid, deeply-discounted rights issue, whereby existing investors were almost forced to take up rights issues at such attractive terms or see their holdings shrink and share price drop.

First, Great Northern announced an issue of $60 million worth of new shares at par. But the big shock was that shareholders could pay for their new shares effectively on hire purchase in installments. In Great Northern's case, payments could be made over 16 months until April 1908. This was a completely new idea on Wall Street. Almost simultaneously, another of Hill's companies, Northern Pacific, sought to raise $93 million in new shares at par value. It offered even longer, two years, to pay. Initially, this was hailed as innovative on Wall Street and was well received.

But the instant Livermore saw it, he could see the real story, which was Hill's desperation to raise cash. The deal was too good, and Livermore saw right through it for what it was. When he saw the advertisements, he knew that capital on Wall Street had effectively dried up, and this was the only way

Hill could get the money he needed. From that moment on, Livermore knew for certain that a crash was coming. At the time, he said: "The advertisements struck me as more than ominous."

That morning, Livermore rushed into Ed Hutton's office waving the advert he had torn from the pages of the *New York Times*: "Just look at that ad, will you. This is when I should have begun. The time to sell is right now."

Hutton agreed with his friend but still advised caution and said they should wait before plunging in short. But Livermore told him: "Ed, this is a signed confession on the part of the bankers. What they fear is what I hope. This is a sign for us to get aboard the bear wagon. It is all we needed. If I had $10 million, I'd stake every cent of it this minute."

Because Livermore was now totally reliant on credit from Hutton, he was forced to hang back. So when he did get the chance for some action, it was much less than he wanted to put down. He sold as much short as Hutton would let him. Livermore remembered: "He wasn't content with only the inferences a sane man could draw from the amazing advertisement. It was enough for me but not for most people in the office."

But eventually, Livermore got his short line away. A few days later, the St Paul Fire and Marine Insurance Company came out with its own rights issue attempting to beat the railway companies to any new funding that was available. That finally convinced Ed Hutton that Livermore was right. Both men sold Great Northern and other top stocks short. Immediately, the market broke and Livermore was in profit straightaway as Wall Street began its inexorable march downwards. There was no spare money and as the share prices fell, the two rights issues were in immediate trouble.

Livermore remembers the euphoria: "My reputation and my credit was reestablished in a jiffy. That is the beauty of being right in a broker's office, whether by accident or not. But this time, I was cold-bloodedly right, not the result of a hunch or skillful reading of the tape but as a result of my analysis of conditions affecting the stock market in general. I wasn't guessing. I was anticipating the inevitable. It did not call for any courage to sell stocks. I simply could not see anything but lower prices. And I had to act on it. The whole list was as soft as mush."

Livermore held his nerve and sold more shares short, as many as Hutton would allow him. Eventually, there was a small rally as some players tried to squeeze the bears but it wasn't sustained. Jake Peters suffered his first bear market decline and was badly hurt. Peters kept predicting the bottom and advising Livermore to cover his shorts. But Livermore told him: "It isn't time for these corpses to rise to the surface. They are not quite dead yet."

Livermore just kept on selling into every rally, especially the railway stocks. They all collapsed except one, and that was The Philadelphia and Reading Railroad (P&RR). It was controlled by Pierpont Morgan, and the number of shares in circulation with the public was very small.

Despite the fact that there were easier targets around, Livermore, for reasons best known to him, started shorting the shares. But the price hardly moved. Then, one day, he sold 8,000 shares through two different brokers simultaneously. He then sold a further thousand. The share price cracked and he took a 25 per cent profit off the top almost immediately. Cracking the P&RR was to him a personal triumph, and even the great Pierpont Morgan couldn't have failed to notice that feat.

By the end of February of 1907, Livermore had cleaned up.

In the middle of February, he found himself with $400,000 profit from his short position in eight of the biggest companies on Wall Street. All eight stakes were moving slowly downwards. And then he gave them all a short-term shove by selling larger parcels short and exiting quickly. It worked, and the shares moved sharply down. He now had a large profit, and caution entered his head again. He had made back everything he had lost and was good to the tune of $400,000 again. But the success made him fearful and he was also anxious to go to Palm Beach for the season. So he bought in all his shorts and, once again, his money was safely in the bank.

The attractions of Palm Beach were many and, for Livermore, the anticipation of going was almost as good as being there. He totally loved Palm Beach and was always desperate to get there. The relatively new resort had been created by Henry Flagler, a founder of Standard Oil and partner of John D. Rockefeller.

Flagler believed the 16-mile long island, a wilderness of brush when he first saw it, was unique. So much so that he ploughed tens of millions into the area from 1890 onwards. First, he made it connectable to New York by building a new railway, which eventually would run the entire length of Florida. Then, he started construction of the first of four major hotels he built in Palm Beach, called the Royal Poinciana. The Poinciana was built entirely of wood and had 1,100 guest rooms. Within a few years, Palm Beach became the playground of New York society, and figures like Joseph Kennedy built grand houses on the beach.

Livermore found he mixed easily with the society figures that inhabited Palm

Beach. His great passion for fishing the dark blue waters of the Gulf Stream was almost insatiable. The Gulf Stream comes within three miles of Palm Beach, and large fish travel in the stream on their way north. It was the fish that Livermore was interested in: the giant sailfish; bluefin tuna; hammerhead sharks; tiger fish; mako sharks; marlin; king mackerel; and tarpon. The variety that could be caught off the Florida coastline was staggering.

So with all that on his mind, the next day he left for Palm Beach for six weeks. As he recalled: "I came down to Florida for a fishing trip. I had been under a pretty severe strain, and I needed my holiday." But that was a little disingenuous. What Livermore really needed was time to reflect on the roller-coaster of the previous six months. For all his understanding, he realized there was so much more he did not understand. There was plenty to reflect on. He was not yet 30 years old and had almost half a million dollars. Did it get any better than that? He didn't think so.

To make sure his reflections went completely undisturbed, he rented a fishing boat with just him, the captain and a steward. He intended to spend a few weeks cruising in his rented boat off the coast of Florida and not return to land if he didn't have to. He was completely out of the market by then and enjoying some very fine fishing. He even stopped reading the newspapers.

But he had only been at sea for a few days when a smaller boat, owned by a friend, pulled up alongside and Livermore was invited to share some lunch. The friend brought some newspapers on board, which Livermore tried to avoid. But he found himself gingerly glancing over his friend's shoulder to see the headlines, which told him that the market had rallied very strongly.

Instantly, he told the skipper of his boat that his holiday was over. He immediately went down to his cabin, swiftly packed his bag and hopped over to the smaller boat. As he explained later: "I didn't know what I might or might not do. But I knew that my pressing need was sight of the quotation board."

Livermore went ashore with his friends and straight over to E. F. Hutton's Palm Beach office. He knew instinctively that the big rally made no sense at all: "Moderate rallies from time to time were reasonable. But the bear market was not over, and here was Wall Street, or the fool public or desperate bull interests, disregarding monetary conditions and marking up prices beyond reason or letting somebody else do it."

The E. F. Hutton office was abuzz and the presence of Jesse Livermore was warmly welcomed: "When I walked in, I found there were a lot of chaps I knew. Most of them were talking bullish. They were of the type that trade on the tape and want quick action."

Although more or less unknown on Wall Street, Livermore was the star turn at Huttons, and he knew it. As he recalled: "Of course, people always magnify a fellow's winnings and the size of the line he swings. The fellows in the office had heard that I had made a killing in New York on the bear side, and now they expected that I would again plunge in on the short side."

There was no ticker tape in the Palm Beach office, but as soon as the prices were relayed by telegraph from New York, they were chalked up on what was called the quotations board. Livermore said: "The moment I saw how far the recovery in prices had gone, I no longer felt the need for a vacation. I had not thought of just what I was going to do when I came ashore. But now I knew I must sell stocks."

For some reason, his eye immediately focused on the quotation of the Anaconda Copper Mining Company, whose price had been driven up seemingly by a concert party. The stock had risen to 300, and Livermore liked the look of it. As he said: "It was an old trading theory of mine that when a stock crosses 100, 200 or 300 for the first time, the price does not stop at the even figure but goes a good deal higher so that if you buy it as soon as it crosses the line, it is almost certain to show you a profit. Timid people don't like to buy a stock at a new record high, but I had a history of such movements to guide me."

Although Livermore was a raging bear, he was tempted to trade Anaconda long. He realized that the current rally would probably last a while longer and that it was not quite right to plunge in short. But as he said to himself: "I might as well pay myself wages for waiting." He bought 32,000 quarter shares of Anaconda at around 75. It was a very big order, some $2.5 million worth. Then he booked himself into a hotel to wait.

The following day, he was at Huttons at opening time. But there had been violent storms between Palm Beach and New York the previous night and the telegraph was down. It remained silent until it clattered at last. Ominously, the only quote that came over the wire for Anaconda that day showed it had fallen to 292. Livermore had lost $80,000, getting on for a quarter of his net worth. He recalled that moment: "I wanted quick action. Well, I was getting it."

Overnight, Livermore suspected that he had been right about the bear market and wrong about Anaconda. He realized he had bet the wrong way and wondered why he had acted against what he felt to be right. He recalled his own old proverb: "The only thing to do when a man is wrong is to be right by ceasing to be wrong."

The storms passed, and the next day the telegraph was working at its normal speed. Anaconda came back to nearly 303 but then began falling back. Now he definitely knew he was wrong and realized the movement in Anaconda was what he called a "fake movement" and that he had to get out before he did himself real damage. When Anaconda fell to 301, he told the clerk to sell out his entire position: "All I've got". Then he could only wait and hope.

As Livermore went to sit down and wait for his confirmation notes, he was accosted by a couple of brothers, both experienced traders who had made their reputations in commodities. The elder brother shouted across that Livermore would be sorry he had sold his position. Livermore wondered how he knew he had sold: "I knew that he was supposed to be very clever and always traded on inside news, but how he knew my business so accurately was beyond me." It turned out that the older of the brothers had learned Morse code and he was able to know everybody's buy and sell orders before they were actually fulfilled in New York. That advantage would last until 1910, when the key tappers were replaced by keyboards.

When Livermore realized what was going on, he resolved to limit his trading in the Palm Beach office in future.

Back in New York, the Hutton office had to get rid of 32,000 quarter shares of Anaconda. The New York brokers were very experienced and knew that if they dumped the lot at once the price would crack and their client would lose heavily. But they knew better than that and fed it out in 5,000 share parcels. The first parcel went at 299 ¼ and the last at 298 ¾. From the pattern of selling, Livermore realized that there was no real demand for the shares, and he had been very lucky to emerge with only a small loss.

Straightaway he knew what to do to profit from the situation. As he explained: "The moment I got the report of the sale of the last of my long stock, I started to do what I had really come ashore to do and that was to sell stocks. I simply had to. There was a market, after its outrageous rally, begging to be sold. People were beginning to talk bullish again, but the course of the market told me that the rally had run its course. It was safe to sell them, and it did not require reflection."

Anaconda broke open the next day. Livermore just sold and sold its shares until he was up to his limit. He recalled that moment: "My growing paper profit kept reminding me that I was right, hour by hour. Naturally, I sold some more stocks – everything. It was a bear market, and they were all going down."

At that point, with $5 million or so at stake in the market, he decided he was going home. He said: "I was needed in New York. Who needed me? I did. Palm Beach was far too remote, and too much valuable time was lost to telegraphing back and forth."

And he was proved right when the market crashed precipitously on March 25th after some panic selling. But rumors flew round that it was part of a corner by Ed Harriman, Henry Frick, William Rockefeller and Jacob Schiff. There was no corner, but it turned out the financiers were trying to assemble a $25 million fund to be able to go into the market and restore confidence. They even tried to tempt Jack Morgan, the son of Pierpont Morgan, into the pool. But his father refused and the pool broke up. But the rumors of such an operation proved to be enough on their own to boost confidence and provoke a sharp rally. The market dropped and rallied continuously.

Livermore spent the whole of the spring and summer selling shares short and covering and then selling short again, taking care not to risk his growing fortune on fake rallies. It was a game of cat and mouse between him and the market. As he admitted: "The market had frequent rallies much as before, and I kept covering and putting them out again...I had lost every cent of the $300,000 I had made out of the San Francisco earthquake break. I had been right and nevertheless had gone broke. I was now playing safe – because after being down, a man enjoys being up. Even if he doesn't quite make the top."

In hindsight, Livermore was over-cautious and could have made three or four times the money he did in that period with just a bit less caution, but as he said: "The way to make big money is to be right at exactly the right time. In this business, a man has to think of both theory and practice. A speculator must not merely be a student, he must be both a student and a speculator."

He readily admitted his caution was now his enemy, and he would be hampered if he could not find a way to bet big and be consistent when he could clearly see where the market was going. But as ever, and throughout his life, consistency was never a talent that he really possessed. As he admitted: "I did pretty well even if I can see now where my campaign was tactically inadequate."

As the summer arrived, the market started to go sideways as investors were unsure of the future. The action dried up, and Livermore's thoughts returned to leisure activities. The intense in-and-out activity of the past four months had exhausted him. He knew the bear market was not over but realized there would be no real movement in the market for months: "It was a cinch that there would be nothing done in a big way until long in the fall."

It was fashionable for New York's movers and shakers to vacation in Europe in the summer of 1907, and Livermore decided to join them: "Everyone I knew had gone or was going to Europe, so I thought that would be a good move for me."

In the four months since he had returned to New York from Palm Beach, he had managed by dint of small deals, with little risk, to double his fortune. He now had $750,000 on hand.

Once again, he closed all his positions and caught a steamship for Europe.

He crossed the Atlantic to Cherbourg and then went by train to Paris. From there, he travelled to Aix-les-Bains, a French resort in the south east of the country. Aix-les-Bains enjoyed natural hot sulphur-infused springs that were reputed to have great healing qualities. The springs fed baths carved out of the rocks many hundreds of years earlier by the Romans. The resort was very popular with Wall Street types and had been made famous from frequent visits by Pierpont Morgan and Queen Victoria. Morgan built a house there, where he used to entertain his French mistresses every summer. Many Wall Streeters went there hoping to bump into Pierpont Morgan and take in some of his wisdom and influence. Livermore was just as obsessed with Morgan and his reputation as the next man, and he also hoped for a meeting or even just a sighting.

Livermore thoroughly enjoyed himself in Aix-les-Bains and remembered: "It was good to be in a place like that with plenty of money and friends and acquaintances and everybody intent on having a good time." He and his friends spent their time drinking, eating, gambling, lounging in the Roman baths, swapping anecdotes, stories and jokes about Morgan most of the time.

There were also plenty of French girls, seemingly on tap and willing to do almost anything for the rich American financiers who descended on their country every year. He remembered: "Wall Street was so far away that I never thought about it."

There was no talk of the stock market, and it was the only place Livermore ever managed to completely forget what he did for a living. He knew he had enough money to last for a long time with plenty left over for when he finally got back to New York. That summer was the most carefree and relaxed period of his life he had ever enjoyed, and he was determined to make the most of it.

But he knew that in September he was headed back to New York, and he hoped for a long period of effortless moneymaking as the bear market hotted up. He had never been as sure of anything in his life.

Then he made the mistake of picking up a copy of the Paris edition of the *International Herald Tribune*. He idly read a small article about the American Smelting Company, affectionately known by its nickname of Smelters. Smelters had been founded by the Rockefellers and was a bellwether stock at the time. The newspaper report stated that Smelters had increased its dividend from seven to eight per cent and had sparked a share rally in New York. Livermore had expected the market to drift for the summer, but he was unprepared for a big rally. It was a signal to him that the big fall was closer to hand than he had originally thought. With that taster, he opened the financial pages and, as his eyes scanned the tables of share prices, he realized that the market was heading for a precipitous fall anytime soon. He recalled years later: "That changed everything for me sitting in Aix." The news simply meant that the bull cliques were still fighting desperately against conditions. Livermore believed that there was a concert party of insiders falsely running up the market against the big fall they knew was coming. He found that sort of behavior offended his sensibilities: "I knew that the bull manipulation was foredoomed to failure in that bear market...I knew there was only one thing to do to be comfortable, and that was to sell Smelters short." He thought: "The insiders have as much as begged me on their knees to do it when they increased the dividend rate on the verge of a money panic. They dared me to sell that stock short." At least that is what Livermore believed.

There were no stockbroker's offices in Aix-les-Bains so, instead, Livermore went to the local telegraph office and sent a telegram to E. F. Hutton in New York with instructions to sell as much Smelters short as they could. By the time he got a reply and confirmation, the stock was already off six points.

Livermore had intended to leave for Paris at the end of August, spend three weeks in the French capital before leaving for Southampton and returning to America by the beginning of October. But instead, he left for Paris that night by train. Interestingly, Pierpont Morgan also made plans to return to New York early and sailed for home on August 21st.

Livermore immediately booked passage for New York on the fastest steamer available and arrived back in New York a month ahead of his original schedule. He got straight to work. That same day, he was in E. F. Hutton's office selling the top shares short. They all produced positive results, and he started to build his positions in the leading stocks. Although he stayed in profit, he had to wait a long time for any real action to develop.

Livermore's continued bearishness was based on a sound proposition – that the supply of money was being squeezed to market brokers. The trigger for the squeeze was the San Francisco earthquake and the Boer War, which had sucked nearly two billion dollars out of the world economy. Half of that was from the financial damage done by the Boer War and the consequent drop-off in world trade. Of course, the contraction was gradual over a period of a year but it was nonetheless happening, and it seemed only a few people were aware of it.

However, Livermore quickly discovered that the line of least resistance was upwards. But he instinctively believed that the market was ready to turn.

He had not spent all his time in Aix-les-Bains engaged in hedonistic activities. Whilst he was there, he gave great thought to the problem of market timing. He gradually dreamed up a new system of trading he called "market probing." His new strategy was exactly the opposite to his previous one of plunging straight in when it felt right.

He resolved in future to think every move through to its conclusion before he acted and to decide his complete strategy in advance of trading a stock, especially what his final target position was to be. Having decided that, he would then issue probes. For instance, if he planned to take a 1,000 share position, his first trade would be 200 shares. It was simple enough, and if the first trade went up, as he predicted, he would put on a second equal tranche. If it didn't, he would wait and get out if the loss was more than 10 per cent. Then he would probe again, repeating himself. Only when the probes were continuously going the right way, would he complete his purchase and wait. Obviously, the new system would mean losses that could last a long time, but he figured it was far more preferable than risking everything on every trade.

In line with his new system and way of thinking, he decided to send out probes in the four most traded categories of the period. He sold small parcels of shares short: two in each category, eight shares in all. To his surprise, he found a small profit in each. In line with his new system, he increased his takes gradually. It worked, and so the system became a hallmark of Jesse Livermore's trading style for the rest of his life.

It was to be especially useful as the beginning of October 1907 dawned.

CHAPTER 12

Stock Market Meltdown

Credit crisis threatens America

September - October 1907

From the latter part of September onwards, the credit markets were, as Jesse Livermore put it, "megaphoning warnings to the entire world." But a belief that the boom times would go on kept the stock market high despite the fact that the economies of the world were gradually running out of hard cash.

The writing was well and truly on the wall when, at the beginning of October 1907, the Bank of England increased its base interest rate from four per cent to six per cent. The huge increase, in a period of a few days, reflected more than anything the tightening cost of credit. The rate was increased in order to stem the outflow of gold from London to the United States, which was reaching crisis proportions. The newly installed governor of the bank, Sir William Campbell, took the unprecedented step of warning London's big banks immediately to stop lending to the United States, which he believed was wildly over extended. The bank even threatened to increase base rates to seven per cent if the lending continued.

President Theodore Roosevelt didn't help matters when he gave a speech to New York's prestigious Gridiron Club accusing Wall Street figures of engaging in excessive speculation in copper, mining and railroad stocks. He called them "malefactors of great wealth."

And there were other factors that had contributed to the tightening of credit markets. The Armstrong Laws finally had been passed in 1907 and they restricted the ability of America's life insurance companies to lend money as they liked and as they had done in the past. Henceforth, the insurers would only be allowed by law to put their money into treasury bonds and the like.

The global situation, although by no means as dire as in the United States, was deteriorating fast. The financial markets in Japan and Egypt were in turmoil. The Bank of England was forced to send $3 million of gold to Alexandria to support the Egyptian economy. Smaller banks were failing in Tokyo every day. The German, Dutch and Danish markets faced financial collapse after credit dried up and interest rates in Germany rose to 10 per cent.

Jesse Livermore had been proved right in his predictions. Insiders had been off-loading huge lines of stock to the general public over the summer by means of concert parties and other trickery. It turned out that all of the rallies had been fake rallies.

Livermore had been steadily selling stocks short from the very beginning of the month on his belief that the tightening credit would force a collapse in equities. But the New York Stock Exchange had been left untouched by the growing crisis, and it could still borrow as much as it wanted. The stock exchange's line of credit was called 'call money' and secured by the value of shares and commodity stocks offered by brokers to the banks every night to secure the necessary cash to keep the exchange liquid.

Traditionally, call money, as its name suggests, was available on demand to Wall Street's brokers provided there was sufficient security available, and there always was. The daily interest rates on call money were extremely high as the loans were very short term. The lending was very profitable for New York's banks, and it was the last to be withdrawn.

Credit was especially important to the stock market as everyone traded on margin. For their part, bankers were happy to provide unlimited amounts of cash to stockbrokers provided of course they had the funds to lend – which they always did.

The money was allocated out on the floor of the New York exchange in an area traditionally called the Money Post. The area was actually marked by a wooden post, and the prevailing interest rate was always released at midday and pinned to it.

By 1907 the system of lending was very refined and, in reality, it was only the bigger brokers who borrowed money. They passed funds to their smaller brethren, often lending money out themselves as principals when they were very flush in the good times.

So much so that by the middle of the afternoon, every broker in the exchange knew where they were for the day, what their position was and how much they needed to borrow. There was an unwritten rule that no bank could refuse to make a loan, and the system was very smooth and ran like clockwork, provided there was enough cash to lubricate it.

Livermore got early warning of the crisis from a broker friend of his. He said that the brokers themselves were no longer lending to their fellow brokers and were suddenly letting the banks do all the heavy lifting. The reason was simple: the big brokers believed the small brokers were not creditworthy.

The way the integrity of the system worked was that the large brokers could not refuse a loan to any member of the exchange who was solvent and credit worthy. The problem was that the larger brokers knew the smaller ones could not pay them back in the current environment. So they simply didn't turn up at the Money Post and so, technically, they had not refused to make a loan. But whilst the banks were still lending, it mattered little.

As in many significant global disasters, the actual collapse was triggered by a totally unrelated event.

In the first week of October 1907, there was an attempt to corner the shares in a company called United Copper by three financiers: two brothers, Augustus and Otto Heinze, and their partner Charles Morse. The Heinzes were former commodities traders and Morse had originally made his money trading in ice. The three of them owned various minority stakes in banks and finance houses. They had timed their operation at a period when many of America's leading industrialists and financiers were in Europe, thereby eliminating any possible high level interference with their plans.

It took a vast amount of ready cash to finance the operation, and it turned out that the three men did not have enough and the corner failed when the share price of United Copper suddenly skidded 35 points in two hours. The problem, which the three financiers had failed to allow for, was the falling value of copper itself. It gradually fell from 22 cents a pound to 12 cents.

Within a few days, United Copper's share price had collapsed from $60 to $10. It forced all three financiers into bankruptcy and their companies with them. It was the trigger for a panic.

The banks and the trusts that had lent the Heinzes and Morse money for the operation found that their security was less secure than they believed. In fact, the whole edifice was unsubstantial and the debts were by no means covered by what had been pledged. Around three quarters of the money was lost, much of it by the trust companies.

And so began a game of real life dominoes. The weakest went first, and the smaller finance houses that had flourished in the boom went into bankruptcy one by one. There was no hiding place. The panic culminated with intense pressure on America's third largest trust company, the oddly named Knickerbocker Trust, run by Charles Barney.

The Knickerbocker was in fine fettle and had not actually lent the Heinzes and Morse any money for their United Copper venture. But it was damned by association, as its chairman Charles Barney had been very closely associated with the Heinzes in earlier ventures.

Everyone assumed the Knickerbocker Trust had lent them money that had not been paid back and therefore also assumed that the Knickerbocker must be in financial trouble. Perception took over from reality in a very big way. Although it had lost no money from the collapse of United Copper, everyone believed it had.

The first sign of trouble was when a queue of customers began to form at the front door of the Knickerbockers' headquarters at the junction of 34th Street and Fifth Avenue. The Knickerbocker had $60 million of assets and 18,000 deposit accounts, and it appeared that, suddenly, all 18,000 wanted their money out – in cash. But the Knickerbocker only had $10 million in cash on hand.

It seemed the more the Knickerbocker managers explained it had not been involved with the United Copper Company, the less it was believed. Confidence in its operations had completely disappeared, and it was guilt by association. The sudden lack of belief was disastrous for a trust company, especially one as large as The Knickerbocker.

Charles Barney, its blameless chairman, who had wisely declined to get involved, desperately sought a meeting with Pierpont Morgan of J. P. Morgan. But Morgan refused to see him and Barney was forced to resign by his fellow directors, creating a management vacuum that only served to make matters worse.

The run started in earnest on Friday October 18th and, by the following Tuesday, the lines of customers stretched round two blocks. Then the management had a bright idea. They ordered the van loads of cash that were arriving at the back door to unload in full view of everyone at the front doors as a show of confidence. The purpose was to convince everyone that there was not a problem and that there was plenty of cash. But it had the opposite effect, and seeing the cash attracted more customers, more publicity and more withdrawals. That Friday and the following Monday, the Knickerbocker paid out $9 million to its depositors.

Then, in the first three hours of opening on Tuesday October 22nd, over $3 million in cash was paid out. By midday, the cash had run out and the Knickerbocker Trust temporarily closed its doors and waited for its fate to be decided by others.

With the Knickerbocker in terminal trouble, every single trust in the city was vulnerable and queues formed around many of them as cash was transferred from savings accounts to mattresses. There were no weak trusts left, they had already closed. The stronger ones just kept paying out; it would have been suicide not to.

The queues at the banks were a lot smaller; they still retained their customers' confidence but not so the 21,000 regional banks that held their surplus cash in the big New York banks.

When the regional banks started to withdraw their cash from the New York banks, the liquidity crunch was complete.

On October 23rd, it all came to a head in the afternoon at the Money Post in the New York stock exchange. The banks could no longer lend any money to the stockbrokers because they didn't have any to lend. And they wanted every cent they had already lent paid back. When it didn't materialize, loans were simply rolled over and everybody made good. The crisis was wallpapered over. Livermore remembered: "Reports from the money crowd early indicated that borrowers would have to pay whatever the lender saw fit to ask. There wouldn't be enough to go around. That day, the money crowd was much larger than usual. When delivery time came that afternoon, there must have been a hundred brokers around the Money Post, each hoping to borrow the money that the firm urgently needed. Without money, they must sell what stocks they were carrying on margin – sell at any price they could get in a market where buyers were as scarce as money. And just then, there was not a dollar in sight."

From there being unlimited money to finance margin trading, there was suddenly literally none available at any rate of interest. The banks were all too busy saving themselves and didn't even turn up at the stock exchange on Thursday October 24th 1907. Livermore was surprised. It was beyond anything he had witnessed or read about before: "It made me think. I had seen a smash coming, but not, I admit, the worst panic in our history. It might not be profitable to anybody if it went much further." With that in mind, he decided to go down to the floor of the exchange to see what was happening for himself.

At first, everyone was calm and believed the lack of credit was temporary, existing loans were simply rolled over and a "sticking plaster" was applied to the problem. The plaster stayed stuck on for a few hours. By two o'clock there was still no activity at the Money Post, and Livermore realized that the next few hours were make-or-break for everybody. As he said: "Finally, it became plain that there was no use in waiting at the Post for money. There wasn't going to be any." Livermore went off to tell Ed Hutton what he had seen. It turned out Hutton didn't need any warning. He told Livermore: "My God, Jesse, I don't know what's going to happen. I never saw anything like it. It can't go on and something has got to give. It looks to me as if everybody is busted right now. You can't sell stocks, and there is absolutely no money in there." E. F. Hutton & Co itself was sound. It had virtually no long positions in the market, nor did its clients. Being in a net short position, it had no reason to borrow. Without any general liquidity in the market, Hutton was too frightened to cover any of its clients' short positions, and Ed Hutton advised Livermore to stay put. As he told him: "There is no money anywhere, and you can't liquidate stocks because there is nobody to buy them. The whole street is broke at this very moment, if you ask me."

Livermore remembered: "The optimists and the wishful thinkers, dreading the pain of a small loss at the beginning, were now about to suffer total amputation without anaesthetics in a day I shall never forget, October 24, 1907."

The chairman of the stock exchange pondered what to do, and did the only thing he could. He picked up the phone and called James Stillman, president of National City Bank, America's largest commercial bank, who in turn picked up the phone to Pierpont Morgan, the head of J. P. Morgan & Co, which was de facto America's central bank. The stock market finally ran out of hard cash at midday Thursday October 24th. There was no money and no loans left to be rolled over.

Meanwhile, customers of the Knickerbocker Trust continued to wait patiently outside its doors. Many had set up tents and deck chairs. The New York Police started a system of ticket numbers so people in the queue could go and get a meal.

New York held its breath to see what would happen next.

CHAPTER 13

Enter Morgan

Livermore makes $1 million in a day

October - November 1907

N ow everyone knew there was only one man who could save America and its financial system and that was Pierpont Morgan, the 70 year-old head of America's largest and richest financial institution, J. P. Morgan & Co. Morgan was the only man who had the know-how and the financial clout to effect a rescue.

In October 1907, America was in a difficult and vulnerable place as it was the only developed country that did not have a central bank. The Federal Reserve would not be created until six years later, and it left J. P. Morgan & Co as essentially the country's central bank.

It was effectively up to Pierpont Morgan to singlehandedly save America, and he wasn't feeling best disposed as he wearily started his task.

Morgan had been forced to return earlier than he would have liked from the Triennial Episcopal Convention he was attending in Richmond, Virginia as a lay delegate. He was extremely influential in church circles and he looked forward to the Convention every three years and spending a few days with America's senior church leaders afterwards.

He had delayed his return as long as he dared, lest news of his premature return to New York promoted even more panic on the stock market. He also had to give his servants time to hurriedly open up the house, which had been closed for the summer. He finally returned by train to New York on the evening of Saturday October 19th.

That evening, he was briefed on the situation by his partners at J. P. Morgan & Co. Later, after his partners had left for the evening, George Baker of First National Bank and James Stillman of National City Bank came for supper. He asked the two powerful bankers if they would be his eyes and ears as the crisis unfolded.

Baker and Stillman, in particular, were the two most powerful commercial bankers in America, and Morgan had chosen his allies well. Their interests were mutually exclusive. Stillman ran National City Bank, which eventually became Citibank. The 57-year-old was the son of a powerful industrialist and had become president of the bank 16 years earlier, a protégé of its creator Moses Taylor. Small and dark but always immaculately turned out, Stillman was known as a "master of silence." He valued silence more than any other attribute and was called by one reporter: "The coldest proposition in America." The bank was capitalized at close to $40 million.

George Baker, 67, was regarded as a banking genius. A prodigy at the age of 23, he was one of the junior founders of First National Bank in 1863. He became president in 1877 at the age of 37.

With two powerful allies signed up, and all three of them agreeing to sing from the same hymn sheet, Morgan could rest easier that Saturday night, as he fell asleep. On Sunday, he rested all day, ready for what he knew was to come.

And come it did.

On Monday October 21st, Morgan walked to his office at 23 Wall Street. It was a long walk, but he needed the exercise as he was trying to shake off a cold. On the way, he was continually accosted by people he knew wanting his help. When he arrived at the office, countless presidents of New York banks and trust companies were waiting to seek his help and advice, mainly to rescue their companies – some that he could help save and some he couldn't.

The trust companies were the most difficult to help. These were quasi-banks that had sprung up from nowhere to take deposits from the general public and supposedly lend that money prudently back to the general public. But over time, their lending had expanded into all sorts of risky areas, including loans for share purchases. The trusts were lightly regulated and less well capitalized than mainstream banks.

The banks didn't like the trusts and would have preferred to see them all go under. But they were frightened of contagion.

Morgan also had to worry about the stock market, which was hovering on a precipice. Jesse Livermore had also become personally very worried even though he was showing huge paper profits on his short holdings. Although Livermore was by then nearly $1 million to the good in his brokerage account, it was not yet real money. He still had to buy in the shares he had sold short to turn it into real cash. If he couldn't cover his shorts and buy back the shares he had sold, then he would not the able to deliver them to the buyers and collect his profit.

Above: Jesse Livermore in Palm Beach, Florida on Christmas Day 1924. Palm Beach was his vacation resort of choice for almost 40 years.

nder to Young Men To-Day
40 Years Ago, Livermore Says

Left: The earliest surviving image of Jesse Livermore taken around the turn of the 20th Century. By this time, Livermore was already a wealthy man and making headlines in the financial press. His youthful good looks made him just as successful with women as he was with making money.

Right: The original stock market ticker tape machine, supplied by Western Union to stock brokers and bucket shops across America. At one point in his heyday, Jesse Livermore owned more than 80 ticker tape machines installed across his various homes and offices.

Below: The Haight & Freese Bucket shop in Boston, which Livermore frequented in the early 1900's. Prices were chalked straight up on the boards as they came off the ticker. That price prevailed until the next one came. Livermore graduated to this more upmarket establishment after learning his trade in the rougher bucket shops with no seating and sawdust on the floor. Livermore's ability to beat the 'shop' led to his being banned from them all.

Stock market panic on Wall Street in 1907

Above: Crowds gather in Wall Street in March 1907. The New York Stock Exchange fell almost 50 percent from its peak the previous year. It caused widespread panic leading to runs on banks and trust companies. Livermore benefitted by being short of the market, just as he would be in 1929.

Left: Jesse Livermore's first wife, Nettie Jordan, photographed in 1910. The couple were married in 1901 and then estranged the same year. For the next seventeen years they saw each other occasionally when it suited them. They did not divorce until 1918. This picture shows her not long after Livermore had become one of Wall Street's most successful operators. All three of Livermore's wives were petite brunettes and the sort of girl he liked to marry. However for his mistresses he preferred them blonde and blue eyed.

Left: Edward Hutton of E.F. Hutton & Co, which was Jesse Livermore's principal stock broker until 1909. Livermore kept an office in Hutton's building and was the brokerage's best client for many years.

Above: Charles Pugh and his family manipulated Jesse Livermore in 1908 to do their bidding. Under cover of Livermore's trading, Pugh liquidated half of his portfolio of stocks at good prices before he died.

Above: James Stillman, chairman of National City Bank, the biggest commercial bank in America. He teamed up with Pierpont Morgan to save the financial system in 1907.

J. P. Morgan & Co., the centre of power in America in 1900

Above: An early twentieth century view of the exterior of the elegant 'second empire' style Drexel Building, designed by the architect Arthur Gillman and home of the offices of J. P. Morgan & Company. Located at 23 Wall Street, on the southeast corner of Wall and Broad Street, it was demolished in 1913 to make way for J. P. Morgan's new headquarters.

J. Pierpont Morgan: the most powerful man in America

Above: J. Pierpont Morgan pictured in 1902 when he was at the height of his powers and worth a quarter of a billion dollars. His fortune and his influence dwarfed that of any other man in history then and since. In 1907, he singlehandedly saved the world from financial disaster.

Above: Former Ziegfeld Follies dancer Dorothy Livermore, the second wife of Jesse Livermore, pictured in fancy dress costume at a Palm Beach party in 1925. She and her husband lived a fabulous life with unlimited riches at their disposal between 1918 and 1931.

The Livermore yachts

Left: *The Anita* was a 200-foot schooner purchased by Jesse Livermore in 1907 after he made $3.5 million selling shares short. It was the first of many yachts.

Right: The *Venetia* was a 300-foot schooner which Livermore was persuaded to buy by yacht broker Joe MacDonald in 1907, even though he already owned the *Anita*. He kept the yacht on Lake Michigan and lived in it whilst he traded at the Chicago Board of Trade.

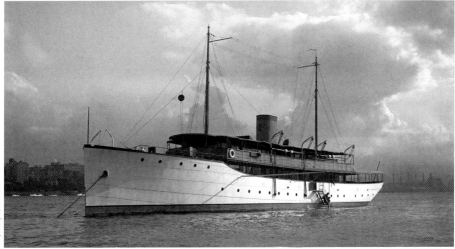

Left: The original *Athero* which was the sixth yacht Jesse Livermore owned, like the others, bought from yacht broker Joe McDonald. It was too big to be moored at Great Neck and was sold when he took delivery of *Athero II*.

Above: *The Athero II* was built especially for Jesse Livermore in 1925 and ultimately cost $3 million. It was the last yacht designed by Henry Gielow before he died. It was built by George S Lawley & Sons in Boston. In the winter of 1926/7 the Livermores cruised the Caribbean for nine weeks on its maiden voyage.

The Livermore mansion on Long Island Sound

Above: Evermore was Jesse Livermore's main family home in Long Island, where his two children were brought up by him and his wife Dorothy between 1918 and 1931. But the family crumbled under the weight of his money, and the house was sold off for a fraction of its value by his wife after their divorce.

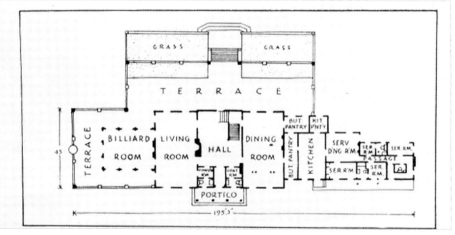

Above: A floor plan of the house as presented in a sale catalogue.

Left: Evermore was bought for $250,000 and another $1 million was lavished on it by Livermore and his wife, Dorothy.

Above left: The Loggia at Evermore. It was reckoned to be the finest example of a Renaissance style loggia in America.

Above Right: The front porch with its imposing columns.

Left: The dining room with its columns and windows overlooking the grounds.

Right: The illustration shows the enviable position of the property, which stood in eleven acres of landscaped grounds at Kings Point, Great Neck, Long Island.

Below: The balustrade and terrace at the rear of the house overlooking Long Island Sound.

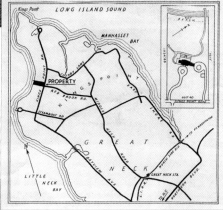

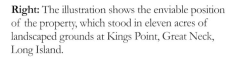

Below: An aerial view of the main house and the grounds.

Above: The Livermore family leave the courthouse in Mineola, Long Island, on July 11th 1927 after a hearing for the arraignment of James Monaghan, one of the burglars who robbed them at their home on May 29th, 1927.

Left: The Royal Poinciana Hotel was where Jesse Livermore stayed when he first went to Palm Beach in the early 1900s. At over 1,000 rooms for 2,000 guests, it was the biggest hotel in the world and the largest wooden building ever constructed.

Above: The five hundred dollar bill was popular with Jesse Livermore in the early thirties, when he carried a bundle around in his pocket primarily to give to his wife for gambling at the Beach Club at Palm Beach.

Left: Ed Bradley, the famous proprietor of the Beach Club in Palm Beach, on the cover of *Time* magazine. The club was a semi-legal gambling establishment in the 1920s and '30s. Jesse Livermore was one of his biggest gamblers.

Above: The Breaker's Hotel in Palm Beach, Florida. It became Livermore's hotel of choice in Palm Beach because of its proximity to the sea and the gaming tables of the Beach Club owned by Ed Bradley.

The New York Stock Exchange in the early 1920's

Above and below: The floor of the New York Stock Exchange in the early 1920's.

Left: An external view of the entrance to the New York Stock Exchange.

Above: The New York Curb Exchange. Members of the Curb Exchange traded outside until they moved to a permanent building in the 1920's.

Below: On September 16th 1920, the financial district is rocked by a bomb blast at 23 Wall Street. Thirty people were killed outright, eight more subsequently died of their injuries. More than 400 people were injured. The perpetrators were Galleanists and part of anti-capitalist agitation in the United States at that time.

Left: Empty chairs and silent stock tickers in front of quote boards for the New York Stock Exchange after the close of a trading day.

Right: Traders fixated on a typical Wall Street quotation board, pictured in the early thirties.

Above: Recording the price of Cotton Seed Meal at the Cotton Exchange, Memphis, Tennessee.

For the first time, Livermore realized that the stock market was not as durable an institution as he had assumed. It required money – lots of money – to lubricate it.

Every day that week, the market looked more and more shaky and no one could be sure if it would reopen the following morning. If the stock market did not open, and without cash, most members of the stock exchange would go broke, Livermore along with them. He was only rich on the credit side of E. F. Hutton's books of accounting.

Like everyone, Livermore was waiting to see what Pierpont Morgan would do. It gradually became clear that only he could save the market and save Jesse Livermore.

By midday, Pierpont Morgan decided to leave his office at 23 Wall Street and not go back until the crisis was over. He was besieged and needed peace and quiet to think and to plan. So he decided to move his personal office to his home, a handsome brownstone at Madison Avenue and 36th Street, where he could work in peace.

His house contained a vast library, which had east and west wings. It was the perfect venue for the tortuous and frequent negotiations he knew were to come. The rooms were very grand and dominated by rich wood panelling and large tapestries. No one could fail to be awed and intimidated by the opulence.

Morgan's first task was to examine the books of the Knickerbocker Trust, the country's third largest, to see if it could be saved. There were urgent requests from its president Charles Barney for a meeting, but Morgan refused. He knew Barney well, and meeting him would bring emotion into any decision he made. Instead, Morgan seconded a committee of young bankers to be his auditors. He sent these young men out in pairs to look at the books of every institution in trouble that needed cash.

Morgan sent two of his best, Henry Davison of First National Bank and Ben Strong of Bankers Trust, into the Knickerbocker and told them he wanted a report on its financial health that night. As they sat in the trust's back office, poring over the books, they could see the depositors lining up outside trying to get their money out. The Knickerbocker's total assets were valued at $60 million, and Davison and Strong had to verify that they exceeded its liabilities. Or not.

That night, Davison and Strong went back to Madison Avenue and told Morgan that The Knickerbocker was insolvent. With that information, Morgan did not intervene to stop the run, which ran its course the following day when the cash ran out.

Letting the Knickerbocker go was a big decision and probably the hardest Morgan had to make during the whole crisis. But he knew if he saved the Knickerbocker, he would have to save everyone that came afterwards, and at this stage he had no idea what condition they were in. He said after the decision had been made: "I can't go on being everybody's goat. I've got to stop somewhere."

With that difficult decision made, Morgan took charge of shoring up the healthy trusts. If good security was available, he would lend them hard cash. If not, they would be allowed to fail.

Morgan was constantly on the phone to the Secretary of the Treasury, George Cortelyou, in Washington. Cortelyou told Morgan he would provide him with as much liquidity (i.e. hard cash) as he needed to ship into the trusts, provided they were solvent. Cortelyou also said that he was ready to deposit money in the New York banks to help shore up their deposits. Then he got on a train to come to New York.

But Morgan still had to decide where he would draw the line. After the Knickerbocker, Davison and Strong had gone into the Trust Company of America (TCA) and done a similar audit. They would deliver their report to Morgan the following morning. TCA had assets of $100 million, but less than 10 per cent of that was in readily accessible cash.

Meanwhile, Morgan was personally directing the liquidation of TCA's assets to allow it to get hard cash to pay to the depositors lined up outside. The trust survived to the close of business that day.

Morgan had two big problems to solve. The trusts needed hard cash and the banks needed deposits to bolster their reserves so they could release more cash to support the trusts.

At around 10 o'clock, Morgan was informed that the secretary of the treasury had arrived in New York. Morgan walked down to the Manhattan Hotel at Madison and 42nd Street where George Cortelyou was booked in.

They were also joined by James Stillman, George Baker and four other top commercial bankers. It was a very fruitful meeting, and Cortelyou agreed to make $25 million immediately available.

Afterwards, Morgan stayed on to have a late supper with the Secretary and retired to his bed just after two o'clock, exhausted. The strains of the last few days had finally got to him and he felt his cold getting worse. The next morning, his valet had trouble waking him up. When the servant finally roused him, his voice had gone and he seemed dazed. Morgan's personal physician, Dr Markoe, was called and prescribed a host of throat sprays, gargles and lozenges to keep the cold at bay.

That morning, Wednesday the 23rd, there were plenty of immediate problems. The Knickerbocker collapse had effectively put the Trust Company of America in play and long queues had formed outside its offices. New York's newspaper headlines that morning had not helped. One read: "Trust Company of America: J. P. Morgan to help." It was ostensibly good news, but its customers had not realized that TCA needed help. On reading their newspapers, many headed to the trust's offices to get their money out – just in case. The contagion Morgan feared was starting to happen. And the truth was that he had not yet made the decision as to whether he would save TCA. The newspapers were wrong.

After he had left Cortelyou, Morgan had sent messengers ordering the presidents of the big trust companies to come to his home early the following morning.

Morgan knew none of these men and would be meeting them for the first time. He had watched the rise of the trusts as a force in American finance with the maximum of disinterest. Now they had forced his interest.

He was stunned when he discovered that none of the trust presidents knew each other and were all meeting for the first time. It was a complete contrast to the banking sector, which was akin to a club run on the old boy network – where everyone knew everyone.

Morgan was not used to such a lack of familiarity and there were a lot of introductions and explanations necessary before they could get down to business. It made consensus difficult. But things changed after Ben Strong delivered a positive report on TCA's financial health. He explained that its assets were sound and intact. The only negative was a lack of liquidity. TCA president Oakleigh Thorne told Morgan that he only had $1.2 million of cash left and would not be able to stay open until the three o'clock closing time.

Morgan had heard enough, and he finally drew his line in the sand. He decided to save TCA. He famously declared, in words that have become immortalized and used time and time again by bankers in the years since: "This is the place to stop the trouble, then."

Morgan told the trust presidents that he would supply the liquidity, but they would have to supply the solvency. To kick start the process, the trust presidents pooled together to provide loans of $8.25 million to allow the Trust

Company of America to stay open for at least two days. First National Bank and National City Bank also agreed to loan $3.25 million in contingency money. For his part, Morgan agreed to keep buying the Trust's assets as necessary and paying cash on the nail. But he also had some ideas to make life easier for all the Trusts.

It had become apparent to him that the maximum a Trust company's cashiers could pay out physically in a day was around $8 million, working at normal speed. He told the Trust presidents that their tellers were working too efficiently and must henceforth "work inefficiently." Morgan told them to slow their tellers down and to count cash three or four times before handing it over. This cut the physical amount that could be doled out per day to less than $4 million. Later, he would slow the cashiers down to $3 million and then $2 million a day. It was typical of Morgan's ingenuity in a crisis. The Trust presidents, all meeting him for the first time, were awestruck by the simplicity of his plan and the difference they knew it would make. Of all the things Morgan did to save America's financial system that fall of 1907, this was arguably the single most important.

But Morgan wasn't finished with his ploys. He knew that there were risks for Trust customers emptying accounts and keeping their money under the mattress. Already, burglaries had gone up over 1,000 per cent since the crisis began. Morgan personally phoned newspaper editors and told them to run as many burglary stories as they could, as often as they could. He literally wanted to scare people from taking their money out of the Trusts. The deception had the desired effect.

Having dealt with the Trusts, Morgan sought a permanent solution to recapitalize the New York banks. They too were starting to see queues forming and were having to pay out between $2 and $4 million an hour to depositors. He made sure that the Secretary of the Treasury's cash injection that day of $25 million was well publicized.

But he knew that wouldn't be enough, so Morgan called his old friend, oil tycoon John D. Rockefeller, and told him about the problems in New York. Rockefeller immediately arranged to deposit $10 million of his own personal cash into National City Bank, instantly making it the best financed bank in New York. Rockefeller also put out a news release to the Associated Press agency stating he was confident about the future and would de depositing more of his cash, up to half of his net worth, into accounts at New York's banks.

The news had the effect Morgan wanted: headlines in all the newspapers.

ENTER MORGAN

Rockefeller was thought to be America's richest man, and he knew that New Yorkers would follow his lead. Money began to pour into the big New York banks, which could then lend it to the weaker ones. Wednesday the 23rd had been a momentous day, and Morgan had strained every sinew to save TCA and had managed it.

That night, he returned to the Manhattan Hotel to brief George Cortelyou on the day's events. In the midst of talking, he fell asleep in his chair, cigar in hand. After half an hour, Cortelyou woke his friend and walked him back to his house, pledging to stay in New York with him until the crisis was over.

Before he retired that night, Morgan dictated a telegraph message to his son, Jack, who was stationed in London at J. P. Morgan & Co's subsidiary Morgan Grenfell. It read: "We have had tremendous day STOP Whole financial district thronged with people STOP As far as human foresight can tell, believe we have passed the crisis STOP Thursday will decide. All Well."

Whether Morgan believed those words as he dictated them will never be known, but with the banks and trusts stabilized, he knew he must turn his attention to the stock market, which had already run out of money.

On Wednesday afternoon, the New York banks were reluctant to continue to make the short-term loans to facilitate daily stock trades. This despite the fact that overnight interest rates had risen to the annual equivalent of 90 per cent. By Thursday morning, they had withdrawn from the market altogether despite their loans now commanding 150 per cent interest. The stock market only existed because of unlimited liquidity supplied by banks, and when it stopped there was an existential threat.

That decisive moment came at 11 o'clock on the morning of Thursday October 24th when the president of the New York Stock Exchange, Ransom Thomas, picked up his telephone and called James Stillman, president of the National City Bank. He asked Stillman if he could call on him within the hour. When he arrived, Thomas told Stillman that he was going to have to close the exchange two hours early and he was not sure, if he did that, if it would ever reopen. Stillman always made it his practice to listen in silence, with an impassive face, to anybody who brought a proposition to him. Stillman was said to use silence as an art form. But not this time. Stillman told him immediately to do nothing of the sort, but Thomas answered that he had no choice. Stillman pondered for a moment and said: "Mr Thomas, we'll have to go and see Mr Morgan about this." With that, Thomas agreed to defer his decision for half an hour – until half past one.

Stillman picked up Thomas in his own chauffeur-driven automobile, which was standing by on the curbside. They went straight to Morgan's house on Madison Avenue. Stillman didn't hesitate and threw his coat to the startled butler, who took them straight through to the library after grabbing Thomas's overcoat from his back. The butler had orders to admit Stillman, day or night, and to take him straight to Morgan, wherever he was.

Thomas walked in a daze and was in absolute awe. He had never met Morgan before, let alone visited his home.

As they stood in the library, Stillman nudged a silent Thomas, who eventually spoke: "I beg your pardon, Mr Morgan, but the exchange will have to close early this afternoon. There is no money on offer." Morgan waved his hand and said: "At what time do you usually close it?" Thomas was astonished that Morgan did not know the exchange's opening hours and replied "Why at three o'clock." Morgan found stock trading a "vulgar" activity and had little interest in it – he only bought and sold whole companies, hence his ignorance of its opening times.

Morgan wagged his finger at Thomas and said: "It must not close one minute before that hour today." Morgan asked Stillman what he thought would happen if the exchange did close early. Stillman replied: "It will be nothing short of catastrophic, and I do not believe it will ever open again." Morgan said that it was inevitable that over 50 stock broking firms would declare bankruptcy by the end of the day if that happened.

Both men looked at Morgan and he looked straight back of them, stroking his beard. After at least 10 seconds of silence, when the only sound was the wood crackling in the large hearth, he said: "Go back to the exchange and tell them that there will be money for them." Thomas inquired: "Where?" Morgan replied "From the banks."

Thomas didn't hesitate for a second and ran from the room, shouting to the butler for his coat. Stillman's driver was waiting and, within eight minutes, Thomas was back at the exchange, down at the Money Post shouting out the good news. No one asked for details, such was their faith in Pierpont Morgan's word. Still, it was a nervous half hour whilst the brokers waited in silence round the Money Post for something to happen.

After Thomas had left the house, Morgan and Stillman huddled together discussing how to make good on their promise. Time was not on their side. Morgan called one of his own personal brokers into the room. It so happened that John Atterbury, of Van Emburgh & Atterbury, was in an adjacent room working on liquidating TCA's stock holdings. Morgan told Atterbury to go to the stock exchange and lend out some money. He told him "$10 million should be enough."

Atterbury went out of the room. The butler already had his coat in his hand, as if anticipating his master's next move. Morgan's chauffeur was at the door with the car engine running, ready to take Atterbury to the exchange. By 2:30pm Atterbury approached the Money Post. No one needed telling why he was there or who he was. Everyone knew that John Atterbury was Morgan's man. Word went round as soon as he got out of the car and entered the great double doors at the front of the building. Meanwhile, Morgan and Stillman had sprung into action. As soon as Atterbury had left the house, they called for messengers, and Morgan's secretary quickly wrote personal notes to the presidents of all the major New York banks. They were asked to be at his house by three o'clock at the latest. They all knew what it was about and some were already on their way, having anticipated the call. Some of them knew Pierpont Morgan very well indeed and knew he would not let the market go.

But Morgan was under huge pressure. He had not eaten lunch and his cold was bad. Instead of eating, he was chain smoking cigars to keep him going whilst he prepared to put up the performance of his life. As the bankers filed into his library and sat down, Morgan didn't waste any time coming to the point.

Morgan informed them that the stock exchange would close forever unless $25 million was lent that night. Shocked at the number, suddenly every banker in the room was talking at once. They told Morgan there was no money to lend and that they were "loaned up to the hilt." Morgan declared: "You've got your reserves." When they replied they were up to the legal limit, Morgan said: "Use them. That's what reserves are for." There was little further argument as no banker wanted the exchange to fail. The 12 bank presidents present pledged an average of $2 million each to a fighting fund, and $23.6 million was raised.

Meanwhile, back at the exchange, John Atterbury called for quiet. According to witnesses, the noisy hub instantly ceased. Over 100 principals of most of New York's larger stockbrokers strained to listen. Atterbury raised his hand and declared: "I am authorized to lend ten million dollars." A loud cheer rang out and the brokers surged forward as security men stood in front of Atterbury lest he was knocked over. He shouted: "Take it easy! There will be enough for everybody." With that, order was restored as they stood in an orderly queue whilst Atterbury wrote down their names and their requirements for money. Atterbury didn't tell them where the money was coming from. He simply took down the name of the firms and how much they wanted to borrow. He told them they would know which bank would lend them the money and where to take their security later: "You will be told where your money is." Instead of the predicted $10 million, the final tally was $19 million, but Atterbury used his discretion and authorized all the loans. He knew his boss well enough. The brokers all burst into spontaneous applause and sang "For He's A Jolly Good Fellow" in honor of Pierpont Morgan, whom they knew had personally rescued them from oblivion that evening. An hour later, Atterbury returned and told the brokers where to get their money.

That afternoon, with the market liquid again, Jesse Livermore covered his shorts and actually banked $1 million profit. Finally, it was real money. As he said: "That was the day I remember most vividly of all the days of my life as a stock operator. It was the day when my winnings exceeded one million dollars. It marked the successful ending of my first deliberately planned trading campaign. What I had foreseen has come to pass. But more than all these things was this: a wild dream of mine had been realized. I had been a king for a day."

Livermore was exultant that night, as he had finally cracked how to operate on the big board.

Up to then, he had never been as successful at the stock exchange as he had been in the bucket shops. As he explained: "I knew that someday I would find out what was wrong and I would stop being wrong. It was rather a sort of feeling that the same old stock market that so baffled me would one day eat out of my hand. I just felt that such a day would come. And it did on October 24th 1907."

That evening, many New Yorkers knew they would have to file for personal bankruptcy the following morning. But for Livermore and a small coterie, they had all become millionaires after reading the market right. They included many of Hutton's customers and Hutton himself, who had followed Livermore and shorted the market heavily. But for every winner there were 20 losers, and any sense of victory was extinguished by sympathy for the bulls who had lost everything.

Meanwhile, over at Madison Avenue, Pierpont Morgan met with John Atterbury and did the accounting. When they had finished, both men realized how close a call it had been.

By now, word of that day's events and Pierpont Morgan's role in it had got out. Morgan found himself the centre of global attention. He never spoke to newspaper journalists, but that evening he was forced to issue his first ever press release and was quoted saying: "If people will keep their money in the banks, everything will be all right." Because of who he was, it was seen as almost a royal command, and Americans across the nation heeded his advice.

The cash crisis was over, but the stock market crisis just gathered pace. Friday October 25th saw another black day on the stock exchange and the brokers would need another $10 million that night, on top of the $19 million at the close. This time the money was more easily forthcoming; Morgan saw to it.

Livermore sat on his hands for most of the day waiting to see what would happen, refraining from plunging in again. He watched and waited and didn't like what he saw. There were no buyers at all in the market for anything: "At one time, there wasn't a single bid for Union Pacific. Not at any price! Think of it! And in other stocks the same thing. No money to hold stocks, and nobody to buy them."

As Jesse Livermore pondered the wreckage of Thursday and Friday, he realized that Monday would be a crucial day on the exchange, and he had it in his power to almost dictate what would happen. No man understood more, at that moment, about what was happening to the market than he did. He had foreseen the crisis and ridden on the back of it for all its worth. As he said: "I certainly pushed my luck to the limit. What is the use of being right unless you get all the good possible out of it?"

So Livermore made his plans and decided he would sell 10,000 shares of Union Pacific on Monday morning and smaller quantities of the six highest dividend paying stocks he could find. But as he pondered, he also realized the dangers of what he planned as he mused to himself: "There was a certainty that all that I had to do to smash prices still more was to send in orders to sell ten thousand shares each of Union Pacific and of a half dozen other good dividend-paying stocks, and what would follow would be simply hell. It seemed to me that the panic that would be precipitated would be of such intensity and character that the board of governors would deem it advisable to close the exchange. It would mean greatly increased profits on paper. It might also mean an inability to convert those profits into cash."

Livermore, of course, had no idea how close it had come on Thursday to what he feared actually happening. He also knew such an action would delay any recovery in stocks he knew must surely come soon. As he explained: "I was beginning to figure after all that bloodletting that such a panic would do much harm to the country generally."

Suddenly, Livermore had one of his hunches. In an instant, he changed his mind and decided, instead of leading a further downturn, he would reverse himself and do the exact opposite and buy those same shares on Monday morning. As he later explained: "I had practically covered all my shorts and it seemed to me there was a chance to buy stocks cheap and help the needed recovery in prices at the same time – if nobody hammered the market."

Across town, exactly the same sort of thoughts were going through the head of Pierpont Morgan himself. Somehow, Morgan had to stop the sell-off as share prices underpinned everything. Morgan knew, from his own youthful days trading stocks, that there would be a few big short sellers leading the sell-off. He asked John Atterbury who he should reach out to. Atterbury had just two words to say to his boss: "Jesse Livermore." Morgan told Atterbury to seek out Livermore and ask him to do the right thing for his country.

Atterbury did not know Livermore personally, but he knew a broker who did. He asked for an introduction which was duly made; Jesse Livermore was not about to say 'no' to a meeting with the legendary John Turner Atterbury. Atterbury asked his broker friend to bring Livermore to his office at 5 Nassau Street that evening.

When Livermore got there, Atterbury was too cute to come right out and ask him to stop selling shares short – that might have provoked the opposite reaction. Instead, he asked him what he thought about the state of the stock market.

Livermore remembered the meeting with Atterbury years later: "He listened with great interest to what I told him the market was going to do when the real selling began, after another push or two. When I got through, he said he might have found something for me to do later in the day."

Suddenly, Atterbury came to the point: "I have sent for you because we hope you will not sell any more stocks. The market can't stand much more pressure. As it is, it will be an immensely difficult task to avert a devastating panic. I appeal to your patriotism. This is a case where a man has to work for the benefit of all."

Livermore remembered: "He was very tactful. I suppose he thought that, having planned to smash the market, I would consider his request as equivalent to throwing away the chance to make about ten million dollars."

By now, Livermore had worked out that Atterbury must have sent for him on behalf of the great Pierpont Morgan himself. And Atterbury as good as confirmed it. Livermore looked him in the eye and said: "Go back and tell Mr Morgan that I fully realized the gravity of the situation even before you sent for me. I not only will not sell any more stocks, but I am going to go in and buy as much as I can carry." It was exactly what he wanted to hear, and Atterbury breathed a sigh of relief. He leaned over his desk to shake Livermore's hand.

The coming of the weekend was a huge relief to Morgan and gave him two days to find a permanent solution. By Friday evening, the US Treasury was low on funds itself and some of the smaller banks had closed their doors forever on Friday afternoon after running out of cash. The big banks were okay, but the rest were very shaky and needed as much liquidity as they could get. Morgan knew he had to restore confidence permanently.

So Morgan marched off to the Manhattan Hotel again late on Friday. He pitched an idea to George Cortelyou, whereby the US Treasury would create an alternative form of liquid asset that could be instantly traded between banks, an instrument everyone would have confidence in. He came up with the idea for a government backed loan certificate and wanted Cortelyou to authorize the Treasury to issue it for Monday morning. He told Cortelyou he needed to set up a counter at the Treasury's New York clearing house where banks could swap securities and bond and share certificates in return for the loan certificates which the Treasury would swap for cash on demand. The certificates, generally known as scrip, became the paper equivalent of cash. They enabled banks to get hard cash on demand, no questions asked, from the Treasury's New York vaults. It was another touch of Morgan genius. Although Cortelyou was reluctant to increase money supply in the US economy by $100 million virtually overnight, he saw the necessity.

But as soon as Morgan had effectively solved the banking crisis, another sprung up. The city of New York had been inadvertently caught up in the middle of the crisis. During September, it had been in the middle of renewing its own long-term financing. The crisis had halted the fund raising, and Mayor George McClellan called at Madison Avenue asking for help. He told Morgan that the city had begun to run out of money to pay wages and its day-to-day bills. After all his problems that week, Pierpont Morgan found it an easy issue to resolve. He arranged for J. P. Morgan & Co to quickly buy an emergency issue of $30 million worth of city bonds, but on very preferable terms with a six per cent coupon attached.

When John Atterbury returned to Madison Avenue and reported back his conversation with Livermore, Morgan decided to let the stock market take care of itself the following week. He chose not to intervene to support the market other than supplying it with enough ready cash to function. He would leave Jesse Livermore and his ilk to take care of the recovery in stocks that was surely coming after the hammering of Thursday and Friday.

But Morgan had one final task before he could rest. He sent messages out to New York's senior clergymen and asked them to come to Madison Avenue on Saturday morning. When they arrived, he told them they were his "spiritual relations committee." He asked them to spread the word to all priests to preach calm in Sunday services across America. He knew America's citizens listened to their priests and invariably did whatever they advised.

On Saturday afternoon, Morgan travelled down to his country home, Cragston in Highland Falls. He took his own Pullman carriage and promptly fell asleep for the whole journey. Sunday brought a torrential downpour. Cragston overlooked the Hudson River, and Morgan would spend the whole day in his conservatory gazing at the water and thinking. All across America, from their pulpits, priests of all denominations told their flocks not to panic.

As the rain fell on the conservatory roof, Morgan found his thoughts continually returning to Monday morning and what speculators like Livermore would do. He hoped that he would be a man of his word and do what he promised. A great deal depended on it. Morgan, for all his street smarts, had not realized how much America's financial institutions depended on the stock market to value its assets. The value of those assets was now crucial to any recovery.

Morgan needn't have worried. Jesse Livermore was resolute and knew what he had to do. He was also aware of the risks, but as he said: "I made up my mind that since it was unwise and unpleasant to continue actively bearish, it was illogical for me to stay short so I turned and began to buy."

That morning Ed Hutton had fully expected Livermore to continue to hammer the market and was stunned when his buy orders started coming in. Hutton immediately reversed himself and started to buy as well, without actually talking to his friend. When the other Hutton clients heard what was going on, they too turned round and started to buy. But Livermore had got the drop on them: "After my brokers began to buy in for me, I got bottom prices. I kept my word. I bought one hundred thousand shares that day, for the long account. I did not sell another stock short for nine months." And when the rest of the street saw the buy orders coming out of Hutton, they followed suit. The market began its recovery. Although shares had come a long way down, the ripple effect from Livermore's buying meant the exchange stabilized. This was vitally important as bankers headed to the New York clearing house to swap share certificates for loan certificates and much needed cash. It was Jesse Livermore's finest hour, although he never really knew it.

The following week was the best week of Livermore's life. The request from Morgan himself to help save Wall Street had buoyed Livermore up and he was on cloud nine. As he remembered: "I do not suffer from delusions of grandeur, but I said to friends that my dream had come true and that I had been a king for a moment."

He also felt good about himself – that he was now a buyer and not a seller: "The stock market at one time that day certainly was at the mercy of anybody who wanted to hammer it; in fact, you know how I feel about being accused of raiding the market and about the way my operations are exaggerated by the gossip of the Street."

Livermore was now attracting almost hero status in the offices of E. F. Hutton & Co. Following him in the past week had made a lot of people in the office rich, not least the principals of Hutton themselves. As he said: "Our office made a great deal of money. My own operations were so successful that they began to be talked about and, of course, were greatly exaggerated. I was credited with starting the breaks in various stocks. People I didn't know by name used to come and congratulate me. They all thought the most wonderful thing was the money I had made. They did not say a word about the time when I first talked bearish to them and they thought I was a crazy bear with a stock market loser's vindictive grouch. That I had foreseen the money troubles was nothing. That my broker's bookkeeper had used a third of a drop of ink on the credit side of the ledger under my name was a marvellous achievement to them."

Livermore's activities had also started to receive attention from the New York newspapers. As he remembered: "The papers said that Jesse Livermore, the Boy Plunger, had made several millions. Well, I was worth over one million after the close of business that day. But my biggest winnings were not in dollars but in the intangibles: I had learned what a man must do in order to make big money; I was permanently out of the gambler class; I had at last learned to trade intelligently in a big way. It was a day of days for me."

Pierpont Morgan read the articles with a wry smile. Livermore's actions had helped him immensely and he believed he was in the clear, although he knew there was still much work to be done to completely stabilize the situation. The $100 million issue of scrip had worked like a dream. J. P. Morgan & Co had taken its new New York City bonds to the window and exchanged them for cash and was two per cent to the good on the annual interest rate. The crisis may have been difficult for Morgan personally, but his bank was making money at every turn.

As a result, Monday October 28th to Thursday the 30th went by relatively quietly and Morgan was able to work normal hours, eat normally again and begin to recover from his cold. But it was a false dawn.

On Friday November 1st, Morgan had one of the biggest shocks of his life and found his reckoning that the crisis was over to be wrong when John Atterbury delivered him bad news. Atterbury had just heard that one of the New York stock exchange's biggest stockbrokers, Moore & Schley, was about to collapse. He told Morgan that Moore & Schley had on its books a large quantity of Tennessee Coal & Iron (TC&I) shares, a controlling stake. It appeared to own the shares outright, something it was not supposed to do. Stockbrokers were agents, not principals, and the firm had stepped over the line of proprietary behavior, putting it at risk. Worse than that, its boss Grant Schley had also personally, along with a wealthy wine merchant called George Kessler, bought millions of dollars worth of TC&I shares at $135. Kessler had already gone bankrupt as banks called in his loans and Schley was on the edge.

TC&I was a major steel producer based in Alabama and potentially a very valuable asset.

The collapse of the TC&I share price to $30 meant the value of the broker's security had collapsed with it. The shares stood on Moore & Schley's books at an average buying price of $135.

Morgan knew that if Moore & Schley went down, there would be a new wave of panic. Initially, Morgan offered Grant Schley an emergency loan of $5 million, which was refused as being inadequate. Schley finally explained that his brokerage owed millions to banks who were calling in $35 million of those loans immediately. Normally Schley would have sold a portion of its TC&I shares to cover it. But the value had dropped so much that a sale would not be enough. And any offloading of so big a stake would probably see the price collapse again. It was an impossible situation with no immediate solution. And there was another problem. Moore & Schley did not actually own the controlling stake in TC&I itself. The stake was held as collateral from two syndicates that had gradually assembled a controlling stake in TC&I. Schley had lent money to the two syndicates and then pledged the shares to banks, which lent it the money. The messy situation was made even messier when it emerged that John Gates, the prominent financier and owner of Republic Iron & Steel Company, was behind the two syndicates and had hoped to take control of TC&I via the back door.

Gates was a potential savior of Moore & Schley but he was on the high seas in the middle of the Atlantic on a steamer returning from Europe and was unreachable. Morgan immediately saw his chance to save Moore & Schley and make himself a lot of money in the process. In truth, he effectively had no choice to save the broker but it was also a once-in-a-lifetime business opportunity.

Morgan searched for solutions and quickly found one. J. P. Morgan & Co controlled the U.S. Steel Corporation, America's largest steel producer with 65 per cent of the domestic steel market. Morgan called its president and asked him to buy TC&I at the generous price of $90 a share, three times the market price and valuing the company at $45 million.

A takeover would negate the need for More & Schley to sell its shares on the open market, depressing the overall market even more. U.S. Steel could well afford the price tag, as its annual profits were $200 million and it was valued at over a billion dollars on Wall Street. The takeover would solve all Grant Schley's problems and he agreed to it, although he knew John Gates would not be happy. Morgan shook Schley's hand on a deal. In the interim, whilst the takeover was finalized, Morgan told Schley he would advance his firm $25 million, more or less unsecured.

But by then, the rescue of Moore & Schley became a sideshow as Pierpont Morgan was almost immediately drawn into another crisis situation. Whilst he was negotiating with Grant Schley, the presidents of Trust Company of America and the Lincoln Trust were waiting for him in the lobby. They told him they would have to close their doors for good on Monday morning. Despite all Morgan's efforts to promote calm, depositors were continuing to queue at their doors for cash. Morgan didn't understand the problem and told them that cash was available in exchange for good security.

But that was the problem. The Trust Company of America, even though shares had mildly recovered, had become technically insolvent and the Lincoln Trust Company was not far behind.

Instantly, Morgan realized he had made a mistake neglecting the stock market and being blasé about falling share prices. He realized that the precipitous fall in shares the previous week was beginning to undermine the rest of the rescue. He cursed himself for being so stupid and realized this particular new crisis had been brought upon by himself.

So on Saturday evening, Morgan ordered over 40 of New York's top bankers and Trust presidents to gather at his house to meet with the executives of the two Trusts in trouble. This time, he would try and fashion a rescue plan that would stick. He put the bankers in the east wing of the library and the Trust presidents in the west wing.

Morgan knew that the bankers were prepared to let the two Trusts go down or to shift the responsibility for saving them onto Morgan himself. But that was the last thing Morgan wanted to happen, and he needed leverage to prevent it happening. He soon found it.

Morgan thought that bankers were unlikely to be happy if he allowed Moore & Schley to collapse. He also realized that if he didn't proceed with his purchase of Tennessee Coal & Iron, that is exactly what would happen. He decided to tell it to them straight and apply blackmail tactics.

Morgan went into the east wing and announced that U.S. Steel was calling off its takeover of Tennessee Coal. Immediately, the bank presidents knew what Morgan was up to. He didn't need to spell it out. They begged Morgan to change his mind and let the takeover proceed. He gradually told them his terms and it became a game of high stakes bluff.

Talks continued well into Saturday night but without much progress. Around midnight, Morgan upped the pressure and told the banks that he had also decided to withdraw the $25 million he had lent Moore & Schley in short term funding.

It is said that sometime after midnight, with the bankers still calling his bluff, he locked the bronze doors of the library and put the key in his pocket. The reluctant bankers had no way of leaving. As Ben Strong recalled: "He was up to his old tricks: confinement of his adversaries, a deadline, then abrupt appearance of the menacing host after long hours of bargaining."

When Morgan reappeared at around four o'clock in the morning, he unlocked the door and told the bankers that the whole system would collapse on Monday morning if the Trusts were not bailed out. Exhausted, at last they took him seriously. Morgan wanted $25 million committed there and then, and he had a memorandum document prepared and ready to sign. At a quarter to five early on Sunday morning, he targeted Edward King, the self-appointed leader of the Trust presidents. King was beaten down by all-night bargaining and Morgan told him: "Here's the place, King, and here's the pen." King meekly signed along with the rest of the Trust presidents. Soon afterwards, the bankers capitulated and signed the loan agreement. Morgan finally let them all go home at quarter to six in the morning.

On Sunday afternoon, Morgan was as good as his word and U.S. Steel signed heads of agreement to buy TC&I at $90 a share, enough to save Moore & Schley. But that proved the easy part. Now came the difficult bit. The takeover was subject to President Theodore Roosevelt agreeing to waive Anti-Trust provisions contained in the Sherman Anti-Trust Act. U.S. Steel already had a 60 per cent share of the steel market and the merger of U.S. Steel and Tennessee Coal was anti-competitive and would never have been allowed to proceed in normal circumstances.

Getting approval was more difficult than it sounded, as a big part of Roosevelt's central policy was based on breaking up monopolies and restoring competition to the major industries of America. This takeover flew right in the face of that.

Roosevelt had made breaking up monopolies a focus of his presidency. To allow this one to go through would be an act of treachery towards his own people.

Morgan despatched his two top steel executives, Henry Frick and Judge Gary, overnight by train to Washington to ask Roosevelt to grant a waiver before the market opened on Monday morning. There were no scheduled trains on a Sunday night so Morgan rang the president of the railroad and a locomotive engine was hitched up to Morgan's personal Pullman carriage to get them to Washington.

When they got to the front gates of the White House, Roosevelt's chief of staff gave orders that they were not to be admitted. He refused to let them in to see the President.

They checked into their hotel and called Morgan, who was woken up by his valet. Morgan wasn't surprised and put a call into James Garfield, the Secretary of the Interior. Garfield immediately realized how vital it was and he personally arranged for a meeting with the President before breakfast the following morning. By then, it was less than an hour before the stock exchange was due to open.

Garfield briefed the president and impressed upon him the urgency of his decision. Roosevelt sat down with secretary of state, Elihu Root, and the two men were forced to review the proposed takeover and had only half an hour to decide. Roosevelt relented as he recalled: "It was necessary for me to decide on the instant before the Stock Exchange opened, for the situation in New York was such that any hour might be vital. I do not believe that anyone could justly criticize me for saying that I would not feel like objecting to the purchase under those circumstances."

The news of the presidential waiver was telephoned instantly to Morgan by Frick and Gary from the Oval Office – five minutes before the exchange opened at 10 o'clock. The news was received with euphoria and there was a huge, instant confidence boost felt across the whole of New York and confirmed by the leading trade paper of the day, *Commercial & Financial Chronicle*, which reported that "the relief furnished by this transaction was instant and far-reaching." The stock market duly had its best day since the crisis had begun. Jesse Livermore saw his decision to go long vindicated in a big way, and he had made almost as much profit on paper from his long positions as he had from his shorts the previous week.

It only remained for *i*'s to be dotted and the *t*'s to be crossed. On Tuesday November 5th, at half past eleven, many of New York's leading industrialists, bankers and financiers gathered in Pierpont Morgan's vast library. The carriages and chauffeur-driven automobiles lined up along 26th Street from Madison Avenue to Park Avenue.

The meeting went on all day as a decision was made to put Trust Company of America and the Lincoln Trust into effective administration. It would be controlled by five trustees from the other big Trusts but with a promise backed by J.P. Morgan and others to pay 100 cents on the dollar to depositors, past, present and future.

Then, Judge Gary and Henry Frick presided over board meetings of both U.S Steel and Tennessee Coal & Iron. Both boards agreed to the takeover, and bankers' drafts and share certificates were handed over to complete the transaction and make it final.

At midnight, Morgan arranged for the Waldorf Hotel to send over four urns of strong coffee and six hampers packed with food, along with waiters, to serve to the 100 plus people camped out in his house.

At dawn, Edward King held a small press conference confirming the details of the plan to save TCI and Lincoln. He was followed by Judge Gary and Henry Frick confirming that the takeover of TC&I by U.S. Steel had been approved by both boards of directors and been declared unconditional.

After that, the panic was effectively over. The runs on the Trust companies ended and people started re-depositing their cash. Somehow, the realization that Roosevelt would waive his beloved Anti-Trust laws signalled the right message to investors and depositors.

For Morgan, it was a profitable four weeks in prestige and hard cash. He was hailed as the savior of America. He had also made hundreds of millions of dollars profiting from the distress of others. His cash handouts were secured loans with high coupons accompanied by warrants. His purchases were all at bargain distress prices. Later, the assets of Tennessee Coal & Iron were valued at $1 billion. At $90 a share, his U.S. Steel paid just under $45 million for the whole company. But it was enough for Grant Schley to be able to pay off his own debts and those of his firm.

On Wednesday November 6th, John Gates walked down the gangway of his steamer after six days at sea. He had been out of the United States for two of the most tumultuous weeks in its history. An absence the cost of which was in the hundreds of millions. But it was all over, and there was nothing he could do. Later, he accused Pierpont Morgan of all sorts of malfeasance in buying Tennessee Coal & Iron and snatching it from his grasp. There was no doubt that Morgan had made hundreds of millions from the 1907 crisis, but in the process he had also saved the American financial system from total collapse. Nothing John Gates could say, or do, could take away from that.

But Gates exited the crisis with his fortune and reputation largely intact. Not so Charles Barney, the most high profile of all New York financiers, whom it seemed everyone blamed for starting the crisis. He was personally disgraced and, nine days later, on Thursday November 14th, he shot himself in the stomach. It was a well-planned suicide, and he lived long enough to say goodbye to his wife and children and make the necessary changes to his will in the four hours before he died. His will later revealed bequests to his family of $2.5 million.

Barney was the real innocent victim of the crisis. He had lent no money for the United Copper corner, and before the unfair and unjustified run on its deposits, his Knickerbocker Trust been solvent and successful.

The crisis may have been over, but the recession it had triggered was not. America's economy went into deep decline. Industrial production fell dramatically by 11 per cent in the next 12 months and imports by a staggering 26 per cent as demand for goods fell away. Unemployment soared to eight per cent and bankruptcies multiplied. The biggest effect was felt in the number of immigrants entering the United States. From an annual run rate of 1.2 million it fell to less than 750,000 people in 1909.

The *Commercial & Financial Chronicle* trade newspaper called the 1907-1908 recession "an industrial paralysis and prostration" and said it was the "very worst [recession] ever experienced in the country's history."

CHAPTER 14

The Corn Trade Experiment
First serious trades in commodities

November 1907

At the end of 1907, Jesse Livermore was still not 30 years old and yet he was worth $3 million and counting. It was an astonishing turnaround from the previous year, when his net worth had been less than zero.

On Monday November 5th, the stock market crisis concluded and Livermore instinctively knew that a period of calm and sideways movement on Wall Street was likely for the next few years.

As he began making plans for his new life as a very rich man, he started house hunting for an apartment – money no object. He also started looking for a yacht, big enough to live on in Palm Beach, where he planned to spend a lot of time in the future. He was also considering buying his own rail car so he could travel in similar style to his hero Pierpont Morgan.

He was also attracting unwanted attention from newspaper reporters. With his large profits and subsequent prolific spending, it was inevitable. *The Chicago Tribune* was tipped off about his $200,000 purchase of a yacht berthed on Lake Michigan. In a front-page article, it called him a "beardless fortune hunter of 28" who had spent five years building his fortune.

The Daily Globe in Boston did a more revealing piece and Livermore actually spoke on the record to one of their reporters. He told them: "I prefer not to discuss my personal affairs. Few men in Wall Street know me, and I prefer not to be known. When a man has been successful down there, Wall Street is looking for him. There are those who have won fortunes in the markets and heralded their success, but I prefer to enjoy my gains as quietly as I won them."

The purchase of a 200-foot yacht did not exactly square with that philosophy.

Surprisingly, the newspaper articles attracted little attention in New York and, for the most part, Livermore continued to be ignored in New York and was able to operate quietly and in peace. But his next move was in Chicago.

131

With the start of his vacation in Palm Beach still two months away, he found he needed some action before he went away. With nothing doing on the stock market, he turned his attention to commodities, namely agricultural futures. The futures market was based at the Chicago Board of Trade (CBOT), the world's largest futures exchange, which was founded in 1848.

Chicago was a hub of physical shipments of grain and it was the natural centre for trading commodities. The market was usually very liquid and there was no limit to the size of deals it could handle. It was possible to trade in New York, but everything of consequence came out of Chicago anyway. Livermore established trading accounts at half a dozen brokers but this time with no loyalty to any particular one.

All through 1907, there had been a growing frenzy as agricultural commodity prices kept rising in line with the stock market. Wheat, corn and oats were the main traded products. A poor harvest in Argentina started the upward movement. Then there was news of hoarding in Russia and an export ban. Then plagues of insects destroyed crops, seemingly across the world. There was no good news.

The sustained upward advance drew the attention of all the top commodity traders, and it became obvious that corners were being attempted. Then the rains came in America, making the dirt roads impassable and crops started to rot on the stalks or in wagons that couldn't be moved. It increased the frenzy even more, and all grain became very overvalued. None was being physically delivered at the traded prices; it was all speculation of future prices. Seemingly nothing would stop the upward advance in prices.

Jesse Livermore was certain that the oncoming recession – certain after the financial shenanigans in New York and the credit crunch – would cause commodities to drop in physical demand and consequently price. He couldn't understand why the market kept going up.

Even though he was anxious to get to Palm Beach, it became a short-selling opportunity he could not ignore. As he settled into his new apartment, he looked forward to some big profits.

First, he used his new system of probes. The probes were initially positive and he was soon short 10 million bushels of both wheat and corn. He said: "I had studied the grain markets for a long time and was as bearish on corn and wheat as I had been on stocks."

His wheat position showed a healthy profit straight away, but he was very surprised when corn went the opposite way. Livermore was also convinced there was a big oversupply of corn in the country and was baffled by the rise in price.

Soon he found out why. A notorious commodities speculator called James Patten from Chicago was attempting to run a corner, force the price up and control the market.

The 58-year-old had spotted an opportunity after he travelled to the west of the country to see the state of the crop for himself. He came back sufficiently encouraged to start buying every bushel of corn that was available. Patten, who owned his own brokerage called Patten Brothers, was notorious for running corners in every form of commodity. Patten Brothers was a powerful force in the market.

Livermore remembered what suddenly became a very difficult situation: "Patten had run up the price, and I had quite a loss. I knew there was much more corn in the country than the price indicated. The law of demand and supply worked as always. But the demand came chiefly from Patten."

What Patten knew that Livermore didn't was that heavy rain and the relatively warm seasonal weather had made the dirt roads of the west impassable. The crop was there, but it couldn't be delivered. In those conditions, farmers relied on a freeze to make the roads hard and passable again. Livermore explained: "There was an acute congestion in the movement of corn. I remember that I used to pray for a cold spell that would freeze the impassable roads and enable the farmers to bring their corn into the market. But no such luck."

His losses on corn rose to around $300,000, not life threatening because he had profits on wheat to offset. But it became apparent that Patten would not let him off the hook easily. Patten kept a very close eye on all the short sellers, including Livermore. As he ruefully recalled: "He knew he had me, and I knew it quite as well as he did. But, as I said, I was hoping I might convince the weather that it ought to get busy and help me. Perceiving that neither the weather nor any other kindly wonder-worker was paying any attention to my needs, I studied how I might work out my difficulty by my own efforts."

Livermore decided to clear the decks and arm himself for battle. He sold his wheat position and made around $200,000. But getting out of corn was almost impossible when Patten was effectively the only buyer at current market prices: "The problem in corn was infinitely more difficult. If I could have covered my ten million bushels at the prevailing prices, I instantly and gladly would have done so, large though the loss would have been. But, of course, the moment I started to buy in my corn, Patten would be on the job as squeezer-in-chief, and I no more relished running up the price on myself by reason of my own purchases than cutting my own throat with my own knife."

At this stage, Livermore had thrown in the towel on making a profit. It was now all about minimizing losses. So he put in an order to buy five hundred thousand bushels of corn every eighth of a cent it went down from the prevailing price. That was effectively a stop on realizing a cash loss, although his paper loss was mounting as the price rose.

Then he had another idea: he decided to change the conversation and open the front on another battlefield.

He sought the help of the powerful Armour family, but the family patriarch, Jonathan Ogden Armour, turned him down. Even so, Livermore became desperate to show people that he and Ogden were on the same side, acting together.

To put pressure on Patten, Livermore decided to enter the market for oats where Patten was also attempting to corner the market in opposition to the Armours, who were determined not to be intimidated. He knew the Armour family believed the oats market belonged to them and that they did not care for Patten. As Livermore explained: "If the market thought the Armours were selling, they would follow. Knowing how the traders' minds worked, it was a cinch that they would instantly think that Armour was gunning for Patten."

In the first stage of his plan, Livermore put in short orders through four brokers to sell 200,000 bushels of oats at market price. The scattered selling was designed to make the brokers think that the Armours were trying to break Patten's oats corner. Livermore hoped that the market would also think the Armours were going after Patten on corn and would sell off their corn holdings next.

It worked like a dream, just as Livermore had planned it. He remembered later: "My dope on the psychology of the Chicago traders was absolutely correct."

The price of oats broke and, with it, Patten's corner. When the brokers saw how easily Patten had been seen off, by what they thought was an assault by the Armours, they figured (as Livermore hoped they would) that corn was next.

But any figuring proved unnecessary, as Livermore got very lucky. To his surprise and delight, the Armours started selling their holdings of corn to take advantage of the run on Patten. The market broke open and as the sell-off started suddenly – Patten was overwhelmed and unable to figure out what was going on. He sat on his hands as he waited to understand what the market was doing. It was the break Livermore needed, and he was able to buy six million bushels first and then the remaining four million he needed at well below the previous day's close. He then sold off his 200,000 bushels of oats at a loss of only $3,000. A delighted Livermore said: "That was pretty cheap bear bait. I covered the entire line of ten million bushels within one-half cent of the price prevailing at the time I started to cover on the traders' selling."

Overall, he managed to get out of his positions in corn at a loss of $225,000. His loss from the whole caper was less than $30,000, which was a great result as he had been staring at a $1 million-plus loss at one point.

And it soon became apparent how close to absolute catastrophe Livermore had come. Corn broke upwards and Patten re-established his grip on it. It went up 25 cents a bushel and Livermore would have been wiped out with a $2.5 million loss. As he said: "There is no telling what I would have had to pay."

CHAPTER 15

The Life of Reilly

Buys yacht - luxury lifestyle begins

November 1908

So Jesse Livermore was finally ready for his winter vacation – but this time with a difference. He was now a very, very wealthy man by anyone's standards and could afford anything and everything he wanted to buy. He was also ready for a better lifestyle, which he felt he needed and deserved after the harrowing time of the past 15 years of his life.

His first move was to leave the hotel life behind and move into his own apartment on the Upper West Side. The freehold apartment at 194 Riverside Drive was part of a seven-storey block that had been built in 1901 by famed New York architect Ralph Townsend. The block was typical of the Townsend inspired neo-renaissance buildings constructed at the turn of the century.

The apartment between 91st and 92nd Street had splendid views of the Hudson River and was accessed from its own private cul-de-sac. Measuring 6,000 square feet in all, it had 13 rooms and the building had three apartments per floor. It enjoyed high beam moulded ceilings, hardwood parquet floors and tiled fireplaces. The apartment enjoyed huge bay windows with banquettes and spacious walk-in closets.

The apartment was already filled with beautiful furniture left by the previous owners who, ironically, had lost all their money in the stock market crash. Livermore enjoyed the services of the full-time concierge in the lobby and got a good sensation every time he passed through the entrance doors, which were flanked by giant stone lions' heads on each side.

He also ordered a private Pullman railcar, just like the one owned by Pierpont Morgan, at a cost of over $100,000.

But most importantly of all, he finally fulfilled a lifelong dream to own his own yacht. And not just any yacht. The *Anita* was a 202-foot long steel-hulled, triple-screw yacht, better known as a schooner in yachting circles. The boat was 10 years old and cost him $120,000 from John Flagler, the industrialist. The

Anita was registered at the Columbia Yacht Club, based at Lake Michigan in Chicago. As he was beginning to spend time in Chicago trading commodities, he saw no reason to change that and he continued to fly the red, white, and blue pennant of the club on the ship's stern. As soon as the deal was done, he had the captain sail the *Anita* directly to Palm Beach so it was there waiting for him as he started his winter vacation. He recalled: "I am really daffy about fishing, and this was the time when I was going to fish until my heart's content from my own yacht, going wherever I wished, whenever I felt like it."

Livermore couldn't wait, and the anticipation in the week before he left almost overwhelmed his senses. He truly was living a dream. By 1907, Palm Beach had become a synonym for turn-of-the-century indulgence, and Livermore intended to do just that – indulge himself.

Livermore realized that he had to learn to live the life of a rich man from now on. He strongly believed that there was no point having lots of money if it was never spent. So to go with the yacht, he ordered himself three sets of a traditional yacht owner's uniform: blue blazer, grey flannel slacks and a captain's peak hat.

This time, he did not sell out all his positions and kept the same shares he had bought on November 4th after Pierpont Morgan had asked him to. As soon as his affairs were in order in New York, he closed up the apartment and took the train and headed down to Palm Beach. When he got to the station, he went straight to the quay to board the *Anita* for the first time as owner. He loved the fuss the twelve-man crew made of their new owner.

For the first week, he spent most of his time aboard the *Anita*. The weather was extraordinary even for the time of year and his mood couldn't have been better. How easy it was to enjoy life with $3 million in the bank, he mused to himself as he got used to being able to afford anything that took his fancy. As he recalled: "I cruised about in Florida water, having a grand old time. The fishing was great. Everything was lovely. I didn't have a care in the world, and I wasn't looking for any." He was so happy he even invited his estranged wife, Nettie, to come and spend a week aboard with him.

He found the cook on board the *Anita* was not the best, but he was immediately unable to do anything about that so he would leave the yacht in the evening and dine at the Breaker's Hotel, formerly the Palm Beach Inn, which was situated directly on the beach and owned by Henry Flagler. The giant seaside hotel had 425 rooms, which were full of New York society at that time of the year. The hotel was fully booked and it was impossible to get a room, and Livermore was glad he had his yacht to escape back to every night. Sometimes, he might take back a young lady he had just met in the Breaker's bar and sometimes he might not. Whatever his fancy, the same lady rarely returned twice.

He mingled and mixed easily and began to get to know the Palm Beach regulars. They knew very little of Jesse Livermore except that he was a new rich man in town with one of the biggest boats in the harbor. He was not short of friends.

The chef at the Breakers was superb. He described dinner in the restaurant as "exquisite." After dinner, he enjoyed coffee, brandy and a cigar on the famous veranda directly over the top of the lapping waves. He found the atmosphere in Palm Beach unlike anywhere else in the world. He just lapped it up and was in a form of seventh heaven, living a lifestyle he barely believed was possible. Those few months at the beginning of 1909 were certainly the happiest times of his life.

After a few weeks, he heard about the famous Bradley's Beach Club built by the legendary Colonel Ed Bradley and his brother Jack Bradley. The Beach Club was adjacent to Breaker's, and Livermore was immediately accepted as a new member.

Livermore sought out Bradley and proceeded successfully to ingratiate himself with the club's famous owner. Bradley himself had been an army scout during the Apache wars and was involved in the capture of the great Apache chief, Geronimo. He had reputedly known Billy the Kid and Wyatt Earp. Although they came from totally different backgrounds, he recognized Livermore as a kindred spirit straightaway.

The club, situated north of the Flagler Memorial Bridge, had been open for only eight years and the prime attraction was that it was within walking distance of the Breakers Hotel and the Royal Poinciana Hotel. Joseph Kennedy was a leading member.

Ed Bradley had recently bought his brother's shares in the club and was now the sole owner.

The beach club was primarily a casino, which was rather inconvenient as gambling was illegal in Florida. But Bradley circumvented that by declaring it a private club for members only. Whether that made it legal was highly debatable, but as no one sought to challenge Bradley's view, the club remained open under Henry Flagler's patronage.

Evening dress was mandatory after seven o'clock, and the club was also unusual as its rules allowed and indeed encouraged women to gamble, a custom almost unheard of in the United States.

In fact, it was women who had saved the club. When it opened in 1898, it was very poorly patronized and was on the brink of closure. Just in time, Bradley's wife Agnes had the brilliant idea of letting women gamble at the tables. The club's fortunes changed overnight and it never looked back.

The club was very female friendly, another first in America, and Bradley decorated it in green and white with special soft lighting that flattered a woman's complexion. Up to now, gambling clubs had always had harsh bright white lighting to discourage cheating. But that wasn't necessary at the Beach Club as no one dared cheat in an Ed Bradley-owned establishment. Colonel Bradley had his own way of dealing with things.

Despite allowing women to gamble, Bradley had a strict rule that a woman must be escorted. He had no intention of turning his club into the sort of clip joints that many other Palm Beach establishments had inadvertently become.

The club's success was also helped by the fact that the owner was a professional gambler himself who owned a string of highly successful racehorses. He understood the needs and desires of his members.

Soon, Livermore was dining at the beach club as well. He found it had an even better chef than the Breakers. Installed at the Beach Club was a culinary genius called Gene Braccho, to whom Bradley was rumored to pay a salary of over $20,000 a year, 10 times the going rate. Braccho was worth every cent and his reputation ensured that the dining room, which could seat 212 people, was packed every night for two sittings. Braccho travelled to New York for a week every year to sample the best the city could offer and bring it back to Palm Beach.

Bradley played his part and bought the best ingredients for his kitchens, regardless of cost. Even though the restaurant charged the highest prices of any venue in America, it still lost money. But whilst the patrons went on to the casino and gambled the night away, it didn't matter.

Even though Bradley was the perfect host, he also had strict rules. Drinking and smoking was forbidden in the gambling parlor but encouraged in the dining room and outdoor areas. Occasionally there were problems. Drinking was rather out of control in the pre-prohibition years in the United States, especially amongst young people. So Bradley established a minimum age of 26 for entry into the club in an attempt to curb excessive drinking. If a member did imbibe too much and lost control of himself, a message went out that there was a telephone call for the offender, who was then met by Bradley at the phone booth and told: "Young man, you're drinking a little heavily tonight, come back tomorrow and everything will be settled." It was Bradley's code for a member to leave. If the member did not get the message, strong young men from the state of Tennessee, who looked after the club's security, would make sure he did. The next day, their membership was revoked and there was no second chance.

Tom Bohne, Bradley's secretary, was effectively manager of the club and once described the conditions for membership to a local magazine: "Only gentlemen are allowed membership. A woman had to be escorted at all times by a gentleman member. No one under 26 years old is permitted in the club, even in the dining rooms. Ed's logic was that a young man was likely to claim he was 22, thinking that 21 was required, so they would know he was not 26."

Eventually, Bradley would interview all new members himself. If he liked them, they were in. If he didn't, membership was declined for unspecified reasons by letter a few weeks later.

Bradley actively discouraged Palm Beach locals from becoming members. He did not want them to gamble everything away and inevitably bear him a grudge. Even when New Yorkers lost everything they had, Bradley would often refund them half their losses and retain their goodwill. He knew he would eventually get the money back anyway.

The limits at the casino were even higher than in Monte Carlo, and Bradley only wanted those people to gamble who could afford to lose. When they won big, he took great pleasure in going up to them, shaking their hands and converting their chips back to cash, personally reeling off thousand dollar bills from the 100 such bills he was reputed to carry on his person at all times.

Most of all, he wanted members to enjoy themselves at the club. As Tom Bohne explained: "Many a time, when the customer would win, why, Ed would be tickled. He'd really be pleased because so many would lose. If a member could get some pleasure out of it, extending his time at the table, being seen, and enjoying passing checks back and forth, that was Ed's idea of entertainment. And that's just what it was."

As a result, Ed Bradley was very well thought of by the residents of Palm Beach. Its most prominent citizen, James Owens, Mayor during the war years, later called Bradley: "One of the finest men I ever knew, whose word was just better than most people's bond, and he contributed a great deal to the growth and development of Palm Beach and its beauty and loveliness."

Despite owning America's most successful club and being the perfect host, Ed Bradley was quiet and secretive out of hours. That character trait, a combination of outward flamboyance yet inner secretiveness, meant that he and Jesse Livermore got on well. They quickly became fast friends, although they were both initially extremely reticent with each other.

They developed a mutual respect and understanding. Livermore loved to gamble at Bradley's, and the two swapped stories of the stock market and casinos. Bradley told Livermore stories about what he called "the art of being lucky." Bradley believed that luck was an actuality and, when combined with endeavor and hard work, was an unbeatable combination in any man. According to Livermore biographer Richard Smitten, Bradley reputedly told him: "A person either works for a living or gambles for a living. In fact, life is a gamble, but if a person chooses to take up gambling for a living, it has to be studied intelligently and worked at, at least twice as hard as any other profession."

As well as sailing and gambling, Livermore's other indulgence was women. Eventually, his lust for the opposite sex attracted the attention of the gossip columnists. Especially when he was reported to have taken up with the 46-year-old society singer Lillian Russell, who was the girlfriend of legendary businessman and Palm Beach regular Jim Brady. But Livermore was never involved with Lillian Russell. It was a newspaper myth. It was a cover for his married friend Alex Moore, who had stolen Russell from Brady. Livermore, Russell and Moore became an inseparable threesome in Palm Beach, baffling the gossip columnists on the true nature of their relationship.

After three months, the season was coming to an end and Livermore knew he must return to New York and earn his living again. Since the turn of the year, he had spent over $400,000 on his apartment, yacht and railcar. He had spent another $50,000 just enjoying himself for three months in Palm Beach and nearly as much at Bradley's gambling tables. He was $500,000 light, and his bank account had diminished to $2.5 million. His annual overhead was now over $100,000 a year maintaining his new assets, especially the yacht. At that rate, he would be poor again soon and he knew he must pull himself together and get back into the groove of winning on Wall Street again. But that was to prove easier said than done.

CHAPTER 16

Newspaper Notoriety

Lady Luck rescues new 'Cotton King'

1908

As his vacation wound down in Palm Beach, Jesse Livermore's thoughts turned back to Wall Street and he contemplated his return to New York. In Palm Beach, everyone was talking about a wealthy cotton trader called Theodore (Teddy) Price who had just lost everything when he had tried to corner March cotton contracts in Chicago.

Livermore's ears pricked up suddenly as he sought to learn more about the man they were talking about. He discovered that the 46-year-old Price had already gone spectacularly broke 15 years earlier and then re-established himself. His background was as a southern financier but he had an unrivalled knowledge of cotton and an uncanny ability to package a deal. He had followed his father into the business at the age of 21 and risen to head his own brokerage, called Price McCormick & Co.

His first failure had come in 1890, when he was attempting to corner cotton after he had advance knowledge of the crop failure of 1890. At first, he bought and made a respectable profit. But, inexplicably, he reversed himself and went short with obviously consequences; the corner failed and he lost a staggering $13 million on the trade. Both he and his firm went bankrupt.

But Price was anything but a pessimist, and he picked himself up, dusted himself off and gradually rebuilt his reputation. By 1907, he had repaid his creditors every cent of the $13 million and made himself a million dollars on top. He had also become a journalist of some repute, writing newsletters and editing the prestigious Commerce & Finance magazine.

What he lacked however was a trader's instinct and, for the second time in his life, in early 1908, he managed to lose everything he had once again. His latest failure came as a complete surprise to everyone, and Livermore christened it his "second Waterloo in the cotton market."

The story sparked Livermore's interest, and he studied Price's first failure as part of his own education and tried to analyze where Price had gone wrong. He said: "Price tried to corner cotton. But McCormick did not have the vision or the courage of his partner and got cold feet on the very verge of success. Instead of making a killing, they made one of the most sensational failures in years."

The more Livermore looked into the story, the more he admired Price's recovery from his first bankruptcy and the fact he repaid his creditors when he had no legal obligation to do so. The effect on Livermore of the Price affair was startling, and for the first time in a few months, he stopped thinking about fishing and started thinking about the market again. But he had no notion of the dramatic effect Price was to have on his own life.

And so it was a very tanned and relaxed Jesse Livermore who returned to New York in late February 1908, this time in his own private Pullman railcar, which had just been delivered. He quickly reopened his new apartment on the river on the Upper West Side. He settled back in quickly and loved his new residence and its splendid views of the Hudson River.

Livermore quickly resumed his New York life. But after his success and his new riches, he no longer felt as comfortable at E. F. Hutton's office as he had in the past, when he was just one of the boys seeking a living. Ed Hutton realized that this might pose a problem and he gave him the ultimate client accolade of his own office with his name on the door and the services of his own secretary. He was now Hutton's star client, and they were determined to look after him. Not only did he bring huge commissions to the brokerage, but it was also very profitable to follow him in and out of the market.

His new status made little difference, the stock market was still going nowhere and his portfolio was static. He looked at resuming trading in agricultural futures, but after his close shave on grain, he was in no mood to rush into that. He realized he had been very lucky and didn't fancy pushing his luck again.

After a month, the bored Livermore wondered where to turn to for some immediate action. On an impulse, and recalling the Teddy Price story, he decided to relocate temporarily to Chicago to trade in cotton. Chicago was the centre of global cotton trading and Livermore felt a need to be close to the source of the action. He temporarily abandoned New York, much to the disappointment of Ed Hutton.

Once in Chicago, he opened accounts at all the major cotton brokerages at the Chicago Board of Trade, the world's oldest futures exchange.

For the first few weeks, he stayed in hotels but then decided almost on impulse to buy a second yacht to live in on Lake Michigan. To own two yachts was undeniably reckless, but Livermore could easily afford it. His yacht broker, Joe MacDonald, found a yacht called the *Venetia* for sale at the Columbia Yacht Club. It was owned by Morgan Plant, owner of the Plant railway company. It was much too big, but it was the only one available large enough to live on. The *Venetia* dwarfed the *Anita* at 310 feet, with a beam of 51 feet and displacing 580 tons. With eight staterooms and four bathrooms, it had a crew of over 20. He wrote a check for $200,000 to Morgan Plant, and the *Venetia* was his. He moved in straightaway and got down to work.

This time he focused exclusively on cotton and staked everything on July cotton contracts. The 1908 cotton harvest was spectacular and 13.5 million 500-pound-bales were harvested. The prevailing price was 9.2 cents a pound and the harvest was worth a record breaking $625 million, a trader's paradise, and by mid-April the price was understandably very weak.

Because of a potential glut of cotton, it seemed that everyone in Chicago was bearish. In fact, it seemed that everyone was selling July cotton, as Livermore observed: "You know how people are. I suppose it is the contagion of example that makes a man do something because everyone around him is doing the same thing. Perhaps it is some phase or variety of the herd instinct."

Most traders were selling July cotton and anticipated a collapse in the price. The price duly did drop and Livermore observed all this, but he also saw that the time frame for the short sellers to buy back in was shrinking fast. He didn't see how they could pull it off, so he bought 100,000 bales – there was plenty available: "It seemed to me that I could have offered a reward of one million dollars for the capture, dead or alive, of a single trader who was not selling July cotton and nobody would have claimed it." Despite that, Livermore kept buying and the rest of the market kept selling. That is, until the end of the second week in May, when he found he owned 120,000 bales, around $5.5 million worth of cotton. The price started to go up and, with 10 minutes to go before the market closed one Saturday afternoon, Livermore was on the hunt to see what was available to buy and he got another 20,000 bales. At the close, the price was up on his late buying. Now everything depended on how it opened on Monday morning.

Chicago had a direct telegraph link to the Liverpool Cotton Exchange in England. Because of the time difference, Liverpool opened first and, on the morning of Monday May 11th, it opened well up, peaking at $9.90, 30 per cent above the low in April.

Unsurprisingly, the bears got very nervous and everyone suspected there was a corner going on but no one knew who was running it. Livermore was not surprised and said: "That just showed me that my deductions had been sound and that I was trading along the path of least resistance."

That was all very well, but Livermore now had a large holding of July cotton to sell. The market was fragile and would not be able to absorb it. Despite the price action and the unsettling of the bears, there was little cotton available to buy and no sign of any panic that he would have expected. Livermore had 140,000 bales to sell, which had cost around $6.5 million. If he couldn't find any buyers, he was potentially in plenty of trouble and he suddenly began to realize just how much. On paper, his cotton holdings were worth $7.5 million: but only on paper. As and when he began to sell, he knew the price would collapse.

But then, an extraordinary thing happened.

On the morning of Tuesday May 12th, *The New York World* newspaper, with a circulation of over one million a day, splashed a story on its front page about an unknown speculator who had cornered the cotton trade. That morning, completely and blissfully unaware, Livermore was strolling along the boardwalk on Lake Michigan to the offices of one of his brokers, when a friend collared him at the entrance and said: "That was quite a story in *The World* this morning." Livermore asked: "What story?" The friend replied: "What? Do you mean to tell me you haven't seen it?" Livermore said: "I never see *The World* – what is the story?" The reply came: "Why it's all about you. It says you've got July cotton cornered." Livermore just about kept his composure. He was stunned but tried not to show it. As he shuffled inside, he knew if it was true then he was out of danger and a very large potential profit loomed. Straightaway, he saw on the telegraph that prices had shot up in Liverpool that morning.

He sent a messenger out for the paper, and when he opened it up, there it was splashed above the fold on the front page: "July Cotton Cornered By Jesse Livermore." He recalled later: "Of course I knew at once the article would play the dickens with the market. If I had deliberately studied ways and means of disposing of my 140,000 bales to the best advantage, I couldn't have hit upon a better plan. It would not have been possible to find one." That article at that very moment was being read all over the country either in *The World* or in other newspapers quoting it. It had been cabled to Europe, and that was plain from the Liverpool prices. The market was simply wild, no wonder with such news. The cotton bears took cover and started buying.

The Chicago market opened at 10 o'clock, and by ten minutes past 10, Livermore no longer owned any cotton. He sold or, as he described it, "let them have it" all: 140,000 bales. And he managed to get the top market price prevailing at around $9.90 against his average purchase price of around $8. He remembered: "The traders made the market for me. All I really did was to see a heaven sent opportunity to get rid of my cotton. I grasped it because I couldn't help it. What else could I do?"

When he was given the confirmatory slips at midday, Livermore realized he had made a profit of almost $2 million on his investment, a third of it in 10 minutes at the opening. The money had simply been handed to him. If the newspaper article had not appeared, he would have had immense trouble exiting the position at a profit. As he said: "Selling 140,000 bales of July cotton without sending the price down was a trick beyond my powers. That is one trouble about trading on a large scale – you cannot sneak out as you can when you pike along."

The New York Times of Friday May 15th later put the story right: "J. L. Livermore, who has been one of the successful traders in the cotton market for a year, is said to have unloaded long line at the high prices yesterday, but the idea that he had cornered the market was generally discredited in the trade."

The New York Times had the truth; Livermore had got very, very lucky again. By the end of June, the price of July cotton collapsed to $6.40 a bale, the correct price. He had inadvertently run his first corner but only in the eyes of a few rumor-mongers and reporters and a very slow news day at The New York World.

Livermore had no idea where The World got the story from or why they published it, as it was completely untrue. Livermore's holding was no more than one per cent of the entire stocks of July cotton. He would have needed to have $30 million in capital to have established a corner, and even the most basic of research would have established that the story was untrue.

Although his $2 million profit had been pure luck and nothing really to do with him, it suddenly gave him overnight legendary status. As Livermore remembered: "One of the biggest men in cotton in the entire world met me a day or two later and said: 'That was certainly the slickest deal you ever put over, Livermore. I was wondering how much you were going to lose when you came to market that line of yours. You knew this market was not big enough take more than fifty or sixty thousand bales without selling off, and how were you going to work off the rest and not lose all your paper profits was beginning to interest me. I didn't think of your scheme. It certainly was slick.' I had nothing to do with it, I assured him as earnestly as I could. But all he could do was repeat: 'Mighty slick, my boy. Mighty slick. Don't be so modest.'"

After that, Livermore was rarely out of the newspapers and he gained a new moniker to add to the boy plunger. Now, he was alternately called 'The Cotton King.' With the money burning a hole in his pocket, he returned to New York to adoration. But he was very conscious walking around New York that it was a false moniker: "There is not enough money in the world to buy the columns of *The New York World* or enough personal pull to secure the publication of a story like that. It gave me an utterly unearned reputation at that time."

Livermore called it "a crown that was pressed down upon the brow of an undeserving trader."

He was suddenly famous, with what he called "newspaper notoriety."

And it was the reason why he finally came to meet in person Teddy Price.

CHAPTER 17

Under the Influence: Cotton Fiasco
Seduced by Teddy Price

August 1908

In the middle of 1908, Jesse Livermore found himself even richer than he had been a few months earlier. His net worth was now over $5 million and he was enjoying life in New York again. This time he was determined that his profits would stay in the bank and he was looking forward to a period of relative inaction.

His new fame attracted begging letters and letters requesting trading advice and share tips. He threw them all in the bin unopened. He simply wasn't interested in any distractions or anything that could affect his trading psyche.

But one letter he did open was from Teddy Price requesting a meeting: "Of course, I immediately answered that I'd be glad to see him at my office at any time he cared to call. The next day, he came."

Livermore was in awe of Price's reputation. He was honored that someone like Price wanted to meet him. As he admitted: "I had long admired him. His name was a household word wherever men took an interest in growing or buying or selling cotton, people quoted Teddy Price's opinions to me. I remember once, at a Swiss resort, talking to a Cairo banker who was interested in cotton. When he heard I was from New York, he immediately asked me about Teddy Price, whose market reports he received and read with unfailing regularity. "I had always thought Price went about his business scientifically. He was a true speculator, a thinker with the vision of a dreamer and the courage of a fighting man – an unusually well-informed man, who knew both the theory and the practice of trading cotton. He loved to hear and to express ideas and theories and abstractions, and at the same time there was mighty little about the practical side of the cotton market or the psychology of cotton traders that he did not know, for he had been trading for years and had made and lost vast sums. After the failure of his old Stock Exchange firm of Price McCormick & Co, he went it alone. Inside of two years, he came back, almost spectacularly. I remember reading that the first thing he did when he got on his feet financially was to pay off his old creditors in full."

The full repayment of his old debts impressed Livermore immensely. It is exactly what he would have done himself, despite the lack of a legal obligation to do so. But Price was down on his luck having lost a second fortune, something else Livermore was very familiar with.

In early June, Teddy Price arrived at the entrance to 194 Riverside Drive, and the concierge brought him up to Livermore's apartment. As both men sat on the brown leather sofas in front of the large bay window with the late morning sun glinting off the Hudson, they chatted about the markets. Price was a long time coming to the point. When he finally did, he proposed to Livermore that they formed what he called "a working alliance." Price would supply information – information that was not yet public knowledge – and Livermore would trade on the basis of it. Livermore was immensely pleased that Price had come to him with a proposition to be partners. Price flattered the younger man and told him he had a "special genius" that he did not possess himself.

Livermore was very flattered but not stupid enough to believe all the praise Price heaped upon him. Of course, Livermore knew that his success as a cotton trader, so far, had been down to blind luck and that he was actually no genius at all – just a lucky punter. He was slightly surprised that a worldly man like Teddy Price could not see that. So Livermore, although he could see the merit of his scheme, put him off and replied: "I do not think I could run in double harness, and I am not keen about trying to learn."

Price was not for taking no as an answer and insisted that, together, they would be an ideal combination. Eventually, Livermore had to be more blunt and told him that he did not want to have anything to do with influencing other people to trade. He told him: "If I fool myself, I alone suffer and I pay the bill at once. There are no drawn-out payments or unexpected annoyances. I play a lone hand by choice and also because it is the wisest and cheapest way to trade. I get my pleasure out of matching my brains against other traders – men whom I have never seen and never talked to and never advised to buy or sell and never expect to meet or know. When I make money, I make it backing my own opinions. I don't sell them or capitalize them. If I made money in any other way, I would imagine I had not earned it. Your proposition does not interest me because I am interested in the game only as I play it for myself and in my own way." Price vainly tried to convince him that he was wrong but Livermore stonewalled him, unwilling to be swayed. Price finally backed off, and for another hour they congenially discussed cotton trading and its vagaries. Price told him many stories of the market, for which Livermore was all ears. Then he asked Livermore about his July cotton success. He was totally honest about his lucky profit. But Price no more believed him than anyone else had.

Before he left, Livermore offered Price some money to help him get back on his feet. He said: "I would consider it a privilege if you would allow me to be of financial assistance to you." Price turned him down flat. He had not come for Livermore's money but his trading expertise. The refusal greatly impressed Livermore.

After he had gone, Livermore wondered to himself why he had been so determined to resist the proposition. And then he remembered the promises he had made to himself not so many years before: "When I said that a speculator has a host of enemies, many of whom successfully bore from within, I had in mind many mistakes. I have learned that a man may possess an original mind and a lifelong habit of independent thinking and still be vulnerable to attacks by a personable personality. I am fairly immune from the commoner speculative ailments, such as greed and fear and hope. But being an ordinary man, I find I can err with great ease." Livermore firmly believed that would be the end of the matter and that any talk of a partnership was dead: "I would have sworn that our business paths would never cross. I was not sure I'd ever see him again. But on the very next day, he wrote me a letter thanking me for my offers of help and inviting me to come and see him. I answered that I would. He wrote again. I called. I got to see a great deal of him. It was always a pleasure for me to listen to him; he knew so much and he expressed his knowledge so interestingly. I think he is the most magnetic man I ever met."

It was the first of many meetings and the two men got to know one another very well, even spending a couple of weeks together in Palm Beach. Price shared many an afternoon with Livermore on the shaded upper deck of the *Anita* and then of an evening at the Beach Club casino. Livermore remembered the conversations well: "We talked of many things, for he is a widely read man with an amazing grasp of many subjects and a remarkable gift for interesting generalization. The wisdom of his speech is impressive; and as for plausibility, he hasn't an equal. I have heard many people accuse Teddy Price of many things, including insincerity, but I sometimes wonder if his remarkable plausibility does not come from the fact that he first convinces himself so thoroughly as to acquire thereby a greatly increased power to convince others."

Livermore analyzed Price very carefully. He was anxious to learn as much as he could about cotton at the feet of an acknowledged expert. He remained flattered that Price was so interested in him and wanted to spend more time talking with him: "Of course we talked about the market matters at great length. I was not bullish on cotton, but he was. I could not see the bull side at all, but he did. He brought up so many facts and figures that I ought to have been overwhelmed, but I wasn't. I couldn't disprove them because I could not deny their authenticity, but they did not shake my belief in what I read for myself. But he kept at it until I no longer felt sure of my own information as gathered from the trade papers and the dailies. That meant I couldn't see the market with my own eyes. A man cannot be convinced against his own convictions, but he can be talked into a state of uncertainty and indecision, which is even worse, for that means he cannot trade with confidence and comfort."

Slowly, Price was bamboozling Livermore, taking over his mind like a professional hypnotist would. Much later, Livermore would readily admit this and his foolishness at allowing it to happen: "I cannot say that I got all mixed up, exactly, but I lost my poise; or, rather, I ceased to do my own thinking. I cannot give you in detail the various steps by which I reached the state of mind that was to prove so costly to me. I think it was his assurances of the accuracy of his figures, which were exclusively his, and the undependability of mine, which were not exclusively mine, but public property. He harped on the utter reliability, as proved time and again, of all his ten thousand correspondents throughout the South. In the end, I came to read conditions as he himself read them – because we were both reading from the same page of the same book, held by him before my eyes. He has a logical mind. Once I accepted his facts, it was a cinch that my own conclusions, derived from his facts, would agree with his own. "When he began his talks with me about the cotton situation, I not only was bearish but I was short of the market. Gradually, as I began to accept his facts and figures, I began to fear I had been basing my previous position on misinformation. Of course, I could not feel that way and not cover. And once I had covered, because Price made me think I was wrong, I simply had to go along. It is the way my mind works. You know, I have done nothing in my life but trade in stocks and commodities. I naturally think that if it was wrong to be bearish, it must be right to be a bull. And if it is right to be a bull, it is imperative to buy."

Suddenly in mid-July, Livermore changed track. He became completely hooked on Teddy Price and they became partners, just as Price had wanted the year before. Before he knew it, Livermore, on Price's insistence, was long 60,000 bales of cotton. He put out his probes, 20,000 bales at a time, and initially it went well and the price went up.

But what really changed his mind was when Price told him he was in discussions with Farmers Alliance, the cotton growers association.

Livermore admitted he was unwell at the time and suffering from a mystery virus for which his doctor could prescribe no cure. Whether it affected his judgement he could not tell, but soon he was the owner of 160,000 bales of cotton. Simultaneously, he had a big position in wheat and was still long the stock market.

Livermore also found himself hindered by the publicity he was receiving. Previously, no one knew who he was but now it seemed everyone knew him. His moves in the markets were reported in the newspapers, and everyone was interested in him.

His personal life was also in the spotlight, and he was never out of the Chicago and New York gossip columns. Everyone in Chicago knew of the young millionaire who lived on one of the biggest yachts on Lake Michigan with a crew of 20 on hand to indulge his every whim.

He was also worried that his luxury lifestyle was altering his judgement. He was aware that he was no longer the hungry young man and wondered whether it showed in the quality of his decision making.

Newspapers as far away as Los Angeles continually reported what he was up to. The *Los Angeles Times* reported that he was running a cotton corner and that he owned all the stocks of cotton in New York's warehouses. The *Chicago Daily Tribune* ran a profile of Livermore that read: "A fair haired, beardless man of 31, younger looking by ten years than his age who sits in a back room of a brokerage house and issues orders to a score of busy clerks in a gently modulated voice, has possessed himself of every bale of cotton not under contract in the warehouses of great New York. And he is smilingly watching the painful contortions of a group of grizzled bears on the New York Cotton Exchange."

Those fanciful articles put the cotton price up briefly by $3.50 a bale, but this time Livermore did not have the good sense to get out and it fell back again very sharply.

Whilst he was focusing on cotton, the price of wheat was rising: "I was not only long of cotton but I was carrying a heavy line of wheat. My fool efforts to bolster up cotton had increased my line to about 150,000 bales. I may tell you, by this time, I was not feeling very well."

Livermore never made excuses for his own actions but he decided to go away for a short break. He was not in the mood for either of his yachts. Any hedonistic activity just felt wrong with the state he was in. So he went away to think and found a small hotel in Sandy Hook in the Bayshore area just outside Manhattan. Sandy Hook is the break that splits lower New York Bay from the Atlantic Ocean. It is perfect for long contemplative walks. But the few days walking did Livermore little good as he decided to focus all his efforts on getting the cotton trade right and excluded everything else. He made the decision to put all his eggs in one basket.

He began to act out of character and started to break his own rules, as he remembered later: "It seems incredible that knowing the game as well as I did, and with an experience of twelve or fourteen years of speculating in stocks and commodities, I did precisely the wrong thing."

The right thing to do was to sell off the losers and increase his holding in the winners. But he did the opposite. As he admitted: "The cotton showed me a loss and I kept it. The wheat showed me a profit and I sold it out. It was an utterly foolish play, but all I can say in extenuation is that it wasn't really my deal, but Price's. Of all speculative blunders, there are fewer greater than trying to average a losing game. My cotton deal proved it to the hilt a little later. Always sell what shows you a loss and keep what shows you a profit. That was so obviously the wise thing to do and was so well known to me that even now I marvel at myself for doing the reverse."

The sell-off of his wheat holdings became one of the most catastrophic decisions of Livermore's life and certainly the biggest mistake he had made up to that point: "And so I sold my wheat, deliberately cut short my profit in it. After I got out of it, the price went up twenty cents a bushel without stopping. If I had kept it, I might have taken a profit of about eight million dollars. And having decided to keep on with the losing proposition, I bought more cotton."

He was astonished at himself and virtually every single day, after he sold his wheat, the wheat price accelerated and the cotton price declined. He kept score of his daily theoretical loss had he made the opposite decision and this took him into a sort of death spiral of false hope: "I remember very clearly how every day I would buy cotton, more cotton. And why do you think I bought it? To keep the price from going down. If that isn't a super sucker play, what is? I simply kept on putting up more and more money – more money to lose eventually. My brokers and my intimate friends could not understand it and they don't to this day. Of course, if the deal had turned out differently, I would have been a wonder."

One of the things that sustained Livermore was a deal supposedly worked out by Teddy Price with the Farmers' Alliance, an organization that represented cotton growers throughout the south. Under the arrangement, Alliance farmers had undertaken not to sell the new crop of cotton at less than $9.90 a bale, therefore putting a floor under the price and considerably lessening Livermore's risk.

The farmers were very eager to make the agreement. For decades, they had been held to ransom by the Chicago Board of Trade and other cotton exchanges, forced to accept low prices for their cotton bales. The basic problem was overproduction. There was always a natural glut of cotton, which forced prices down, and the buyers had previously held all the cards. This was a chance for the farmers to fight back and stand up to buyers.

In the past, whenever farmers started to sell the crop the price always dropped, sometimes dramatically and they lost millions as a result. Most cotton farmers were living day to day, paying interest on huge debts they had built up over time. Cashflow was always a vital consideration. Price understood this, but Livermore did not.

Price had persuaded them that this year would be different and Livermore could dictate the price they received. Of course, Livermore was not dealing with the growers himself. That was down to Price, and he had no way of judging the true situation and could only go on what Price told him.

Initially, the arrangement worked and it served to put a floor on the price of a bale of cotton as it rose to as high as $12.50. Livermore was encouraged.

Up until that point, Livermore had endured losses but was reassured by the deal with the farmers. But Price had not told him the whole story – he knew that eventually the farmers would crack and begin selling. But this time, Price had always been unsure whether it would hold although he did not tell Livermore this. The agreement relied on the premise that the growers would not panic and hold out. But there were all sorts of issues for the farmers, not the least of which was cashflow.

At the end of the second week of August, the wheels finally came off the

Livermore/Price bandwagon. It had come down to a straightforward stand-off between Livermore and a bunch of cotton bears. It was almost about who would blink first. Livermore blinked.

If Livermore had retained the support of the growers, he would have won. But, just as Price thought, the Farmers Alliance fell apart and individual members began to sell off cotton at prices well below $9.90. It very quickly became every man for himself. At some point, Price must have realized that the agreement wouldn't hold and that was when he joined the bears and took the other side against his partner.

Inevitably, on August 12th, the price of cotton suddenly collapsed as the growers released their cotton stocks all at once. Price went short and the onslaught of the bears overwhelmed Livermore. The price of a bale of cotton dropped by as much as $4 overnight. Selling orders overwhelmed buying orders by as much as 20-1.

Livermore lost the battle and the New York Times reported that the price of cotton had fallen $4.25 in one week. Livermore's defeat was mainly the result of treachery from his partner. Price had bought cotton heavily in the weeks before the articles came out, but as soon as they appeared he double-crossed his partner, selling out all his holdings and more besides. Livermore had no idea what was going on until he read of it in the New York Times: "Most of the selling was done by an operator who was supposed to be in harmony with the bull leaders."

The big mystery was why Livermore carried on adding to his position for so long when he knew it was a mistake. It was something he could hardly explain to himself.

It was as if Price had put a spell on him. As he admitted: "The market was not going my way. I am never afraid or impatient when I am sure of my position, but the market didn't act the way it should have acted had Price been right. Having taken the first wrong step, I took the second and the third, and of course it muddled me all up. I allowed myself to be persuaded not only into not taking my loss but into holding up the market. That is a style of play foreign to my nature and contrary to my trading principles and theories. Even as a boy in the bucket shops, I had known better. But I was not myself. I was another man – a Teddy Price person." As he got deeper in, more and more people came to Livermore and told him the dangers on relying solely on the advice of Teddy Price. But he did not seem to hear and carried on buying to hold the price up. By the end, he had bought 440,000 bales of cotton worth in excess of $25 million.

Although his friends suspected that Price was now acting to the contrary, no one told him outright of Price's treachery. There were newspaper rumors that Price was bearish and heavily short cotton.

When he realized that he had been double-crossed, Livermore knew he had to cut on his losses and get out himself. During the third week of August, he did just that. When word got out, the price broke again and Livermore suffered losses of $4 million. By August 22nd, it was all over as the price briefly dipped below $6.50.

By the time Livermore realized how exposed he was, it was too late. As he explained: "I lost nearly all that I had made out of all my other deals in stocks and commodities. I was not completely cleaned out, but I had left fewer hundreds of thousands than I had millions before I met my brilliant friend Teddy Price. For me, of all men, to violate all the laws that experience had taught me to observe in order to prosper was more than asinine. Instead of standing or falling by my own observation and deductions, I had merely been playing another man's game. It was eminently fitting that my silly plays should end with that."

CHAPTER 18

Ultimate Betrayal
The treachery of Teddy Price

August 1908

Jesse Livermore was left with around $300,000 after everything he owned was unwound. He had lost around $4.5 million on the cotton deal. He retreated to his home and locked the door. He told the concierge to admit no one and his telephone was left unanswered. He needed to understand what he had done, and he could only do that alone. As he explained: "To learn that a man can make foolish plays for no reason whatever was a valuable lesson. It cost me millions to learn that another dangerous enemy to a trader is his susceptibility to the urgings of a magnetic personality when plausibly expressed by a brilliant mind. It has always seemed to me, however, that I might have learned my lesson quite as well if the cost had been only one million. But fate does not always let you fix the tuition fee. She delivers the educational wallop and presents her own bill, knowing you have to pay it, no matter what the amount may be. Having learned what folly I was capable of, I closed that particular incident and Teddy Price went out of my life. "I had been a millionaire in rather less than a year. My millions I had made by using brains, helped by luck. I had lost them by reversing the process."

On his own, often in the dark, Livermore agonized over what had happened. It wasn't all doom and gloom. His stock holdings, which he had held for nearly a year after the promises he made to Pierpont Morgan, were on the rise as the stock market recovered. But it was a natural consequence and a purely accidental, although welcome, profit.

Livermore tried to be philosophical about what had happened, although he found it difficult as the wounds he had suffered at the hands of Teddy Price were just too raw. There was also the fact that Price had come out well and made as much as Livermore had lost, simply by being on the opposite side when he was supposed to be on his side. Livermore ruefully recalled: "The recognition of our own mistakes should not benefit us any more than the study of our successes. But there is a natural tendency in all men to avoid punishment. When you associate certain mistakes with a licking, you do not hanker for a second dose, and, of course, all stock-market mistakes wound you in two tender spots – your pocketbook and your vanity. But I will tell you something curious: A stock speculator sometimes makes mistakes and knows that he is making them. And after he makes them, he will ask himself why he made them; and after thinking over it cold-bloodedly a long time, after the pain of punishment is over, he may learn how he came to make them, and when and at what particular point of his trade, but not why. And then he simply calls himself names and lets it go at that."

But in this instance, Livermore did not let it go. He bottled it up and even went into denial about what had happened.

Then, he focused a lot of his time on an analysis of mistakes. He wanted to know why he had made a catalogue of mistakes in his cotton trading even after he realized that Teddy Price could no longer be relied upon.

The fictional biography of Livermore, written by Edwin Lefèvre and called *Reminiscences of a Stock Operator*, contains no details of the betrayal by Teddy Price that led to the losses. It glosses over what happened and Livermore seemingly provides a disingenuous analysis of the affair. But it was Price's dishonesty that defeated Livermore's spirit. The betrayal hurt him badly, both emotionally and financially.

In the end, all Livermore could do was to airbrush it from his life as Lefèvre did in the pages of *Reminiscences of a Stock Operator*. What he did vow was never to make the same mistake again and never to have a partner again, that was the only way he was able to rationalize it: "If a man is both wise and lucky, he will not make the same mistake twice. But he will make any one of the ten thousand brothers or cousins of the original. The mistake family is so large that there is always one of them around when you want to see what you can do in the fool-play line."

The betrayal continued to haunt him for 10 years until it was faded from his memory by his later successes and by observing the travails that eventually befell Teddy Price. He got over the loss of the money relatively quickly: "Losing money is the least of my troubles. A loss never bothers me after I take it. I forget it overnight. But being wrong – not taking the loss – that is what does the damage in the pocketbook and to the soul."

It was clear that being betrayed had caused serious damage to his heart and soul. In Lefèvre's book, Livermore finally dismisses the incident and says he allowed himself to become overextended and broke the golden rule of the 19th century speculator Dickson G. Watts. As Livermore recounts, Watts tells a story about a man who asks his nervous friend what is the matter: " 'I can't sleep,' answered the nervous one. 'Why not?' asked the friend. 'I am carrying so much cotton that I can't sleep thinking about it. It is wearing me out. What can I do?' 'Sell down to the sleeping point,' answered the friend."

As for the loss of some of his possessions, Livermore accepted that philosophically. His loss was smoothed out a little when the long positions he had kept in the stock market came good. He found himself with an unexpected $500,000 profit, which he gleefully took. He adapted to just being rich rather than very rich. As he said: "As a rule, a man adapts himself to conditions so quickly that he loses perspective. He does not feel the difference much – that is, he does not vividly remember how it felt not to be a millionaire. He only remembers that there were things he could not do that he can do now. It does not take a reasonably young and normal man very long to lose the habit of being poor. It requires a little longer to forget that he is used to being rich. I suppose that is because money creates needs or encourages their multiplication. I mean that after a man makes money in the stock market, he very quickly loses the habit of not spending. But after he loses his money, it takes him a long time to lose the habit of spending."

The first casualty was Livermore's second yacht, the *Venetia*, and then the railway car. Both fetched good prices. He also cut down his extravagant living by half although he kept the apartment and the *Anita*.

With that, he decided to take an early holiday, and in the first week of September, he travelled down to Palm Beach intent on going on a long cruise on the *Anita* whilst he still had some money left.

Straight after the cotton losses, he had resumed trading in stocks but found it very difficult. But the real blow came in the downward spiral of his trading. It was as if he knew the game was up, and everything he touched turned rotten. He had lost his mojo overnight. In short, he was a loser and couldn't shake off that notion. As he tried to turn things around, he found himself losing big sums of money: "Luck was against me. I ran up first against illness and then against the urgent need of two hundred thousand dollars in cash. A few months before, that sum would have been nothing at all; but now it meant almost the entire remnant of my fleet-winged fortune. I had to supply the money and the question was: Where could I get it? I didn't want to take it out of the balance I kept at my brokers' because, if I did, I wouldn't have much of a margin left for my own trading; and I needed trading facilities more than ever if I was to win back my millions quickly. There was only one alternative that I could see, and that was to take it out of the stock market."

Whilst sailing the Atlantic, he received some truly bizarre news that brought about an urgent appeal for cash from his wife, Nettie. Although he and Nettie had effectively separated in 1901, they had remained married and Livermore continued to pay her living expenses and provide a house for her. There was a lingering affection on both sides. So when Nettie called for help, he felt obliged to come running.

The money was needed urgently at the beginning of September to pay the legal fees of his brother, Chester Jordan. Jordan had killed his wife and then cut her up into small pieces to cover up the crime. He admitted his crimes to the Police and his lawyers decided to run a defense of insanity to try and save him from execution, his certain fate on conviction. Why Nettie Livermore felt obliged to try and save the man who had brutally murdered her sister-in-law is unknown. And why Livermore felt so obliged to pay out what was said to be $200,000 for his defense is also unrecorded. Livermore declined to explain or even discuss, and it has since remained a mystery. Somehow he managed to find the money and was forced to cut short on what proved to be his last trip aboard the *Anita* before ownership was passed to a stockbroker to settle a debt of $50,000.

The Boston lawyer Nettie wanted to hire, William Schorton, demanded a $75,000 legal war chest. Livermore scraped it together and then attempted to make it back in double quick time and, in so doing, broke another of his golden rules. As he freely admitted years afterwards: There isn't a man in Wall Street who has not lost money trying to make the market pay for an automobile or a bracelet or a motorboat or a painting. I could build a huge hospital with the birthday presents that the tight-fisted stock market has refused to pay for. In fact, of all hoodoos in Wall Street, I think the resolve to induce the stock market to act as a fairy godmother is the busiest and most persistent. "Like all well-authenticated hoodoos, this has its reason for being. What does a man do when he sets out to make the stock market pay for a sudden need? Why, he merely hopes. He gambles. He therefore runs much greater risks than he would if he were speculating intelligently, in accordance with opinions or beliefs logically arrived at after a dispassionate study of underlying conditions. To begin with, he is after an immediate profit. He cannot afford to wait. The market must be nice to him at once, if at all.

He flatters himself that he is not asking more than to place an even-money bet. Because he is prepared to run quick – say, stop his loss at two points when all he hopes to make is two points – he hugs the fallacy that he is merely taking a fifty-fifty chance. Why, I've known men to lose thousands of dollars on such trades particularly on purchases made at the height of a bull market just before a moderate reaction. It certainly is no way to trade."

CHAPTER 19

Six Lean Years

Going nowhere slowly - the lost period

1909 - 1914

At the beginning of 1909, Jesse Livermore was desperately trying to recover from his losses in cotton. Instead, he managed to lose what cash he had left and was forced to liquidate virtually all his assets. He called that period of four months the crowning folly of his career as a stock operator: "It beat me. I lost what little my cotton deal had left me. I kept trading – and losing. I persisted in thinking that the stock market must make money for me in the end. But the only end in sight was the end of my resources."

Livermore was getting into debt and he did the rounds of virtually all the stockbrokers in New York, anyone who would give him credit to trade. As he said: "I went into debt, not only to my principal brokers but to other houses that accepted business from me without my putting up an adequate margin. I not only got in debt but I stayed in debt from then on. It was a spiral and there was no way out."

So began a period of six years that would prove to be utterly miserable for Jesse Livermore. It was a period when he could virtually do nothing right, even when the market turned bullish in 1910. As he ruefully admitted: "There I was, once more broke. I was sick, nervous, upset and unable to reason calmly. I was in a frame of mind in which no speculator should be when he is trading. Everything went wrong with me. Indeed, I began to think that I could not recover my departed sense of proportion. Having grown accustomed to swinging a big line – say, more than a hundred thousand shares of stock, it scarcely seemed worthwhile being right when all you carried was a hundred shares of stock. After the habit of taking a big profit on a big line, I wasn't sure I would know when to take my profit on a small line. I can't describe to you how weaponless I felt."

He was worse off than at any point in his life. His state of mind was utterly

165

in the wrong place. As he said: "I was incapable of assuming the offensive vigorously."

In the past, when Livermore had made mistakes, he had used the lessons of the mistakes to recover and find his way back. As he explained: "After all those long years of success, tempered by mistakes that really served to pave the way for greater successes, I was now worse off than when I began in the bucket shops. I had learned a great deal about the game of stock speculation, but I had not learned quite so much about the play of human weaknesses. There is no mind so machinelike that you can depend upon it to function with equal efficiency at all times. I now learned that I could not trust myself to remain equally unaffected by men and misfortunes at all times."

The loss of money did not bother him. He had adapted from being the playboy prince with two yachts to being poor extremely well. It was the loss of his judgment that rankled: "Money losses never worried me in the slightest. But other troubles could and did. I studied my disaster in detail and of course found no difficulty in seeing just where I had been silly. I spotted the exact time and place."

He realized that his past success was now causing his present failure. His sudden rise to extreme fortune and then more extreme fortune, albeit very lucky, had completely skewed his judgment and his perspective.

But his realization of the problem was very gradual. It took several years to work out as he explained: "A man must know himself thoroughly if he is going to make a good job out of trading in the speculative markets. To know what I was capable of in the line of folly was a long educational step. I sometimes think that no price is too high for a speculator to pay to learn that which will keep him from getting the swelled head. A great many smashes by brilliant men can be traced directly to the swelled head – an expensive disease everywhere to everybody, but particularly in Wall Street to a speculator."

With his credit running out in New York, he had a decision to make. As he said: "I was not happy in New York, feeling the way I did. I didn't want to trade because I wasn't in good trading trim. I decided to go away and seek a stake elsewhere."

He decided to return to Chicago and the scene of his past triumphs (and failures) in commodities: "The change of scene could help me to find myself again, I thought. So once more I left New York, beaten by the game of speculation. I was worse than broke, since I owed over $100,000 spread among various brokers."

His move was also prompted by a falling out with Ed Hutton. For reasons that were never made clear, Livermore was forced to vacate his office at E. F. Hutton & Company and give up the secretary provided for him by the broker. His name was removed from the office door at the end of June 1909. The story was significant enough to make the front page of the New York Times on July 21st 1909. The story reported that he had been "missing" from his accustomed place at the offices in 35 New Street for several weeks. The paper also reported that enquiries by its reporters had been met with "some impatience" by Ed Hutton.

Livermore had no more use for the office as, by mid-year, he moved to Chicago lock, stock, and barrel and said his farewells to New York. He found a small residential hotel and arranged for his family and friends to pick up the tab. Getting credit to resume trading in Chicago was not a problem. His reputation could not have been higher in the windy city after his cotton exploits. Everyone, it seemed, wanted Jesse Livermore for a client as his high frequency trading yielded substantial commissions. He remembered: "I went to Chicago and, there, found a stake. It was not a very substantial stake, but that merely meant that I would need a little more time to win back my fortune. A house that I once had done business with had faith in my ability as a trader and they were willing to prove it by allowing me to trade in their office in a small way. I began very conservatively. I don't know how I might have fared had I stayed there."

But his move to Chicago was interrupted after a few months by a strange telegram he received from the office manager of a leading New York stockbroker, which was run by the brother-in-law of the great railwayman and investor Charles Pugh.

The telegram asked him to come to New York at once to meet the senior partner of the brokerage, who was Pugh's brother-in-law. Livermore was reluctant to leave, having just re-established himself in Chicago. But the urgency left him with little choice, and he caught a train the next day.

He was met at Grand Central Station by the sender of the telegram, who immediately took him to see Pugh's brother-in-law. The stock broking house was long established and had been founded in the 1870s by the current incumbent's father, who was now very wealthy himself and now looked after other wealthy families besides his own. But the brokerage was sustained by Charles Pugh, the husband of the founder's daughter.

Pugh was worth as much as all the other clients put together. The 60-year-old was the leading light of the Pennsylvania Railroad Company and had founded the Baltimore, Chesapeake & Atlantic Railway Company. He was also a board director of over a dozen banking and insurance companies. He was thought to own cash and assets worth $250 million, two thirds of which was in stocks and shares.

And it was because of Charles Pugh that Livermore was called back from Chicago, although he wasn't immediately to know that.

For reasons best known to him, Livermore never revealed the name of the senior partner, referring to him only by the pseudonym Dan Williamson.

After some pleasantries, Williamson asked Livermore if he would come and trade at his brokerage with what would effectively be an unlimited line of credit. The broker told Livermore that his house wished to do business with him and handle all his stock market trades. It was not the sort of offer Livermore got everyday, and he at first appeared confused.

Livermore told Williamson that he hadn't any money to out up as margin. Then he decided to be completely frank and said he hadn't any money at all. Williamson cut to the chase and took out his checkbook and immediately wrote him a check for $25,000

According to Livermore, Williamson told him: "For you to deposit in your own bank. You will draw your own checks. I want you to do your trading in our office. I don't care whether you win or lose. If that money goes, I will give you another personal check. So you don't have to be so very careful with this one – see?" Livermore mused: "I knew that the firm was too rich and prosperous to need anybody's business, much less to give a fellow the money to put up as margin. And then he was so nice about it." Livermore allowed himself to be seduced despite the illogicality of it: "Instead of giving me a credit with the house, he gave me the actual cash so that he alone knew where it came from, the only string being that if I traded I should do so through his firm."

Livermore allowed his natural suspicions to be suppressed as Williamson told him: "The idea is simply that we want to have a customer in this office who is known as a big active trader. Everybody knows that you swing a big line on the short side, which is what I particularly like about you. You are known as a plunger."

But Livermore wasn't entirely convinced and so resisted, but Williamson tried again: "I'll be frank with you, Mr. Livermore. We have two or three very wealthy customers who buy and sell stocks in a big way. I don't want the

Street to suspect them of selling long stock every time we sell ten or twenty thousand shares of any stock. If the Street knows that you are trading in our office, it will not know whether it is your short selling or the other customers' long stock that is coming on the market."

Suddenly Livermore understood what he wanted: to cover up his brother-in-law's operations with his own reputation – and that was fine with Livermore. After that, he didn't hesitate and took the check. As he remembered: "He was offering me a chance to come back and come back quickly. I took the check, banked it, opened an account with his firm and began trading. It was a good active market."

The conditions were right, and Livermore suddenly found his mojo again. He multiplied the stake five times to $125,000 inside three weeks. But when he attempted to repay the loan, he was met with a surprise. It was refused. As Livermore remembered: "I made the mistake that I have regretted more than any other I ever made in my Wall Street career. It was responsible for long and dreary years of suffering. I should have insisted on his taking the money. I was on my way to a bigger fortune than I had lost and walking pretty fast. For three weeks, my average profit was 150 per cent per week. From then on my trading would be on a steadily increasing scale. But instead of freeing myself from all obligations, I let him have his way and did not compel him to accept the twenty-five thousand dollars. Of course, since he didn't draw out the twenty-five thousand dollars he had advanced me, I felt I could not very well draw out my profit. I left the money undisturbed and resumed my trading. I was getting on very nicely."

Up to then, Livermore had been trading on the long side. But then he suddenly switched to the bear side and was shorting stocks. And when he decided to sell short 8,000 shares of Baltimore, Chesapeake & Atlantic, the problems began.

Williamson called him in and said: "Jesse, don't do anything in Chesapeake & Atlantic just now. That was a bad play of yours, selling eight thousand short. I covered it for you this morning in London and went long."

Livermore was shaken to his core at this turn of events, but since it wasn't really his money he had to go along with it. As he remembered: "I was sure Chesapeake & Atlantic was going down. The tape told it to me quite plainly; and besides I was bearish on the whole market, not violently or insanely bearish, but enough to feel comfortable with a moderate short line out. I said to him: 'What did you do that for? I am bearish on the whole market and they are all going lower.' But he just shook his head and said: 'I did it because I happen to know something about Chesapeake & Atlantic that you couldn't know. My advice to you is to not sell that stock short until I tell you it is safe to do so.' What could I do? That wasn't an asinine tip. It was advice that came from the brother-in-law of the chairman of the board of directors. He was not only Charles Pugh's closest friend, but he had been kind and generous to me. He had shown his faith in me and confidence in my word. I couldn't do less than to thank him. And so my feelings again won over my judgment, and I gave in."

But Livermore was proved to be right, and being bearish on the railway had been a good call. Equally, being long also proved disastrous. At that moment, as he remembered: "The first thing I knew was not only had I lost all my profit, but I owed the firm one hundred and fifty thousand dollars besides. I felt pretty badly about it, but he told me not to worry."

Williamson was unconcerned and told Livermore: "I'll get you out of this hole. I know I will. But I can only do it if you let me. You will have to stop doing business on your own hook. I can't be working for you and then have you completely undo all my work in your behalf. Just you lay off the market and give me a chance to make some money for you. Won't you, Jesse?"

It was an extraordinary situation, but Livermore decided to go along with it. He effectively did nothing for six months. When he went back into the office, there was a surplus in his account and he also owned 10,000 shares in a railroad called Southern Atlantic, also controlled by Charles Pugh. Those shares quickly lost Livermore $200,000, but the process was repeated and the loss was made up again six months later. This went on for two years.

What had happened was that Jesse Livermore had unwittingly lent his name and his reputation to Charles Pugh in order that he had cover to liquidate his not inconsiderable share portfolio. And all through this time, there was enough surplus in the account for Livermore to go travelling and enjoy a few months in Palm Beach. Livermore followed the path of least resistance even though it went against all his best instincts.

Finally, Livermore worked out what was going on. He heard a rumor that Charles Pugh was ill and could be dying, and suddenly everything made sense. If the portfolio had been sold off quickly, the value would have dropped. But because it was being sold off underneath the cover of Jesse Livermore buying the shares, a large chunk of the Pugh portfolio was fed out slowly to willing punters at a premium price.

Livermore remembered many years later: "Finally, I tumbled. It was plain that I had been used. It made me angry to think it, but still angrier that I had not tumbled to it quicker."

A very angry Livermore returned to the brokerage, drew out what cash there was in his account and quit the firm. Livermore was upset, as an opportunity to make good money in a good market had been denied him. 1909 and 1910 had been good trading years, and they were drawing to a close. The rumors of possible war in Europe sent the market in a sideways swoon. As Livermore recalled: "That was the loss of a great opportunity. The market, you see, had been a fine trading market. I was right. I mean, I was reading it accurately. The opportunity to make millions was there. But I allowed my gratitude to interfere with my play. I tied my own hands. After that, there was practically no opportunity for me to make big money. The market flattened out."

Livermore realized that his role had been as a 'beard' for Charles Pugh: "Every time his firm did a few thousand shares in any one stock, the Street jumped at the conclusion that Charles Pugh was buying or selling. I was being used as a smoke screen, particularly for Pugh's selling. Charles Pugh fell sick shortly after I went in. His ailment was early diagnosed as incurable."

It was much later that Livermore began to see those two years when he was Charles Pugh's stooge in a better light. It came after Pugh died in 1914: "I have always considered this the most interesting and most unfortunate of all my experiences as a stock operator. As a lesson, it cost me a disproportionately high price. It put off the time of my recovery several years."

Livermore didn't blame Pugh personally, as he probably did not know what was going on. It was the brother-in-law who had duped him: "He was a very shrewd boy, as slick as they make them; farsighted, ingenious, daring. He was a thinker, had imagination, detected the vulnerable spot in any man and could plan cold-bloodedly to hit it. He did his own sizing up and soon doped out just what to do to me in order to reduce me to complete inoffensiveness in the market. He did not actually do me out of any money. On the contrary, he was to all appearances extremely nice about it. He loved his sister, Mrs. Pugh, and he did his duty towards her as he saw it."

But when the dust had settled, Livermore had missed out on the bull market of 1910. It was a period when he could have made up his millions and got his career back on track. But he was sidelined as the estate of Charles Pugh was liquidated. As he described it: "The greatest opportunity of a lifetime was before my very nose. I could not put out my hand and reach for it."

After that, Livermore faced three more years in the wilderness. That period in the three years before the outbreak of the First World War was static. The market neither dropped down nor went up. It was in a seemingly perpetual move sideways, a mode in which a trader like Jesse Livermore could not function profitably. As he recalled: "Things drifted from bad to worse. I not only lost all I had but got into debt again – more heavily than ever. Those were long lean years, 1911, 1912, 1913 and 1914. There was no money to be made. The opportunity simply wasn't there, and so I was worse off than ever."

Somehow, Livermore survived this time in the wilderness with no money by relying on the largesse of others or, as he often put it, "the kindness of strangers."

As he said: "It isn't uncomfortable to lose when the loss is not accompanied by a poignant vision of what might have been. That was precisely what I could not keep my mind from dwelling on, and of course it unsettled me further. Five years is a long time for a man to be poor. Young or old, it is not to be relished. I could do without the yachts a great deal easier than I could do without a market to come back on."

CHAPTER 20

Official Bankruptcy
The ultimate humiliation

1915

By the beginning of 1915, Jesse Livermore was well and truly broke. He had tried earning a living in Chicago and had then moved back to New York, having exhausted his credit in the windy city.

At the end of 1914, he had run up debts at various stock and commodity brokers that added up to over $1 million. As he confirmed: "I tried other brokers' offices. In every one of them, I lost money. It served me right because I was trying to force the market into giving me what it didn't have to give – opportunities for making money. I did not find any trouble in getting credit because those who knew me had faith in me. You can get an idea of how strong their confidence was when I tell you that when I finally stopped trading on credit, I owed well over one million dollars."

But the debts were not pressing, as they were spread thinly over 20 or so brokers anxious to continue to do business with Livermore. None of them pressed him for repayment and all seemed to have faith that he would bounce back and repay them at some time in the future. They showed remarkable trust.

By this time, all his toys were gone, including the two yachts, the apartment and the railcar. The *Venetia* had actually been signed over to one of the Chicago broking houses where he owed money.

By then, he was living in Bretton Hall, a residential hotel on Broadway and 86th Street. It was a dramatic comedown, only made easier by the fact that his family was paying his accommodation bills. This time, he was really on his uppers and had no spare cash at all. He was relying on handouts from his parents and brother and sister, Elliot and Mabel. He had been very kind to them when he had plenty of money, and they were happy to support him in his hour of need. He would also, when he was in need, retreat to the house his wife owned. Despite having been separated from Nettie for 14 years, they

173

were still married and still enjoyed occasional conjugal relations.

But Livermore knew he couldn't carry on living like that, depending on the kindness of strangers. He was in deep trouble psychologically, and his judgement had been shot to pieces. So much so that for the first and last time in his life, he uncharacteristically blamed the market. As he said: "We ran smack into a long moneyless period; four mighty lean years. There was not a penny to be made. As Billy Henriquez once said: 'It was the kind of market in which not even a skunk could make a scent.'" Regardless of who Billy Henriquez was, the point was well made. As Livermore admitted: "It looked to me as though I was on a date with destiny. It might have been the plan of providence to chasten me."

As 1915 dawned, he really was in a bad place. Especially with the market once again showing signs of life: "The trouble was not that I had lost my grip, but that during those four wretched years the opportunities for making money simply didn't exist. Still I plugged along, trying to make a stake and succeeding only in increasing my indebtedness. After I ceased trading on my own hook, because I wouldn't owe my friends any more money, I made a living handling accounts for people who believed I knew the game well enough to beat it even in a dull market. For my services, I received a percentage of the profits – when there were any. That is how I lived. Well, say, that is how I sustained life.

"Of course, I didn't always lose, but I never made enough to allow me materially to reduce what I owed. Finally, as things got worse, I felt the beginnings of discouragement for the first time in my life."

Livermore was continually analyzing his own behavior and trying to understand himself: "Everything seemed to have gone wrong with me. I did not go about bewailing the descent from millions and yachts to debts and the simple life. I didn't enjoy the situation, but I did not fill up with self-pity. I did not propose to wait patiently for time and providence to bring about the cessation of my discomforts. I therefore studied my problem. It was plain that the only way out of my troubles was by making money. To make money, I needed merely to trade successfully. I had so traded before and I must do so once more. More than once in the past, I had run up a shoestring into hundreds of thousands. Sooner or later, the market would offer me an opportunity."

Livermore really believed that, and it had sustained him for those long hard years. Eventually, he stopped blaming the state of the stock market and realized he was 100 per cent responsible for what was happening to him as it dawned on him what the root cause of the problem was. As he explained: "I convinced myself that whatever was wrong was wrong with me and not the market. Now what could be the trouble with me? I asked myself that question in the same spirit in which I always study the various phases of my trading problems. I thought about it calmly and came to the conclusion that my main trouble came from worrying over the money I owed. I was never free from the mental discomfort of it."

Finally, he had discovered what was wrong. It was like a eureka moment after a long period of misery. Once he knew what was definitively wrong, he could finally start the process of making it right and solving the problems.

He also knew the debt itself was not a problem. As he explained: "It was not the mere consciousness of my indebtedness. Any businessman contracts debts in the course of his regular business. Most of my debts were really nothing but business debts; due to what were unfavorable business conditions for me, and no worse than a merchant suffers from, for instance, when there is an unusually prolonged spell of unseasonable weather."

The debts weren't a problem whilst no one was chasing them, but as soon as they did it became a real problem for him psychologically. Jesse Livermore was just not made to deal with debt collectors. As he freely admitted: "As time went on and I could not pay, I began to feel less philosophical about my debts. I'll explain: I owed over a million dollars – all of it stock-market losses, remember. Most of my creditors were very nice and didn't bother me; but there were two who did bedevil me."

There was one particular creditor who dogged him, a John Pierson, to whom he owed a mere $500. The chap couldn't believe that Livermore didn't have $500 to pay his debt. Pierson threatened to seize his furniture and anything else he owned. But by then there was nothing left and all Pierson could do was harass him.

The pressures from Pierson, a rather unpleasant individual, grew intense. It was that pressure that made Livermore begin to realize that his problem was entirely psychological: "I quite cold-bloodedly reached the conclusion that I would never be able to accomplish anything useful so long as I was worried, and it was equally plain that I should be worried so long as I owed money. I said to myself: 'I must go through bankruptcy'. What else could relieve my mind?"

Of course, it was easier said than done. Bankruptcy was not a natural state for a man like Jesse Livermore to face at the age of 38 – especially when he had previously enjoyed the lifestyle one of the richest men in America. He also knew it would be a salacious story in the newspapers, and he wasn't wrong. As he said: "It was more than unpleasant. I hated to do it. I hated to put myself in a position to be misunderstood or misjudged. I myself never cared much for money. I never thought enough of it to consider it worthwhile lying for. But I knew that everybody didn't feel that way. Of course, I also knew that if I got on my feet again I'd pay everybody off, for the obligation remained. But unless I was able to trade in the old way, I'd never be able to pay back that million."

Once he had made the decision, he was determined to carry it through despite a few false starts. He was scared stiff of reading about his own demise in the newspapers, so he took some precautions to ease the eventual pain.

Before declaring himself bankrupt, Livermore decided to go and see every one of his creditors to explain what he was doing and why: "I nerved myself and went to see my creditors. It was a mighty difficult thing for me to do as most of them were personal friends or old acquaintances. I explained the situation quite frankly to them. I said: 'I am going to take this step not because I don't wish to pay you but because, in justice to both myself and you, I must put myself in a position to make money. I have been thinking of this solution off and on for over two years, but I simply didn't have the nerve to come out and say so frankly to you. It would have been infinitely better for all of us if I had. It all simmers down to this: I positively cannot be my old self while I am harassed or upset by these debts. I have decided to do now what I should have done a year ago. I have no other reason that the one I have just given you.'"

Although it was not part of his original purpose of going to see them, to his amazement one-by-one the creditors forgave his debts and issued him with a waiver. For reasons not at all clear to him, they did not want to be listed as a creditor of Jesse Livermore. All of his big creditors effectively cancelled their debts to the tune of over $900,000.

When he finally added up the schedule of his debts and handed them to his accountant, they came to just over $100,000.

His accountant drew up the paperwork for a 'voluntary petition in bankruptcy' but refused to accept payment. Seemingly, that was the attitude of everybody but the eight creditors listed on the petition.

It was with a very heavy heart that he walked up Fifth Avenue on his way to the Federal District Court on Wednesday February 17th 1915 and sat with his court-appointed referee. He expected a long drawn out bureaucratic process, but it was over in an hour and a half. When he left the building, he felt a mighty sense of relief as if the weight of the world had been lifted from his shoulders. But nothing could have prepared him for the following day's newspapers. The *New York Times* screamed out from above the fold on page five: "Cotton King a bankrupt – Jesse L. Livermore loses millions he made in Wall Street." It was extremely disagreeable for him to see his name in the newspapers in that manner. But his demeanor instantly changed when he looked at the front page and read the news of Edward Stone, the first American citizen to be killed on the battlefields of the First World War. Then he realized how lucky he was to be walking down Park Avenue with the early spring sunshine on his face and his whole future still ahead of him.

Livermore remembered that day for the rest of his life: "I had always paid my debts in full, and this new experience was most mortifying to me. I knew I'd pay off everybody some day if I lived, but everybody who read the article wouldn't know it. I was ashamed to go out after I saw the report in the newspapers."

It did not take long for it to have the desired effect. After getting over the initial shock of the *New York Times* article, the feeling of doom and gloom quickly wore off. As he said: "I cannot tell you how intense was my feeling of relief to know that I wasn't going to be harried any more by people who didn't understand how a man must give his entire mind to his business if he wishes to succeed in stock speculation. My mind was now free to take up trading with some prospects of success, unvexed by debts."

The next problem was to find some capital. One problem with bankruptcy was that he was not allowed to incur any fresh debt whilst the bankruptcy stood. So he needed someone to give him some money as a gift.

It became more and more urgent as he could sense that the mood of the market was changing. A situation was beginning to develop that February from which he knew he could profit. It was the first opportunity he had sensed for four years, and he was anxious to participate.

The market had remained depressed since 1907 and European countries, especially Britain, had used the opportunity to buy cheap US stocks and shares. By 1914, the Europeans owned $4 billion of railway company shares, with $3 billion belonging to the British. Railway shares were very attractive as they were secure and bought at depressed prices, well below asset values.

They were also very liquid and, if sold under the gold standard system, the cash could be used to buy gold to ship back to Europe.

At the outbreak of the First World War, that is exactly what started to happen. England, France and Germany suddenly needed cash urgently and began an immediate sell off of all their American holdings. Then, the cash was quickly being converted into gold and shipped out of the United States. Almost instantly, it caused a huge drain on America's gold reserves and supplies of hard cash started to run very low. And this time there was no Pierpont Morgan to save the day.

The sudden outflow of gold posed a twin threat: an internal drain of currency from the banking system and an external drain of gold to Europe. To stem the flow, three days after war was declared, the stock exchange was shut on orders of the Treasury Secretary, William McAdoo. McAdoo, backed by Democratic President Woodrow Wilson, had prepared for the crisis even though the new Federal Reserve Bank Act, passed the previous year, was not yet in action.

Despite that the lessons of the 1907 crash had been well learnt.

In 1913 McAdoo had enacted a law, passed in 1908, but never used, called the Aldrich-Vreeland Act, which allowed for the issue of bonds, which legally were the equivalent of hard cash. The bonds could be issued by the major commercial banks at will and were backed by the Federal Government. Suddenly unlimited cash was available and customers withdrawing cash, instead walked out with bonds that were legal currency ensuring the liquidity of the system and preventing financial collapse. Banks could literally issue unlimited hard currency and as the stock market was closed asset values were effectively frozen. It was innovative but it worked.

The stock exchange closure gave America breathing space and McAdoo proved something of a financial genius. He quickly promoted and ramped up US exports to a needy Europe so starting to earn much needed gold that would be required to eventually redeem all the US securities held by Europeans. It took four months to build up gold reserves before the stock exchange could reopen.

McAdoo's efforts outshone those of Pierpont Morgan, seven years before. The US economy had a smooth landing although stocks and shares fell heavily once trading resumed in December. But nothing like what had happened in October 1907. The US public were also filled with confidence and this time kept their money in the banks and were soon re-depositing the bonds. In no time at all the stock market recovered and began its long march upwards.

OFFICIAL BANKRUPTCY

Livermore watched all this happening from the sidelines. They were exactly the sort of conditions in which he could use his techniques to make millions. But he never saw the closure of the stock market coming and was glad to be out of the game when it happened. When it reopened he watched shares fall but saw the American economy starting to boom, profiting from the war in Europe. They were perfect conditions for a speculator like him.

The next step was to get another stake but that proved difficult. As he explained: "I owed all my friends. I couldn't very well ask them to help me again just because they had been so pleasant and friendly to me when I knew that nobody was in a position to do much for anybody. It was a mighty difficult task, getting a decent stake, for with the closing of the Stock Exchange there was nothing that I could ask any broker to do for me. I tried a couple of places but no use."

Finally he went to see Charles Pugh's brother-in-law, the broker who had duped him in 1909, six years before.

CHAPTER 21

Dramatic Return to Form
Makes $5 million, pays off debts

1915 - 1917

J esse Livermore wasn't really one for eating humble pie. It gave him no pleasure to return to the offices of Charles Pugh's brother-in-law, known as Dan Williamson, and almost beg for a stake to get him going again. Williamson listened as he always did, but this time he didn't write him a check as Livermore had hoped. He merely said: "When you see something that looks good to you and you want to buy five hundred shares, go ahead and it will be all right."

Livermore left his office more than a little peeved. As he said: "I admit I was a little sore to think that he didn't give me a decent stake but I thanked him and went away. He had kept me from making a great deal of money and the office had made a lot in commissions from me. But, anyhow, I realized that, such as it was, there was my chance to come back."

Even though Livermore was in a cautious mood for his comeback, this was a setback. 500 shares was a small line for someone who had often dealt in trades a hundred times bigger. He had intended to trade very conservatively, and his small stake meant he had to scale his plans down even more. It would make his financial recovery a very slow affair.

He was faced with an out and out obvious bull market, so that was one less decision he had to make. As he remembered: "It was a bull market. That was as plain to me as it was to thousands of traders. But my stake consisted merely of an offer to carry five hundred shares for me. I had no leeway and I couldn't afford even the slight setback at the beginning. I must build up my stake with my very first play. That initial purchase of mine of five hundred shares must be profitable. I had to make real money. I knew that unless I had sufficient trading capital, I would not be able to use good judgement. Without adequate margins, it would be impossible to take the cold-blooded, dispassionate attitude toward the game that comes from the ability to afford a

181

few minor losses such as I often incurred in testing the market before putting down the big bet."

In those early days of April 1915, Livermore found himself at a critical stage of his life. He realized only too clearly that it was make or break. If he failed again, there was probably no way back. As he said: "It was very clear that I simply must wait for the exact psychological moment."

He laid the ground very carefully and spent a whole six weeks doing nothing but studying the ticker tape. He kept away from Pugh's office to avoid the temptation of plunging in suddenly and he was, more than ever, acutely aware of his own weaknesses. The tribulations of the last six years had not been lost on him. As he revealed: "A trader, in addition to studying basic conditions, remembering market precedents and keeping in mind the psychology of the outside public as well as the limitations of his brokers, must also know himself and provide against his own weaknesses. I have come to feel that it is as necessary to know how to read myself as it is to know how to read the tape.

"So day after day, broke and anxious to resume trading, I sat in front of a quotation-board in another broker's office where I couldn't buy or sell as much as one share of stock, studying the market, not missing a single transaction on the tape, watching for the psychological moment to ring the full-speed-ahead bell."

Gradually his mind began to focus on the shares of Bethlehem Steel, run by Charles Schwab. Bethlehem was America's second largest steel producer. Livermore knew there was going to be tremendous demand for steel across the world over the next few years, and neither Bethlehem's share price or the price of steel itself was reflecting that in its share price. Bethlehem owned iron ore mines and was sitting on stocks of ore waiting for the price to go up. It was also stockpiling armor plate, anticipating demand as the US government expanded the armed forces.

Livermore thought Bethlehem was very undervalued and that the price could treble within the next year. As soon as the market realized the potential, he was certain it was going up but equally certain he must be sure before he plunged in. He decided to wait until it crossed par. He explained: "It has been my experience that whenever a stock crosses 100 or 200 or 300 for the first time, it nearly always keeps going up for 30 to 50 points – and after 300, faster than after 100 or 200. One of my first big coups was a share I bought when it crossed 200 and sold a day later at 260. My practice of buying a stock just after it crossed par dated back to my early bucket-shop days. It is an old trading principle."

Livermore was desperate to resume trading in his old style with a big line. But he knew he must first make back his stake: "I was so eager to begin that I could not think of anything else; but I held myself in leash. I saw Bethlehem Steel climb, every day, higher and higher, as I was sure it would, and yet there I was, checking my impulse to run over and buy five hundred shares. I knew I simply had to make my initial operation as nearly a cinch as was humanly possible.

"Every point that share went up meant five hundred dollars I had not made. The first ten points advance meant that I would have been able to pyramid, and instead of five hundred shares I might now be carrying one thousand shares that would be earning for me one thousand dollars a point. But I sat tight, and instead of listening to my loud-mouthed hopes or to my clamorous beliefs, I heeded only the level voice of my experience and the counsel of common sense. Once I got a decent stake together, I could afford to take chances. But without a stake, taking chances, even slight chances, was a luxury utterly beyond my reach. Six weeks of patience – but, in the end, a victory for common sense over greed and hope."

Livermore watched as Bethlehem Steel went all the way up to $90: "I really began to waver and sweat blood when the stock got up to 90. Think of what I had not made by not buying when I was so bullish. Well, when it got to 98, I said to myself: 'Bethlehem is going through 100 and, when it does, the roof is going to blow clean off.' The tape said the same thing more than plainly. In fact, it used a megaphone. I tell you, I saw 100 on the tape when the ticker was only printing 98. And I knew that wasn't the voice of my hope or the sight of my desire, but the assertion of my tape-reading instinct. So I said to myself: 'I can't wait until it gets through 100. I have to get it now. It is as good as gone through par.'"

He could contain himself no longer and rushed to the brokers and put in an order to buy 500 shares of Bethlehem Steel. The price was $98 and he got half his five hundred shares at $98 and the other half at $99.

A day later, the stock was at $114 and he had enough profit to buy another 500 shares. The next day it hit $145 and he cashed out with a $38,000 profit. No profit had ever felt sweeter than the profit he made that day. As he said: "You would not have believed it was the self-same man trading. As a matter of fact, I wasn't the same man, for where I had been harassed and wrong I was now at ease and right. There were no creditors to annoy and no lack of funds to interfere with my thinking or with my listening to the truthful voice of experience, and so I was winning right along."

Suddenly, Livermore could not put a foot wrong and he rode the bull market hard. He had $38,000 of his own money and $50,000 of his broker's loan to play with, potentially a leveraged stake of $500,000, and it felt good. As he said: "All of a sudden, I was on my way to a sure fortune." Soon he was sitting on a cash pile of his own of $200,000.

Then, on the afternoon of May 7th 1915, a German submarine torpedoed the *RMS Lusitania*, a Cunard Line ship and one of the biggest passenger vessels on the high seas. The *Lusitania* had left New York bound for Liverpool on May 1st. The ship was fired at only 11 miles off the coast of Ireland as it neared Liverpool harbor. From the torpedo hitting, it took only 18 minutes to sink after a series of internal explosions. Of the 1,959 passengers and crew, 1,198 were killed that day including 128 Americans.

The news of the sinking reached the market the following day and instantly caused the bull market to temporarily reverse, catching all the bulls out, including Livermore who lost $150,000 overnight. Stocks dropped 20 per cent inside half an hour of opening, but by the close had recovered to being only 10 per cent down.

He was doing well up to that point, but took his losses on the chin. As he said sanguinely: "No human being can be so uniformly right on the market as to be beyond the reach of unprofitable accidents. What I can tell you is that, on account of what I lost through the *Lusitania* break and one or two other reverses that I wasn't wise enough to foresee, I found myself at the end of 1915 with a balance at my brokers of about $150,000. That was all I actually made, though I was consistently right on the market throughout the greater part of the year."

The stock market rose 82 per cent during the year and the Dow Jones closed at 99.15.

Considering he was officially bankrupt at the start of 1915, the state of his bank account was quite an achievement. But without the *Lusitania* sinking, it would have been ten times better.

But the *Lusitania*'s sinking had only temporarily delayed the bull market as it roared on in 1916.

Suddenly there was a huge demand for goods from American factories from every country of the world, especially those at war. Cash and gold rolled in, and Wall Street boomed like it never had before. It was a one-way market as Livermore said: "It was plain to everybody that the Allied purchases of all kinds of supplies here, made the United States the most prosperous nation in the world. We had all the things that no one else had for sale, and we were fast getting all the cash in the world. I mean that the wide world's gold was pouring into this country in torrents. Inflation was inevitable, and, of course, that meant rising prices for everything."

Once he realized that the virtuous circle had been closed, he had no more inhibitions: "I was rampantly bullish in a wild bull market. Things were certainly coming my way so that there wasn't anything to do but make money. It made me remember a saying of the late H. H. Rogers, of Standard Oil Company, to the effect that there were times when a man could no more help making money than he could help getting wet if he went out in a rainstorm without an umbrella. It was the most clearly defined bull market we ever had."

Nearly $1 billion in gold flowed into the country during this period from Europe and Russia. In the space of three years, America exported $7 billion worth of goods, mainly armaments to those countries at war.

The 1915/1916 bull market was the most effortless in stock market history. It was unprecedentedly profitable for ordinary punters; the rise in the market was wholly upwards with hardly any corrections at all. The American public piled into stocks, and the profits were more widely distributed than in any other bull market in the history of Wall Street. But this time, ordinary Americans kept their money in the market causing it to boom further. Virtually no one took any profits and just reinvested in more shares. Livermore observed this folly and said: "The game does not change and neither does human nature."

Livermore was bullish but also cautious, looking for the next bear market he knew could be just around the corner: "I was as bullish as the next man, but of course I kept my eyes open. I knew, as everybody did, that there must be an end, and I was on the watch for warning signals. I wasn't particularly interested in guessing from which quarter the tip would come and so I didn't stare at just one spot. I was not, and I never have felt that I was, wedded indissolubly to one or the other side of the market. That a bull market had added to my bank account or a bear market has been particularly generous I do not consider sufficient reason for sticking to the bull or the bear side after I receive the get-out warning. A man does not swear eternal allegiance to either the bull or the bear side. His concern lies with being right."

"And there is another thing to remember, and that is that a market does not culminate in one grand blaze of glory. Neither does it end with a sudden reversal of form. A market can and does often cease to be a bull market long before prices generally begin to break. My long expected warning came to me when I noticed that, one after another, those stocks which had been the leaders of the market reacted several points from the top and – for the first time in many months – did not come back. Their race evidently was run, and that clearly necessitated a change in my trading tactics. In a bull market, the trend of prices, of course, is decidedly and definitely upward. Therefore, whenever a stock goes against the general trend, you are justified in assuming that there is something wrong with that particular stock. It is enough for the experienced trader to perceive that something is wrong. He must not expect the tape to become a lecturer. His job is to listen for it to say 'Get out!' and not wait for it to submit a legal brief for approval."

Livermore was the first to spot that a reversal was on the cards. He noticed that the leading stocks had slowed to a halt and dropped off just below their peaks and started to move sideways. The less attractive stocks carried on going up which kept the bull market strong. He observed sagely: "There was no need to be perplexed into inactivity, for there were really no crosscurrents. I did not turn bearish on the market then, because the tape didn't tell me to do so. The end of the bull market had not come, though it was within hailing distance. Pending its arrival, there was still bull money to be made. Such being the case, I merely turned bearish on the stocks, which had stopped advancing and, as the rest of the market had rising power behind it, I both bought and sold. The leaders that had ceased to lead, I sold. I put out a short line of five thousand shares in each of them; and then I went long of the new leaders. The stocks I was short of didn't do much, but my long stocks kept on rising. When finally these in turn ceased to advance, I sold them out and went short – five thousand shares of each. By this time, I was more bearish than bullish because obviously the next big money was going to be made on the down side. While I felt certain that the bear market had really ended, I knew the time for being a rampant bear was not yet. There was no sense in being more royalist than the king; especially in being so too soon. The tape merely said that patrolling parties from the main bear army had dashed by. Time to get ready."

Suddenly Livermore found he was short 60,000 shares, made up of 5,000 shares in each of America's top 12 quoted companies. And then he stopped and waited and watched. He didn't have to wait long and, after a month, the entire market became quite weak and prices of all stocks went into reverse.

Very quickly, he had an average profit of four points in each of the 12 stocks. He doubled up to 10,000 in each a line of 120,000 shares out short. With that, he stopped. As he explained: "I had my position. I was short of stocks in a market that now was plainly a bear market. There wasn't any need for me to push things along. The market was bound to go my way, and, knowing that, I could afford to wait. After I doubled up, I didn't make another trade for a long time. About seven weeks after I put out my full line, we had the famous 'leak' and stocks broke badly. The leak (which was a news wire piece, albeit premature) said that President Wilson was going to issue a message that would bring back the dove of peace to Europe in a hurry."

The infamous leak accurately forecast a peace initiative from the President and any hint of peace in Europe was bad news for the stock market. It would be eagerly seized upon by speculators, including Livermore.

That news came to Livermore's attention on December 20th 1916. He was in the Palm Beach branch office of Chicago stockbroker Finlay, Barrel & Company with a friend. He did not trade there but went to look at what the market was doing. He had a lot at stake; even though his bear position had never been out of profit, he knew it was vulnerable to good news.

In the early afternoon, a news article ostensibly written by W. W. Price of the *Washington Star* the capital's evening newspaper, came over the telegraph. It said that President Wilson was brokering a peace initiative to end the war. The piece had not appeared in the newspaper and did not appear to be on general release but had been sent over the paper's new wire service system, which at that point had very few subscribers. It so happened that Finlay, Barrel & Company was one of those subscribers.

Livermore knew this news should have caused the market to break wide open, but it hadn't, and he couldn't understand why not.

Livermore hurried over to the offices of E. F. Hutton but nothing similar had been received, which was perhaps unsurprising as Hutton did not subscribe to the *Star*'s news wire. Livermore was still surprised as he thought such momentous news would, by now, have been re-transmitted on every wire service across the country.

All the other official news organizations and the newspapers were silent; it seemed the message had been sent only to clients of the *Star*'s news service. Livermore scanned the official sources for confirmation without success.

Livermore took the piece seriously because of it was attributed to W. W. Price. Price was the *Washington Star*'s White House correspondent and one of 150 journalists accredited to the White House. Price had gained the confidence of President Wilson and the columns of the *Star* were scrutinized every

evening by White House watchers, many of them other journalists. He had
produced many scoops since 1914 when he first got the job. The *Star*'s news
wire had been started in part due to the demand for his daily articles and the
valuable revenues that could be obtained from syndicating them out to other
newspapers. It was only by chance that Finlay Barrel's Chicago HQ subscribed
to the service and pushed it out to its branch offices – and that Jesse Livermore
just happened to be in the office that day at that hour. And back in New York,
it so happened that Bernard Baruch subscribed to the service, as he did all the
newswires, and the same thoughts were going on in his head as they were in
Livermore's.

Later, as Livermore stood in the office of E. F. Hutton in Palm Beach, another
wire service to which Hutton subscribed that had finally picked up Price's
story and the news finally arrived. Now he knew the story had some status. He
could only assume that the delay had been because political correspondents
had no idea of the gravity of such a story and the affect it would have on the
stock market.

The whole stock market boom had been predicated on a boom in trade to
Europe. If peace came, that could end sharply. As the rumors spread, the stock
market dropped like a stone and Livermore covered his whole position. As
he said: "It was the only play possible. When something happens on which
you did not count when you made your plans, it behooves you to utilize the
opportunity that a kindly fate offers you. For one thing, on a bad break like
that you have a big market – one that you can turn around in – and that is
the time to turn your paper profits into real money. Even in a bear market, a
man cannot always cover one hundred and twenty thousand shares of stock
without putting up the price on himself. He must wait for the market that will
allow him to buy that much at no damage to his profit as it stands him on
paper."

Livermore had not expected the break that happened. He didn't quite
believe the rumors that the war would soon be over and a peace brokered by
President Wilson. So he had no choice but to take his profits. As he explained:
"My experience of thirty years as a trader is that such accidents are usually
along the line of least resistance on which I base my position in the market.
Another thing to bear in mind is this: Never try to sell at the top. It isn't wise.
Sell after a reaction if there is no rally."

By the end of 1916, from being a raging bull and then a raging bear, and
calling the market changes, Livermore had amassed $3 million as he carried

on enjoying his winter holiday in Palm Beach. Despite the year end fall, the Dow closed down only five per cent at 95 at the end of 1916. Livermore had called it all absolutely perfectly.

He was 39 years old and a rich man again: not quite as wealthy as he had been for that short period in 1907, but rich beyond most men's dreams. He summed up his year: "I cleared about three million dollars in 1916 by being bullish as long as the bull market lasted and then by being bearish when the bear market started. As I said before, a man does not have to marry one side of the market till death do them part."

With money in his pocket again, he had already made his peace with Ed Hutton. But the relationship was never the same, and he did not get his office back although his trading account was re-opened and he still used the Palm Beach office of E. F. Hutton when he was on vacation.

He left a small short line in shares and wheat open over the holiday period.

This vacation was devoted to fishing and gambling. Devoid of his yacht, he stayed at The Breakers Hotel and rented a small fishing boat. This vacation he did not turn off from the market and intended to carry on trading throughout, so favorably did he read market conditions. As he said: "I used to go to my broker's branch office regularly and I noticed that cotton, in which I had no interest, was strong and rising."

The outset of 1917 saw much talk about the efforts of President Wilson to broker a peace in Europe, as forecast in the infamous leak. Wilson's efforts were the talk of Palm Beach and there was a degree of confidence in the President's eventual success.

But Livermore was mystified that with peace supposedly close at hand, the stock market and wheat ought to be going down and cotton up.

Then, one sunny afternoon on the last day of January 1917, he stopped his fishing early and hurried down to E. F. Hutton's office. He remembered: "I had not done anything in cotton in some time. At 2:20 that afternoon I did not own a single bale, but at 2:25 my belief that peace was impending made me buy fifteen thousand bales as a starter."

Almost immediately came news that the peace initiative had fallen apart.

After the market had closed, Germany announced it would be waging 'unrestricted submarine warfare' late on January 31st 1917. It was due to come into effect the next day. It was effectively a blockade of the Allied countries by Germany, and any shipping attempting to run the blockade would be fired upon, which meant American ships. It was the nearest thing Germany could do to the United States of America short of declaring war. President Wilson's reaction three days later was to break off diplomatic relations with Germany.

That very afternoon, after the market closed, the news of President Wilson's reaction came through and traders were left hanging overnight. The atmosphere in Palm Beach, where most of Wall Street was vacationing, was extremely tense. There was certain to be a big break in prices of all shares and commodities at next day's opening. Livermore was short shares and wheat but long cotton, a decision he had made a few hours earlier.

The main stocks opened eight points or more down. Livermore once more covered all his short positions in stocks and wheat. He was short 50,000 shares of US Steel amongst others and made enormous profits that morning. By the end of the day, he was up $1.5 million.

But it was not all good news. Livermore was long 15,000 bales of cotton and was showing a paper loss of $350,000. For once, he was unsure what to do. As he admitted: "I was not so clear as to what I ought to do in cotton. There were various things to consider, and while I always take my loss the moment I am convinced I am wrong, I did not like to take that loss that morning. Then I reflected that I had gone south to have a good time fishing instead of perplexing myself over the course of the cotton market. And, moreover, I had taken such big profits in my wheat and in stocks that I decided to take my loss in cotton. I would figure that my profit had been a little more than one million instead of over a million and a half. It was all a matter of bookkeeping, as promoters are apt to tell you when you ask too many questions.

"If I hadn't bought that cotton just before the market closed the day before, I would have saved that four hundred thousand dollars. It shows you how quickly a man may lose big money on a moderate line. My main position was absolutely correct, and I benefited by an accident of a nature diametrically opposite to the considerations that led me to take the position I did in stocks and wheat."

Despite his loss in cotton, there was a cause for massive celebration that night at Ed Bradley's Beach Club. Whilst most of the members had lost big that day and were down in the dumps, Livermore and his friends were celebrating in a big way.

But the cotton loss still bugged him. As he explained: "If things had turned out as I had figured, I would have been 100 per cent right in all three of my lines, for with peace stocks and wheat would have gone down and cotton would have gone kiting up. I would have cleaned up in all three. Irrespective of peace or war, I was right in my position on the stock market and in wheat and that is why the unlooked-for event helped. In cotton I based my plans on something that might happen outside of the market – that is, I bet on Mr. Wilson's success in his peace negotiations. It was the German military leaders who made me lose the cotton bet."

When Livermore returned to New York in the middle of February, he had a special mission to perform. His first act was to visit all the creditors to whom he owed money from his 1915 bankruptcy. Two years before on exactly the same date, 17th February, he had visited all his creditors to deliver the bad news.

This time, he had checks in his hand for over $1.2 million to deliver to 25 addresses in New York City. To each one he added 4.5 per cent annual interest for two years. It was a poignant moment when he arrived unannounced at the addresses of each of the people who had extended him credit and whom he had let down.

There was a certain amount of quiet satisfaction as he handed them a cream envelope containing a check and saw the stunned looks of surprise on their faces.

Many of them didn't want to accept his offer of interest on the debt, but he insisted. He recalled later: "I paid back all the money I owed, which was over one million dollars. It was a great pleasure to me to pay my debts. I might have paid it back a few months earlier, but I didn't for a very simple reason; I was trading actively and successfully and I needed all the capital I had. I owed it to myself, as well as to the men I considered my creditors, to take every advantage of the wonderful markets we had in 1915 and 1916. I knew that I would make a great deal of money, and I wasn't worrying because I was letting them wait a few months longer for money many of them never expected to get back. I did not wish to pay off my obligations in driblets or to one man at a time, but in full to all at once."

There was one creditor he didn't pay off that day and that was Mr John Pierson, to whom he owed $500. He waited until Pierson had heard the others creditors had been paid. Of course, Pierson could no longer chase Livermore for the debt, and so Livermore made him squirm for all the unpleasantness two years earlier. As he remembered: "The man I paid off the last of all was the chap I owed the five hundred dollars to, who had made my life a burden and had upset me until I couldn't trade. I let him wait until he heard that I had paid off all the others. Then he got his money. I wanted to teach him to be considerate the next time somebody owed him a few hundreds."

Even after paying off his debts, he had nearly $3 million left. He bought an annuity worth $500,000, ostensibly controlled by his estranged wife, Nettie, but for his benefit. He wanted to make sure he couldn't touch the money himself so that he always had something in reserve. He explained: "The reason I did this was because I knew that a man will spend anything he can lay his hands on. By doing what I did, my wife was safe from me. More than one man I know has done the same thing, but has coaxed his wife to sign off when he needed the money, and he has lost it. But I have fixed it up so that no matter what I want or what my wife wants, that trust holds. It is absolutely safe from all attacks by either of us; safe from my market needs; safe even from a devoted wife's love. I'm taking no chances." He added: "I don't expect I will ever need it, but I want to make sure that if I lose every other dollar I've got, I will still have the means on which to live."

CHAPTER 22

War and a Coffee Scam

Roasters outwit Livermore

1917

When President Wilson declared war on Germany on April 6th 1917, shortly after congress had voted in favor of a declaration, Jesse Livermore was out of the market and in one of his periods of relative inactivity. Livermore had foreseen the outbreak of war but could not predict what the stock market's reaction would be.

War was by no means certain, and President Wilson had only garnered the support of the American people after a document called the Zimmermann Telegram was published. The telegram was so called because it was sent by Arthur Zimmermann, the German Foreign Secretary, to the German ambassador in Mexico, Heinrich von Eckardt. It proposed that Germany would offer Mexico assistance to annexe Texas and other parts of the southwest if America entered the war against Germany. The telegram was intercepted and decoded by British army intelligence officers. The code for the encrypted message had been cracked by a group of code breakers in London, known internally as Room 40 because of their secret location in the heart of Whitehall, a region of London almost exclusively occupied by government offices. Decoding that telegram was the most significant event of the First World War. It was also one of the most foolish and inept diplomatic communications ever sent and virtually guaranteed that Germany would ultimately lose the war.

Its publication outraged ordinary Americans and made President Wilson's mission much easier. The final declaration of war came after Germany sank seven US merchant ships on the way to Europe.

Livermore was certain that the stock market would decline but was unsure for how much and for how long. Conscious of how easily he had previously let millions of dollars of profits slip through his fingers, he resisted the temptation and stayed on the sidelines whilst all the time studying the markets and looking for opportunities. Wealth preservation became his main priority.

The market went on a swoon throughout 1917, although Livermore was a modest bear and read the market reasonably well. But the war made him doubly cautious of committing to stocks and shares, and he preferred the safer waters of commodities during this period.

It was Livermore's opinion that America's entry into the war guaranteed that the price of commodities would rise sharply: "It was as easy to foresee that as to foresee war inflation. Of course, the general advance continued as the war prolonged itself, and I now had the time, the money and the inclination to consider trading in commodities as well as in stocks."

But much of the price rise had already happened by the time Livermore was ready to plunge in. He had been focusing on the easy money in stocks and had missed the commodities boom which had seen everything rise from between 100 per cent and as much as 400 per cent inside two years.

But there was one commodity that hadn't taken off, and that was coffee. The reason was clear; at the outbreak of war, all supplies had been diverted from war-torn Europe to the United States, and there was a glut that had forced the price down. Coffee was the one commodity selling below pre-war prices.

And for all intents and purposes, it was set to stay that way. The Europeans weren't in the market for luxuries, and coffee was certainly considered a luxury on the war-torn continent. But the low price depended on there being a plentiful supply of ships to carry the raw coffee from South America to its export markets.

But suddenly there wasn't as German U-Boats began sending record numbers of Allied merchant ships to the bottom of the ocean. All available shipping was being used for essential supplies and coffee wasn't considered one of them, even by hedonistic Americans.

Livermore figured there would be little capacity to ship coffee anywhere and, despite the huge current glut, the supply must eventually dry up. He remembered: "It didn't require a Sherlock Holmes to size up the situation. Why everybody did not buy coffee I cannot tell you. When I decided to buy it, I did not consider it a speculation. It was much more of an investment. I knew it would take time to cash in, but I knew also that it was bound to yield a good profit. That made it a conservative investment operation – a banker's act rather than a gambler's play."

After a long period of inactivity sitting on his money as the stock market see-sawed on war news, Livermore plunged into coffee in November 1917. He bought a modest physical supply and focused on buying options for future delivery. He carried the options until July 1918, and they showed a loss throughout. When the contracts expired, he took the $600,000 hit. But he had not changed his opinion, so he shrugged his shoulders and realized he had been too early into the market. He was soon buying again at lower prices of around eight cents a pound. This time he really piled up coffee and bought three times his original stake. As he said: "I was sure my views were sound. I had been clearly wrong in the matter of time, but I was confident that coffee must advance as all commodities had done."

This time it was different and the price started to rise almost as soon as he had finished taking in his new line. As he remembered: "The sellers of the contracts I held were the roasters, who had bought the coffee in Brazil confidently expecting to bring it to this country. But there were no ships to bring it."

As soon as they realized there were no ships, the US based roasters dumped their holdings. The lack of ships came exactly as Livermore had forecast, albeit almost a year later. But he was sanguine about it: "The punishment for being wrong is to lose money. The reward for being right is to make money. I had been made to wait a year, but now I was going to be paid both for my waiting and for being right. I could see the profit coming – fast. There wasn't any cleverness about it. It was simply that I wasn't blind."

The coffee price started to roar away and Livermore was sitting on a huge physical pile of coffee as well as plenty of options. His potential profit was in excess of $5 million.

Then the unexpected happened. The roasters, realizing that they had read the market wrong, were set to lose tens of millions of dollars of profit. So, in an audacious move, they appealed to the US government for help.

Coffee was an everyday commodity for millions of Americas and not a remote commodity such as wheat and cotton. With the price set to rise dramatically, the cost of a cup of coffee for ordinary Americans was also set to rise. So the crafty roasters hired publicity experts in Washington and instigated a public relations campaign alerting American consumers to what was happening and accusing speculators, like Livermore, of being responsible for the situation. In reality, traders like Livermore had simply bought coffee and options at the prevailing price, which the roasters had willingly sold them and were glad to have been taken out of a hole. Now they turned on their savior.

The roasters were pushing at an open door and American consumers swallowed the story. It so happened that the Wilson government had passed into law many safeguards against war profiteering, and the roasters saw an opportunity to get back some of their losses at the expense of Jesse Livermore.

So the roasters took their case to the Price Fixing Committee of the War Industries Board, which Wilson had set up to adjudicate on pricing disputes and eliminate profiteering.

Livermore was amazed. He was only one of many speculators who had seen what he had seen; yet the roasters singled him out alone as the greedy speculator who was set to cheat the American people.

The roasters had chosen their target well as there was no way Livermore could appeal to the American public and put his side of the story, even though he knew they were being conned by the roasters. He was on a hiding to nothing. Livermore hired some of his own publicity people to try and explain to the American public that the price of coffee that consumers actually paid often had little to do with the raw price of the commodity. In this case, the coffee bean and that the bulk of any price rise was in the cost of shipping and roasting the beans, and his buying had made very little difference to the cost of a cup of coffee. But consumers had deaf ears and understood the simpler argument much better.

Livermore lost the public relations war. He described it so: "It was simply that the fellows who had sold me the coffee, the shorts, knew what was in store for them, and in their efforts to squirm out of the position into which they had sold themselves, devised a new way of welshing. They rushed to Washington for help and got it. They made a patriotic appeal to that body to protect the American breakfaster. They asserted that a professional speculator, one Jesse Livermore, had cornered, or was about to corner, coffee. If his speculative plans were not bought to naught he would take advantage of the conditions created by the war, and the American people would be forced to pay exorbitant prices for their daily coffee."

The roasters completely outwitted Livermore and portrayed themselves as "patriots who were willing to help the Government curb profiteering actual or prospective." They pitched a very good case to the Price Fixing Committee of the War Industries Board. At the hearing, the roasters openly accused Livermore of trying to corner the coffee market and force prices up.

The Committee did not need much convincing and took the roasters at their word.

Their decision was a foregone conclusion, and the Committee unilaterally fixed a maximum price for raw coffee at nine cents a pound and also imposed a time limit for closing out existing coffee future options contracts. Livermore accused the Committee of carrying out only a superficial investigation that caused the New York Coffee Exchange to close down. He said the Committee had been misled by the roasters, who had manipulated the situation for their own ends. But his protest fell on deaf ears. He had been completely outmaneuvered by the roasters. An exasperated Livermore called it "the unexpectable" and pronounced it as a "hazard of investing."

When the decision from the Committee came down, Livermore immediately liquidated his coffee positions and managed to get out without loss. As he said: "There was only one thing for me to do, and I did it; and that was to sell out all existing contracts. Those profits of millions that I had deemed as certain to come my way as any I ever made failed completely to materialize."

Livermore was livid. As he explained: "I was and am as keen as anybody against the profiteer in the necessaries of life, but at the time the Price Fixing Committee made their ruling on coffee, all other commodities were selling at from 250 to 400 per cent above pre-war prices while raw coffee was actually below the average prevailing for some years before the war. I can't see that it made any real difference who held the coffee. The price was bound to advance; and the reason for that was not the operations of conscienceless speculators, but the dwindling surplus for which the diminishing importations were responsible, and they in turn were affected exclusively by the appalling destruction of the world's ships by the German submarines. The Committee clamped on the brakes.

"As a matter of policy and of expediency, it was a mistake to force the Coffee Exchange to close just then. If the Committee had left coffee alone, the price undoubtedly would have risen for the reasons I have already stated, which had nothing to do with any alleged corner. But the high price – which need not have been exorbitant – would have been an incentive to attract supplies to this market."

Livermore was right and the low price of raw coffee destroyed growing coffee as a profitable business. Growers simply switched to other more profitable crops. Coffee beans rotted in warehouses and at the docks as it wasn't worth paying the high cost of shipping to get them to market. Americans paid more for their coffee anyway as shipping prices went up.

As supply dwindled and price controls ended, the price of raw coffee shot up and consumers paid a higher price than they would have done had the Committee done nothing. As Livermore explained: "When the Coffee Exchange resumed business later on, coffee sold at twenty-three cents. The American people paid that price because of the small supply, and the supply was small because the price had been fixed too low."

Livermore's conscience was clear. He had no intention of profiteering. To him, it was a legitimate commodities deal and he had been conned out of a huge profit by the unscrupulous roasters who had manipulated the American government into a short-term course of action. As he said: "I have always thought that my coffee deal was the most legitimate of all my trades in commodities. I considered it more of an investment than a speculation. I was in it over a year. If there was any gambling it was done by the patriotic roasters. They had coffee in Brazil and they sold it to me in New York. The Price Fixing Committee fixed the price of the only commodity that had not advanced. They protected the public against profiteering before it started, but not against the inevitable higher prices that followed. Not only that, but even when green coffee hung around nine cents a pound, roasted coffee went up with everything else. It was only the roasters who benefited. If the price of green coffee had gone up two or three cents a pound, it would have meant several millions for me. And it wouldn't have cost the public as much as the later advance did."

Livermore considered his coffee escapade, as he later called it, to be an "exercise in education." He later wrote about it as a case study into unexpected events that can catch even the savviest speculator out. As he explained: "Post-mortems in speculation are a waste of time. They get you nowhere. But this particular deal had a certain educational value. It was as pretty as any I ever went into. The rise was so sure, so logical, that I figured that I simply couldn't help making several millions of dollars. But I didn't.

"On two other occasions I have suffered from the action of exchange committees making rulings that changed trading rules without warning. But in those cases my own position, while technically right, was not quite so sound commercially as in my coffee trade. You cannot be dead sure of anything in speculative operation. It was the experience I have just told you that made me add the unexpectable to the unexpected in my list of hazards."

Publicly, Livermore pretended he was relaxed about what had happened. But he had not only lost $5 million in guaranteed profit, he had also had his name besmirched publicly and it rankled with him: "The theory that most of the sudden declines or particular sharp breaks are the results of some plunger's operations probably was invented as an easy way of supplying reasons to those speculators who, being nothing but blind gamblers, will believe anything that is told them rather than do a little thinking."

In this instance, it was clear that Livermore thought that the Price Fixing Committee of the War Industries Board had done little thinking when it fixed the price of raw coffee so low. The price of coffee for ordinary Americans shot up anyway as the roasters cashed in, taking advantage of lower raw commodity prices to jack up profits at the retail counter. It was an education for Livermore at the hands of the wily roasters, and it was an education he never forgot.

It was the third time he had been taken for a mug: first by Teddy Price, secondly by Charles Pugh and his brother-in-law, and thirdly by a bunch of crafty and unscrupulous roasters. Each time, he estimated, it had cost him around $5 million: a total of $15 million inside ten years. He vowed he would not let it happen again.

From now on, he would take a leaf out of Price, Pugh and the roasters' books and cease to be the nice, honorable guy who always played by the rules, always paid in cash and always told the truth. Now he vowed to play a rougher, tougher and less honest game against his opponents.

There would be no more Mr Nice Guy.

CHAPTER 23

The Great Escape

Margin trading and short selling under threat

1917

After his successes in 1916, Jesse Livermore believed he had earned the respect of his contemporaries on Wall Street. He craved respectability and at last he thought he had it.

But that is what he didn't get when he was accused of nefarious deeds over his coffee trading and later the famous leak of information over President Wilson's peace initiative at the end of 1916.

He brushed off the criticism over his coffee trading relatively easily but not so easily the accusations that he had illegally profited from inside information direct from the White House.

Livermore had made $1.5 million by selling out his short positions in December 1916 and people believed he had been part of a sophisticated scam. Two months later, his name was all over the newspapers for all the wrong reasons.

The unwelcome publicity came about from an inquiry instigated by Sherman Whipple, counsel for the House of Representatives House Rules Committee.

Livermore had never heard of it, but the Committee was an ancient institution formed in 1789 and vested with great powers. From 1880 onwards, it was generally reckoned to be the most powerful government committee in Washington.

As general counsel for the committee, Whipple was a very influential man, and in some quarters in Washington, the mere mention of his name would cause a room to fall silent.

People began whispering in his ear about the huge profits that had been made on the stock market by speculators in December 1916 from a so-called leak of information from the White House. Whipple and others began to suspect foul play, and he initiated an inquiry by the House Rules Committee. The main targets were Jesse Livermore and Bernard Baruch, principally because they had been the biggest beneficiaries.

The chief complainant was a veteran Boston stock trader, 60 year-old Tommy Lawson. Lawson was a one-time associate of Livermore in Palm Beach, and the two had cooperated on stock purchases in the past. Lawson had been heavily invested in the market in December 1916 and lost virtually his entire fortune. He was adamant that Livermore and Baruch had been recipients of inside information and had bribed journalists to get it. He insisted on an investigation and said if everybody had had the benefit of the same information then he and others would not have lost money.

The inquiry was to be chaired by Congressman Robert Henry. The trouble was that Whipple and Henry had little understanding of how the stock market worked and even less on how newspapers worked, or the new wire services that transmitted news instantly by telegraph.

The committee hearings, nicknamed the leak committee, convened at the start of February 1917. Significantly, it heard evidence from Bernard Baruch and Jesse Livermore and a host of bankers, traders and brokers. The hearings were notable for the sheer number of extraordinary untruths told to the naïve committee by almost every witness.

Bernard Baruch, a stock trader with a very high reputation, set the scene and he even lied to the committee. He told them he had made profits of only $400,000 on December 16th and 17th when he had actually made $3 million from acting on the leak. Livermore, more modestly, told the committee he had made $1 million when he actually made $1.5 million.

Approximately 30 traders, bankers and brokers were called to give evidence and, apart from Baruch and Livermore, every one of them denied that they ever sold shares short, i.e. sold shares they didn't own. One by one, the witnesses openly lied to the House Rules Committee. In reality, all of them sold shares short on a daily basis.

The committee was not entirely convinced and afterwards said it would examine the books of the 400 stockbrokers active that day in New York to find out who profited from the news. Sherman Whipple never got to the bottom of it, and nor did he publish the results of his investigation of 400 stock brokers' books of account.

After the inquiry had concluded, Whipple made a statement to the effect that the Committee found that short selling and trading on margin – staples of the stock market for many years – was "questionable." Whipple took the view that for every dollar of profit made by a short seller, a member of the American public also lost a dollar. He stated that it was his main concern that short sellers were stealing from the American public. Whipple said: "It has been brought out in this inquiry, as it never was before, how the public is made to foot the bill of the Wall Street speculator."

Whipple didn't name Bernard Baruch, but he made it clear he disapproved of his short selling methods. Of the 35,000 shares that Baruch had admitted he sold short, Whipple assumed that these had been purchased on margin by thousands of ordinary people across America who had lost a combined $400,000. It was a simplistic view that was undoubtedly false. At the other end of Baruch's deals were other speculators who believed that the stock market was going to continue its move upwards although Whipple and the committee failed to grasp this.

But simplistic or not, the House Rules Committee had the power to influence Congress and few now realize how close the US Congress came in 1917 to enacting a bill that would have banned short selling and trading on margin outright.

Whipple confirmed it when he said: "There will be pressure on Congress to favor the passage of bills which will make both short selling and marginal trading illegal. When that is done, there will be eliminated the dangerous elements in the stock exchange."

He added: "The thing upon which short selling lives is marginal trading. If there were no marginal trading there would be no stock in a position to be lent. You see when a person buys a stock on margin, not only is he is engaged in a gamble, but he lays his stock open to be hypothecated or borrowed by the short seller. If there is no stock held by brokers on margin then there is no one who owns stock outright who is going to lend it to the short trader."

Despite his naivety in other areas, Whipple appears to have got that analysis exactly right.

His words seemed to be backed up as a series of bankers came to testify and were asked the same question: "How much money had they lent to the stock market as of today for marginal trading?" The sums proved to be extraordinary: Francis Hine of First National Bank said his firm currently had lending for such purposes of "between $75 million and $80 million". William Simonson confirmed that National City bank had lent out and average of $73 million every day to finance margin trading.

Behind all this was the simple fact that the inquiry had been called for on a false premise - a grudge. It had been instigated by Lawson and other speculators who had lost money in December 1916 and who had bent Whipple's ear in Washington, seeking retribution.

Another problem for the committee was the number of people who claimed credit for the leak and for sending a mystery telegram to brokers' offices. Amazingly, it appears that the committee never asked W. W. Price to give evidence or to explain what really happened on December 16th 1916.

But all that was brushed under the carpet as Whipple tried to get congress to pass new laws which would fundamentally change Wall Street forever. Whipple was really worried about the bribing of reporters and the fact that it could spread to government officials. As he stated: "We have shown what can be done with inside information. We have shown whether or not men could make millions out of advance information. It can now be seen whether there is enough in it to bribe a government official to get information. If a man can obtain $100 through advance information, he will not pay much for it. But if he could obtain millions, he could afford to pay more."

For Whipple it was a real concern, and he was genuinely frightened about the possibility of the corruption of American public servants when such big sums of money were at stake. Whipple was actually a far-sighted man, as the Teapot Dome scandal was to prove four years later.

The Committee never got to the bottom of the leak, which was really President Wilson's fault and not the result of any nefarious activity; Wilson was guilty of being indiscreet with a friendly reporter, and that was all there was to it. It was cock-up rather than conspiracy but one which could have so easily ended Jesse Livermore's career overnight if short selling and margin trading had been banned in 1917. And it came very close to being so.

In the end, the hearings claimed only one innocent victim: President Wilson's brother-in-law, a man called Wilmer Bolling. He was forced to resign from the stockbroking firm of F. A. Connolly & Co. Bolling had seen the news come over the wire and realized its significance only because of his connection to the White House and his knowledge of the stock market. He had naturally disseminated it, and as a result no one believed he wasn't part of the scam despite his tearful protestations.

There is also some evidence that Whipple knew he was being lied to by virtually every witness, when he stated: "Any question of false statements will be considered by the committee in executive (closed) session in Washington, which will make its report on February 27th."

There never was any report and the lies were seemingly brushed under the carpet in a practice that seemed routine in Washington, when it was faced with awkward truths, during those boom years after the turn of the century.

It was left to the governing committee of the New York Stock Exchange to make any changes it deemed necessary. It issued a statement saying that it "disapproved of the employment of newspaper representatives for the purposes of obtaining confidential information or privileged information. Hereafter, a member disregarding this policy of the exchange will be liable to a suspension for a period not exceeding a year."

Its official resolution read "that the indirect or direct employment of representatives of the press by a member of the New York Stock Exchange or by his firm for the purposes of obtaining advance or confidential information is an act detrimental to the interest and welfare of the exchange."

The Exchange also adopted a new resolution that seemingly had far wider powers and may have given the Governing Committee the leeway to target short sellers and even margin sellers. It read: "[the governing committee] may by a vote of a majority of its existing members suspend from the exchange for a year any member who may be adjudged guilty of any act which may be determined by said committee to be detrimental to the interest or welfare of the exchange."

Everyone was unsure exactly what it meant or what its intention was, and there were an anxious few months before traders could do business comfortably again.

The rulings had no effect on Jesse Livermore and Bernard Baruch, who were effectively left untouched. They had no need for membership of the Exchange to carry on their day to day trading.

When Jesse Livermore read the transcripts of both hearings, he was astonished at the naïveté of both the rules committee and the Governing Committee although he didn't complain.

But the inquiry and the subsequent publicity severely irritated Livermore and damaged his reputation at a time when he was trying to build one for his new business. As he remembered: "The professionals in Wall Street and the newspaper writers got into the habit of blaming me and my alleged raids for the inevitable breaks in prices. After the coffee episode, I was so successful in other commodities and on the short side of the stock market that I began to suffer from silly gossip. At times, my selling was called unpatriotic – whether I was really selling or not."

Livermore was furious that his buying and selling operations were severely exaggerated in newspapers, and he was accused of all sorts of things he had nothing to do with. He was described as a raider, and the newspapers were full of stories of raids he had supposedly carried out. He was adamant that newspaper reporters did not understand the stock market. Nor did members of congress: "No manipulation can put stocks down and keep them down. There is nothing mysterious about this. The reason is plain to everybody who will take the trouble to think about it for half a minute. Suppose an operator raided a stock – that is, put the price down to a level below its real value – what would inevitably happen? Why, the raider would at once be up against the best kind of inside buying. The people who know what a stock is worth will always buy it when it is selling at bargain prices. If the insiders are not able to buy, it will be because general conditions are against their free command of their own resources, and such conditions are not bull conditions.

"When people speak about raids, the inference is that the raids are unjustified; almost criminal. But selling a stock down to a price much below what it is worth is mighty dangerous business. It is well to bear in mind that a raided stock that fails to rally is not getting much inside buying, and where there is a raid – that is, unjustified short selling – there is usually apt to be inside buying; and where there is that, the price does not stay down. I should say that in ninety-nine cases out of a hundred, so-called raids are really legitimate declines, accelerated at times but not primarily caused by the operations of a professional trader, however big a line he may be able to swing."

Livermore was so cross that he attempted to sue the *National Financial News* magazine for criminal libel after it published a story about him being a "big bear" and accused him of deliberately sending out his staff and "paid agents" to spread pessimism in the stock market. But a judge ruled that the terms "bear" and "spreader of pessimism" could not possibly be libelous. After that, Livermore never tried to sue anyone again for libel, having realized it was fruitless and any judge would be unlikely to look upon his plight favorably.

More realistically, Livermore adjudged the whole affair a very lucky escape. If short selling and margin trading had been banned, Wall Street would have been changed forever and people who earned their living from it, people like him, would have ceased to exist.

A year later, at the dawn of 1918 Livermore breathed a very deep sigh of relief. A bullet, perhaps a fatal one, had been dodged.

CHAPTER 24

Divorce, Marriage, Family

Dottie steals his heart

1917 - 1918

J esse Livermore was never a man who enjoyed a conventional personal life. His extraordinary relationship with his first wife, Nettie Jordan, defied any sort of rational analysis. Although they were together as man and wife for less than a year, they remained married for 17 years even though the marriage had broken down within a few months of their wedding ceremony in December 1900.

The root cause was haste. They had wed two months after they had met and were virtually strangers on their wedding night. When things were going well for him, the marriage was fine. However, at the first sign of financial trouble, she upped and left him.

The crunch came when he told her he needed to pawn her jewelry to raise money. When it came to a choice between keeping her jewelry or her husband, Nettie chose the jewelry.

She fled to her parents' home in Indianapolis with the jewels, said to be worth $30,000 and her father locked them in his safe. After that she made periodic visits back to New York, and the two remained friends despite the circumstances of her leaving. Livermore was still enamored of his wife despite her treatment of him; and when he could afford it, he bought her a very comfortable house in Long Island where she chose to live quietly. She told her husband that whilst he continued to be a stock market speculator she could not live with him and could not come to terms with the vagaries of the career he had chosen.

The two never lived together again although they continued to allow each other conjugal rights on her occasional visits to New York and his to Long Island. They also vacationed once a year together in Palm Beach.

And that was the routine for almost 17 years. Livermore had strange views about the sanctity of marriage. Although he no longer loved his wife and she felt the same about him, the marriage contract continued to bind them together. She could never quite forgive him for trying to re-possess her jewels, and he could never quite forgive her for running off with the jewelry in his hour of need.

But Nettie Livermore undoubtedly manipulated her husband's sense of guilt and the strong sense of loyalty he felt towards his wife. None more so than when he ponied up $200,000 in 1908 to pay for her brother Chester's fight to avoid the electric chair for murdering and dismembering the body of his wife. The money was paid over to Chester's lawyers at a time when Livermore could barely afford it. And when the legal maneuverings failed and Chester Jordan was denied clemency and executed for the crime, Livermore somehow got the blame.

Neither of Livermore's parents, Hiram or Laura, had ever liked Nettie; and the Jordans certainly did not like their daughter's choice of husband either, although they were happy to take his money when he had it. In truth, the whole Jordan family was, in reality, a bad bunch on the make. It took Livermore more than 16 years to see through them and to attempt to make the break.

In 1916, as Livermore approached his forties, he suddenly began to feel mortal and yearned for a proper family. He realized that this wasn't going to happen with Nettie, who had shown no desire to have children.

By 1917 he was a rich man again and, unlike the other times he had been rich, this time he felt unfulfilled. The novelty of being the consummate playboy around town had worn off, and he gazed jealously at men of similar age with their happy families and mostly, as he saw it, chocolate box and seemingly blissful existences.

A year later, by the time Jesse Livermore celebrated his 40th birthday, he was worth $8 million after all of his old debts had been settled. He had an office near Times Square and was living in the Hotel Netherland, one of New York's more fashionable hotels on Fifth Avenue.

His financial problems and bankruptcy had been long forgotten, and he was well known and respected again on Wall Street – his name was always in the newspapers.

It was true that he had more girlfriends than he could count and enjoyed an enviable lifestyle, but now he yearned for a family and a more stable existence.

One of his best friends was Florenz Ziegfeld Jr, a 50-year-old theatrical impresario he had first met across the gambling tables at the Beach Club in Palm Beach. The two men had become best friends and partied virtually every night in Palm Beach and New York. Ziegfeld became Livermore's closest friend for more than two decades and an important figure in his life until his death in 1932.

Along with his first wife, Anna Held, Ziegfeld created an eponymous Broadway show called The Ziegfeld Follies. The show consisted of dancing girls, elaborate backdrops and the latest music of the day. He had had the idea for the show when he was in Paris in the early 1900s. He went to see a cabaret act called the Folies Bergère and thought something similar would go down well on Broadway, but as a proper stage show.

As he returned home on a steamship, during the crossing he and his wife worked it all out and, by the time they disembarked in New York, they had conceived a plan. Ziegfeld looked for financial backers and soon found some, including William Randolph Hearst, the publisher. Ziegfeld sold them on the idea that they would get to hang out with the girls after the show. It was an easy pitch to make.

In 1907, the Ziegfeld Follies opened on Broadway and was an instant success. He copied the Paris show but on a bigger scale, adapted for a New York audience.

The secret of the show's success were the beautiful New York girls chosen personally by him and outfitted with elaborate costumes by his wife. He designed equally elaborate sets. He also had the works of the great composers George Gershwin, Jerome Kern and Irving Berlin reworked and adapted to suit the show. It was a winning formula, and from the first performance, the theatre was packed.

The Ziegfeld Follies quickly became a very valuable Broadway theatrical property, playing to sell-out audiences every night. It made Ziegfeld a very wealthy man and, inevitably, the fame and fortune changed his life and expectations. He divorced his wife in 1913 and married Billie Burke, a famous actress of the time.

As a result, Ziegfeld became a famous personality in his own right, continually profiled in newspapers and magazines across America. He always told reporters that it was the girls, their personalities and ability to attract publicity that made the show famous. Soon, many of the girls were stars in their own right. The show's star, Fanny Brice, previously an unknown singer, became the most famous woman in America.

The success of the show was also to have a big impact on Jesse Livermore's life.

One of the lesser-known Ziegfeld girls was a brown haired 22-year-old diminutive beauty called Dorothy Wendt, a New York native of Brooklyn. Wendt had unusual green eyes and a very open face that made her seem as though she was perpetually laughing. She also spoke well and was of good stock. Her mother was from a fine family and her father a wealthy Brooklyn wholesaler.

Unlike the other girls in the line-up, she eschewed publicity and kept to herself. As a result, she became something of an enigma amongst the eligible bachelors of New York.

Florenz Ziegfeld brought her to the attention of Livermore and told him she was perfect wife material. But he also told him that Dorothy was not like the others and would need wooing.

By then, Livermore was even more determined to straighten his life out, get married again and start a family. He had dallied with many of the girls appearing in the Ziegfeld Follies but never found one he would want to spend a second night with.

It became almost a ritual and, every night, after the show, they would all adjourn to the bar at the Hotel Netherland and one, or sometimes even more than one, would end up in Livermore's suite until morning. But Dorothy used to go home to Brooklyn every night and rarely attended the after-parties.

So Livermore did not notice Dorothy until he saw her on stage one night during one of his infrequent visits to see a show he was already very familiar with. As soon as he spotted her in the line up, he wondered if this was the girl that Ziegfeld had told him about. That night, he went back stage and introduced himself. At 40 years old, Livermore was no longer the youthful boy plunger or the young Robert Redford lookalike that he was in his youth. But he still cut a handsome figure. Dorothy was overwhelmed by his presence in her dressing room; she had heard all about the handsome financier from the other girls.

She accepted his invitation, and Livermore took her to dinner that night at the St Regis Hotel and then drove her all the way back home to Brooklyn. She gave little away during the dinner, and Livermore was unsure what sort of impact he had made, if any.

Dorothy was intrigued and asked her boss about him the following morning. Ziegfeld was full of praise for his friend and told Dorothy she could do no better. Then he tipped off his old friend about the enquiry.

But Dorothy Wendt was to prove no easy catch. Although she didn't socialize with the other girls, she had a host of respectable male admirers and a full social calendar. But Livermore persisted and eventually won her round, and she gradually shed her other beaus.

Despite her fine looks, Dorothy's real appeal was her bubbly personality; she had a way with words and a turn of phrase that other girls did not. But even as they became close, she resisted all Livermore's attempts to get her into his bed. Gradually, Livermore fell in love with her and she with him.

Very quickly, they decided to marry. But Dorothy was shocked to discover he was still technically married to his first wife and didn't quite believe the story he told her about Nettie and their relationship. So his relationship with Dorothy turned into a holding operation until he had disposed of Nettie; a scenario that had suddenly become very urgent and was proving far from easy.

In 1917, he finally told Nettie he wanted to be free, and for the first time, their relationship turned nasty when she refused. There appeared to be no reason for the refusal other than bloody mindedness. Still, Livermore thought she would agree if the settlement terms were generous enough. But it still proved very difficult.

After a 17-year separation, Livermore had mistakenly thought that an amicable divorce would not be a problem. But he didn't reckon on the determination of Nettie. She liked, and had got used to, being Mrs Jesse Livermore. Divorce in the early 1900s was still a social stigma, and she didn't want any of it.

The battle of the Livermore divorce soon seeped into the gossip columns as Nettie resisted and told Livermore that they would stay married come what may. To him, this was unacceptable and the relationship, after 17 years of relative harmony, became extremely hostile. At the height of the battle for a divorce, Nettie made clear her position to a reporter: "I will never divorce him. He may harass me and hurt me, but I will never stoop to divorce. If Mr Livermore has some other woman in mind that he would like to marry, he will find that idea hard to carry out. It will be quite impossible, as I will never release him. He may torment me and humiliate me, but I will stick by him."

The divorce became a staple of the New York gossip columns. Few readers understood that the Livermores had effectively lived apart for close to 17 years, and so they took Nettie's side. They saw a poor, wronged wife on one side and a greedy mistress on the other. Dorothy was portrayed as a home wrecker, and it was a very upsetting time. She resigned from the Follies line up, and Livermore bought her a house on Signal Hill in Lake Placid where she could hide out and he could visit at weekends. He also showered her with gifts of expensive jewelry. The most expensive was an engagement ring made of platinum with a giant emerald. It was said to have cost $150,000.

In an attempt to buy off Nettie, Livermore agreed to give her the Long Island house, a new automobile and $1,000 a week in alimony, but still she did not buckle.

The divorce battle became very acrimonious and moved from the gossip columns onto the newspaper front pages. There was a much-publicized battle over a 1902 black Rolls-Royce sedan that Livermore had bought new and parked in Nettie's garage, safe from his creditors many years earlier. He had almost forgotten about the car and now tried to reclaim it. Equally, she was determined to keep hold of it since it had been in her possession for nearly 15 years. The car had cost $6,000 and because of a shortage of cars during the war years, it was now worth much more.

Livermore, somewhat foolishly, employed a high profile private detective called William Jerome to repossess it by force. The 59-year-old was a former New York County District Attorney and reckoned to be one of America's best private detectives. But he proved no match for Nettie Livermore, who outsmarted and humiliated him. She had him arrested and charged with stealing her car. He was held overnight until Livermore arranged bail. When that didn't work, Livermore went to court. The judge eventually found for Livermore after he took a dislike to Nettie and her behavior, and so Livermore got his car back.

Finally, Nettie was worn down by the publicity and saw that her husband was intent on getting what he wanted and marrying Dorothy. On November 18th 1918, Nettie filed for divorce in Reno, Nevada. She was apparently persuaded when Livermore agreed to sign over the trust fund annuity worth $500,000 he had set up for himself and which she had technical control of anyway. Two weeks later, the divorce was made final on December 1st.

The next day, Jesse Livermore and Dorothy Wendt were married in the St Regis Hotel, the scene of their first date 18 months earlier. Inscribed inside the gold wedding ring Livermore placed on her finger were the words: "Dotsie forever and ever J. L."

The evening ceremony, which was over in less than 15 minutes, was presided over by a magistrate called Peter Barlow. Present were Livermore's parents, Hiram and Laura; his brother Elliot and his second wife Myra; and his sister Mabel and her husband Arthur. Dorothy invited a dozen of her close relatives from Brooklyn. The only outsiders present were Flo and Billie Ziegfeld. Afterwards, they all had dinner in a private room at the St Regis.

The venue could not have been finer. It was New York's best and most expensive hotel. Situated on Fifth Avenue, four blocks from Central Park, the 18-storey building was owned by John Jacob Astor IV who had built it 14 years before as a companion hotel to his Waldorf-Astoria 20 blocks up the road.

Livermore booked all the rooms and suites on the 18th floor for his new extended family. The newly married couple spent their first night as man and wife in the 3,500-square feet Presidential Suite with its fabulous views of Central Park. The next day, they left on Livermore's newly re-purchased private Pullman railcar for Palm Beach, where they spent a two-week honeymoon doing what Jesse Livermore liked best: fishing by day and gambling by night. For the second week, they were joined by the Ziegfelds and went cruising on Livermore's new yacht, he had named the *Athero*, although nobody knew why.

During those two weeks, their eldest son Jesse Jr was conceived. They returned to New York to a fifth storey penthouse at 8 West 76th Street on the upper west side, which Livermore had purchased the previous summer. It had views of Central Park and the Hudson River. A week after they arrived back in New York, Dorothy told her delighted husband that she was pregnant. On September 19th 1919, Jesse Jnr was born.

Four years later, on April 23rd 1923, Paul Livermore was born and the family was complete.

CHAPTER 25

The Effortless Millions

Deals galore as he makes $15 million

1919 - 1922

When the war ended on November 11th 1918, the stock market spiked and then began an inexorable move down that was to last for two years as America came down from the war boom economy and the world faced the reality of the traumatic post war years. Livermore was short for most of the time and added to his millions effortlessly.

War ruined the economies of the victors and defeated alike. The Allies had spent a total of $58 billion between them, including Britain, which spent $21 billion. The United States, in its brief time at war, spent $17 billion. Germany spent a relatively modest $20 billion and was ordered to pay ruinous reparations to the victors.

The cessation of hostilities was, as expected, very bad news for the stock market. From late 1918 to the end of 1920, the Dow Jones Industrial Average almost halved, falling from around 115 to a low of 60.

Jesse Livermore had almost $6 million in capital not fully utilized because the opportunities available were sparse. He was also ever conscious about losing it. The ease of losing money concerned him greatly, and he sought a safer way to do business. The first was a virtually total switch from trading in stocks to trading in commodities. The second was to structure his business operations to make the maximum use of his talents and produce a stable rather than an uncertain income.

Livermore was anxious to set up his business on a more formal basis, rather than being a one man trading operation. He was tired of working out of stockbrokers' offices and for a long time wanted a base of his own. He had in mind becoming a kind of boutique merchant bank – assisting and even handling public offerings. It came to fruition when he finally resolved to get into business properly and formed J. L. Livermore & Company. He acquired permanent offices at The Trinity Building at 111 Broadway, on the fringe of

215

Wall Street's financial district. The building had been constructed in 1905 in the neo gothic style of the time and then it was one of the tallest buildings in New York at 278 feet high. Livermore leased a suite of offices on the 11th floor of the 21-storey office block.

He was as proud as any man could be when he moved into his new office with a secretary and a few young assistants who had answered his advertisements and whom he had recruited from the top American universities. Soon he installed some ticker tape machines and set up direct telegraph links with his main brokers and the Chicago grain pits.

Although Livermore carried on his bearish selling throughout 1919 and 1920, his main focus was on commodities and his exploits were continually being reported in newspapers. The press was obsessed with commodities trading in this period and Livermore's every move was reported on. Being long commodities and short stocks proved a winning combination for two years. As a result, the millions started to pile up, and Livermore's annual earnings of $3 million in the years up to 1923 were only limited by his own caution.

He also started to make real money from his new business, which became one of organizing buying pools and consulting on public offerings. Fees of $1 million a time were obtainable if he was successful, and he generally was.

In an effort to add respectability to his new firm, Livermore bought a seat on the New York Curb Exchange for $5,000. It didn't mean very much but gave him certain privileges on New York's second trading arena. The curb exchange, as its name implied, traded outside but Livermore's timing proved good, and in 1921 its members bought a building on Greenwich Street in Lower Manhattan and became respectable.

Respectability went to his head, and on the first Monday of September 1920, on Labor Day, Livermore did something very uncharacteristic. Through his lawyer, he issued a press release calling the end of the bear market permanently. It was a strange and uncharacteristic thing for him to do, but he felt in his new role as chairman of J. L. Livermore & Company that it was the sort of thing he should be doing. He was enjoying the new status of running his own company instead of just being a share speculator. He envied the reputations of men like Jack Morgan (Pierpont's son who now ran J. P. Morgan) and wanted to emulate them.

The press release also proved to be a very good call. The market had bottomed in August and was at the start of a very gradual rise.

There was also another reason behind the press release – profit.

The truth was that Livermore had switched his direction two months before in early summer. He was now a bull and was growing impatient at the market's seeming inability to catch up with events. He decided to give the market a shove. It worked and further proved that he had the Midas touch where making money was concerned.

The success of the press release inspired Livermore to make a serious attempt to shed some of his anonymity and reputation for reclusiveness. He became media friendly and was suddenly very sensitive about what was being written about him.

Meanwhile, in late 1921, he got his first big deal for his new company when he was asked to run the management of a pool formed to put up the share price of a company called Seneca Copper and float it on the main exchange. Seneca was a company controlled by a small merchant bank called Lewisohn Brothers. Seneca traded on the over the counter market at around $12 a share.

Livermore was contacted by Walter Lewisohn, whose father, Leonard, had started Seneca Copper. When Lewisohn's father died in 1902 he left him $2.5 million, mainly in Seneca Copper shares. But the shares and the company had languished without the guiding hand of Leonard Lewisohn at the helm. Walter Lewisohn had no sentimental attachment to his father's company and wanted the share price up so he could cash in his inheritance.

Livermore was tasked with running a pool of buyers to get the price up. He was also asked to make the company and its activities well known on Wall Street and get it a higher profile.

Livermore described what he saw as his role in getting the price up: "Activity is all that the floor traders ask. They will buy or sell any stock at any level if only there is a free market for it. They will deal in thousands of shares wherever they see activity, and their aggregate capacity is considerable. It necessarily happens that they constitute the manipulator's first crop of buyers. They will follow you all the way up and they thus are a great help at all the stages of the operation. To get a professional following, I myself have never had to do more than to make a stock active. Traders don't ask for more. It is as well, of course, to remember that these professionals on the floor of the Exchange buy stocks with the intention of selling them at a profit. They do not insist on its being a big profit; but it must be a quick profit."

The initial plan was for Livermore to buy shares that would be paid for by Lewisohn Brothers until there were enough independent buyers at the higher price. The agreement allowed him discretion to buy shares in on behalf of the Lewisohn family. Livermore's trading quickly saw the share price double. But demand was fundamentally weak and Walter Lewisohn simply ended up owning a lot of shares at relatively high prices. Livermore explained it so: "If the demand is what it ought to be it will absorb more than the amount of stock I was compelled to accumulate in the earlier stages of the manipulation; and when this happens I sell the stock short – that is, technically. In other words, I sell more stock than I actually hold. It is perfectly safe for me to do so since I am really selling against my calls. Of course, when the demand from the public slackens, the stock ceases to advance. Then I wait."

After four months of trading, Livermore had got the price up to $24 a share and, with his in and out trading, made himself a quarter of a million dollars in the process. But it was all built on sand, and on January 19th 1922, the shares suddenly dropped to $18.75, a 25 per cent fall on the day. It is thought that Livermore dumped all his shares on that day and took his profits, leaving Walter Lewisohn with losses in excess of $1 million. Without support, the shares later fell back to the original price, causing Lewisohn another big loss. But Livermore believed he had the situation under control. As he explained: "Whatever the reason may be, the stock starts to go down. Well, I begin to buy it. I give it the support that a stock ought to have if it is in good order with its own sponsors. And more: I am able to support it without accumulating it – that is, without increasing the amount I shall have to sell later on. Observe that I do this without decreasing my financial resources. Of course, what I am really doing is covering stock I sold short at higher prices when the demand from the public or from the traders or from both enabled me to do it. It is always well to make it plain to the traders – and to the public, also – that there is a demand for the stock on the way down. That tends to check both reckless short selling by the professionals and liquidation by frightened holders – which is the selling you usually see when a stock gets weaker and weaker, which in turn is what a stock does when it is not supported. These covering purchases of mine constitute what I call the stabilizing process."

But Livermore was given no time to put the "stabilizing process" into action. On January 20th 1922, the relationship ended suddenly and Lewisohn cancelled Livermore's contract and refused to pay for the last shares he had bought on his behalf. It was a relatively small deal of 200 shares with a value of under $5,000. But Lewisohn believed that these shares were actually owned by Livermore himself and thought he had been duped.

Livermore had done nothing wrong, but his behavior appeared underhand.

Certainly he was now playing by new rules and had changed his philosophy after he had been severely bruised by his treatment at the hands of Teddy Price, Charles Pugh and the coffee roasters. He had resolved to be a lot tougher in looking after number one, and Walter Lewisohn was the unfortunate first victim of that change of outlook.

Walter Lewisohn eventually realized losses of over $2 million on Seneca shares and lost two thirds of his fortune. The setback had greater personal consequences. Lewisohn became very depressed over the losses and his own stupidity. At the same time, news of an affair with Leonora Hughes, a dancer, was made public in newspapers. It all became too much for him and he had a nervous breakdown. He was finally committed to Blythewood Sanatorium in Connecticut by his own family.

When it all became public on September 14th 1923, Livermore hired David Cahn, a lawyer, to represent him. Cahn issued a statement stating that his client had "at all times acted in good faith". Whether that was true or not was extremely doubtful. By this time, Livermore hardly cared; he was making money hand over fist and just moved on to his next deal, happy that this time he was the victor rather than the vanquished.

For Livermore it was all part of the game. He believed that the people who hired him to get their stock prices up were relatively unsophisticated and did not understand his methods. They believed the stock market was a one-way escalator, and once a stock was going up it would continue in the same vein. But Livermore knew this was not the case. As he explained: "There comes a weak day. The entire market may develop a reactionary tendency or some sharp-eyed trader may perceive that there are no buying orders to speak of in my stock, and he sells it and his fellows follow. As the market broadens, I of course sell stock on the way up, but never enough to check the rise. This is in strict accordance with my stabilizing plans. It is obvious that the more stock I sell on a reasonable and orderly advance, the more I encourage the conservative speculators, who are more numerous than the reckless room traders; and in addition the more support I shall be able to give to the stock on the inevitable weak days. By always being short, I am always in a position to support the stock without danger to myself. As a rule, I begin my selling at a price that will show me a profit. But I often sell without having a profit, simply to create or to increase what I may call my riskless buying power. My business is not alone to put up the price or to sell a big block of stock for a client but to make money for myself. That is why I do not ask any clients to finance my operations. My fee is contingent upon my success.

"What I have described is not my invariable practice. I neither have nor adhere to an inflexible system. I modify my terms and conditions according to circumstances.

"A stock which is desired to distribute should be manipulated to the highest possible point and then sold. I repeat this both because it is fundamental and because the public apparently believes that the selling is all done at the top. Sometimes a stock gets waterlogged, as it were; it doesn't go up. That is the time to sell. The price naturally will go down on your selling rather further than you wish, but you can generally nurse it back. As long as a stock that I am manipulating goes up on my buying, I know I am all hunky, and if need be I buy it with confidence and use my own money without fear – precisely as I would any other stock that acts the same way. It is the line of least resistance. When the price line of least resistance is established, I follow it, not because I am manipulating that particular stock at that particular moment, but because I am a stock operator at all times.

"When my buying does not put the stock up I stop buying and then proceed to sell it down; and that also is exactly what I would do with that same stock if I did not happen to be manipulating it. The principle marketing of the stock, as you know, is done on the way down. It is perfectly astonishing how much stock a man can get rid of on a decline.

"At no time during the manipulation do I forget to be a stock trader. My problems as a manipulator, after all, are the same that confront me as an operator. All manipulation comes to an end when the stock you are manipulating doesn't act as it should: quit. Don't argue with the tape. Do not seek to lure the profit back. Quit while the quitting is good – and cheap."

Next, Livermore turned his attention to a company called Mexican Petroleum, this time on his own account.

He formed a pool to bet against the future of the oil company, better known on Wall Street as 'Mexican Pete.' Livermore had analyzed Mexican Petroleum and concluded that its oil reserves were not what they were made out to be and that, instead of being positive, were actually negative and running out. He may have been right about the oil reserves, but he had overlooked the cash reserves of the company and its strong cashflow. 'Mexican Pete' paid a generous dividend and had the ability to pay out that dividend for many years to come regardless of what happened to its oil reserves.

Soon the whole of Wall Street was abuzz with news of the deal, and this became its problem. Everyone knew Livermore and his group were short, and seemingly the whole of Wall Street sought to take the opposite side in a market that was generally rising.

At first, Livermore sought to deny that he was involved in shorting Mexican Petroleum at all. But unfortunately he had bought many of his shares at the New York Curb Exchange in person and there were first-hand newspaper accounts of his trading.

His fame was now hindering him, and whenever Livermore appeared at any exchange in person, it was very big news. Reporters and traders hung off his every utterance. One newspaper reported his dealings in 'Mexican Pete' word by word as he bid for $1 million worth of stock in a few hours at the Curb: "Four and five sevenths for 1,000 Mexican – same for another 1,000, sold," wrote one reporter; "In a two hour visit to the exchange, Livermore bid for 10,000 shares and picked up 5,000 shares, nearly a million dollars' worth of stock." So his denials carried little weight when faced with that sort of evidence of his trading.

Livermore and his pool of investors appeared to be trying to create a corner in the shares, which was highly unusual in such a big company. The fact that the attempted corner was public knowledge and the pool had nearly $25 million of shares made it even more unusual.

Whilst the Livermore pool was selling, the price was static, but the bulls were just looking for a break. At the height of the pool's action, Livermore was sleeping in his office at night with his hand firmly on the tiller, countering any concerted buying in Mexican Petroleum with strong selling. He knew he was in the fight of his life and much depended on it.

The break came on June 6th 1922 when the well-known actress Lillian Russell died unexpectedly at the age of 61. Livermore was a close friend of Russell's of 15 years, from the days when they had caroused together in Palm Beach. He couldn't go to the funeral in Pittsburgh but felt he was obliged to attend her memorial service in New York a fortnight later, on June 16th. The bulls got wind of it and laid a trap.

For the whole of the first half of June, Livermore had not left his office during market hours, sleeping on a camp bed, as he monitored the situation minute by minute. Now he adjudged it was safe to go out for a few hours.

When Livermore left to go to the memorial service, which was being held in the New York Hippodrome, a theatre on Sixth Avenue, the bulls got word and fell upon the shares in a buying frenzy. The price went up 8.5 points in an afternoon as they furiously bid up the price.

So instead of falling, as Livermore and his associates expected, the stock rose by 75 points before they had a chance to cover. The following day, Livermore knew the game was up and, ten days later, the pool was down $8.5 million. He had effectively lost control during his fateful absence from his office.

But even after Livermore was beaten, a problem remained. He was short almost the entire float and, as the float was in the hands of the opposing bull pool, he had no choice but to come to terms.

The stock had effectively been cornered by the bulls and there were no shares left on the open market for him to buy. He sought an accommodation and the leaders of the pool on the other side settled with him at $225 a share.

It appears that 20 individuals were involved in the pool, and total losses were $8.5 million. Livermore's share of that loss was $2 million.

Normally, Livermore was open about his losses and would discuss them, but not this one; it was too embarrassing. The pool had been Livermore's idea and he had attracted investors into it. His credibility was on the line especially if the news got out, which it inevitably did.

The whole affair was recorded by newspapers which gleefully reported the huge losses suffered by Livermore's pool of investors.

Livermore was livid, he didn't mind the losses but he did mind the reporting of them. His response the following day was to "deny, deny, deny." He blatantly told The New York Times: "The man who wrote that story must have been inexperienced in the ways of Wall Street not to have given me at least enough sense to have gone short of practically the entire floating supply of the stock. If the man who wrote that story only knew how much Mexican Petroleum I purchased the afternoon I was supposed to have been at the Hippodrome, such stories would not gain circulation."

But the stories were true. He had gone short equivalent to the float of Mexican Petroleum and put himself in a certain losing position. It was a ludicrous place for such an experienced operator like Livermore to find himself. It was the stupidest mistake of his life, and he was totally shocked at his own ineptitude.

His response was to commission a public relations campaign, and he sought to spin the story to one of success for him and his partners. As far as Livermore was concerned, his investments in Mexican Petroleum had shown him and his pool a $2 million profit, and this was the story he put about. It was picked up by some unknowing newspapers across rural America. But insiders in Wall Street knew the truth, and the New York newspapers printed stories that were pretty close to what had really happened.

When the dust settled, Livermore was thoroughly fed up with his performance in the Mexican affair. He decided he needed to get away and take a rest. On August 6th, he sailed with his wife on the liner *Aquitania* for an extended trip to Europe and told his staff he would not be back until September 12th. He realized that nothing was going to happen on the stock market during the summer.

In a bid to rebuild his reputation he actively befriended reporters from *The New York Times* and told them: "The stock market is now passing through a period of midsummer dullness and probably will be for some time." But he left the newspaper in no doubt that America was still gripped in a bull market that would not abate for some time. He predicted that there was an advance of between 50 and 100 points still to be made.

Livermore had big plans for the fall of 1922 and promised to keep his new friends at the *Times* fully up to date with his plans. And indeed he did, as the newspaper faithfully reported his trip to Europe and when he would be home. On July 12th, it reported his plans to be away for a month. On August 4th, it reported he had sailed, and on August 24th reported that he was on his way home aboard the *Olympic* liner.

The charm offensive towards *The New York Times* was alien to his character, but he was desperate to distance himself from the loss of other people's money. He was anxious to build a business and keep his reputation as a savvy operator, although in the case of the manipulation of Mexican Petroleum he had been anything but.

The plan seemed to work because as soon as he was back, Livermore got offered a very big deal indeed. He was appointed to handle the public offering of Mammoth Oil Company by its controlling owner, Harry Sinclair of the Sinclair Pipeline Company.

Mammoth was potentially a very exciting company. On April 7th, the US government had awarded Mammoth a lease for the development of the Teapot Dome oil reserve in Natrona County, Wyoming. Mammoth would develop the oilfield as a partner with the government. It was a plum deal.

Teapot Dome was a US Navy-owned oilfield. In the early 1900s, the US Navy had converted from coal to oil powered ships and the government, under President Taft, had wanted it to have its own independent supplies of oil.

In 1921, without explanation, President Harding reversed that policy and by executive order transferred control of the oilfields from the Navy to the Department of the Interior.

The Interior Secretary was a man called Albert Fall, who almost immediately leased the oil production rights at Teapot Dome to Harry Sinclair. Sinclair formed a new company called Mammoth Oil to exploit the rights. The lease was issued without any competitive bidding, which was supposedly allowed under the Mineral Leasing Act of 1920.

The lease terms were deemed extremely very favorable to Mammoth, and investigations began into the transfer in April 1922. But the investigations were deemed to be routine and had no effect on the flotation in October 1922.

Livermore was ecstatic at getting his first really big deal, and he put every effort into making it a success. The public offering was timed for October 9th. It was a relatively simple sell as the company's only asset was the 9,321 acres of Teapot Dome. Drilling had already started, and nine exploratory wells had struck oil. Mammoth announced grand plans to build oil storage tanks capable of holding 1.6 million barrels of oil. Harry Sinclair said he would build a separate pipeline to get the oil to market. It appeared to be a bonanza for investors with very little risk.

Livermore told The New York Times: "I have thoroughly investigated the properties and I am convinced there is nothing theoretical about the prospects."

Not surprisingly, the flotation was a huge success, and the offering was oversubscribed with the book being closed on the same day of the offering. Interestingly, Livermore did not reveal how many shares had been sold and at what price they had been offered. The first deal on the Curb Exchange was quoted at $43 and 8,000 shares were sold. During the first day's trading, over 40,000 shares were traded and the stock closed at two points down on the opening. Some $1.7 million worth of shares changed hands on the first day. Livermore is believed to have made himself $500,000 from the flotation.

The Mammoth flotation ultimately sparked a Senate Committee investigation in late 1923, and the figures were made public at hearings before the Committee. It was the third investigation in which Livermore had been involved dating from his market activities in 1922. Livermore initially tried to evade a subpoena issued by the committee to appear and was finally served by a US Marshall. His failure to appear caused the hearings to be postponed three times.

At the hearings it emerged that 109,000 shares were allotted at $40, and applications for 151,000 had been received.

The hearings were very enlightening as it was revealed that no shares remained in public hands and they had all been subsequently repurchased by

Harry Sinclair. Livermore testified that ultimately shares worth $10 million had been repurchased by his syndicate at prices between $40 and $56.

Livermore, rather disingenuously, maintained he had made the sum of just $9,916 from his role in the flotation. He maintained throughout that he was an innocent party and there had been no shenanigans. When he was asked by Senator Walsh of Montana why shares had to be repurchased by his syndicate, he replied: "To furnish a stable market. That is why I was retained." Livermore explained that many of the purchasers of the original subscription of shares had been people he described as "professionals" who were certain to sell the stock at the first opportunity for a profit. He stated: "Unless there was a buying agency to take these offerings, the public would have no confidence in the issue."

The senators, collectively, were left bemused by Livermore's answers but he was far too clever for them and tied them up in knots. When one senator attempted to untie the knots and asked about the apparent dual capacity in which Livermore was hired – on the one hand to sell the stock and on the other to buy it back, a seemingly pointless exercise – he said to him: "First, you were a distributor for the stock and then an agent for its recovery." Livermore replied: "Harry Sinclair expressed disappointment over the results of efforts to create a market and said he would rather pocket the loss necessary to regain complete control than to allow a few thousand shares to remain out to be kicked about. He told me to get all outstanding shares for him as cheap as possible." Livermore further explained that in order to maintain an orderly market, he was forced not only to engage in buying during the process but to periodically sell shares as well. He called it "preventing a runaway market".

But then Livermore was undone when evidence was produced by Senator Smoot of Utah that showed Livermore had at one point bought in more shares than actually existed. In fact, it appeared that he had bought a lot of shares that he himself had sold short.

In the end, the Senators just didn't know what to make if it and Livermore wasn't about to enlighten them on the real reasons for the Mammoth floatation and subsequent re-privatization.

It all became academic in 1927 when the Supreme Court took away the licenses from Mammoth Oil, deeming Harry Sinclair had obtained them by fraud. The Teapot Dome scandal became the biggest public corruption affair in US history. An investigating Senate committee, chaired by Senator Robert La Follette of Wisconsin, eventually uncovered a huge fraud by the Secretary of the Interior, Albert Fall.

At the outset La Follette believed Albert Fall to be innocent of any corruption. But then La Follette's office in the Senate building was burgled and ransacked, and he strongly suspected Fall was behind it. So Senator Thomas Walsh of Montana was appointed to lead an inquiry into the affair, which would take two years. Albert Fall proved to be a genius at covering his tracks and records of the transactions kept disappearing, and the inquiry initially concluded that the lease had been awarded legitimately.

But Fall was undone by his growing wealth. Questions began to arise as to why Fall had become so rich, particularly when he purchased a cattle ranch in Montana. When his finances were investigated, it was revealed he had received large sums of money from Sinclair and others.

The Supreme Court cancelled the Teapot Dome lease in October 1927, ruling it had been fraudulently obtained and the oilfield was returned to the Navy. Fall was found guilty of accepting bribes in 1929 and sentenced to a lengthy spell in prison. He was the first cabinet member in history to go to jail. Questions remained, however, as to why President Harding had transferred the oil leases away from the Navy and why it had taken so long to prosecute Fall. And why none of the bribers, including Harry Sinclair, was ever found guilty.

But none of this dented Jesse Livermore, who had long ago made his profits and moved on to other things. But there were other consequences.

Jesse Livermore had so much publicity during 1922 that he was finally hauled in front of a Federal Trade Commission (FTC), which was investigating the effect of speculators like him on the country's stock markets. The Committee of Inquiry, under the auspices of the United States Senate, had become concerned with behavior on Wall Street. It was the second inquiry Livermore had faced in five years. This time, the Senate was particularly interested in commodity trading, something it could relate to more easily than share trading.

The committee was chaired by Victor Murdock, who was also chairman of the FTC. It travelled around the country holding hearings. Initially, Livermore did his familiar disappearing trick unwilling to be questioned again on his activities in the stock market. But finally, on October 6th 1922, Livermore sat in front of the investigators at a public hearing in New York's Federal Building.

He faced a strong grilling from a panel of lawyers about his short selling tactics, which they believed frequently drove share and commodity prices down.

He attempted to defend short selling in the grain markets. Far from being harmful, Livermore argued that short sellers were essential for market harmony. He said short sellers "took up the slack" and kept the market on an even keel. He told the panel: "I am not a gambler. I am a speculative investor."

He went on to describe the way he operated: "The only way to make money in the market is to forecast the future; I must determine what the future will bring. I have a basis for every play I make. Whenever I play, it is because I think from observation and experience that the trend of the market is this way or that."

Livermore described a gambler as something entirely different: "The gambler is the man who walks into a broker's office and asks 'How can I make a thousand dollars quick?' and a clerk suggest this or that stock. The man buys it and then sits back and prays the market will go his way."

During the hearings, Livermore was forced to admit that he would not be able to tell a blade of wheat from oats or any other grain, yet he admitted he had dealt in millions of bushels of both during his lifetime.

The chairman pointedly asked Livermore whether he believed that a farmworker, who typically earned between $5,000 and $10,000 for a lifetime toiling in the fields, lost out because of his short selling. Livermore appreciated the irony of the question but fiercely defended short sellers such as himself. He told the committee: "How would the farmer market his grain if there was no trading on the stock exchange? If there were no exchanges, what would happen when the grain was all harvested and offered for sale? The speculators take up the slack and carry the commodity until such time there is a sale for it."

Chairman Murdock responded to this by asking Livermore: "But you think nothing of selling several hundred thousands of bushels of wheat or something else that you haven't got and never expect to have. Do you think it is right for a man to sell a commodity which he hasn't got and wouldn't know if he saw it?"

Livermore became agitated at this point and rose to his feet to give his answer. He almost shouted "absolutely." Then added more quietly: "You're talking about selling short. Why, every sale in the world has the element of selling short. Suppose I was a big manufacturer and you as a dry goods man wanted to buy a bill of goods from me. I'd sell you the goods wouldn't I? Even if I didn't have them, I'd sell short. As a matter of fact, the men who sell short are the lifesavers of the market on critical days. For instance, when a report of war comes and the market is affected, everyone wants to sell. Who will buy then if it weren't for the shorts? The next day, after rumors straighten things out and everyone wants to buy, the shorts become the salesmen. On the bad days, I tell you, the shorts keep a market from going crazy."

By now, Livermore had the whole committee in a virtual trance and in the palm of his hand. They seemed mesmerized, and as he looked at them, he decided to go for broke: "Several years ago, I went short 50,000 shares of US Steel. Then I went south for a vacation. A few days later, one of those submarine messages hit the market an awful blow. A number of persons offered me thousands of shares of US Steel at eight and ten points off the market. I would have been a fool if I hadn't taken my profit and bought these shares. I was keeping the market steady, for it was only men like myself who were willing to do any buying."

It was a bravura performance and the first and most eloquent explanation and defence of short selling in the world's stock markets, then and since.

But then Livermore ruined it by declaring that stories of operators like him manipulating commodity markets by making corners was a myth. He called such stories "just newspaper talk". He added: "There is no such thing as a bear raid when the market drops. For it wouldn't be profitable to the raiders. So far as group action is concerned, men trading on the stock exchange would not trust each other." Livermore stated that he always played alone and that his operations never influenced the market in any way.

It was total poppycock and not believed by anyone. It completely neutralized his earlier brilliant defence of short selling, and an opportunity was ultimately wasted.

But he was so rich by this time that he really did not care. He held the government pygmies in Washington in utter contempt. He was making so much money so effortlessly that he thought it would never end.

CHAPTER 26

Respectability is Bought

Great Neck House Purchase

1922

After Dorothy Livermore announced to her husband that she was pregnant with their second child in September 1922, Livermore decided that they needed a proper house in the country to permanently escape the heat of the New York summer. Previously they had decamped to Palm Beach, Lake Placid, or Saratoga, or they had rented a house for the summer in Long Island.

With one child and another on the way, Dorothy made it clear to her husband that she would prefer to live permanently out of the city. Livermore agreed, and they both decided they wanted to live on Long Island and set their hearts on living in Great Neck on the North Shore.

Great Neck is a peninsula covering 11.4 square miles set between Manhasset Bay and Little Neck Bay with Kings Point at its furthest reach. It is one of the most ponied areas of New York State, set 16 miles from the centre of Manhattan at the eastern edge of the city, with a population of around 4,000 living across nine suburban villages.

For hundreds of years, before the mid-1800s, Great Neck was an exclusively farming community, supplying vegetables and grain direct to New York City. Excellent rail, road and boat connections were established to Manhattan so the produce was fresh every day. Eventually these fast connections attracted people wanting to escape the fast pace of living in New York. And so, gradually, the vegetables were replaced with people.

Great Neck was gradually gentrified and became a fiefdom of wealthy New Yorkers, initially Jewish traders. It became a very special place, built entirely by new money. Judith Goldstein, who wrote the definitive history of Great Neck, called it: "America's most fascinating suburb."

After the Jews, it became a home away from home for writers and eventually earned itself a reputation as the literary hub of America. After the writers came

229

the actors and the stars of Hollywood and Broadway. Great Neck became part of America's psyche as the fictional setting for F. Scott Fitzgerald's novel *The Great Gatsby*. Goldstein said Great Neck "reflected the tensions, dramas and dreams" of America.

It seemed that only large grand houses were built in Great Neck, especially in the village of Kings Point where the water silently lapped the shore. Amongst those who built houses were automobile barons Walter Chrysler, William Durrant and Alfred Sloan.

The house that caught the eye of Jesse Livermore was on sale through the real estate broker, I. G. Wolf & Co. It was called Augustina at Locust Lawn and was on the market for around $250,000. It was considered a bargain and had cost a rumored $600,000 to build 22 years earlier.

Livermore heard about the house through Walter Chrysler when they were gambling together at the Beach Club in Palm Beach. Chrysler spent a lot of time at the tables and became a great friend of Livermore. One night, he told him he had just bought a house at Great Neck from the fashion designer Henry Bendell. As he described its 12 acres of beautiful waterfront, Livermore became more and more entranced by what he was hearing. Chrysler explained he was currently renovating and had renamed it Forker House. Then he indicated that the house next door was also for sale and said he was worried that the low price might attract the wrong sort of buyer. With that, Livermore's ears pricked up and he asked Chrysler how he would feel about having the Livermore family as his neighbors. Chrysler said he would be mighty pleased if that were to happen. He called over his wife Della, who chatted to Dorothy about the house.

As soon as he got back to New York, Livermore contacted the Long Island office of I. G. Wolf, which had 72 real estate brokers working out of it. One thing led to another and one September morning, the Livermores got on a train at Penn Station. 25 minutes later they alighted at Great Neck Station.

There was great excitement at the offices of I. G. Wolf that the great Jesse Livermore was coming to view a house. The brokers at I. G. Wolf were all over Livermore and his wife when they arrived from Manhattan, and a car took them straight to the property.

The house had originally been built by Senator Thomas Palmer, who represented the state of Michigan. It turned out that Palmer was related to Ed Hutton through his marriage to Elizabeth Merrill. Palmer bought the 11 acres with the prime intention of building a new grand house, principally for his retirement. First he had to demolish the old farmhouse that sat on the site, then he spent $600,000 building the new house and another $100,000 landscaping the gardens. When it was complete, he lived in it with his wife for ten years.

When Palmer died in 1913 at the age of 83, his widow found the house far too big for her to handle and sold it to the developer John Kiser. Kiser had grand plans but in the end decided that the cost of conversion was too high and passed the house onto August Janssen, a well-known New York restaurateur who also was an amateur real estate developer. He renamed the house Augustina, a combination of his name and that of his daughter, Tina. Janssen lived in it for a while but he too found the cost of upkeep too high. The house needed an owner with very deep pockets, and one was soon found.

The Georgian style colonial house was located at the best position on Kings Point Road. The house was approached from the road by a graded blue stone driveway that circled in front of the magnificent porticoed front elevation.

As soon as the car entered the driveway, both Livermores knew it was exactly what they had been looking for. The location and the seashore set an idyllic scene, and they fell in love.

The 11-acre grounds were entirely landscaped and rose in a gentle slope over wide sweeping lawns, commanding a magnificent view of Long Island Sound across to the shores of Connecticut.

The house was built of brick and limestone topped with a natural slate roof and four huge double chimneys. At the back, there was a full-length canopied terrace with stone steps down to the lawns and shrubs and bushes in front. There was also a side terrace that surrounded the loggia. Both terraces were fully tiled with beautiful granite balustrades.

Inside the house, visitors were greeted by an imposing entrance hall. There were only three reception rooms but they were all huge. They consisted of a drawing room, a dining room and the loggia, latterly used as a billiard room. There was a full-size kitchen and laundry room. The rest of the ground floor was made up of servants' rooms.

Upstairs there were eight bedrooms, each with an en-suite bathroom. There was a separate nursery with its own bathroom. There were also six servants' bedrooms

The house had been built with a full size basement, which contained a bar, recreation/leisure room and, a proper hairdressing salon complete with resident barber.

The separate stucco style garage block could take four large cars at ground floor level. On the first floor were seven rooms, which consisted of a flat for the chauffeur and the resident caretaker. The garage block had also been fireproofed by Senator Palmer so that if one of his cars caught fire, not uncommon in those days, the house would be safe.

The landscaped gardens were tended to by a team of gardeners and were described as "manicured" in I. G. Wolf's brochure. They contained masses of maple, oak, blue spruce and pine trees.

The prime feature was the magnificent 450-foot water frontage to Long Island Sound. The house was separated from the water by grass first and then by a narrow private sandy beach. Attached was a hefty concrete and steel pier that could accommodate a 200-foot yacht and two secondary jetties for smaller boats. There was also a wet boathouse and numerous outbuildings.

The house came complete with a staff of servants, a butler and housekeepers, plus a flock of gardeners. More to the point, they could move in straightaway, and when August Janssen agreed to throw in much of the furniture and fittings for the $250,000 asking price, the deal was as good as done.

Livermore did not even bother with a survey or to haggle the price. He simply said "yes."

One of the attractions for Livermore was the road and rail links to Manhattan. The house was three miles from Great Neck Station, which connected to the city via the Long Island Railroad. Road connections were also superb, and he could be chauffeured into his office every day. There was also the option for Livermore to sail his new yacht, the *Athero II*, then in the design stage, into Manhattan direct from the pier at the bottom of the garden to a jetty on the East River at 26th Street.

Within three quarters of an hour of leaving his house he could be at his office at 111 Broadway by car, train or fast boat.

As soon as the purchase was approved and the keys handed over, the Livermores set out on an extravagant restoration of the house that would ultimately cost more than $1 million. The main objective of the restoration was to install every modern convenience that was available in 1922. The house was completely electrified and all the electrics upgraded to provide modern lighting and floor level electrical sockets. In the basement, Livermore installed three giant oil burners fed by an outside fuel tank. One boiler took care of the heating, another hot water for baths and the third was for the kitchens and sinks. Livermore swore to his wife that they would never ever run out of hot water, one of the main bugbears of wealthy people in the early 1900s when running hot water was the number one luxury in America. Huge commercial fridges were installed in the rooms off the kitchen.

The kitchen staff was upgraded to four people to make and serve food. Livermore ordered his wife to hold two dinner parties a week so they could get to know their well-to-do neighbors. He told Dorothy that she and her staff were totally in charge of entertaining, and he wanted to do it on a large scale.

Finally, they renamed the house 'Evermore' in celebration of their own relationship.

At last they felt like a proper family, and when young Paul arrived a few months later, the newly decorated nursery complete with nanny was waiting for him.

The renovation of the house was an ongoing project, and Dorothy was assisted by her mother, Reena. When they had decided the color scheme for a room, Livermore approved it and wrote out a check to pay for it. This went on for months. There was no budgeting and Dorothy and her mother just assumed there was unlimited money to do the job. And they assumed correctly.

When the refurbishment was complete, the two women started a buying spree for furniture and *objets d'art* that defied any comparison. $305,000 of jade ornaments were purchased to display in the public rooms; then $200,000 worth of silverware and $110,000 on furniture, some of it Chippendale.

The new house also gave Livermore the opportunity for the first time to indulge his love of firearms. He had always owned a small collection of weapons, but now he could let rip and really enjoy himself. He started buying guns until his collection had over 150 in it. But he was not satisfied with it just being a static collection.

He decided that Evermore was big enough for him to build a firing range. So he excavated a long trench right by the beach at the left hand side of the house. It was dug out between the end of the lawns and the beginning of the sand. He brought a mechanical digger in to excavate down over seven feet and made the trench 112 feet long. Old railway sleepers were shipped in and mounted vertically to line the trench from beginning to end. At the end, a two-inch thick steel plate was placed with railway sleepers in front to prevent ricochets. The whole family learned to shoot and all became proficient, particularly his son Paul who picked up a gun when he was three years old for the first time and eventually became a crack shot to Olympic standard. He also purchased a clay pigeon rack that he used to shoot over Long Island Sound.

One of his other jobs was to extend the 200-foot jetty by another 50 feet and reinforce it so it could cope with his new yacht. His new yacht, *Athero II*, when it arrived from the shipyard in Boston, would be moored at the specially extended jetty. He also bought a new Chris-Craft runabout that was capable of taking him to Manhattan if he felt like enduring the sometimes rough sea voyage.

Gradually, Evermore became the Livermore family playground, outfitted with no regard to the cost. His wife, her mother and his children lived a life wanting nothing and having every whim attended to by servants. It was not the best way to raise a family, but it was the only way Jesse Livermore knew. The eventual repercussions would be horrific, but for now no one cared.

For the next seven years, the Livermores were deliriously happy as Dorothy tended to her family and Jesse built up his business in New York. It was the best of times.

CHAPTER 27

The Piggly Wiggly Affair

Another day, another controversy

1923

At the beginning of 1923, Jesse Livermore got involved in yet another controversial operation in the stock market when he was approached by a southern gentleman from Memphis called Clarence Saunders. Saunders, a rotund 41-year-old, was one of the American business geniuses of the age.

Clarence Saunders had left school at 14 and done various small time jobs. At 19 he went to work for a wholesale grocer, earning $8 a week. Two years later, he set up his own wholesale grocery operation. It became a huge learning operation as he sought to refine the art of food retailing. In 1919 he switched his principal operations from wholesaling to retailing when he opened the first self-service store in the world, curiously called the Piggly Wiggly Store.

Piggly Wiggly was a phenomenon, a revolution not seen before or since in US retailing. It grew like topsy into a chain of retail self-service stores situated mostly in the south and west, with its headquarters in Memphis. In June 1922, barely three years after it started, Piggly Wiggly went public on Wall Street and issued 200,000 shares. Clarence Saunders became a very wealthy man. He bought himself a huge plot of land in Memphis and built a pink marble mansion, nicknamed locally as the Pink Palace.

After the flotation of Piggly Wiggly Stores Inc, Saunders proceeded to sell franchises to would-be grocery retailers across America. In the process, he became the first man to create a national franchise operation. He was helped by the fact that in 1917 he had had the foresight to patent his concept of a 'self-serving store'. Whether the patent could be upheld seemed irrelevant; entrepreneurs flocked to buy a franchise.

The self-service system was certainly unique for its time. In a Piggly Wiggly store, customers entered through a turnstile and walked between four aisles, organized into departments. Crammed into those four long aisles were 600 items, mostly packaged goods, then itself a relatively new concept. Every item was clearly priced, which was another first. The customers selected goods on the way and put them in a wicker basket provided by the store. Eventually, walking through a wooden railed maze, they ended up at a cashier who checked the goods out and packed them in the customers' own bags. And what's more, the customers preferred the experience to the traditional counter service grocery store.

The success and growth of Piggly Wiggly was unprecedented, so much so that many other independent and chain grocery stores changed to self-service in the 1920s.

By 1923, Piggly Wiggly had over 2,000 stores across America and nearly $200 million in annual sales.

But Saunders was never destined to be remembered for his real legacy as the man who started self-service shopping. Today, he is remembered as the last man to run a corner in a publicly listed company.

It all started in late November 1922, when a group of bears formed a pool to drive down Piggly Wiggly's stock. The bears seemed to believe, against all available evidence, that Piggly Wiggly was not the growth company it had been portrayed as and was overvalued. But it was all a mistake. The bears had got it confused with a company with a similar sounding name. It turned out a small group of franchised stores in the East had gone into receivership over real estate-related problems. The stores had no financial connection with the publicly quoted Piggly Wiggly, their demise had been purely the result of some bad real estate deals on the stores.

The bear raid surprised and enraged Saunders and, in response, he began to buy in his own shares in order to protect the value of his own holdings and those of other Piggly Wiggly stockholders, many of whom were his close friends and family.

But he quickly realized that as much as he understood retailing, he was out of this depth in the stock market. So he called in Jesse Livermore to help.

Saunders asked Livermore to form a buying pool to get the price of the shares up and to keep them up. It was exactly the sort of job Livermore relished. He advised Saunders that he should sponsor a secondary public offering and appoint Livermore to handle that as well.

Livermore assured Saunders that it was his area of expertise, and Saunders was soon persuaded to grant the persuasive Livermore *carte blanche* to handle it and see off the bears. He was perfectly suited to the task.

Livermore recounted how the Piggy Wiggly deal came to be done in his fictional biography *Reminiscences of a Stock Operator*: "Assume that there is an individual that has a block of stock which it is desired to sell at the best price possible. It is a stock duly listed on the New York Stock Exchange. The best place for selling it ought to be the open market, and the best buyer ought to be the general public. The negotiations for the sale are in charge of a man. He – or some present or former associate – has tried to sell the stock on the Stock Exchange and has not succeeded. He is – or soon becomes – sufficiently familiar with stock-market operations to realize that more experience and greater aptitude for the work are needed than he possesses. He knows personally or by hearsay several men who have become successful in their handling of similar deals, and he decides to avail himself of their professional skill. He seeks one of them as he would seek a physician if he were ill or an engineer if he needed that kind of expert.

"Suppose he has heard of me as a man who knows the game. Well, I take it that he tries to find out all he can about me. He then arranges for an interview, and in due time calls at my office.

"Of course, the chances are that I know about the stock and what it represents. It is my business to know. That is how I make my living. My visitor tells me what he and his associates wish to do, and asks me to undertake the deal.

"It is then my turn to talk. I ask for whatever information I deem necessary to give me a clear understanding of what I am asked to undertake. I determine the value and estimate the market possibilities of that stock. That and my reading of current conditions in turn help me to gauge the likelihood of success for the proposed operations."

Livermore also negotiated himself an exceptional deal for running the pool to get the share price up where it should be. He would get a 20 per cent share of the value of the uplift of the shares that were in public hands.

He considered himself very skillful in negotiating such deals as he explained in *Reminiscences*: "If my information inclines me to a favorable view, I accept the proposition and tell him then and there what my terms will be for my services. If he in turn accepts my terms – the honorarium and the conditions – I begin my work at once.

"I generally ask and receive calls on a block of stock. I insist upon graduated calls as the fairest to all concerned. The price of the call begins at a little below the prevailing market price and goes up; say, for example, that I get calls on one hundred thousand shares and the stock is quoted at 40. I begin with a call for some thousands of shares at 35, another at 37, another at 40, and at 45 and 50, and so on up to 75 or 80.

If, as a result of my professional work – my manipulation – the price goes up, and if at the highest level there is a good demand for the stock so that I can sell fair-sized blocks of it, I of course call the stock. I am making money; but so are my clients making money. This is as it should be. If my skill is what they are paying for, they ought to get value."

As soon as the terms were agreed, Livermore sent some of his young analysts on the train to Memphis and told them to go through the books, visit Piggly Wiggly stores and talk to customers and staff. The young men returned to New York gushing about Saunders and talking up the company's prospects. Instead of being overvalued, the young men told Livermore the company was seriously undervalued. This was all he wanted to hear.

Livermore immediately sensed what had happened and that the bears had somehow got this one wrong. There was already the sense of a bull market and Piggly Wiggly was a highly successful and undervalued company – what could go wrong?

Livermore explained in *Reminiscences* how he would sort the problem out: "The first step in a bull movement in a stock is to advertise the fact that there is a bull movement on. Sounds silly, doesn't it? Well, think a moment. It isn't as silly as it sounded, is it? The most effective way to advertise what, in effect, are your honorable intentions is to make the stock active and strong. After all is said and done, the greatest publicity agent in the wide world is the ticker, and by far the best advertising medium is the tape. I do not need to put out any literature for my clients. I do not have to inform the daily press as to the value of the stock or to work the financial reviews for notices about the company's prospects. Neither do I have to get a following. I accomplish all these highly desirable things by merely making the stock active. When there is activity, there is a synchronous demand for explanations; and that means, of course, that the necessary reasons – for publication – supply themselves without the slightest aid from me."

To put his plan into action, he advised Saunders to borrow $10 million against the value of his own holdings from a consortium of banks. Livermore advised Saunders to form a separate company he called Piggly Wiggly Investment Company Inc to handle the operation.

Livermore told Saunders he saw this as an easy assignment. He knew Piggly Wiggly was an excellent investment, and with $10 million at his disposal, he knew he could not fail to really push the stock up. As he said: "I make the stock active in order to draw the attention of speculators to it. I buy it and I sell it and the traders follow suit. The selling pressure is not apt to be strong where a man has as much speculatively held stock sewed up – in calls – as I insist on having. The buying, therefore, prevails over the selling, and the public follows the lead not so much of the manipulator as of the room traders. It comes in as a buyer. This highly desirable demand I fill – that is, I sell stock on balance."

But he must have questioned his own philosophy as he managed to buy half of the outstanding float within two weeks and the prevailing price of $42 rose only 15 per cent as the bears kept selling. Livermore was surprised and he had intended to stop there. But when the price hardly moved, he was forced to carry on and ended up buying a lot more stock than he had intended. But it worked, and as he kept buying, the bears broke and the price suddenly doubled to $80.

In the process, the outstanding float was reduced to barely anything.

Within the month, Livermore had pushed the once-moribund shares from $42 to $125 as the bears were routed. On one glorious day, Tuesday March 20th, as the early spring sun shone on Wall Street, Piggly Wiggly shares jumped $52 as bears panicked and sought to buy in stock they had earlier sold short. *The New York Times* reported: "Fully one-third of the brokers on the floor were crowded about the Piggly Wiggly post."

At the end of the day, it emerged that Livermore's campaign had brought in 198,872 shares on behalf of Saunders at an average price of around $70. Livermore had spent nearly $14 million and, by now, Saunders himself was overstretched.

But it wasn't enough for Clarence Saunders, who now smelled the blood in the water. That Tuesday, some of the bears had been flushed out and taken their losses. But many still remained, almost taunting Saunders. Saunders was determined to have the ultimate revenge on the remaining bears; he wanted to bankrupt them and destroy them totally. For him, it became personal. He virtually ordered Livermore to corner the shares. Saunders said: "I want to beat Wall Street professionals at their own game."

Livermore, for once, cautioned against such a plan. He had realized that the original bear raid on Piggly Wiggly had been a mistake and that the bears now realized that they had been confused by a company with a similar name. Saunders and Livermore had a disagreeable conversation on the telephone, after which they agreed to disagree. Livermore later heard that Saunders had been bad-mouthing him and his methods.

So on the evening of Sunday March 11th, Livermore phoned Saunders at his home in Memphis and asked him to get on the train on Monday morning and come to New York for a crisis meeting

When Saunders arrived at Livermore's office on Monday morning he immediately showed him a copy of a letter he said he had written to him on Saturday. The letter said that Livermore was resigning the account. He told Saunders he had no desire to bankrupt people who were his friends. He also tackled Saunders about reports of what bad mouthing he had heard. Saunders was taken aback by Livermore's resignation and told him firmly that his reports were wrong.

At 11 o'clock that morning, it was announced to the stock exchange that Livermore and Saunders had parted company. Afterwards Livermore issued a statement through his lawyer confirming he was resigning the account but giving no reasons. Later Saunders told *The New York Times*: "Mr Livermore gave as his reason in his letter for terminating suddenly and without warning his relationship with me that he understood I had made some statements reflecting his character and his handling of the market operations for me. But it appeared that after he wrote the letter, he had changed his mind about these reports."

The relatively stable market that Livermore had provided for the shares instantly disappeared after he resigned and a degree of panic ensued. Curiously Livermore, for reasons best known to himself, later put out a statement saying that he had been sacked by Saunders. He told friends it was to protect his contractual position with Saunders who owed him hundreds of thousands of dollars in fees.

Then the mystery deepened. Rumors abounded that Livermore and his associate, Frank Bliss, a veteran Wall Street trader, had sold shares short themselves and had a dual interest in the outcome.

With Livermore gone, Saunders was determined to press on and destroy the bears. He almost succeeded in his objective. He controlled almost the entire 200,000 shares float outstanding and then he publicly asked the short sellers to deliver the shares he had bought. He said he would let them buy back the stock at $150. He set a deadline of three o'clock on Thursday 23rd March. If the bears did not deliver the shares they had sold him, he declared that his price after three o'clock would be $250.

Saunders believed that the bears owed him 25,000 shares and that another

20,000 were owed to others. He told *The New York Times*: "More than 25,000 shares, even with the extra day allowed, are short to me on delivery. And there are still thousands of additional shares due on marginal accounts to others which must be liquidated in the settlement."

Saunders was on a crusade to punish Wall Street, and he declared: "As long as I live, I will not be president of any company again that has its stock traded on the New York Stock Exchange where the gambler and the speculator have such free rein to ply their trade."

The bears needed $7.5 million to buy back shares they had sold, and they faced losses of around $4 million. There were no shares left in the open market for them to buy, and they had to come to Saunders who held all the aces.

Saunders believed he had the bears by the neck that night and explained his rationale to the *New York Times*: "It was strictly a question of whether I should survive and likewise my business and the fortunes of my friends or whether I should be licked and pointed to as a boob from Tennessee."

It had turned out that Clarence Saunders was no boob, and until he attempted the corner of his own company's shares, he had never even purchased a single share in his life.

But he couldn't have foreseen the reaction of the Business Conduct Committee of the New York Stock Exchange. It suddenly suspended trading in Piggly Wiggly, pending an investigation. Worse, they allowed rumors that the shares were to be suspended to percolate through the market for at least half an hour before the announcement, which saw the shares drop to $85 on the day from a high of $124. Saunders lost some $30 million on paper, but in reality he was left holding shares worth $17 million against a loan of $10 million. But he could no longer sell the shares.

Bears were left needing to buy some 50,000 shares but with no shares to buy. The suspension froze the situation and gave the bears some breathing space. Saunders, who originally believed he could wrest $20 million in profit from the bears, was potentially in trouble if the shares were not allowed to trade again quickly.

The Stock Exchange committee was in an invidious position. It was faced with 50,000 more shares being sold than actually existed. It was the first time that had occurred, and it circled the wagons to protect its own against the outsider.

The New York Times reported it so: "It is understood that it was found by the Business Conduct Committee as a result of this investigation that there was not sufficient stock available to satisfy the requirement of a normal market."

Initially, Saunders and his lawyer, E. W. Bradley, co-operated with the Committee and agreed that the shares could be suspended temporarily. But the suspension, lifted eventually, proved to be longer than they imagined – and longer than they could hold out as the bankers put them under pressure to repay loans, now secured by an illiquid stock.

By now Saunders owed $14 million to his bankers and yet could not get delivery of the shares he had bought because of the suspension. The banks he owed money to panicked and started selling off his stock on the unofficial market and the price dropped. The bears took advantage of lower prices to buy in the stock to deliver to Saunders, which he had to pay for. And so a downward spiral began.

When all the shares had been bought and sold, Saunders owed his bankers $6 million and was eventually forced to declare personal bankruptcy and resign as chairman of Piggly Wiggly Stores Inc.

The stock market historian Robert Sobel summed it up well when he said: "It is fitting that the first major corner of the 1920s bull market began with a Livermore-Bliss victory, the wreck of a business man, an avoidance of responsibility on the part of the Exchange – all in connection with a stock named after a pig."

After the dust settled, the role of Jesse Livermore was seen as having echoes of what had happened to Walter Lewisohn. Most people concluded that Livermore and his associate Frank Bliss had behaved less than honorably in the end.

Piggly Wiggly was described by Jon Markman, author of the annotated edition of *Reminiscences of a Stock Operator*, as: "One of Livermore's most notorious operations."

Livermore shrugged it off as just one of those things. He did not blame himself but the naïveté of his client towards the stock market: "Of course, there are times when a pool may be wound up at a loss, but that is seldom, for I do not undertake the work unless I see my way clear to a profit. This year I was not so fortunate in one or two deals, and I did not make a profit. There are reasons, but that is another story."

As for Clarence Saunders, he was never the same again. He started two more chains of shops but his innovatory talent was gone and the market had moved on. They both failed. He was forced to sell off the Pink Palace and the surrounding lands. The mansion was purchased by the local council, and developers snapped up the surrounding land. It became the famous residential estate called Chickasaw Gardens.

As a consequence of all this Clarence Saunders never got the credit he deserved for inventing the self-service supermarket and considerably improving the lot of America's housewives. His name and his achievements have been forgotten.

It was a sorry end to a sorry tale.

CHAPTER 28

Legendary Status Is Conferred
Publication of fictional biography

1923

Jesse Livermore's return from the Wall Street dead and his amassing of a new stock market fortune of $8 million conferred on him a kind of legendary status. In 1915, he had been down and out and officially bankrupted with barely a cent to his name. Seven years later, he was one of the biggest movers and shakers on the street and revered by fellow traders. So much so that he was approached by a reporter called Edwin Lefèvre who wanted to write his biography. The thought of a biography of his life appalled Livermore, who was nonetheless flattered at the approach especially by such an esteemed journalist as Lefèvre. Rather than turning Lefèvre down flat, Livermore deflected the request and prevaricated. He resolved to get to know Lefèvre better.

Lefèvre was arguably the leading journalist writing about Wall Street. The 50 year old was renowned for his writing prowess. Trained as a mining engineer when he graduated, he immediately went into journalism, which led him to a career in stock broking, where he focused his writing on Wall Street. Lefèvre was unique because he wrote financial fiction as well as non-fiction, seemingly moving effortlessly between the two.

When his father died unexpectedly, he inherited a sizeable fortune that he invested himself, turning it into an even bigger fortune consisting of a portfolio of shares. As a consequence of managing his own portfolio and his work as a stockbroker, Lefèvre became intrigued at how stocks and shares rose and fell. He found he made as much money if he left the portfolio alone as he did when he actively managed it. So he left it alone and became a full time writer.

In 1901, he had a collection of short stories published called *Wall Street Stories*. From that, he went into fiction and used Wall Street as his subject. He was fascinated by people like Livermore and the other Wall Street titans of the age such as Pierpont Morgan, E. H. Harriman and the like. He liked to say the two big motivations of Wall Street were "love and greed" and that it was the meeting place of the "greed stricken." No one disagreed with his assessment.

By 1908, he was making considerable amounts of money from both his writing and his share portfolio. So much so that he and his wife Martha moved to a large country estate in East Dorset, Vermont.

Then came his big moment in life. Still aged under 40, Lefèvre's writing attracted the attention of the newly-elected President Taft, who appointed him as a US Ambassador. In 1919, Lefèvre went to Europe to serve in France, Spain and Italy for four years. They were four fantastic years. But his diplomatic career was suddenly cut short when Taft, a Republican, failed to be elected for a second term of office and was put out by Woodrow Wilson, a democrat. Wilson had no need for Lefèvre's services and so he returned to writing, briefly working for the *New York Sun* newspaper. He also resumed writing books, and that led him to Jesse Livermore's door.

A few months later, Livermore turned down Lefèvre's idea of a biography, saying he could not possibly reveal the stories of his career and name names. But he did suggest to Lefèvre that he might attempt a fictional biography where all the names, including his own, were altered and disguised but which would otherwise be a true story of his life and, as far as possible, in his own words.

Lefèvre was intrigued but was not quite sure it would work. So he initially suggested they collaborate on a series of magazine pieces along the lines Livermore had suggested. The series of articles were published in 1922 in *The Saturday Evening Post*. The 12 articles were a big success, written in first person fiction telling the story of a share trader on Wall Street called Larry Livingston, who was really the embodiment of Jesse Livermore. Few people realized it was the life of Livermore at the time.

The articles became the basis of the book and the two men agreed to co-operate to publish what eventually became *Reminiscences of a Stock Operator*.

Lefèvre had no problem finding a publisher. He was a personal friend of George Doran, founder of the George H. Doran Company of New York. Doran was one of the most successful publishers in America. The firm had been started in Toronto in 1908 and moved to New York a few years later. Doran quickly built it up to be one of the biggest book publishers in the country. He specialized in British authors and published P. G. Wodehouse, Arthur Conan-Doyle, Somerset Maugham and Virginia Woolf. Doran was also the first port of call for former American ambassadors writing their memoirs – hence Lefèvre's connection with the firm.

When Lefèvre first presented the idea, Doran was worried about the possible legal implications. He insisted on meeting Livermore personally. Any doubts that Doran may have had were dispelled when they met. Livermore readily agreed to put aside his legal rights with respect to the book and signed a full waiver. He gave his permission for publication in writing and also pledged his wholehearted support for the project

But despite that, Doran privately said he did not have particularly high hopes for the book, which he described as "eccentric". But he was also clever enough to know that in publishing, no one really knew anything.

Reminiscences of a Stock Operator was published on May 25th 1923. Surprisingly, it attracted little attention at the time and was not considered the great classic it is now, possibly because people doubted its veracity and assumed that Lefèvre, with his reputation for fiction, had simply made it up. No major newspaper reviewed it. Livermore was particularly upset when *The New York Times* chose to ignore its publication and did not review it. Apparently the owner of *The New York Times*, Adolph Ochs, also believed that it had been made up by Lefèvre and ordered his editors to leave it alone.

Less than a thousand copies of the first edition were printed and it had no separate dust jacket. It was bound in an insipid beige-yellow cloth that the printer had lying around in his factory. The 299-page book had a cover price of $2.50.

It was described inside as not just being a novelized memoir, but rather the most acute commentary of stock market speculation ever written; essential reading for the professionals and also for anyone foolhardy enough to try to ride the tails of the professionals.

The finished book was padded out from the 12 articles into 24 chapters and was rather a mish mash – some episodes were an extraordinary retelling of Livermore's derring-do on Wall Street but others were rambling accounts of stock market techniques and personal opinions. The last half dozen chapters, for instance, were not related to Livermore at all and were taken from previous articles that Lefèvre had written about share manipulation and were then adapted to the style of the book.

The book was told in the first person and, aside from the last six chapters, contained almost certainly all of Livermore's words, deciphered by Lefèvre. The difference in the quality of the writing in the chapters was quite stark. But that didn't seem to matter, and the first thousand copies were quickly snapped up by eager buyers as word got around.

Readers were ensnared by the truthfulness of the narrator, who didn't hold back about his own lack of competence, poor judgment and self-inflicted misfortunes.

Despite the relative lack of publicity, a second edition was quickly rushed out by Doran and, this time, some money was spent making it look good. The cloth binding was changed to a pleasant shade of green and over 2,000 were run off. Some additional money was found for a proper dust jacket designed with black text on a green card. The strap line described the book as "The inside story of the stock market and the man who found a 'system' that worked." The dust cover also called Livermore, or rather Livingston, "The greatest speculator of the century." The publisher said he was "The first operator of such magnitude to tell the secret of his success and of others' failures." It described how Livermore drew a "sharp distinction between gambling and intelligent planned speculation."

The second edition also sold out quickly and a third run was planned, this time with 4,000 copies. The same design and binding was used but this time the book was published under the imprint of Doubleday Doran. Doran often collaborated with Doubleday until the two companies merged in 1927, making Doubleday Doran the biggest book publisher in the English language.

Despite the book's success, *The New York Times* continued to ignore it but that didn't stop it becoming arguably the most enduring of any book written about Wall Street. Of the eight books written by Lefèvre, it is easily his best known and has become a classic of American business writing.

The book's sales were adjudged a big success and prompted Edwin Lefèvre to collaborate on another fictionalized biography of a Wall Street figure told in the same way. It was called *The Making of a Stock Broker*, and the 341-page book was published in July 1925. The stockbroker was called John Wing. It was thought to be a thinly disguised pseudonym for John Prentiss, a retired broker. It was also published by the George H. Doran Company.

The book was well received but not a best seller in the way that *Reminiscences* had become. But *The New York Times*, finally realizing its mistake in ignoring *Reminiscences*, published a full-page review of *The Making of a Stock Broker*. But it didn't help the poor sales.

Reminiscences easily outsold Lefèvre's new book. Doran published another edition in 1930 and again in 1931 to capitalize on the publicity Livermore received after the 1929 crash.

Even after sales tailed off, the book refused to die. In 1938, it was licensed by a firm called Sun Dial Press Inc and a new smart hardback edition published. In 1947, Doubleday & Company re-launched the book afresh.

After that, there were regular reprints as the copyright was passed to Livermore's son, Paul.

Reminiscences is the only one of Edwin Lefèvre's books that has endured, and regular new editions are still published 90 years later as every generation of new share traders catch up with the book. No one knows how many editions have now been published, but at least half a million copies have now been sold.

CHAPTER 29

Big Office, Big Staff & Big Money

Move into the big time of Wall Street

1923 - 1924

In March 1923, Jesse Livermore achieved one of his dreams and moved out of his relatively pokey offices in the Trinity Building into the 18th floor of the Heckscher Building, one of the most prestigious office blocks in Manhattan.

Livermore deliberately moved downtown as he wanted to be away from the hullabaloo and distractions of Wall Street. He found no advantages to being close to the action of the stock exchange and many benefits of being away from it.

The 26-storey Heckscher Building at 730 Fifth Avenue was close to the Plaza Hotel right in the centre of Manhattan at the southwest corner between 56th and 57th Street, adjacent to Park Avenue. There was arguably not a finer office building, or a better located one, in New York.

The building was named after its developer, August Heckscher. Heckscher had come to the United States from Germany in 1867 and made his money in mining. He had intended to retire but became interested in real estate development and, in 1913, bought two old mansions formerly owned by William Whitney and Charles Morse on Fifth Avenue. He demolished both houses to take advantage of the recent New York zoning laws that had been passed in 1916.

In a completely speculative build, he hired the famous architect Charles Wetmore of Warren & Wetmore and gave him a free hand. It was the last office building to be designed in the old style before art deco took over as the style of the time.

The finished building was symmetrically perfect and someone described it as a series of perfect boxes placed on top of each other with only ledges separating them. It was distinctive and effective and crowned with three smaller floors at the top and a mini spire with extensive gilded ornamentation.

The architects actually placed a concrete crown on the top, and today, as a consequence, it is known as the Crown Building.

It topped out at 416 feet high and, afterwards, a 12-foot rooster weathervane was erected, making a total height of 428 feet. In a finishing touch, Wetmore installed three gilded female statues above the entrance in three separate aligned recesses. Below that 'The Heckscher Building' was carved out of the stone and gilded. The building, which formally opened in 1921, was interesting because it had no lobby. The ground floor was given over to showrooms, which were leased exclusively by the famous Miller shoe store.

Like any new building in a prime position, the rents were set high and the lease terms onerous. It took some time to lease the floors, and there were plenty of floors available when Jesse Livermore came looking. He decided instantly this was where he wanted to be and paid the premium rent being asked and signed the onerous lease without hesitation.

Livermore decided that the Heckscher Building would be his home away from home and had to be fitted out as such. He wanted the scale and grandeur of his house at Great Neck to be reflected in his offices, where he would probably spend more of his time.

The 18th floor was bare concrete and ready for fitting out to a tenant's specification. Livermore wanted the office to be designed to his exact specification, to be built around his trading needs. Half of the floor would be taken up by the trading area. Principally he wanted a trading floor that would revolve around him and be totally dedicated to the making of money. Livermore asked the famed architect William Lamb to design the new offices of J. L. Livermore & Company. It was not a given that Lamb would accept the brief. The 30 year old was a prodigy who had started designing buildings in 1911 at the age of only 18.

He had learned his trade at the fabled architectural practice of Carrère & Hastings. It was arguably New York's most prestigious practice of architects and had been founded by John Carrère and Tom Hastings. Both men had graduated from the École Nationale Supérieure des Beaux-Arts in Paris and practiced the Beaux-Arts form of design that came to dominate New York architectural design in the twenties, including the extraordinary New York Public Library.

William Lamb returned from Paris after also gaining a diploma at the École, and it seemed that every practice in New York wanted to hire him. He chose Carrère & Hastings because of the Paris connection, and it promised him a fast track to partnership.

Almost as soon as he arrived at the firm, John Carrère was killed in an automobile accident and Lamb was from then on destined to succeed him. In 1920, he did. When Tom Hastings retired, Lamb and two existing partners, Rich Shreve and Teddy Blake, succeeded him and changed the firm's name to Shreve, Lamb & Blake.

Livermore wooed Lamb with all the charm he possessed. Initially, Lamb told him it was too small a job, but Livermore persisted and told him he wanted him to create the most fabulous office floor ever seen in New York. Livermore told Lamb if he could design the perfect trading floor, it would lead to other commissions for New York's top merchant banks.

William Lamb found it hard to resist the full Jesse Livermore charm offensive and he finally succumbed and set to work. Although he had been reluctant to accept, it was the sort of brief that he really relished, where he could use his full creativity with money virtually no object. As part of the wooing process, Livermore reputedly told Lamb to "fit the floor out first, and set the budget afterwards."

Lamb took the project very seriously, working long into the evenings in late 1922 to satisfy Livermore's demanding brief. His model makers built a scale model in *papier mâché* and clay, never before done for an interior.

Livermore agreed to pay Lamb the staggering sum of $200,000 for the interior design, normally the fee for a whole building. Livermore's only instruction to Lamb was that his design should employ state of the art security. The fit out would eventually cost the staggering sum of $500,000, at that time the most ever spent on an office floor in New York. For his own office, Livermore apparently bought the entire oak paneling of the drawing room of an English manor house and had it expensively shipped over to New York.

When he saw the model, Livermore loved it and changed hardly anything. Lamb's design specified wood paneling throughout and, as was the fashion, the latest wall-to-wall carpeting that hardly anyone chose for offices back then. He also specified floor to ceiling doors throughout. When it was approved, Lamb set the builders to work and within five months it was ready for him to move into. It was completed in the first few months of 1923.

The offices were accessed through a windowless anteroom that was manned by Livermore's personal assistant, Harry Dache, who controlled all access to the building. A corridor led off to the private offices, including Livermore's on the east side of the floor and the trading floor which ran almost the length of the building on the west side.

The front door of the office bore no company name and the concierge would deny the existence of J. L. Livermore & Company to casual enquirers. Only those people on a daily list were allowed access to the lobby and allowed to go up in the lift. At the lift door, visitors were greeted by Harry Dache who kept the key to the main offices in a locked cabinet in the anteroom.

The trading floor was state of the art for the time, with dozens of tickers fed by direct telegraph lines to all the world's major stock and commodity exchanges. There were also direct telephone lines to the 20 or so brokers that Livermore used as well as feeds from all the news wires.

Livermore spent over $35,000 installing the communications facilities, which were then state of the art and the best in the world. All in all, there were over 80 phone lines, 60 direct telegraphs and 40 odd ticker machines installed on the 18th floor. In the middle of the trading floor was an over large conference table so Livermore could hold meetings and keep up with his trading.

Livermore employed approximately 60 people. They were made up of around 20 of the brightest people he could find out of America's top universities. They were lured on the promise that they could trade alongside and directly assist the great Jesse Livermore. A third of the staff were statisticians and the other third back up staff, including secretaries and clerks and the board boys.

The general manager hired to run the office day-to-day was Walter McNerney.

Livermore's trading floor became the centre of all his commercial activity, and his chair and desk in the middle of the floor was a cacophony of wires and telephone receivers as he fired off buy and sell orders. Livermore was described by *The New York Times* as being "quick, nervous and excitable" between the five trading hours of 10 o'clock and three o'clock.

His newly hired staff members were astonished at the intensity of his trading style. A few of them had worked at broker's offices before they came to Livermore and were totally unused to the sheer speed and his ability to retain information and prices in his head.

Along one entire side, the inner wall, were the chalkboards behind a raised platform where the six marker boys stood all day putting up the latest prices for shares quoted on the Dow Jones and most of the world's traded commodities. The marker boys had headsets that were permanently connected to the floor of the New York Exchange. As the latest prices were cried out, they could mark them up direct instead of waiting for the ticker, which at the best of times was 15 minutes behind the market.

Above: Jesse Livermore pictured in 1933 after he had made his first flight on a commercial aeroplane. In those days, flying was very expensive and only for the wealthy few. United Airlines was founded in 1926 and started its own operations in 1931.

October 1929: The Wall Street Crash

Above: Mounted police struggle to keep order with worried investors milling around on Wall Street to learn the latest news of the market crash on Black Tuesday, October 29th 1929. Thousands anxiously waited to discover the extent of their losses some becoming unruly.

Below: A famous photograph of a speculator who had lost everything he had on the stock market.

Three Black Days: October 24th, 28th and 29th

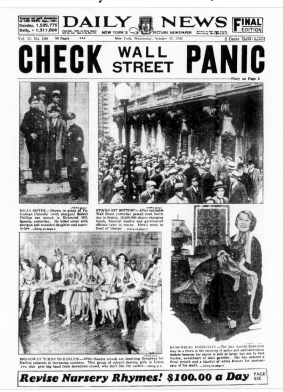

Left: *The Daily News* of Wednesday October 30th 1929 leads with the headline of panic on Wall Street after Black Monday and Black Tuesday. It had been the most hectic day in its history. 16,400,000 shares had changed hands before government officials and financial leaders came to the rescue.

Left: Wall Street clerks worked long hours during the market crash of 1929.

Right: Wall Street back room staff were overwhelmed by the rush of sell orders in October 1929. With no time to go home, stock brokers and their clerks worked until the early hours of October 30th, checking up transactions. They decided not to go home and slept on camp beds in a nearby gym.

Three Legendary Wall Street Traders

Right: Jesse Livermore, was always on the same side as Bernard Baruch, as they cooperated in share pools. But he was always on the other side of trades against Arthur Cutten.

© AP / Press Association Images

Below: Bernard Baruch was the master financier of the age and a close friend of Livermore. But Baruch's fortune endured and increased year on year.

© Baltimore Sun

Above: Arthur Cutten was Livermore's great rival on Wall Street during the 1920's. Initially, he was much more successful until the 1929 crash when he lost much of his fortune.

© Bettmann / CORBIS

Beginning of the end: the meltdown of Jesse Livermore

Above: Jesse Livermore went missing for 26 hours on December 22nd 1933 in New York. After a city-wide police search and fears he had been kidnapped, he returned to his home at 1100 Park Avenue and reluctantly posed for photographers awaiting news.

Right: The stock picture of Jesse Livermore, that was issued by the police after he disappeared.

1934: Jesse Livermore is bankrupt for a second time

Above: Jesse Livermore photographed in the street in 1934 after he filed for official bankruptcy for the second time. Five years earlier, he had been worth $100 million.

Right: Lucille Ballantine attended Jesse Livermore's bankruptcy hearing in March 1934. She claimed that Jesse Livermore promised to give her $150 a month for five years and that she would sue him on his promise.

Divorce from Dorothy and marriage to Harriet

Above: Jesse Livermore married Harriet Metz on December 1st 1934, after his divorce from Dorothy. Harriet Metz had been married four times before and made a widow each time.

Left: Dorothy Livermore on November 29th 1935 with her new husband, Walter Longcope. They were married in 1934 for less than a year. Standing behind the couple, with the family dog, is her 15-year-old son Jesse Jr, her other son, Paul, is on her left.

Above: Dorothy Livermore with her two sons, Jesse Jr and Paul Livermore, photographed at Montecito in Santa Barbara, California, where she moved after her divorce in 1933.

The shooting of Jesse Livermore Jr by his mother

Above: On December 1st 1935, Jesse Livermore's ex-wife Dorothy was arrested for shooting her eldest son, Jesse Jr, and taken to Santa Barbara County Jail. She was later charged with assault with intent to murder by Sheriff James Ross and Sheriff Jack Ross.

Below: On December 1st 1935, Jesse and Harriet Livermore make their way to the Santa Barbara Hospital to visit his son, Jesse Jr, who was critically ill after being shot by his mother.

Right: Jesse Livermore is seen arriving by plane to Los Angeles on December 1st 1935. He and his wife Harriet had flown across the country from St Louis to be at his son's bedside.

Below: Dorothy Livermore being arraigned in a California courthouse on December 2nd 1935 for suspected assault with a deadly weapon with the intent of killing her eldest son. Judge Wagner set her bail at $9,000 which was put up by friends.

Below: Jesse Livermore continued his journey to Santa Barbara from Los Angeles by car to see his gravely ill son.

Above: Dorothy Livermore returns home after a two-day stay in the Santa Barbara County Jail on December 3rd 1935 with Donald Neville, her fiancée at the time of the tragedy.

Above: Dorothy Livermore with her eldest son Jesse Livermore Jr on August 19th 1937. They had gone on vacation to Europe and returned aboard the *SS Conte di Savois*. The trip had been arranged to celebrate his full recovery after she had shot him during an argument. **Inset:** Mother and son at their Montecito home in Santa Barbara, California, on February 26th 1936. Their attorney W. P. Butcher is in the centre of the picture of the newly-reconciled pair.

Above: Jesse and Harriet Livermore with his youngest son, Paul, at New York airport in New Jersey on September 10th 1937. Flying was a regular pursuit for Livermore after 1933.

Left: Edwin Lefèvre, the famous journalist who wrote 'Reminiscences of a Stock Operator' a fictionalised biography in Jesse Livermore's own words. It is one of the best selling business books ever published.

Above top: The first edition of 'Reminiscences of a Stock Operator' by Edwin Lefèvre published in 1923. First editions are now worth over $5,000 each.

Above bottom: Later editions of 'Reminiscences of a Stock Operator' by Edwin Lefèvre sold tens of thousands of copies over the next 90 years as word got around.

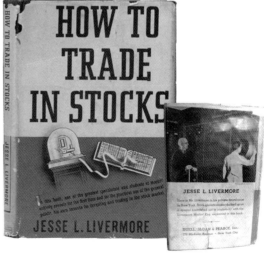

Above: A first edition of 'How to Trade in Stocks' by Edwin Lefèvre with an inscription and signature of Jesse Livermore.

Above right: An old picture of Jesse Livermore's office in the Hecksher Building, 730 Fifth Avenue in New York. is featured on the reverse of 'How to Trade in Stocks.' It shows him at work as boys continually post prices coming off the ticker onto a chalkboard, which Livermore studied all day.

Left: Jesse and Harriet 'Nina' Livermore arriving in New York after a South American cruise aboard the liner *Santa Maria* on February 25th 1936.

© AP/Press-Association Images

Below: The fateful photo taken at the cub room of the famous Stork Club in New York on November 27th 1940 as Livermore and his wife Harriet enjoyed dinner. 24 hours later, he was dead by his own hand.

© Pictorial Parade / Archive Photos/Getty Images

JESSE L. LIVERMORE
1877 — 1940

Above: Jesse Livermore Jr arrives by cab at New York's Sherry-Netherland hotel on Thursday 28th November 1940. 20 minutes earlier, he had been informed that his father had shot himself dead in the hotel cloakroom.

Left: Jesse Livermore's gravestone at Woodlawn Cemetery, Acton, Massachusetts, a short distance from the place of his birth. The simple memorial is marked on the side of his grandparent's grave marker. Livermore was cremated two days after his death, and his ashes were reputedly placed beside those of his mother in the family plot when his wife refused to pay for interment at a mausoleum.

Above: The Sherry-Netherland Hotel next to Central Park. The hotel is situated on the Upper East Side of New York. It was here in the hotel's cloakroom that Jesse Livermore chose to end his own life on November 28th 1940.

The design of the chalkboards was Livermore's own and unlike those of any other trading floor. The board had all the Dow quoted shares plus any others Livermore was interested in. Each stock had its own column running the length of the board. All the day's price changes were recorded in the columns.

All the lighting, artificial and natural, faced the board, and Livermore just liked it that way.

All of the tickers were mounted on high plinths and Livermore preferred to stand up when he was trading and, apart from the noise from the clattering of the tickers, he preferred a quiet, chatterless trading environment whilst he and his assistants worked. At its peak of activity, hundreds of trades were executed every day.

To maintain security, none of the staff left the offices during trading hours and no incoming personal calls were allowed. Livermore wanted total focus and commitment from his staff and did not want them distracted by outside events.

The 60 Livermore employees beavered away with a common purpose, which was making money trading shares and commodities. At the end of the day, the 20 clerks reconciled all buy and sell orders and balanced the books. By the time he went home, Livermore knew the score, not that he hadn't already calculated it in his mind beforehand. The two figures rarely varied.

Adjacent to the trading floor was Livermore's own huge office and a formal boardroom. The boardroom was also mahogany paneled except for a transparent wall of glass that overlooked the trading room. The boardroom had swing glass paneled doors directly into Livermore's office. His desk was huge made of polished mahogany in partners' style as opposed to the roll top desks still favored by most merchant banks. In a completely different style to the somewhat chaotic trading room, his desk had three telephones and a pad of paper plus two trays that read 'in' and 'out', tended to by his personal secretary.

Generally, visitors were discouraged. Those that did come were usually old Livermore cronies such as Tommy Lawson, who always came by when he was in New York visiting from his native Boston. Lawson was now in his sixties and long reconciled with Livermore after they had fallen out in 1917. Livermore was also occasionally visited by Bernard Baruch and Frank Bliss, both of whom he sometimes cooperated with on forays into the stock market.

One of the first deals done out of the new offices was a pool Livermore formed with Bliss to boost the share price of the Computing Tabulator

Company (CTC), which was later to became IBM. The pool quickly doubled the CTC share price from $40 to over $80, and Bliss and Livermore made a million dollars each on the deal. Straight afterwards, they combined on a bear raid on a railroad company called Wheeling & Lake Erie Railroad. The shares initially rose to $100 but quickly fell to $60, netting Bliss and Livermore $800,000 between them. For a time, Bliss, known as the 'silver fox of Wall Street', took an office on the 18th floor until the relationship cooled after a small deal went wrong.

Time magazine reporters once managed to gain access to Livermore at his offices and described it as follows: "The door bearing no name was guarded by a plug-ugly who kept its key locked inside a little green cabinet."

Despite being described as "plug ugly" by *Time*, Harry Dache was actually a very intelligent man. The son of Irish immigrants, he was a veteran of the US Merchant Marine, and his family were Irish immigrants. Dache taught himself six languages, including Latin, and read as many books as he could lay his hands on. He was always at Livermore's side and even travelled with him on vacations, taking care of life's little details.

Livermore allowed very few reporters to penetrate his lair but *Time* became a rare exception when its editor Briton Hadden, who had founded *Time* Inc. with Henry Luce, personally asked him to allow the magazine access to watch him at work. The *Time* reporter wrote: "No one could leave as long as the market was open; only outgoing telephone calls were allowed. Trader Livermore sat in a jungle of telephone wires, his sharp blue eyes glued to the private board, which recorded the minute-by-minute gyrations of his vast paper empire. During trading hours, he was nervous and excited and as jubilant as a boy. At three o'clock, when he the ticker went blank, he bit down hard on his cigar, retired in silence to an inner chamber to study his day's trades. Often, he stayed until eight o'clock."

The New York Times was also granted access to the inner sanctum. The *NYT* was Livermore's favorite newspaper, and he read it every day from when he was six years old to the very last day of his life. Its unnamed reporter was shown into Livermore's office by Harry Dache and fussed over by Livermore's secretary, Nancy Thomas. The reporter was intrigued by Livermore's choice of a female secretary, which at the time was a male preserve in Wall Street.

Livermore did not proffer his hand in the customary handshake. The reporter recorded that he "abhorred physical contact with any male".

Livermore was on the telephone when the reporter entered his office and barely acknowledged his presence as he continued to whisper trading orders into the telephone receiver, covering the mouthpiece with his hand so as not to be overheard.

The writer described the scene: "At 52, Jesse Livermore appeared to be at least ten years younger. Slim and slight of build, his hands were almost womanly in slenderness and smoothness. On his right pinky finger, he wore a huge sapphire in a setting designed for the masculine hand. The morning sun reflected in the stone, which blazed like a baleful eye. His hair, shot through with tell-tale patches of frost, was still predominantly blond; it ran straight back from a high forehead, somewhat bald at the sides and formed a formidable crest above his face. His generous nose supported 'pince-nez' glasses. The eyes were blue, with an owlish stare like that of a professor absorbed with some knotty problem. All in all, Jesse Livermore presented a picture of a cultured, well-dressed man. His double-breasted suit of banker's grey was cut from finest quality cloth and expensively tailored. He wore a spotless white shirt with the new lay-down collar from whose innards a red foulard snaked down from the precise center of his shirt to disappear under the 'v' of his vest. Across Livermore's chest hung a delicate gold chain of simple links. Its ends were hidden in his vest pockets."

At this point, the reporter noticed that Livermore reached from the end of the chain for a gold foil covered pencil. Quickly, Nancy Thomas came in and slid a note pad under his hand on which he immediately scribbled an entire page of notes from his conversation, which was then quickly retrieved by her, presumably for immediate typed transcription.

As soon as his business was over, Livermore transformed himself into a different character, greeting the reporter with a warm smile. He got up and gestured to him to join him in the armchairs situated around an open fire. The Heckscher Building had a central chimney and Livermore enjoyed an open fire in the winter months.

The formal interview then took place for 20 minutes before Livermore hurried to the trading room as Harry Dache showed the reporter out.

The resulting article recorded how Livermore split his time during the working week by going home to Great Neck in Long Island or staying at his Manhattan house. It told how, in the school holidays, he would often be accompanied to the office by his sons Jesse Jr and Paul.

When he was at Great Neck, he would come into the city in the early hours every morning driven by his chauffeur, Eddie Kane, in his canary yellow Rolls-

Royce. In an era when traffic signals were all hand-operated, the policemen operating them ensured Livermore's Rolls never had to wait. It was a service they provided for many wealthy commuters, and the reward was a monthly twenty-dollar bill.

If he was staying in town, the chauffeur would make the short journey to the house or Livermore would walk.

The article failed to record that invariably between the hours of seven o'clock and nine o'clock in the evening, Livermore would visit one of the three or four mistresses he kept in small apartments across Manhattan. It was all part of the lifestyle he enjoyed for that golden ten years between 1922 and 1932 when life was very good and the world was at his feet.

Livermore had good reason for wanting to cozy up to *The New York Times*. It had taken to reporting his periodic proclamations about the stock market with the reverence of the gospel. Now armed with his team of statisticians and researchers working for him at the Heckscher Building, he was able to back up his predictions with reams of background material.

On April 19th he predicted a bear market coming and warned about the number of new companies being floated on the stock market at very high prices. He did not believe the market could absorb all the new issues and that prices would soon fall sharply. He told *The New York Times* he did not want to be considered a pessimist, but added: "I think it is time that the American investing public should be given warnings that the time has arrived when they should thoroughly discriminate in earnest and thoroughly analyze the class of investments and speculative holdings that they possess." He also said that wages were currently too high.

Livermore had kicked the current bull market off in 1921 with similar platitudes, and 18 months later, he said it was coming to an end. His words were soon proved correct, and a very sharp downward period for the Dow began.

Six months later, he changed his mind again and said the fall had gone far enough. In September, he foresaw a new share boom coming in 1924 and wanted to give it a kick-start after being bearish for much of 1923. On October 30th, Livermore issued a new statement to *The New York Times* that immediately set the market alight. In his latest statement, Livermore said that the business future was "hopeful" and that the larger US corporations were now trading at a big discount after the big falls of the previous six months; a fall, which Livermore noted, he had also predicted. He said: "During the past six months, it is my opinion that stocks have discounted to a large extent due to the readjustment process in various industries. And for this reason I believe the future will show good substantial profits to anyone using discretion in buying at prevailing prices the stocks of corporations that are well managed and not overcapitalized."

Livermore also reasoned that, with agricultural commodities selling at record prices since the war, an extended recession looked unlikely: "I don't look for boom times and I don't believe that anyone who has the interest of our country at heart wishes that either, but as long as our farmers are receiving high prices for what they produce and labor is well employed at high wages you cannot very well have bad times in this country."

Livermore noted that the only commodity that was trailing in price was wheat owing to too much acreage being harvested, a hangover from the war years and the export boom.

Livermore's lengthy statement, much of it prepared by the newly employed researchers and statisticians at the Heckscher Building, caused a one-day mini boom on the stock market and 1.4 million shares were traded that day, the highest in nine months.

Proof that Livermore had really arrived as part of the Wall Street establishment came on November 20th when a testimonial gala dinner was held in his honor and where he made the keynote speech of the evening. Livermore was flattered and very honored when the invitation arrived in the mail and he ordered his researchers to prepare for him a formidable speech to deliver. Their resulting effort was full of statistics and reasons why America was set for a prolonged business boom. Inadvertently, the speech kicked off the five-year bull market that was to last until October 1929. In his speech, Livermore focused on the railroad companies that had lost $3 billion of market capitalization in the 15 years since the rail boom had peaked. He said the lost $3 billion would be regained in the months ahead as he predicted that the whole of industry would pick up after the ravages of the post-war years.

Livermore also forecast that railroad companies would receive a boost from Congress whereas other bearish pundits had been predicting new taxes and sanctions against railroad operators, as he said: "Bears and professional tipsters predict that Congress will do something to the railroads. It seems to me, on the other hand, that Congress will do something for the railroads. It will do the very thing that E. H. Harriman, the most far sighted of all our railroad leaders, tried to do in the days when railroad stocks were the favorite of American investors. Congress is going to do everything it can to induce the railroads to consolidate. Therefore I believe, in 1924, that there will be a restoration in confidence in American railroads. New bridges, new extensions, double tracing and terminal expansion will follow with the result that the American working man will remain fully employed at good wages." With those words, Livermore singlehandedly kicked off a two-year revival in railroad shares and he marveled at the power of his own words to do so.

The testimonial dinner rounded off a very successful year in which he had been bearish at the start and bullish at the end, and right both times. His bank balance now stood at close to $20 million, a level he considered very satisfactory.

1923 was the first year when Livermore did not go on vacation mid-year, so when he left for Palm Beach on December 28th it was a mighty relieved man who booked into the Breakers Hotel for three months. It was his first proper vacation with his family and a golden time in his life. He was in love with his wife and his young children and looked forward to indulging them. The routine would hardly vary: fishing by day and gambling by night.

In the past, he had always been rigorous about taking time off and worried about the dangers of over trading, and it was unusual for him to work for 12 months solid. But now he was in a different place as head of his own company that was no longer totally reliant on his skills. When he was away, in Palm Beach or overseas, his team carried on day-to-day business and the 20 traders were allowed discretion to trade within strictly defined limits.

As befitting his new status, for the first time, he took his own telegraph operator with him to Palm Beach and had a telegraph terminal installed into his suite at The Breakers. The daily trades of his protégés would be sent to him to peruse before he fell asleep. As Livermore admitted to the NYT reporter, it was the perfect life: a life he loved living.

When he returned to New York at the end of February 1924, he carried on living that life. His predictions of a mini stock market boom had come true and he was riding it hard. His staff was also doing well and his 20 trading protégés were also showing a profit on his money, something he took great pleasure from. His only disappointment was the lack of work from external sources for flotation advice and buying pools. Livermore had realized that his high profile in the newspapers for making various predictions may be hurting that side of his business, and so he reluctantly decided to withdraw from forecasting the future as a result.

There was also short-term disappointment when the market dipped briefly during the Teapot Dome inquiries that were going on in Washington. All of the dirty laundry surrounding Teapot Dome was coming out and depressing confidence in the stock market. But it was to be short lived.

He had also made a return to the commodities market, particularly wheat, where prices were at historical lows. He made some big profits in March from positions he had taken before he left for vacation and then topped up in Palm Beach.

In the summer of 1924, Livermore made some more big moves in agricultural commodities. He used his system of pivotal points to execute what could have been the perfect trade if he had kept to his own rules. He had been monitoring the price of wheat, which had suffered from a long period of glut as the price reached historic lows. He made a play after the price reached one of his pivotal points and ordered five million bushels. The trading volume in wheat was very large and the glut so big that an order for five million bushels barely ruffled the market. The price moved up slowly and, when it reached its next pivotal point, Livermore bought another five million at 1.5 cents above his first purchase. The second five million was difficult to get and Livermore knew he was right. So far so good.

The next day the price was up three cents and as he recounted in his book, *How to Trade in Stocks*: "An extensive movement had begun which I calculated would extend over a period of several months. I did not however fully realize the full possibilities that lay ahead. Then when I had a 25 cents a bushel profit, I cashed in. I sat back and saw the market advance 20 cents more within a few days. Right then I realized I had made a great mistake. Why had I been afraid of losing something I never really had?"

Livermore was bitterly disappointed with himself – he had forgotten all his own rules. He immediately realized he should have been patient and seen the deal out to the end. He put it down to a lack of courage, saying: "I knew that in due time, when the upward trend had reached its pivotal point, that I would be given a danger signal in ample time."

But this time, he found he did not agonize over his mistake as he might have done in the past. As he explained: "A stock speculator sometimes makes mistakes and knows that he is making them. And after he makes them he will ask himself why he made them; and after thinking over it cold-bloodedly a long time, after the pain of punishment is over, he may learn how he came to make them, and when, and at what particular point of his trade; but not why.

And then he simply calls himself names and lets it go at that. Of course, if a man is both wise and lucky, he will not make the same mistake twice. But he will make any one of the ten thousand brothers or cousins of the original. The Mistake family is so large that there is always one of them around when you want to see what you can do in the fool-play line."

After that, he went straight back in, buying another five million bushels of wheat at 25 cents above his last exit price. This time, he was determined to follow his own rules and to see the deal out.

And there began a series of transactions that lasted into 1925, which included selling wheat short and going into the rye market, which ultimately left him with a $3 million profit. The series of deals reignited his interest in the commodities market and would cause him to make some fundamental changes in his trading habits over the next few years.

It was proving to be another good year and vindication for the money he had invested in the new offices. At the end of the year, he also got a public offering to promote. 1924 had produced a big stock market boom for radio companies, particularly Radio Corporation of America (RCA), the leading radio broadcaster after NBC and CBS.

He was approached by Teddy Luce and William Ingersoll to float their radio set manufacturing company, called De Forest Radio Company. Luce and Ingersoll believed the boom in the broadcasting companies would rub off on them, as they were the company that actually manufactured the hardware. Livermore agreed and said he would sell 75,000 shares at around $24 a share, the same price at which they were traded on the over-the-counter market prior to flotation. The offer would be worth $1.8 million and the entire proceeds used for the company's expansion. No existing holders would sell shares. The issue was well oversubscribed and closed within minutes of the shares being offered.

Although a successful offering, it was small and Livermore hoped for many more as 1925 dawned. But it was not to be. After the boom, the shine once again came off the stock market as it moved sideways for a period. It was neither a bull nor bear market; it was the sort that Jesse Livermore hated and could never make money in. This time, he was determined that his upward progress not be disturbed as it had been in 1909. He had no intention of living through that again. As he explained: "In a narrow market, when prices are not getting anywhere to speak of but move within a narrow range, there is no sense in trying to anticipate what the next big movement is going to be – up or down. The thing to do is to watch the market, read the tape to determine the limits of the get-nowhere prices, and make up your mind that you will not take an interest until the price breaks through the limit in either direction. A speculator must concern himself with making money out of the market and not with insisting that the tape must agree with him. Never argue with it or ask it for reasons or explanations. Stock-market post-mortems don't pay dividends."

So his mind shifted towards commodities in his desire to make money, and he declared for the time being that stocks were dead in the water.

CHAPTER 30

Ups and downs

Battle for supremacy with Arthur Cutten

1925 - 1927

In 1925, Jesse Livermore became disillusioned with trading stocks and shares which were once again going sideways, making it impossible for him to make any serious money. So in a decisive move, he temporarily had all his stock tickers disconnected and put in a store room. He resolved from 1925 onwards to focus on commodities, mostly agricultural products. He knew if the tickers stayed in, he would be tempted to keep trading shares, and he wanted no such temptations.

1925 was not to prove a particularly good year for the Livermores personally. On March 18th, during their winter vacation in Palm Beach, the Breakers Hotel had burnt to the ground. The fire was started by an electric curling iron that had been left on. The Livermore family witnessed the dramatic scene from the hotel grounds whilst urging the staff to recover their luggage before the fire reached their suite. They finished their holiday on a yacht.

A month later on returning to New York, Livermore hurt himself when he fell down an unlit staircase during some home renovations as he was inspecting building work. He suffered severe bruising, a broken arm and multiple fractured ribs on his right side, which were very painful, and he was ordered by Dr Hollister, the family physician, to rest for three months at least.

He recuperated at his Lake Placid home and was virtually immobile for the first three weeks. During his enforced break, he decided to sell his seat on the New York Curb Market as he rarely used it. Since a newspaperman had heard him trading Mexican Petroleum shares in 1922 after he denied he was in the market, he had always been wary of its public nature. The sale surprised him when the seat fetched $25,000, five times what he had paid a few years earlier. He also decided to resign his directorship of the Mizner Development Corporation, in which he had invested $2 million years after advice from his brother Elliot. Mizner, founded by real estate expert Addison Mizner, had been

265

set up to develop the new town of Boca Raton on the Florida coast. Unusually, in addition to investing, Livermore had also agreed to serve on the board of directors. It was one of his few private investments that ever showed him a profit. But now there were rumors of shenanigans, and the accounts had been criticized in the press. It was time for him to leave. By late June, Livermore was ready to return to trading, and he did so with a new enthusiasm.

He was now 48 years old but looked 16 years younger. He retained all his old spirit and instructed his staff and analysts to henceforth focus on grain – at least until the stock market turned up again, which he knew from past experience could take a few years.

But the decision would have unanticipated consequences. The move into commodities was to set him directly against a fabled trader called Arthur Cutten, whose reputation was every bit as good as Livermore's but always on the bull side. In many people's opinion, Cutten's trading skills were sharper even than Livermore's.

Cutten, a Canadian by birth, was 55 years old – seven years older than his great rival. He was the son of a farmer and one of nine children. His rise had taken a similar trajectory to that of Livermore but without the bumps.

From 14 to the age of 20, he worked on his father's farm. But he longed for something more and saved his money until he had $50. Finally, in 1890, Cutten left the farmlands of Ontario and journeyed to Chicago. Like Livermore, he quickly landed a job at a broker for $4 a week. He had very good knowledge of farm production, and he now wanted to learn how to trade the product.

He excelled as a broker's clerk, rising through the ranks to be a manager. After five years, he had saved up $1,000 and learned all that there was to know about trading wheat.

Towards the end of 1895, he made his move and asked permission to open a grain trading account at his employer, A. S. White & Company. His employer advised against it but Cutten could not be dissuaded and instead opened an account at a rival firm.

Inside three months, he had made a small fortune from trading wheat, enough to buy a seat on the Chicago Board of Trade. He resigned from A. S. White and took up full time trading and did not look back.

He traded in all the agricultural commodities and made a large amount of money in futures. Cutten, who often referred to himself as "just a dirt farmer", made enough to buy an 800-acre ranch in 1912. He built a huge mansion on the land.

It was only a matter of time before he came up directly against Jesse Livermore, and that came in early 1925. Cutten had singlehandedly pushed wheat past the $2 a bushel mark for the first time ever.

In late 1924, flushed with success from a summer of profitable grain trading, Livermore had bought wheat at $1.04 a bushel and sold out at $2 a bushel a few months later, making him $10 million, his single biggest profit to date and a marvellous way to start his new career as a dedicated commodities trader. But unknown to Livermore, it had all been down to Cutten's yearlong maneuvring to get the price up.

But Livermore's success in exclusively trading commodities was to be fleeting. It was a bull market extraordinaire which showed no signs of abating, and it seemed everyone was making money from trading wheat futures thanks to Cutten continually pushing the price higher.

After he sold out, Livermore kept an eye on the wheat price and did not believe its rise was sustainable. So midway through 1925, Livermore turned bearish and started shorting grain futures, particularly wheat. But the market did hold up and by the end of 1925, Livermore had lost $9 million on his shorts. At that point, he gave up and took his loss. It reduced his gains for the year to just $1 million.

In the past, Livermore would have retreated from the world after taking this scale of loss. But this time it seemed to hardly trouble him. He realized he had just been plain wrong. As he said: "The man who is right always has two forces working in his favor – basic conditions and the men who are wrong. In a bull market, bear factors are ignored. That is human nature, and yet human beings profess astonishment at it. People will tell you that the wheat crop has gone to pot because there has been bad weather in one or two sections and some farmers have been ruined. When the entire crop is gathered and all the farmers in all the wheat-growing sections begin to take their wheat to the elevators, the bulls are surprised at the smallness of damage. They discover that they merely have helped the bears.

When a man makes his play in a commodity market, he must not permit himself set opinions. He must have an open mind and flexibility. It is not wise to disregard the message of the tape, no matter what your opinion of crop conditions or of the probable demand may be." It was not the first time he had lost heavily on trading wheat, and he knew it would probably not be the last.

Interestingly, Cutten had made just about the same amount going long on wheat, and it turned out he had been on the other side of Livermore's bear trades. Suddenly, the name Arthur Cutten had Livermore's attention and he never again forgot it.

Cutten had also taken notice of Livermore and thought if he could so easily trounce him in the Chicago grain markets then he might be able to pull off the same trick in New York's stock markets. As a direct result of their battle in Chicago, Cutten decided to take Livermore on his own turf and at his own game.

So Cutten closed up his Chicago farmhouse and leased his 800 acres to a manager. He and his wife moved into a rented townhouse on Fifth Avenue, which he established as a new base.

Cutten proved a natural in trading shares, especially as the 1926 bull market finally kicked in. He made some stunning profits in shares like Baldwin Locomotive, RCA, and retail giant Montgomery Ward. In two years, he made more than $50 million, easily eclipsing the performance of Jesse Livermore who had remained bearish and gone into reverse suffering large losses.

So much so that Livermore scaled down his trading to virtually nothing, laying off half his staff and hunkering down. His net worth had declined to less than $5 million, and whilst his losses were not nearly as severe as in years gone by, they still hurt badly. His annual running costs were now as much as $300,000 a year, and he knew he could be broke again if his losing streak lasted. Fortunately, he suddenly found himself making large profits from some land he had bought as part of a consortium called the Mizner Development Corporation in Boca Raton, Florida. Florida was booming and real estate was going up exponentially. His brother Elliot, who had been involved in real estate in Florida all his life, had advised him to get in on the boom, and it had been good advice. He eventually sold all his real estate holdings for a very good return, which eased some of the pain he was suffering on Wall Street.

Livermore remained sanguine about his latest losses. Gone were the days when he would agonize over it for days on end. As he said: "The recognition of our own mistakes should not benefit us any more than the study of our successes. But there is a natural tendency in all men to avoid punishment. When you associate certain mistakes with a licking, you do not hanker for a second dose, and, of course, all stock-market mistakes wound you in two tender spots – your pocketbook and your vanity."

As for Cutten, he reputedly made more money between 1926 and 1928 than any other man in America. He was the highest taxpayer living in Chicago by some considerable margin in 1928.

By comparison, Livermore was struggling, neither losing money nor able to make any. It was another four-year-long losing run where he just about kept the shirt on his back.

Two years later, the two men would duel again with very different results.

CHAPTER 31

Manipulating a Profit

A fortune from Freeport Texas

1927

From mid-1926 to mid-1927, Jesse Livermore combined with Frank Bliss again to run a pool to force up the price of a company called Freeport Texas. Bliss had brought the idea to Livermore and told him he believed the company was seriously undervalued and deserving of their joint attention. The manipulation of Freeport Texas was to prove Livermore's most successful exercise in running up the price of a stock. It turned out to be one of the best investing ideas he ever had.

When Livermore and Bliss first spotted it in April 1926, the price of a Freeport Texas share had already more than doubled in twelve months, from a low of $8 in 1925 to $19. It was the steep rise in a company he had never heard of that pricked Bliss's interest.

Livermore respected Bliss more than he did any other Wall Street operator. He believed he shared his talent for reading the tape. He was also a master promoter, and the legend was that he could "whip up" interest in any stock in any state. He also had a certain technique that enabled him to enter the market and buy and sell large quantities of shares without anyone knowing he was the principal.

Livermore and Bliss had a long history together and had already made money together in Piggly Wiggly, Computer Tabulator Company and Wheeling & Lake Erie Railroad.

The relationship worked because it was one of equal partners. They both put up the capital equally and made the decisions together. Livermore's contribution to the partnership was manipulating stocks, for which he was respected as the master of that game.

Before Livermore and Bliss got involved, Freeport Texas seemed content to be a share that didn't fall because nobody ever sold it. Similarly, there was no inducement to buy the stock. The share was effectively dead and the shareholders seemed content for it to remain that way, which was why the sudden rise in price the previous year attracted their attention.

When Bliss suggested it, Livermore had his staff look at Freeport Texas. They went through the financial reports. Livermore had established a great research set-up on the 18th floor of the Heckscher Building, and the reports he received were professional, objective and unbiased. Livermore's reports showed that Freeport Texas was a very valuable property indeed and totally overlooked by the market.

The company was founded as the Freeport Sulphur Company in 1912. It built and developed its own harbor, called Freeport, on the Texas coast, situated near its sulphur mines. Then it bought up a fleet of ships to transport the sulphur. The company became the largest supplier of sulphur in the world as a result.

Its sulphur mines, spread along the Gulf coast were unsurpassed anywhere for their capacity to supply large quantities of sulphur quickly. The company was a sleeping giant and massively undervalued by any measure. After months of investigation, the bull manipulation of Freeport Texas was on.

Livermore and Bliss began their campaign by establishing how much stock was available and at what price. They immediately took in all the stock that was for sale at around $20. They found that as soon as there was a buyer around, other stock became available. Livermore and Bliss accumulated the stock as quietly and as quickly as they could.

The two men set a target to buy 200,000 shares at an average of $25 each, which they expected would cost them a combined $5 million. In the event, accumulating 200,000 shares took the average buying price up to $30. As they believed, the shares were worth at least $50, so that wasn't a problem.

With the stock bought in, it then had to be boosted and fed out to unsuspecting buyers. Livermore explained how he ran a bull campaign in *Reminiscences of a Stock Operator*: "I didn't give bull tips on to anybody. I didn't have to. My job was to seek directly to influence sentiment by the best possible kind of publicity. I do not say that there should never be bull propaganda. It is as legitimate and indeed as desirable to advertise the value of a new stock as to advertise the value of woollens or shoes or automobiles. Accurate and reliable information should be given to the public. But what I meant was that the tape did all that was needed for my purpose.

"As I said before, the reputable newspapers always try to print explanations for market movements. It is news. Their readers demand to know not only what happens in the stock market but why it happens. Therefore without the manipulator lifting a finger, the financial writers will print all the available information and gossip, and also analyze the reports of earnings, trade condition and outlook; in short, whatever may throw light on the advance. Whenever a newspaperman or an acquaintance asks my opinion of a stock and I have one, I do not hesitate to express it. I do not volunteer advice and I never give tips, but I have nothing to gain in my operations from secrecy. At the same time I realize that the best of all tipsters, the most persuasive of all salesmen, is the tape."

Livermore may not have been completely honest in his assessment of reporters and his relationship with them. At the time, many prominent journalists who reported on Wall Street were suspected of being corrupt and taking bribes to write stories about companies. Amongst the reporters suspected of malfeasance were: Richard Edmondson of the *Wall Street Journal*, William Gomber of *Financial America*, Charles Murphy of the *New York Evening Mail*, J. F. Lowther of the *New York Herald Tribune*, William White of the *New York Evening Post*, and W. F. Walmsley of the *New York Times*.

Certainly Frank Bliss was not beyond bribing reporters.

In *Reminiscences*, Livermore went on to explain how momentum carried everything after the initial manipulation had been carried out: "When I had absorbed all the stock that was for sale, I relieved the market of that pressure, and naturally that made clear for trading purposes the line of least resistance. It was manifestly upward. The moment the fact was perceived by the observant traders on the floor, they logically assumed that the stock was in for an advance, the extent of which they could not know; but they knew enough to begin buying. Their demand, created exclusively by the obviousness of the stocks' rising tendency – the tape's infallible bull tip! – I promptly filled. I sold to the traders the stock that I had bought from the tired-out holders at the beginning. Of course this selling was judiciously done; I contented myself with supplying the demand. I was not forcing my stock on the market and I did not want too rapid an advance. It wouldn't have been good business to sell out the half of my one hundred thousand shares at that stage of the proceedings. My job was to make a market on which I might sell my entire line.

"But even though I sold only as much as the traders were anxious to buy, the market was temporarily deprived of my own buying power, which I had hitherto exerted steadily. In due course, the traders' purchases ceased and the price stopped rising. As soon as that happened, there began the selling by disappointed bulls or by those traders whose reasons for buying disappeared the instant the rising tendency was checked. But I was ready for this selling, and on the way down I bought back the stock I had sold to the traders a couple of points higher. This buying of stock I knew was bound to be sold checked the downward course; and when the price stopped going down, the selling orders stopped coming in.

"I then began all over again. I took all the stock that was for sale on the way up – it wasn't very much – and the price began to rise a second time; from a higher starting point. Don't forget that on the way down, there are many holders who wish to heaven they had sold theirs but won't do it three or four points from the top. Such speculators always vow they will surely sell out if there is a rally. They put in their orders to sell on the way up, and then they change their minds with the change in the stock's price-trend. Of course there is always profit taking from safe-playing quick runners to whom a profit is always a profit to be taken.

"All I had to do after that was to repeat the process; alternately buying and selling; but always working higher.

"Sometimes, after you have taken all the stock that is for sale, it pays to rush up the prices sharply, to have what might be called little bull flurries in the stock you are manipulating. It is excellent advertising, because it makes talk and also brings in both the professional traders and that portion of the speculating public that likes action. It is, I think, a large portion. Whatever demand was created by those spurts I supplied, my selling always kept the upward movement within bounds both as to extent and as to speed. In buying on the way down and selling on the way up, I was doing more than marking up the price: I was developing the marketability."

Bull flurries were a technique Livermore borrowed from studying the techniques of the great 19th century Wall Street speculator James Keene. Jon Markman in his annotated version of 'Reminiscences of a Stock Operator' explains: "Creating 'bull flurries' was a common strategy for pool operators and market manipulators, and you can still see it occur today. Traders are always attracted by shiny objects, just like fish are attracted to silvery lures."

Livermore's objective was to always create a perfectly balanced upward market where there was always a buyer and a seller at the prevailing price. As he explained: "After I began my operations in it, there never was a time when a man could not buy or sell the stock freely; I mean by this, buy or sell a reasonable amount without causing over-violent fluctuations in the price.

The fear of being left high and dry if he bought, or squeezed to death if he sold, was gone. The gradual spread among the professionals and the public of a belief in the permanence of the market had much to do with creating confidence in the movement; and, of course, the activity also put an end to a lot of other objections."

Livermore realized the obvious that, in the end, the job of "subtle manipulation" is so complete that a good company needs no handling at all and the price, once the market has been awakened, will naturally go up to reflect the value. He said: "Everybody now knew that it was a good stock: that it had been, and still was, a bargain. The proof was the rise."

It is unlikely Livermore was specifically referring to Freeport Texas when he made those comments, but the company was his most successful manipulation of a stock and the most profit he ever made on actively manipulating one share. As he said, referring to a previous operation: "It had been, if I do say so myself, a beautiful piece of manipulation, strictly legitimate and deservedly successful. The property of the company was valuable and the stock was not dear at the higher price. There wasn't anything about my manipulation that wasn't normal and sound. As long as the price went up on my buying, I knew I was okay. The stock never got waterlogged, as a stock sometimes does. When you find that it fails to respond adequately to your buying, you don't need any better tip to sell. You know that if there is any value to a stock and general market conditions are right, you can always nurse it back after a decline, no matter if it's twenty points. But I never had to do anything like that.

"In my manipulation of stocks, I never lose sight of basic trading principles. Perhaps you wonder why I repeat this or why I keep on harping on the fact that I never argue with the tape or lose my temper at the market because of its behavior. You would think – wouldn't you – that shrewd men who have made millions in their own business and in addition have successfully operated in Wall Street at times would realize the wisdom of playing the game dispassionately. Well, you would be surprised at the frequency with which some of our most successful promoters behave like peevish women because the market does not act the way they wish it to act. They seem to take it as a personal slight, and they proceed to lose money by first losing their temper."

Freeport Texas was financially sound, hopelessly undervalued and responded well to Livermore's treatment. By the end of the operation, the price had risen from $19 to $74 over a year of being manipulated. At that point, both men divested of their remaining interest in April 1927. The *New York Times* called the rise in price "The most interesting speculative issue on the New York Stock Exchange." Other newspapers called it a "market spectacle." Jon Markman recalls: "Livermore takes pains to explain that he would not manipulate a stock unless he believed it was financially sound."

The manipulation had been helped when Freeport Texas suddenly started paying a dividend in February 1927. The first dividend announced was $2, which was quickly raised to $4 annually, paid out at $1 a quarter.

The pool had remained a virtual secret until the New York Times revealed it on Tuesday April 12th as being the work of Jesse Livermore. The newspaper called it a "startling stock market coup", and one that had made Livermore $4 million personally.

Neither Livermore nor Bliss ever spoke openly about how much money they made or about the whole operation.

But undoubtedly they were helped by the resumption of the dividend payment, which probably doubled their profits. The $4 million profit was very welcome news for Livermore in a period where he had underperformed and consistently lost money for the previous 18 months, mainly at the hands of Arthur Cutten who had continually outsmarted him and been on the other side of many market manipulations Livermore had attempted.

The success was a huge relief, and it was a very satisfied man who read the April 12th edition of the New York Times and decided it was time for another vacation.

CHAPTER 32

Good Times at Great Neck

The halcyon years

1925 - 1927

During the period from 1922 to 1927, the Livermores spent around $7 million buying and refurnishing offices, homes and yachts and another $2 million on personal living expenses.

By 1925, they had finally finished the $1.2 million restoration of Evermore, their country house at Great Neck in Long Island.

They settled down to enjoy a life of unimaginable wealth, where no extravagance was deemed too much and there was an unlimited quantity of money to be spent on anything and everything. By 1926 they employed a staff of 80 people on their yachts and homes and another 60 at Livermore's office, a total payroll of 140 keeping them happy and prosperous.

It marked a period of extraordinary hedonism and lifestyle choices that exceeded anything the much wealthier Morgans, Astors or Rockefellers were spending on themselves at the time.

In addition to Evermore, the Livermores enjoyed two luxurious homes in New York, one on the east side and one on the west, to suit both Jesse and Dorothy's tastes and their convenience. The house on the west side, at 66th Street, was preferred by Jesse. He had always liked the west side as opposed to the tony east side. He bought Dorothy a new co-op apartment at 825 Fifth Avenue and she lavished hundreds of thousands of dollars on it. The apartment was in a new 23-story co-operative building designed by James Carpenter on Lenox Hill and fronting Central Park. It was one of the most prestigious blocks on the east side.

But the rebuilt and refurbished Evermore was the jewel in their crown and was now, arguably, one of the finest country homes in America. It was widely reported that Dorothy and her mother spent $150,000 on just landscaping parts of the garden.

Their immediate friends and neighbors at Great Neck were just as impressive as their possessions. Neighbors Walter Chrysler, Billy Durant, Alfred Sloan and Charlie Chaplin were regarded as business and cultural geniuses and at the time regarded as four of the most upstanding people in America. They naturally clicked with the Livermores and formed a social set on Long Island.

Walter Chrysler had founded Chrysler Corporation and become one of America's richest men. Sloan ran General Motors and was regarded as a management genius as GM overtook the Ford Motor Company as the largest car manufacturer in the word under his command.

Durant was the founder of General Motors, and his techniques had transformed the car industry's finances and broken Henry Ford's domination. Chaplin, then at the height of his powers, was the great comic genius of the age who, at the age of 31, had founded United Artists to give him complete control over his film projects.

Dorothy was the life and soul of the set, and she greatly enjoyed the company of Della Chrysler, Lita Chaplin, Irene Sloan and Clara Durant.

All four men and their wives were very close friends and were frequent visitors to the Livermore home for weekly bridge games. Sloan and Chrysler divided their time between Detroit but were always back in Long Island for weekends. Durant had become a Wall Street speculator on the same scale as Livermore, and both men had much in common. Chrysler was an amateur investor who dabbled in the market for fun but often with sums of over half a million dollars at a time. Chaplin, although in a completely different line of business, was all ears when he was in their company. The odd one out was Sloan. He led a parsimonious life and his passion was bridge; while he rarely missed the Monday night bridge games, he did not indulge in the hedonistic activities at weekends.

But all four families loved the lavish hospitality at Evermore. Twelve house servants were permanently on hand to make guests' lives as comfortable as possible, in addition to cooks, chauffeurs and gardeners. It was old style living at its very best and pulled off impeccably by Dorothy Livermore, then in her early thirties and at the height of her powers as a beautiful and perfection-seeking hostess.

Dorothy lived a carefree lifestyle in the bosom of her close family and her husband's vast riches. She socialized widely in Long Island and New York, with a squadron of servants to back her up as the perfect hostess. She was the exact opposite of her more reserved husband. She was vivacious, highly amusing and very outgoing and generous. Along with her mother, she had lavishly decorated and furnished the house at Great Neck and it was perfect for the extravagant and huge parties that she hosted in the house.

No expense was spared in the house and garden. The most extravagant was undoubtedly the $150,000 that was spent landscaping and planting trees and shrubs in the garden. The rare shrubs, imported from all over the world, were said to have cost $50,000 on their own. $100,000 was spent on silverware, $250,000 on furnishings, $309,000 on jade and $10,000 on an antique needlepoint screen. Chippendale furniture, added later, cost another $25,000

The times they lived in reflected the character of Dorothy Livermore perfectly. The only impediment to her enjoyment of life was prohibition, which had befuddled America and made alcohol consumption rare amongst the law abiding middle classes, although not in the upper or working classes who carried on drinking much as before.

Prohibition was a constitutional ban on the sale, production, importation, and transportation of alcoholic beverages that had been passed into law in 1919 and was ratified as part of the Constitution. It was called the Volstead Act. Outright prohibition had followed a ban of the sale of alcohol of greater than 2.75 per cent strength in 1918. That had been meant to save grain for the war effort but had remained in force afterwards.

President Wilson's administration had introduced prohibition as a last desperate attempt to curb some of the alcohol inspired lawlessness that had swept American cities. Crime was rising fast and it was blamed on alcohol consumption, which was deemed out of control. Wilson's action was a desperate attempt to reverse that rise in crime.

Initially, many Americans supported it in the fight against crime. But it served to drive drinking underground and turned the suppliers into criminals. Inevitably, the Mafia took control of alcohol distribution and created huge fortunes for people like Al Capone, who became a real one-man menace to American society. It also served to spark off massive corruption of police officers who took bribes to turn a blind eye to a law they often did not agree with and saw no point enforcing.

Prohibition started on January 17th 1920. At first it was confusing, as drinking alcohol was not illegal but making, transporting and selling it was. But it soon became apparent that the Federal government lacked the resources to enforce the law and officers on the ground the will. As a result, an American phenomenon called speakeasies were created. Speakeasies were clubs, often situated in basements, that carried on selling alcohol in defiance of authority. By 1925, five years after prohibition started, there were said to be as many as 80,000 speakeasy clubs in New York alone. The consumption of alcohol carried on virtually as before but literally underground and out of view.

The police concentrated on stopping and arresting distributors, mainly importers bringing in liquor from Canada where it was legal, but even that was singularly unsuccessful. For example, Ed Bradley's Beach Club casino in Palm Beach, frequented every winter by Livermore, Chrysler, Durant and Chaplin, had a plentiful supply of good quality alcohol all through prohibition and openly sold it at the club. It was never prosecuted or even raided.

In fact, prohibition never affected the Livermores or their friends at all.

Dorothy Livermore adored the alcohol-fuelled lifestyle that existed in Great Neck and Palm Beach, where she spent virtually all her time. In fact, her drinking became more exciting because of prohibition. Her answer to prohibition was to build a distillery in one of the basement rooms in the house and manufacture her own alcohol for their consumption and that of her neighbors. She hired an expert brewer to brew beer and he made regular deliveries to the homes of Chrysler, Durant and Chaplin and many of her appreciative neighbors in Great Neck.

Dorothy's own alcohol consumption, which on rare occasions started to get out of control, was not at all dampened by prohibition. At first she was a good humored drunk, but as she grew older, drinking turned her into a bad humored drunk. But the bad humored outbursts were infrequent and she was a very popular woman, adored by her husband whom she adored back. Initially, he failed to notice the amount she was drinking and had plenty of other things on his mind.

Most notable was his new yacht, *Athero II*. The new craft was the most technically advanced private yacht built up to then. Livermore had owned over a dozen yachts up to that point, which he had bought and sold according to his financial circumstances at the time. But he had never had a new yacht built to his exact specifications and desires.

It was his ultimate dream and one that took nine years to fulfill.

The new yacht was smaller than the big yachts of the day but designed to be comfortably moored at the jetty at the bottom of the garden at Great Neck and to be able to negotiate the pier in the East River at 26th Street in Manhattan.

The dream started in 1920 after he had settled in at Evermore and had extended the steel and concrete jetty at the end of the garden to accommodate a yacht of up to 200 feet.

He already knew the best yacht designer in America, the legendary Henry Gielow, who ran his own naval architectural practice on the west side of New York. He had first met Gielow in 1907. He also ran a yacht brokerage out of his New York office

Livermore bought and sold all his yachts through Gielow's yacht broker, Joe MacDonald. MacDonald enjoyed the same legendary status in selling yachts to wealthy Americans as Gielow did designing them. It seemed that when MacDonald came on the phone to tell him about a yacht he had for sale, Livermore couldn't say 'no'.

In 1920, he started talking to Gielow about the design of the ultimate private motor yacht, incorporating state of the art technology. Together they sketched out the specification and design of the perfect boat.

Early on, Livermore decided to call the yacht *Athero*. The origin of the name wasn't clear and it appeared to be an ancient word taken from the earliest token of money in the form of the first Greek currency, a name that Livermore found appropriate and that no one else would ever get to the bottom of.

Gielow's office was near Livermore's west side home, and during the design process, Livermore would often visit every other day. It took a year just to lay down the concept of the yacht.

When that was done, Gielow set to work and the first practical drawings emerged six months later. They decided on a length of 171 feet, the maximum Livermore believed it could be to safely navigate the waters between Great Neck and Manhattan. It had a beam of 27 feet and a 13 feet draft to enable it to be easily maneuverable in the narrow rivers. It was specified to have a top cruising speed of 17mph from the new diesel engines that were now available.

The resulting diesel powered yacht would be capable of ferrying him direct from his home to his office in Manhattan or the West Indies or Palm Beach, which ever took his and Dorothy's fancy.

The plans for the *Athero* were changed many times during construction and its specification was upgraded continually so the latest technology could be installed.

It would take many years to finalize the design until Livermore was ready to push the button on construction. Livermore took his usual attitude to budgeting and told Gielow to build it first and do the budget afterwards. When Gielow told him it was looking like it could cost around $2.5 million, making it the most expensive private yacht conceived up to that point, even Jesse Livermore hesitated about splashing out that sort of money. Up to when the keel was laid, there was some doubt whether it would ever be built.

But before he could place the order, Henry Gielow had a heart attack and died in 1925 at the age of 70. His successor was his partner and chief salesman Joe MacDonald who took over the firm. Seeking a boost after Gielow's death, MacDonald applied all the pressure he could to get Livermore to finally place the order. The persuasion and charm offensive worked, and the keel was finally laid a few months after Gielow's death at the shipyard of George S. Lawley & Son in Boston.

Henry Gielow had specified George S. Lawley & Sons to build the boat before he died. Lawley and his son, also called George, were regarded as the best yacht builders in the world at the time. George Sr had started building boats in the east of London at a yard on the River Thames and had moved to America in 1866 to pursue his dream of building really large yachts. He became the go-to-guy for rich Americans wanting the latest specification yacht. His state of the art yard was at an old nail works in Neponset, and it became a magnet for rich men wanting to live their dreams. Livermore visited the yard every month during the construction of the *Athero* and was astonished at the well known people he met in Lawley's offices who were also bitten by the expensive yachting bug.

Livermore was determined that even if it wasn't the biggest, it would be the finest yacht ever built. The 'build it first, budget for it later' approach to the project pushed the cost up another half million dollars. MacDonald described the design brief for *Motor Boating* magazine in 1926: "We were given unusual latitude to put into them the best to be had, regardless of cost, not only in features of construction but in materials and equipment."

At a final cost of over $3 million, it had two of the latest 800hp Bessemer diesel engines that would enable it to get a top cruising speed of 17mph, then the ultimate performance attainable for a big yacht.

The equipment installed was state of the art, from the magnificent tender that ferried guests around port, to the latest galley equipped with oil fired ranges. It was one of the first yachts to have an air conditioning system installed. It was also the first private yacht to be built to eliminate all vibration. Vibrationless yachts became a hallmark of Gielow design and the Lawley yard. Along with it, there was maximum soundproofing and there was virtually no intrusion at all from the engines at low speed.

But perhaps the most important feature of the yacht was the state of the art radio room situated on the deck house. The permanent radio operator also had his sleeping cabin within the radio room so he could keep the *Athero* connected to the world 24 hours a day.

When it was delivered, the Livermores broke from tradition, and it was the first winter they did not spend in Palm Beach. The *Athero*'s maiden voyage was a 1,000-mile trip to the Caribbean, over nine weeks with the Livermore family continuously on board.

As the magnificent yacht sailed into the ports of Bridgetown and Freetown and others on the islands, Livermore was welcomed on the quayside by local dignitaries like a visiting head of state. They were not only anxious to inspect the modern yacht, but according to Livermore, continually pestered him for share tips, and he was astonished at how well known he was in the islands. Livermore enjoyed his carefree sojourn around the Caribbean islands but not as much as he did the lazy days of fishing by day and gambling by night in Palm Beach.

The long voyage around the Caribbean had been a novelty, but they soon missed Palm Beach and its easy living. In 1928, they were back to familiar territory. Almost every winter in the twenties they would take their private rail car to Palm Beach for a three-month break. Although they always had a yacht on hand, they preferred to stay at The Breakers Hotel where they had a year round private suite and staff who catered to their every whim.

But for all the luxuries available to them, the Livermores enjoyed being at Evermore best of all, which became a real family home. They were looked after for the most part by devoted servants.

During those years, especially in the school holidays, Livermore would work from home where he kept a stock ticker in his private office. Then he would teach his two young sons to shoot and show off his private gun collection, kept under lock and key in the basement. Guns had always fascinated Livermore, and as soon as he could afford to indulge in a collection, he did. His youngest son Paul gave long interviews to Richard Smitten, an early biographer, where the gun collection was discussed. It consisted of handguns, shotguns and rifles, and Paul recalled it numbered over 400 separate examples. Livermore taught his wife and two sons all aspects of gunmanship, and they all became expert marksmen. According to Smitten, when Paul was 11 he could fieldstrip a .45 automatic pistol and reassemble it in a few minutes. Whilst he owned a house in Lake Placid, Livermore took his family shooting in the woods but most of it was done on the range he had created near the seashore at Great

Neck and on the clay pigeon shoot over the water.

Life was so good that for a few years Livermore gave up his philandering and resolved to devote himself to his wife and children. The period between 1926 and 1927 truly were halcyon years for the Livermore family. No one could have foretold what was to come.

CHAPTER 33

Shenanigans at Great Neck
The bad times start

1925 - 1927

O n Sunday 29th May 1927, the idyllic and happy lifestyle enjoyed by the Livermore family at Great Neck was rudely and violently interrupted. Two armed robbers, later identified as Arthur Barry and Jim Monaghan, known in crime circles as Boston Billy, held up the Livermores and two house guests and stole jewelry valued at $100,000.

The burglary received national attention because of the value of the jewels stolen and the bizarre nature in which the robbery was conducted.

The two burglars were dubbed 'the gentlemen burglars' by the press because they behaved like the perfect gentlemen through the raid and were dressed in smart suits and neckties.

As well as Barry and Monaghan, there were two other people in the gang: Eddie Kane, Livermore's former chauffeur, and Barry's girlfriend Anna Blake. Kane provided the inside information, which meant the actual burglars knew the exact layout of Evermore and were so effortlessly able to carry out the robbery.

On that Sunday night, they had camped out nearby the Livermore mansion in a clump of trees in the 12-acre garden. The night was warm but they lit a small fire after it grew dark around nine o'clock. They shielded the campfire so it could not be seen, but from their vantage point they had full view of the house, the Livermore yacht, the *Athero II*, and the Chris Craft speedboat moored on the pier.

Although the trees shielded them from the house, they were in full view of the crew of *Athero II*, who appeared to notice nothing. When questioned later, the skipper Captain Howell and second officer Harold Clark said they saw or heard nothing untoward during the evening.

A few hundred yards away, the burglars had concealed a Chrysler Finer 70 Sports Roadster as their getaway vehicle. The car was distinctive, in primrose yellow with a beige hood and brown ribbed upholstery. They had stolen it from the garage of Walter Roesler, one of Livermore's neighbors, by mistake, believing it to belong to the financier. It actually belonged to George Owens, a houseguest of the Roeslers. The plan was to use the car to drive to Long Island station before it got light and to catch the first train at six o'clock into New York and be into the city before the police started searching.

Inside the house, the Livermores were hosting a dinner party for their houseguests Robert Galston, Harry Aronhson and his wife Sadie, who were staying over for the Memorial Day celebrations. There were 12 servants also in residence.

The Livermores and the Aronhsons had left New York together and travelled to Great Neck by sea on Livermore's yacht arriving on Saturday morning. Galston had arrived separately by motor car on Saturday afternoon.

The party was loud and raucous as the five friends enjoyed a carefree dinner. On board the *Athero II*, the crew did their rounds and completely failed to notice the four people huddled around a camp fire in the trees.

An hour before dawn, 28-year-old Barry and Monaghan, 25, made their move. They damped down the fire and changed their clothes from overalls into smart suits, with shirt and tie. Both men donned Fedoras. Monaghan opened his bag and handed Barry a .45 Colt pistol. He also picked out one from the bag. Then they blacked out their faces with the cooling cinders from the fire.

Then, on Monaghan's signal, they sprinted across the lawns, holding a folding ladder they had stolen from the garage. First, they went to the side and snipped the wires to the telephones. When they got to the front of the house, they unfolded the ladder and put it against the balustrades to give them access to the balcony where all the French windows were open. From leaving the camp fire, they were on the balcony within five minutes.

The two, armed with information from Kane, walked into the Aronhson's bedroom first and roused them. Monaghan went to Sadie's side of the bed, shined his torch in her face and placed his hand tightly over her mouth. When he felt it was safe, he withdrew his hand and waved his pistol in front of her eyes. Scared out of her wits, she emitted a small scream but quickly got the message when Barry said to her: "I'll put a bullet through you if you don't keep quiet." She did not need telling twice.

Harry Aronhson was feeling ill and suspected he was suffering from food poisoning. He was in the bathroom sitting on the toilet when he heard his wife's muted scream in the bedroom. He jumped up just in time to see a smiling Monaghan with his finger in front of his mouth, the torch light in his eye and his pistol pointed straight at him. Aronhson knew what he had to do and Monaghan motioned him to walk quietly forward and sit on the side of the bed.

The two were politely asked to hand over their jewels and cash. Barry scooped up Aronhson's platinum wristwatch from beside the bed. Monaghan casually asked for Harry's wallet and found $200 untouched inside. He took it and, smiling, handed him back $2 he told him was for a "cab to the railway station." Aronhson, not a particularly humorous man at the best of times, did not find it funny.

When they had finished, they were ordered to sit on the bed and not move. Monaghan lied to them and told them a third burglar was outside their room keeping guard, they didn't choose to question him or find out for themselves. They sat tight whilst Monaghan and Barry moved into the Livermores' bedroom.

Ten minutes after they had entered the house, they walked calmly to the master bedroom suite and woke the couple after first securing the Colt .22 pistol that Livermore kept in his bedside cabinet.

Then Barry went back and ushered the Aronhsons into the bedroom. They scooped up any loose jewelry and Monaghan asked Livermore to open the safe. When he failed to remember the combination, Monaghan took a jemmy he was carrying and quickly levered the lock open. Livermore was surprised how easily his safe was penetrated by the flimsy piece of metal. To Monaghan's intense disappointment, the safe contained only Livermore and his wife's last will and testament.

Dorothy, still slightly tipsy from the night before, opened up a dialogue with Monaghan, whom she later told police she found charming. She asked him for a cigarette and he obliged, even lighting it for her. Livermore and the Aronhsons sat on the bed astonished as Dorothy charmed the two burglars and embarked on a civilized discussion about their chosen profession and the value of the jewels they were intent on stealing. When Barry removed the matching sapphire rings on her and her husband's fingers, she politely asked him if they could return them as they had sentimental value. Monaghan ordered Barry to give them back, which he did, saying as he passed them over: "I hope they bring you luck." And when she asked him to speak a little softer and walk on tiptoe so as not to wake the two children along the corridor, he duly obliged as well.

Monaghan left Barry to guard the Livermores and the Aronhsons whilst he scoured the house for more jewels. When he returned, they sat the four down, bound their hands and feet and left as silently as they had arrived, just as dawn was breaking. At the gates to the house, Kane and Blake were waiting with the Chrysler and they quietly drove off. After an hour, the Livermores broke free, raised the alarm and the servants came to untie them.

On receiving the call, police rushed to the house and surrounded it. Neighbors were awoken by blazing sirens and flashing lights as over 50 policemen crowded into Great Neck.

After they established the burglars were no longer in the vicinity, the police undertook a fingertip search of the grounds for clues. The senior officers, led by Captain Harold King of Nassau County Police, closely questioned the Livermores, the Aronhsons, Galston and the servants.

With the search of the grounds completed, the policemen fanned out into the neighborhood. The neighbors reported the stolen Chrysler and an APB was put out for the car, which was quickly discovered at Long Island railway station at Manhasset, a few miles away.

It was quickly established that the thieves, finding they had missed the train they had hoped to catch, stole a taxi they found at the station. The taxi, with the keys left in it, belonged to Jack McConnell, who was inside chatting to the station master. They drove the taxi into New York and abandoned it, where the trail went cold.

As soon as the police had questioned them, the Aronhsons packed up and left to be driven home to their apartment at East 67th Street, New York, in Livermore's Rolls-Royce. Any enthusiasm they had for celebrating Memorial Day with their hosts had long disappeared. The Aronhsons, thoroughly traumatized by the experience, would never return to Long Island.

Police soon established that it was the same gang that had carried out a string of robberies at grand houses on Long Island. Boston Billy was soon identified, followed by Arthur Barry.

A hue and cry search was launched for them along the East coast.

The robbery caught the imagination of the American public and received pages of publicity across the country's newspapers. Armed guards were placed at the Livermore house, adding to the drama.

The New York Times reported the robbery the following Monday on its front page, prominently above the fold. The detailed story of the burglary was replayed at great length inside the paper. Jesse Livermore recalled the experience: "The burglars seemed not only without fear but in no hurry. They didn't even modulate their voices. They were business-like enough in some things, but why did they return jewels almost as great in value as those they took? Why did they give into Mrs Livermore's pleading if they were hard boiled yeggmen?"

Livermore was clearly very proud of the courage, valor and the lack of fear shown by his wife in dealing with the burglars. During one conversation in particular, Dorothy had referred to her husband as 'Pops' and managed to persuade Monaghan to give back two sapphire rings worth $70,000. This astonished Livermore. As he said:" That was almost funny. My wife, as far as I could remember, never refers to me as 'Pops,' but she tried it on with those two burglars: 'Now give "Pops" back his ring and stones. I gave them to him and we think a lot of them' and, sure enough, they gave them back."

He continued: "They called me Jesse. That was funny too. They called me Jesse so much and with such an air that I found myself wondering whether I had met them somewhere. I tried to recall if I had heard their voices anywhere. I haven't been called Jesse for years as everybody, my family included, calls me J. L."

Livermore also told reporters that he was amazed with the ease with which the burglars had been able to open his safe with two blows of a chisel and hammer. He said "I told them that there was nothing in there but some papers, but they insisted I open it. Well I tried, and my wife tried, and then I gave them the combination and they tried. Then I asked them why they didn't crack it."

Livermore told reporters he was very surprised that the burglars had such intimate knowledge of his house and the extent that they had been able to effortless and noiselessly move around, to the point where they had not even disturbed his two dogs who usually barked fiercely when they heard strange noises. Livermore added: "I tried to grab the phone just after they came in, but one of them told me they had cut the wires."

Livermore also revealed that the robbers' haul of jewels, valued at $100,000, could have been much more. He said that the bulk of his wife's jewelry collection, worth more than $2 million, was kept in bank safety deposit boxes in New York.

The Livermores quickly left the house to the police to continue their investigations and to question the servants. To celebrate Memorial Day, they decided to go on a two-day cruise on their yacht and quickly packed and left, eager to forget the whole experience which, despite its relative pleasantness, had left them both traumatized.

With all the publicity and the huge police manhunt effort aided by Burns agency detectives and insurance investigators, it was only a matter of time before the perpetrators were apprehended.

Two days after the raid, the stolen taxi was found in New York at Bergen Avenue. It was stripped down by the police and every inch examined and finger printed. The burglars had been very careful, and the only prints found were those of George Owens and his wife on the Chrysler.

In the days after the raid, the family were threatened by hoaxers forecasting a return of the 'gentlemen burglars.' Captain King dismissed the threats, saying: "They are obviously the works of a crank." But King still ordered the number of police men guarding Livermore and his family to be doubled from two to four "just in case."

The Livermore burglary proved the last straw for the insurance company, which retained the services of ace private investigator Noel Scaffa. According to the New Yorker magazine, Scaffa had "an uncannily clever knack of retrieving the stolen valuables of his clients." His technique was to offer a reward and encourage the thieves to try and claim it through him with the inference he would not turn them in and they were safe in his hands. The police hated it, but the insurance companies loved him.

Scaffa employed 20 private agents and claimed to have recovered $6 million of stolen jewels in his career. But this time, it was the police not Scaffa who got the accolades as the drama played out and came to a conclusion less than a week later. The police were aided by nationwide blanket publicity as the American public became obsessed with the story.

After an anonymous tip off, six days after the robbery on June 5th, Arthur Barry and Anna Blake were arrested coming off a train at Ronkonkoma, 50 miles from Pennsylvania. There was a brief scuffle on the platform as Blake immediately gave herself up but Barry ran off up the carriage only to be stopped by two burly policemen at the other end. He was bundled off at high speed into a waiting unmarked Chevrolet car.

The arrest descended into farce as members of the public, witnessing the incident, believed that the police, who did not identify themselves, were the robbers and kidnappers, and that Barry and Blake were the victims. They took the car registration 2 Z 33 number and phoned it in, which started a major operation across two counties to stop the car and occupants and apprehend the two "dangerous" occupants. The hunt only ended when police checked the registration plate and found it was registered to the Nassau County district attorney Elvin Edwards.

When she was caught, Blake was in possession of jewels taken from other robberies, but she had none of the Livermore jewels. The District Attorney believed Barry and Blake were on their way to a drop off with Noel Scaffa, but it was never proved.

Quickly, the police also arrested Barry's brother, William, at their home on suspicion of being involved. The following day, Arthur Barry confessed to the Livermore robbery and turned in Monaghan as well. In return for the confession and for welching on his associate, Eddie Kane, the District Attorney agreed to release Anna Blake and William Barry without charge.

The following day, New York Police raided Monaghan's address at a rooming house in New York provided to them by Barry. But they just missed him.

Later that day, Jesse and Dorothy Livermore were called to the Mineola police station where Barry was being held, but they failed to identify him because of his blacked out face on the night of the robbery. But identification was unnecessary as Barry confessed to 22 other robberies, and it was revealed he was also on the run from jail for assaulting a police officer who was later murdered. His haul from the 23 burglaries to which he confessed, including the Livermores, was later estimated at $2 million. Barry implicated Monaghan as the murderer of the policeman. He also said Monaghan had the Livermore jewels. Barry gave police the name of a fence to whom they had disposed of some of the jewelry. He was Morris Frank, a hairdresser in the Bronx. Frank was quickly arrested but just as quickly released again for lack of evidence.

At his arraignment the following day, Barry said he regretted the burglary: "I was sincerely sorry after I found that Mr and Mrs Livermore were such good sports under the stress of circumstances, but still we went through with the job."

A day later, James Monaghan once again gave the police the slip when he left the Times Square Hotel on Eighth Avenue just before they arrived. But his days appeared numbered as his face stared out from the front pages of every newspaper in America. He was public enemy number one for a few weeks.

Barry was suffering a backlash in prison for informing on his fellow crooks. It was rumored that Monaghan had put out a contract on him even though he was inside. He was put in solitary confinement. Monaghan broke cover a few days later by writing to the *New York Times* claiming Barry had murdered the policeman not him. In the letter, Monaghan called Barry "a rat who would send his own brother to the Chair." Monaghan also wrote that he had proof that Barry had committed the murder.

At his trial a month later, on July 6th, Barry was sentenced to 25 years hard labor. Anna Blake, sitting in court, was in tears. As Barry was sent down, Blake thrust 10 dollars into his hand, knowing she would probably never see him again.

A day after Barry was sentenced, Monaghan's time was finally up. He was spotted entering the room of a motel in Sound View, Connecticut. When police surrounded it, he was shot in the leg as tried to escape out of a back window. He was taken to Memorial Hospital and then straight to jail.

At his arraignment, he faced 21 charges of burglary and seven indictments in all. He pleaded "not guilty." On July 29th, after a week of hearings, he was found guilty and sentenced to 50 years in jail and no remission. He would never be released.

Two years later, on January 6th 1929, Eddie Kane, the chauffeur, was finally arrested in Wisconsin. He pleaded guilty and elected to stay in prison without bail. On May 22nd he was sentenced to three and a half years jail time.

Kane's confession surprised the Livermores more than anything else about the affair. They had refused to accept his guilt until he pleaded guilty. He had been a trusted aide and friend and his involvement shocked them greatly, and from that day it completely changed the relationship they had with their servants.

Kane's trial caused Livermore temporarily to become depressed and he was forced to seek medical help. It took him two months to fully recover and, from then on, armed bodyguards did not leave his side for four years.

There was a postscript to the affair. Barry was serving his sentence at Auburn Prison. In July 1929, he and other inmates shot their way out of the prison during a riot. He remained a fugitive for three years until he was recaptured on October 22nd 1932.

For most of that time, he had been hiding out as a $2 a week lodger on a remote New Jersey farm owned by local farmer Otto Rutter who also lived on the farm in Sussex County. Barry was posing as a salesman for a car windshield wiper company. He always carried a briefcase ostensibly containing samples of wiper blades, but in reality containing a gun and a huge quantity of ammunition to sustain him in a long shoot out if he was ever cornered by police.

The police got a tip-off that he was hiding out in a Sussex farmhouse and began to comb the county.

Barry was finally undone by a local news vendor when he neglected to pay his newspaper bill. During the search, the police questioned the vendor and he told them about a man who ordered every New York newspaper every day and had neglected to pay his bill. When they showed him a photograph of Barry, George Losey the vendor shouted: "That's him, that's the man that owes me two weeks' money", and police knew they had their man.

Losey explained that he had always thought it was funny that a windshield wiper salesman, living on an isolated farm, should be so eager for a complete set of New York newspapers each day.

Losey, clearly sensing that his 15 minutes of fame had come, eagerly agreed to lead the police to the farm and help them catch Barry peacefully. It was a difficult operation for the police and they needed Losey's help. They were all too aware of the likely scenario of a lengthy shoot-out should Barry sense police presence anywhere near the farm.

The police surrounded the farm and sent Losey to the door to enquire about his money. Barry, posing as a James Toomer, came to the door not suspecting a thing.

Losey, on police instructions, deliberately got into a heated argument with Barry over the unpaid bill despite the fact that the hapless fugitive had got his money out ready to pay whilst trying to explain he had simply forgotten about it.

Losey lured Barry outside and the police crept up and were on top of him before he realized what was happening. He had a loaded gun in his pocket but didn't have time to draw it, so engrossed was he in his argument with Losey. Very quickly, Toomer realized it was fruitless to deny he was Barry and he was carted off to jail at Sussex County for the night under heavy guard.

Meanwhile, farmer Otto Rutter was left explaining to police and reporters his utter surprise at sheltering a dangerous fugitive in his farm for over 12 months.

Barry was returned to jail but, amazingly, his story was not over. In 1949, he was released early after serving 21 years of his 25 year sentence for good behavior despite his violent escape in 1929. But he was immediately rearrested for other robberies that the police had discovered he had perpetrated 25 years earlier, which he did not admit at the time. It is believed he died inside.

For the Livermores, however, the story never ended. When Barry escaped, the story was rehashed all over the nation's newspapers yet again. And three years on, when he was recaptured, the story aired again. There was no rest for a family that, by then, had gone their separate ways.

JESSE LIVERMORE - BOY PLUNGER

CHAPTER 34

Build Up to a National Disaster

America binges on shares

January 1928 - August 1929

The seeds of the 1929 stock market boom, the greatest the world had ever seen, were sown seven years earlier, in 1921, when the Federal Reserve slashed its base interest rate from seven per cent to four and a half per cent. The two and a half per cent drop in the space of a few weeks was unprecedented and smacked of unnecessary panic. America had suffered a downturn and its gross domestic product (GDP) had dropped two per cent in 1920 and 1921. But many thought the rate reduction was really to boost the stock market, which was at a low ebb.

Before the rate reduction, the conditions for a sustained period of economic growth were already apparent. Post-war optimism had started a huge exodus of Americans from rural areas into the cities and ferocious economic growth based on manufacturing. Almost overnight, America converted from an agricultural economy to an industrial one, and the period became popularly known as the 'roaring twenties.'

In hindsight, many people believe the rate reduction was an overreaction by the Fed, and it served to kick off a stock market boom that would last for a record eight years, from August 25th 1921 to September 3rd 1929.

It did real damage by effectively compressing a boom that should have stretched over thirty years into just eight with all the pain that that entailed. Apart from a brief reversal in 1924, the Dow Jones Industrial Average rose 500 per cent in a crazy bid for the top – never seen before and never seen since.

Many observers and economists look back now and say if they could change anything, it would be that rate change in 1921; they believe the eventual outcome in 1929 might have been so very different.

The situation in 1921 wasn't helped by a change of Administration. The incoming president, Warren Harding, a Republican, had little idea about economics and wanted to please the American people by quickly tackling the cause of the recession that had started on his predecessor President Wilson's watch. Harding's newly appointed Treasury Secretary, Andrew Mellon, was also inexperienced, and that added to the early missteps.

Harding and Mellon's intentions had been admirable and initially worked like a dream. For the first three years between 1921 and 1923, growth was extraordinary: averaging 10.5 per cent a year. After a breather in 1924, it rose an average of four percent each year for the next five years. Unsurprisingly, the U.S. economy and the stock market overheated.

The effect on the stock market was particularly striking and Jesse Livermore watched prices go up along with the rest of America. He was a more natural bear than he was bull and consequently only participated in some of the rise up to the middle of 1928. After that, he spent a long time either out of the market or trying to find the top.

Livermore recalled the mood: "Prices kept going up and that meant that the end of the bull market was drawing nearer. I did not look for the end on any fixed date. That was something quite beyond my power to determine. But I needn't tell you that I was on the watch for the tip-off. I always am anyhow. It had become a matter of business habit with me."

In fact, from as early as 1927 onwards, Livermore was in no doubt that there would be a sharp reversal at some point – he just didn't know when and lost a considerable amount of money probing the market trying to find the bottom. He wrote off the losses as the cost of being a speculator. He, more than any man, reasoned the market could carry on rising long after it had seemingly reached an unattainable peak. As he said: "The successful trader cannot bet on the unreasonable or on the unexpected, however strong his personal convictions or however certain he may feel, as the unexpected happens very frequently."

Livermore's fears had started in January when the Dow Jones Industrial Average rose by a staggering seven per cent and 111 million shares were traded; double that of the previous January. The unprecedented rise in share prices was fuelled by shares like RCA, which were being manipulated by bull pools such as those of stockbroker Mike Meehan.

At a time when government intervention was desperately needed, nothing was done and, as a result, an eventual stock market calamity became almost a certainty.

At the start of 1929, sitting in his office in New York, Jesse Livermore certainly believed that President Hoover's upcoming inauguration could lead to the market break he had been expecting, especially as Hoover was already exerting pre-inauguration control of the Federal Reserve.

On February 2nd 1929, the Fed sent out a letter to the regional reserve banks across America requesting that it refuse any loans that it believed were destined to finance margin trading on the stock market. Although the letter was issued confidentially, Livermore heard about it almost immediately and guessed that it was just the start of a chain of negative actions from the incoming Hoover administration as it pursued barely disguised efforts to "damp down" the stock market. He was right. On February 7th, the Federal Reserve put out an announcement warning of "the excessive amount of the country's credit absorbed in speculative loans."

The Fed's warnings damped down the market and the Dow Jones fell as borrowing costs to buy on margin rose to 14 per cent. But the decline was brief as Charles Mitchell, chairman of National City Bank, pressured the Treasury Secretary, Andrew Mellon, to talk the market up again – and he duly obliged.

Livermore examined every comma of the Fed's statement so he could truly understand what it was saying and, more importantly, what it was not saying. He was also aware of a huge wrangle going on behind the scenes over the official interest rates. The main row was between the Federal Reserve Bank of New York and Washington. The New York Fed, backed by the new Governor of New York, Franklin Roosevelt, wanted to raise rates from five per cent to six per cent immediately. Washington vetoed it.

It became obvious that something was afoot when the Federal Reserve seemed to be relying on what Livermore called "well meant words" to curb margin lending rather than positive action. The obvious action required was to raise interest rates, which didn't happen.

It became clear that the Fed was trying to pressure the banks to withdraw credit rather than ordering them to. But the banks were reluctant to comply. With interest rates at five per cent, they were lending money to the market at up to 20 per cent and making huge profits.

It later emerged that it was pressure from across the water at the Bank of England that had prevented a rate rise. There was a real crisis going on in London as gold was being transferred from England to America at record rates to finance share speculation. In January, gold imports from London were $7 million alone. Any rise in U.S. interest rates would have just exacerbated the British problem.

Undoubtedly, America should have put its own interests first and the Fed should have raised rates in February to damp down the rampant speculation. When it didn't, an opportunity to avert the trouble that would come later was lost.

For Livermore, these wranglings were a clear signal. It was as clear to him as it had been in 1907 that the market was headed for a big break before the end of the year.

But he would need a big war chest to be able to take full advantage, and Livermore himself was not in the best of financial shape. Four years earlier, he had been worth an estimated $30 million, but his assets had dwindled alarmingly as he lost millions seeking the bottom but instead seeing the market continue to rise.

All through February and early March, Livermore did little else but plan the assault he would make when conditions were right. He sat in his office, chain smoking cigars, determined not to trade until conditions were perfect. His statisticians worked overtime, continually analyzing market data. He picked up everything anyone said about the economy and the stock market, from the President of the United States down to the man who shined his shoes. Nothing escaped him.

President-elect Hoover continually sought to contain and dampen down the stock market. So much so that many observers attributed the ultimate collapse of the market to the president himself. They believe Hoover came into office convinced that it was his duty to prevent a collapse by halting the Wall Street boom by any means he could.

Livermore absorbed it all and analyzed it in his head constantly. Wendy Thomas ran in and out of Livermore's office with files for him to peruse, and she created new ones by the dozen, which his staff filled with newspaper cuttings and data.

Whilst all this frantic activity was going on, Livermore was sanguine. He had, after all, seen it all before. He knew his biggest virtue now was patience. As the market boiled over, he knew that he just had to remember everything he had taught himself. As he explained by comparing his life as a stock speculator to that of a doctor: "The training of a stock trader is like a medical education. The physician had to spend long years learning. He learns the theory and then proceeds to devote his life to the practice. He observes and classifies all sorts of pathological phenomena. He learns to diagnose. If his diagnosis is correct – and that depends upon the accuracy of his observation – he ought to do pretty well in his prognosis, always keeping in mind, of course, that human fallibility and the utterly unforeseen will keep him from scoring 100 per cent of bull's-eyes. And then, as he gains in experience, he learns not only to do the right thing but to do it instantly, so that many people will think he does it instinctively. It really isn't automatism. It is that he has diagnosed the case according to his observations of such cases during a period of many years; and, naturally, after he has diagnosed it, he can only treat it in the way that experience had taught him is the proper treatment."

On March 4th 1929, Herbert Hoover was finally installed as the 31st President of the United States. Hoover was a natural pessimist. He had inherited a booming economy, but he saw it as being overheated and he didn't fail to let everyone know. His inaugural speech in the pouring rain was broadcast to 63 million people round the world. He emphasized his intention to tackle the problems of Wall Street, but that was not his only target. He said his main concern was clamping down on Al Capone and the mafia, ending prohibition, and building up America's defenses.

Hoover's officials repeatedly forecast that the rise in share prices was unsustainable and could not continue indefinitely. Many believe that President Hoover made the collapse in October 1929 inevitable and turned it into a self-fulfilling prophecy. They also accused him of starving America of money supply just when it needed it most. Certainly, if Pierpont Morgan had still been alive, it was clear things would have turned out very differently.

But the irony was despite all the warnings from Hoover and his officials, the opposite was happening, and the market continued to rise through the first half of 1929.

Hoover's words were music to Jesse Livermore's ears. By the middle of March, the plans for the bear assault Livermore was preparing were ready, especially after he heard that the Bank of England was transferring another $22 million of gold to New York that month as British investors joined a frenzy to buy shares on Wall Street.

Livermore's strategy was to see how soft the market was underneath. He wanted a trial run for what he knew might happen at the end of the year. Suddenly, conditions became right for him to move. On March 24th, the market was waiting for the latest statement by the board of directors of the Federal Reserve, which had been in a closed session in Washington for several days.

As a result, there was much uncertainty in the air. Livermore, like the rest of Wall Street knew that something would come out of the meeting, and the longer it lasted, the less positive he guessed it might be. He went home early that night to Great Neck instead of staying in Manhattan as he had for the past few weeks. He wanted time to quietly think.

At 8:30 the following morning, on March 25th, he had made the decision. He called his 20 odd traders into his office and said just three words: "Go, go, go". It was the cue to put into action a plan, a bear raid on Wall Street; something they had discussed for the past two weeks. Now everyone was primed, as Livermore explained his motives: "A man must bet always on probabilities – that is, try to anticipate them. Years of practice at the game, of constant study, of always remembering, enable the trader to act on the instant when the unexpected happens as well as when the expected comes to pass."

At just before 10 o'clock, Livermore took up his place in the trading room, waiting for the tickers to start making the noise that would signal the opening of the market.

As soon as the stock exchange gong sounded, Livermore and his boys began buying and selling shares to a pre-arranged pattern. He was desperate to disguise his intentions in early trading. But as the morning wore on, it became apparent that for every one buy order, there were ten selling orders as the building up of a huge bear position in stocks got underway. Amongst others, Livermore sold American Can, AT&T, American Woollen, Corn Products plus virtually every railway stock and utility.

By 11 o'clock, the newswires started clattering and commentators reported that Livermore had been very active in the first hour of trading. He was selling so many shares it was impossible to keep it secret. By midday, the plan had been fully executed and Livermore and his boys had sold $150 million of shares short, leveraging his equity base of $7 million to the very maximum it would stretch. Whilst he was very confident of success, he was also conscious it would only take a five per cent upswing in the market to wipe him out and that he was pursuing a potentially dangerous strategy should things not go his way.

But in reality, such heavy selling could only push the market one way. After two hours, the market was down one and half per cent giving Livermore some comfort and additional margin on his position. But he was still terribly over extended.

There was no more action that day and the market appeared eventually to absorb his selling comfortably. Livermore held his nerve and bought back nothing before the close. He was, as he described it, "all in."

When the market opened the following morning, the overnight rates for borrowing money for margin trading had shot up to 20 per cent, the highest they had been since 1920. When the new rate was posted on the electric display boards that the stock exchange was now using, a fuse blew, causing waves of laughter to ripple across the trading floor. Then Wall Street blew its own fuse as the market reacted badly to the news. Some investors clearly saw the blown fuse as a bad omen.

There was no cause for laughter over what happened next. Between 10 o'clock and the close five hours later, 8.25 million shares were traded as sell orders poured in, driving prices down. It was the greatest numbers of shares ever traded in a single session up to then and a new world record.

At around two o'clock, Livermore once again gathered his young traders around and told them to buy everything back that they had sold 26 hours earlier. It was executed in less than an hour and when the dust had settled they made $8 million profit, Livermore's single best one-day gain up to that point. In the process, he doubled his capital. Livermore had called the market perfectly and bought back the shorts at precisely the right moment.

That became apparent the next day when Charles Mitchell announced he would increase National City Bank's commitment to lend for margin trading by $25 million. Mitchell's move brought a halt to the decline in share values instantly, and it also caused the rate for so-called 'call money' to drop down to eight per cent.

Charles Mitchell was a consistent cheer leader of the market rise. He thought the Federal Reserve was "meddling dangerously" in areas that didn't concern it. He believed that President Hoover's negative statements were the cause of the market's declines and called upon him to stop making such statements.

After his March coup, Livermore once again retreated into his bunker and waited for conditions to come right to repeat the exercise. In the middle of May, he did again but on a smaller scale. This time, the market break was caused by his selling rather than by the influence of external events. But once again, just as he had on March 26th, he bought back all his positions quickly and banked a small profit of around a million dollars.

The waiting game continued. The European stock markets were already in the doldrums after being starved of cash and, as gold poured into New York from London, Livermore became more and more certain that he was right.

On May 30th, against all expectations, the United Kingdom elected a socialist government and Ramsey McDonald was returned as Prime Minister for the second time. This would have grave implications for a British entrepreneur

301

called Clarence Hatry and potentially grave implications for the world.

All through the summer, Livermore declined to go home to Great Neck. Despite the heat of New York, he clung to his desk, analyzing the data and talking to his contacts on the telephone. In June, another $9 million of gold arrived in New York from London. Hundreds of thousands of American shares were being bought every day by British investors. The Brits were intensely worried about the effect a socialist government would have on Britain's economy and were unwilling to invest in their own country.

And it wasn't only the British. That summer, it seemed that the whole of Europe was buying up Wall Street. American companies were being avidly reported on by European newspapers.

The frenzy seemed never ending and for the first time, newspapers across America began filling their back pages with columns of stock prices, updated every day at market close.

Livermore's research team was now at full stretch and it was uncovering some disturbing statistics. Although the market was rising, it was being led upwards by a small number of stocks. In fact, the majority of shares quoted in New York were actually falling. In June, 614 shares were lower than they had been in the previous January, and only 338 stocks had risen. The speculative frenzy was being played out in fewer and fewer stocks, which were becoming more and more overpriced. Livermore could not think of anything more dangerous.

Americans were withdrawing their savings at record pace to participate. Now that share prices were being published daily in newspapers, they could see what to buy and how their shares were performing daily. Livermore was only too aware of what that meant. He said: "A get rich quick scheme is being played at an increasing break neck speed across America. It is a new national sport that can be played for the price of an evening paper."

Most of the increases were being driven by a surge in turnover and share volumes that bore no comparison to the start of the decade. The more statistics he looked at, the more Livermore knew that a sharp fall was coming. And he was ever conscious of moving too late and losing the benefit of his research and the edge it gave him. As he pondered to himself: "You can transmit knowledge – that is, your particular collection of card-indexed facts – but not your experience. A man may know what to do and lose money – if he doesn't do it quickly enough."

But that summer, the state of the stock market was not the only thing on Jesse Livermore's mind. He had started to be plagued by small lawsuits from various people and organizations with whom he had dealt in the past. Each time, he was forced to settle the suits for a few hundreds of thousands of dollars rather than embark on costly and distracting litigation defending them. The more he settled, the more that seemed to come in.

Livermore rarely lost his temper but when a meritless writ from The Carbonite Company was served on him, he made an exception. Years before he had agreed to invest $500,000 in the company after its directors showed him their patents for a process for decarbonizing piston engines. But the patents did not really exist, and Livermore withdrew from the deal. The directors sued him for breach of promise and Livermore was forced to settle after articles criticizing him appeared in the New York Times. He regarded it as little more than legalized extortion. He was also forced to settle with litigants from a Boca Raton real estate deal in Florida, resulting from his investment in the Mizner Corporation. Finally, he made the decision to settle all his outstanding legal cases so he could focus on the stock market. As much as he hated settling, it was to prove a wise decision.

On July 17th 1929, Livermore called in his whole team to discuss the state of the market. He discovered that in the first two weeks in July, $10 million of gold had arrived from Britain, making $48 million for the year to date. It was clear that the Bank of England was hemorrhaging gold at an unprecedented rate as its citizens continued to invest overseas. Livermore knew then that a sharp increase in British interest rates was inevitable but wished he knew when it would occur.

One of Livermore's advantages throughout this period was the quality of his research team, which by then consisted of some 20 people. His research team was vastly superior to that of the U.S. government or even that of J. P. Morgan. Livermore led the team personally and knew that his information was better than almost anyone else's in America.

On July 17th, the team told him that house building, industrial inventories, steel production and freight movements were static compared to June 1928, and the economy had suddenly stopped growing. They also told him that automobile sales were starting to fall rapidly.

More tellingly his team also reminded him that the Dow Jones index had risen six per cent in the first two weeks of July and that the two sets of information they had presented were not compatible.

Livermore didn't need to be told that in this sort of booming economy, demand for steel and freight capacity should be rising fast, likewise with

303

automobile sales.

It was an early warning that the strong economy was cooling off in spite of what President Hoover and Secretary Mellon had been saying. Despite their pessimism for Wall Street, both men were continually bullish on the state of the American economy.

And Livermore knew that he was the only man in America in possession of all the facts. As July drew to a close, Livermore could not have felt more bearish than he was at that moment. But still, he decided to do nothing. He knew stock markets could behave in a contrary way for very long periods of time. He did not want to move too early.

Just half a mile away, at his offices further up Fifth Avenue, Arthur Cutten was also pondering the future and coming to an entirely different conclusion from Livermore. He had the wholly opposite feeling: that Wall Street had a long way to go upwards before there was any possibility of a reaction. Cutten had made money from his bullish sentiments many times before, and they had never been wrong. He had made himself a fortune of $250 million from following those instincts.

The statistics he had in front of him, culled from official stock exchange sources, told a different story. Cutten was a student of price/earnings (p/e) ratios, a formula he had devised himself for assessing the financial value of a company. He believed that on the basis of price/earnings ratios, shares were not particularly overvalued. During 1928, the after tax p/e ratio of a typical Dow Jones Industrial Average company had increased from 12 to 14, and so far, in 1929, to 15. Cutten did not believe that was high. He was also encouraged by the higher and higher dividends being paid out by quoted companies. In the first nine months of 1929, 1,436 companies had announced increased dividends. In 1928, the number was only 955 and in 1927, it was 755. Profits for Dow Jones quoted companies for the first quarter of 1929 also showed a 31 per cent increase compared to the first quarter of 1928.

The only bad news that Cutten could see was the ever-widening gap between the book value of a company and its market value, which varied between 181 and 420 per cent.

Confident that the figures before him could only indicate share prices going much higher, Cutten doubled up his bullish bet.

The same day that Livermore and Cutten were reviewing the situation and deciding their next moves, Joe Kennedy, the Irish financier, who was back in New York after a spell in Hollywood, conducted his own research – he went to get a shoe shine from Pat Bologna, who polished the shoes of Wall Street's finest. Bologna was taking a break between customers, reading the Wall Street Journal outside his pitch at 60 Wall Street as Kennedy slid into his wooden chair and put his shoes on the foot rests. Kennedy asked: "How's the market Pat?" Bologna replied: "Booming Mr K, just booming." Kennedy asked him if he was making much money, and Bologna nodded and asked him if he wanted any tips. Kennedy nodded back and Bologna replied: "Buy oil and railroads. They are going to hit the sky." As Kennedy walked away, the realization hit him that if the shoeshine boys were now handing out stock tips, then the market must have peaked. The next morning, he sold a million dollars of shares short.

As August drew to a close and the summer heat began to subside, Jesse Livermore started to get the same feelings he had experienced in 1907. But just as in 1907, the market was currently behaving the exact opposite of how he felt. From the middle of August to the beginning of September, shares went on a mini boom as buy orders flooded into stock brokers' offices.

But as this was happening, the experienced market professionals grew even more anxious. All eyes were on Livermore, and his every market move was being scrutinized. He found himself being followed by private investigators working for other financiers and speculators who wanted to know what he was doing and where he was going. Of course, Livermore knew no more than the next man when Wall Street would finally break. He just knew it would.

CHAPTER 35

Seven Incredible Days

Livermore makes $100 million in a week

24th - 30th October 1929

O n Tuesday September 3rd 1929, at around four o'clock in the afternoon, Jesse Livermore was sitting in his office on Fifth Avenue doing what he always seemed to be doing for the past six months – pondering whether a bull or bear he should be.

That day he had watched in wonder as the Dow Jones Industrial Average closed at 318.17 points, an all-time record high. The low point of the decade had been 63.9 on August 24th 1921 and the market had risen 496.51 per cent from the bottom to the top.

As the market continued its inexorable rise, all Livermore could see were warning signs.

For the first eight months of 1929, Jesse Livermore had lost $6 million putting out his bear probes and being knocked back each time. He had been a bear since March and had not participated in the market rise at all, although he had made plenty of money out of it in 1928 when he had been as bullish as the next man.

That July and August, Livermore had stayed in his office in New York despite the summer heat, afraid to trade with the market in such a state of flux. He had spent his days on the telephone seeking market intelligence across the world and pondering when the break he knew was inevitable might come.

The new transatlantic telephone service inaugurated in 1927 made regular voice phone calls to Europe feasible, albeit hideously expensive. The calls were transmitted by radio and the tariff was $25 a minute with a three-minute ($75) minimum. Livermore's monthly account for long distance calls was running at $15,000 to $25,000 a month as he continually phoned contacts in San Francisco, Paris, London and Berlin, sometimes twice a day, weaving his way through the time differences.

Livermore likened the world's stock markets in September 1929 to a "giant jigsaw" to which he "did not have all the pieces." He could feel with every sense he had that a market break was coming, but he just did not know when. $6 million had already gone up in smoke trying to find out why

At just after four, he asked his secretary Wendy Thomas to book him what had become a daily call to London to his contact at the Bank of England, who was by then at his home in the Strand district.

No one in England ever refused to take Livermore's call as transatlantic calls to and from Europe were still extremely rare in 1929, and the recipient felt almost honored to be have been called. It certainly impressed his wife and children when the nightly call came in. But Livermore needed to know what was happening in London, and he needed to know before anyone else. In those days, London was the center of the world and he knew that any break in the market would likely originate from events in London rather than in New York or Washington.

Livermore never revealed the name of his high level contact at the Bank, but the news he had for him that afternoon was well worth the $150 cost of the call. His contact told Livermore that on that very morning, at the monthly lunch of the board at the Bank of England, the Governor Monty Norman had told his directors that "the American bubble had burst."

It was also apparent that raising the interest rate had been discussed at the lunch, and that the long expected, and much delayed, rise in rates would happen before the end of the month. Norman was very worried about the huge outflow of gold from Great Britain to America and Europe. The Bank of England gold stocks had fallen to £137 million ($700 million) as a result. It was not a great position to be in. Norman said that a sharp rise in the interest rate would staunch this and begin the flow the other way.

The other news, which was discussed at the lunch, was that the Clarence Hatry Group – run by the financier Clarence Hatry – was in serious financial trouble. This was valuable news indeed. Livermore did not know Hatry personally, but he was one of the world's best-known financial operators and his companies were quoted in London. If the Hatry companies collapsed, Livermore knew that it, on its own, could provoke a global stock market collapse.

41-year-old Hatry was a very controversial figure. The economist J. K. Galbraith described him as "one of those curiously un-English figures with whom the English periodically find themselves unable to cope." It kind of summed him up. Modern day historians have likened Hatry to Robert Maxwell.

Like Jesse Livermore, Hatry knew how to live a hedonistic lifestyle. He lived in a mansion in Mayfair, just off Park Lane, equipped with one of London's first indoor swimming pools. The pool was situated on the same floor as his bedroom and in a few steps he could go from his bed to the edge of the water. He had spent $350,000 upgrading the house when he moved in in 1924. He also kept racehorses and owned the biggest private yacht in England, called Westward. His office had its own en suite bathroom, another first for London.

Hatry had started as a lowly insurance clerk in London and, as he learnt the insurance business, traded commodities on the side. His big chance came when the insurer City Equitable went bankrupt and Hatry bought the assets, restructured the company and sold it six months later for $1.2 million. He was all cashed up for the war boom and by the end was worth around $3 million. He was into everything, including the very lucrative business of transporting East European migrants to a new life in America.

In 1924, his main company, Commercial Corporation of London, collapsed owing $3.75 million but he emerged unscathed with his fortune intact. He then built a conglomerate with interests in photography, vending and finance. As Galbraith said: "Hatry built up an industrial and financial empire of truly impressive proportions."

By early 1929, the Hatry Group consisted of a clutch of eight separately quoted companies called: General Securities Ltd; Austin Friars Trust Ltd; Dundee Trust; Oak Investment Corporation; Associated Automatic Machines Corporation; Drapery Trust; Retail Trade Corporation; and Photomaton Corporation. It was the fastest growing group of companies in the City of London. Hatry seemingly was into everything and was the first large scale operator of coin-operated photographic booths used for passport and identity photos. The whole group was capitalized at $24 million on the stock market.

But in 1929, he overreached himself as he sought to merge Britain's disparate steel making companies into one group called United Steel Companies, which would be capitalized at $40 million. The consolidation was actually a very good idea but what wasn't known was that the Hatry Group was almost bust because of massive over expansion and that this merger was his last throw of the dice. Debt of $100 million, half of it due to his steel ambitions, was supported by assets of only $16 million. In August, he had tried to persuade Monty Norman to finance the merger and give him a bridging loan, which was refused.

Livermore put the phone down well pleased with himself and what he had heard. He immediately asked Wendy Thomas to send a telegraph to the broker he used in London with some sell orders on all the quoted Hatry companies.

But that was a sideshow; Livermore knew that if the information was correct and Hatry crashed, then it could kick off a run on the world's stock markets. And he knew that the same trigger could happen if the Bank of England raised interest rates. Coincidentally, Livermore had found out earlier that morning that the U.S. Federal Reserve Board would leave interest rates unchanged for September.

Armed with this new information, he was sure that a market break was imminent.

As Livermore absorbed all the news, it was midnight before he left the 18th floor of the Heckscher Building for his townhouse on the west side. The Hatry news gnawed at him all night. He pondered the implications for Wall Street and wondered how many more people were in possession of this inside information. He knew it would take Wall Street days to absorb the news and react, and he needed to know the minute it became general knowledge.

By six o'clock the following morning, he was back at his desk and on the telephone again. London had been open for an hour and he had already made $30,000 on his Hatry shorts as the price fell. But apart from that, nothing seemed to make sense. The market was slowly falling, although RCA, the go-to stock of 1929, was on the rise. He telephoned Michael Meehan, the ace stockbroker who had made millions cornering RCA stock, but he said he was out of the share. Livermore could not tell if he was telling the truth, although he suspected not.

That morning, during Livermore's regular calls to his contacts in Boston, the name Roger Babson kept coming up. He discovered that Babson, a market sage, was giving the keynote lunchtime speech at the annual National Business Conference in Boston. It was the third year running that he had been called to speak at the conference. Babson was a very dull speaker but he had been predicting a spectacular market crash for the past two years. Livermore knew what he said could move the market.

By the time Livermore put down the phone, Wendy Thomas had already placed Babson's file on his desk. Her ability to respond to Livermore's immediate needs was described by people close to him as "uncanny" but it gave him an edge when things got frantic in his office, which they often did. If Thomas hadn't placed Babson's file under his nose that day, he might have forgotten about it and moved on. Her efficiency was to make him a lot of money that morning.

He took a few moments to read the file on Babson. It reminded him that Babson promoted a stock forecasting system he called the 'long swing area method' and published a newsletter. Livermore had studied the system but deemed it amateurish. He said: "It is designed purely for stock market (bearish) minnows." Livermore may have disparaged Babson's abilities as an investor, but he was suddenly interested in what Babson would have to say later in the day. He didn't care what Babson predicted; it was "why he predicted it" that interested him.

After his calls, Livermore read all the newspapers; a daily ritual. He also found the papers full of talk about Babson's upcoming speech. Suddenly, Livermore had a strong hunch – but nothing more than a hunch – that Babson's speech would have a big impact on the market. He took a moment to check himself. Despite his strong personal convictions, Livermore remained very wary of himself. As he readily admitted: "Hunches and the mysterious ticker-sense haven't so very much to do with success. Of course, it often happens that an experienced trader acts so quickly that he hasn't time to give all his reasons in advance – but nevertheless they are good and sufficient reasons, because they are based on facts collected by him in his years of working and thinking and seeing things from the angle of the professional, to whom everything that comes to his mill is grist."

After five minutes of deliberate thought and self-restraint, Livermore decided to go short as much stock as he could sell before the speech went out. He thought there was a very good chance that Babson's words could cause a mini panic if they were as negative as he thought they might be.

Livermore got up and went into the trading room, barking orders at his staff who were just arriving. Then he sat down with his traders and they put together a plan to enact when the market opened at 10 o'clock. Livermore knew he and the team would have around an hour and a half before Babson started talking just before midday.

When the clock struck 10 o'clock they swung into frantic action. Livermore and his boys were extremely good at what they did, and in that hour and a half they sold nearly $15 million worth of stock short.

At just after midday, the Associated Press news ticker bell rang indicating flash news. The AP wire had a bell that alerted subscribers to important news. Livermore went over to the machine and read the headline: "Economist predicts 60 to 80 points stock market crash". The United Press (UP) ticker, only seconds behind, started spewing out the exact text of Babson's speech as he

311

was delivering it. The important bit read: "Sooner or later, a crash is coming which will take in the leading stocks and cause a decline from 60 to 80 points in the Dow Jones barometer."

Livermore had expected something to happen but was surprised by the scale of the reaction to Babson's speech. He thought to himself: "Surely it can't be this easy." He put the trading floor on full alert as the board boys furiously chalked up prices that were coming in over the ticker.

Somehow the story caught the attention of everyone, including America's evening newspapers, many of whom had been given a copy of the speech embargoed for one o'clock and had splashed it on the front page. Babson, who had been unknown to most Americans that morning, was suddenly a national sage. The newspapers quickly called him "one of the world's great economists" and nicknamed him the "prophet of loss." Radio stations soon picked up the story and interrupted their programs with a news flash.

The media reaction to the speech began to become almost hysterical, and Livermore waited for the reaction on Wall Street. He knew that Wall Street professionals would be taking it all in and waiting for a reaction amongst its own before they all followed suit and the herd instinct to come into play. He didn't have to wait long. A few minutes later, the final words came over the UP ticker, stockbroker's switchboards began to light up with private customers calling to sell their shares.

A minor panic began and Livermore leapt into action, selling as many shares as he could get away to add to the earlier sales. His traders started doing the same. Livermore and his men kept selling right up to three o'clock, when the exchange closed. By the close, they had managed to get away another $5 million, making $20 million in all.

The market had fallen over five per cent in two hours and 5.6 million shares had been traded.

Meanwhile, Professor Irving Fisher, who was one of the world's leading economists at Yale University, was asked for his reaction to the Babson speech. The Herald-Tribune carried it exclusively. Fisher rejected any possibility of a crash. By the time Fisher's words were out on AP and UP, the market had closed.

Livermore knew Fisher would be listened to, and he gave orders that every short was to be covered as soon as the market opened the next day.

On the morning of Friday September 6th, Livermore was in his office even earlier, at five o'clock, going through the same routine. At the stroke of ten, and within half an hour of opening, all the shorts of the previous day were covered and he bought in another $5 million worth of shares on top. The market began a rise and by midday had recovered all the losses. Livermore and his team had made over $1.8 million after getting out of their long positions by the market close. The profit, although smaller than earlier breaks, had come out of nothing at all.

It had been a brilliant 24 hours, and the celebrations began in the office and continued at the Sherry-Netherland hotel. That $150 phone call to London had paid off in a big way.

From September 6th and September 21st, Livermore was once again out of the market and did very little other than watch and wait and keep up the phone calls. The telephone account spending increased to nearly $2,000 a day. All this time, the market was gradually falling.

On the afternoon of September 20th, as he put in his usual call to his contact in London, he got his first big break. This time, his Bank of England contact in London told him that the Bank of England discount rate would be raised from 5.5 per cent to 6.5 per cent at midday the following day. He also told him that the Bank expected the Hatry Group to file for bankruptcy within the week. His contact added that Hatry and his board of directors would likely be charged with securities fraud.

Livermore knew that if Clarence Hatry's business collapsed, it would change sentiment. But he also knew there would be a delayed reaction as Wall Street absorbed the news. Livermore's team went through the same exercise and sold short as much stock as it could.

The collection of information continued apace and a week later the Hatry Group finally collapsed and, just as he had been told, Clarence Hatry was arrested on the same day and thrown into jail. The shorts were bought back in, this time for a profit of $2.5 million.

Although everyone was talking about what great shape the American economy was in, Livermore was absolutely convinced a big market break was just around the corner. Elsewhere, Arthur Cutten was again taking a very different view. That same day Cutten was at his desk staring down at the September dividend figures. 193 companies had declared increased dividends compared with 135 the year before. Profits for the third quarter for the 638 companies reporting, quoted in New York, were predicted to be up to 14 per cent on average. Cutten didn't see, with figures as good as these, how shares could go anywhere but up until well into 1930.

Livermore was convinced he knew better. He knew that Hatry's collapse was of great significance. But as Livermore prepared to make his big moves, he knew he was running out of time to get his position on, and he resolved to begin at the slightest upturn.

The market had a wakeup call on October 3rd, when there was a mini crash. It was caused by a speech made by Philip Snowden, the British Chancellor of the Exchequer, when he described the Wall Street boom as a "speculative orgy." On October 7th, The *Financial Times* reported comments made by John Lonsdale, president of the American Bankers Association, who said: "Bankers are gravely alarmed over the mounting volume of credit being employed in carrying security loans, both by brokers and by individuals." The Washington Post's headline that day was "Stock Prices Crash in Frantic Selling."

The bankers had good reason to be worried. The amount of credit available to the stock market speculators every day had grown to $3 billion. Every time bankers attempted to rein it in, private lenders appeared to fill the gap. They knew it was wrong but the situation was out of control.

All Livermore's probes were now showing profits, and he literally decided to throw caution to the wind. Somehow he sensed that this was his big moment – he had never felt so sure about anything in his life.

By this time Livermore had built his own equity up to $20 million from his summer gains. He knew it wasn't enough. But he had prepared his ground well, borrowing what money he could to increase his war chest of cash up to $30 million. The house and the yacht were all borrowed against.

Armed with the $30 million in cash, he set about strong-arming the 20 or so brokers he dealt with to allow him the maximum margin. Some were prepared to give him 30 times, but most gave him 20 times as against the 10 times they normally extended to customers. It meant he could potentially go short on close to $750 million of shares on only $30 million of equity.

It was set to be a tremendous bet on the market going down. But Livermore had no intention of risking being wiped out on a three per cent swing in the market. Although he was sure of what he was doing, he wasn't that sure.

His own lack of courage to go all-in surprised him, as the bet was not as big as it seemed. Livermore knew that if he sold over $750 million worth of shares over the next 10 days, some one per cent of the total value of the stock market, shares could not possibly rise in the current conditions – his selling alone would ensure that. But he was conscious of the presence of bulls like Arthur Cutten, who he knew from past experience were well capable of taking the other side and deploying as much money long as he could short. Cutten had made a rumored $250 million over the past ten years and could potentially leverage that to as much as $2 billion if he chose to. Livermore knew that if Cutten went all in, shares could rise dramatically.

But Livermore believed that even Arthur Cutten could not hold back the tide, and for him it was a one-way bet, which is why he threw everything at it. In truth, Livermore hoped to make $10 or $20 million from his play, and he had no idea of what was coming.

He chose his stocks well, those he thought had no upside whatsoever, and sold RCA, Lehman, National City Bank and most of the utility and railroad companies. It was a huge operation for him and his staff, and in the end, he spread nearly $450 million across over 100 companies and did not use all the leverage he potentially had available. He hoped to be able to sell another $300 million on the way down, lessening the risk and the leverage. But on October 16th, the market dipped sharply and Livermore scaled back his selling, which emphasized to him the need for his extraordinary operation to be carried out in secret.

Over that weekend the *New York Times* carried page after page of economic analysis, with its reporters trying to make sense of the market's decline since its high on September 3rd. The *Washington Post* reporters pointed out that the fall had been led by utility stocks which were hitting new lows and had fallen much faster than the rest of the market. The top 20 utilities were at their lowest levels since late June.

Reporters at the *NYT* emphasized the positives of stable business conditions that prevailed. The newspaper also highlighted the number of shares that had been borrowed and sold short and saw it as a positive because at some point they would all have to be bought back in. But it also saw plenty of negatives such as record amounts of money out on margin and a high degree of nervousness across Wall Street. The article seemed to have little impact, and by Monday October 21st, Livermore's selling was mostly all done.

Once again, Livermore was sleeping on the office couch and didn't dare go home. He didn't have long to wait for action. His selling had already depressed prices and thousands of Americans were being sent margin demands every evening and being sold out of their positions by their brokers when they couldn't meet the calls.

By now there were wild rumors circulating on Wall Street that Jesse Livermore was heading up a powerful bear pool made up of some of America's richest men and they were responsible for the market decline in October.

The rumors gathered pace so much so that Livermore was forced to issue a press statement on October 21st which stated: "In connection with the various reports which have been industriously spread during the last few days through newspapers and various brokerage houses to the effect that a large bear pool has been formed; headed by myself and financed by various well-known capitalists. I wish to state there is no truth whatever in any such rumors as far as I am concerned, and I know of no such combination having been formed by others.

"What little business I do in the stock market has always been as an individual and will continue to be done on such a basis.

"It is very foolish to think that any individual, or combination of individuals, could artificially bring about a decline in the stock market in a country so large and so prosperous as the United States. What has happened in the last few weeks is an inevitable result of a long period of continuous, rank manipulation of many stock issues to prices many times their actual worth based on real earnings and yield returns. The men who are responsible for bringing about these fictitious prices are the men who are directly responsible for what is happening in the stock market today. It is unfortunate for the general public, when such a condition arises, that real sound investment issues have to suffer to some extent along with the readjustment of issues of less merit.

"If anyone takes the trouble to analyze the selling prices of different stocks, as for instance, United States Steel, which is selling around eight to ten times its current earnings, many other issues must look, and have looked for a long time, as selling at ridiculously high prices.

"The Federal Reserve Board through its various warnings and many expressions from very high banking authorities, could not stop the market from going up, so it must be plain and seem utterly ridiculous for any sane person to presume that one lone individual could have any material effect on the course of the price of securities."

On Wednesday October 23rd, the market lost six per cent with an even fall across the day. The margin calls that night were frightening. Livermore was already showing a $8 million cash profit after buying back in a quarter of his position before the market closed. His paper profit was close to $20 million.

On Thursday October 24th, the market had the first of its famous black days and dropped off a cliff at the opening, losing 30 points around 11 per cent. Once again Livermore bought back half his position, some $150 million worth of shares almost at the peak fall. He had made another $14 million. Then he watched the market gain back almost all its fall and sold $100 million more as it clawed back up. At the end of a momentous day, the market ended only two per cent down and a staggering 12.9 million shares had been traded. From the peak on September 3rd, the market was now down 21.5 per cent.

On Friday October 25th, the market made small gains as Livermore once more bought back some of his position and banked another $5 million cash profit. As he sat back in his office that evening, Livermore reflected on the most dramatic week of his life. He had made $27 million and called virtually every single decision correctly. He could not quite believe it himself. He ended the week $200 million shares short and feeling very good about it.

Over the weekend, the newspapers were full of what had happened over the previous five days. The market was open for two hours on Saturday morning and slid down another one and a quarter per cent with 3.5 million shares traded, the second highest volume for a Saturday since the stock exchange was first established. Arthur Cutten, who had gone to Atlantic City for a short vacation, was watching the ticker in his hotel. He told friends that the market would soon recover. Jesse Livermore, at home in Great Neck, took precisely the opposite view.

Livermore was certain that the market would fall on Monday and he was right. October 28th 1929 would forever become known as Black Monday on Wall Street. The market fell 12.82 per cent, a record one-day loss on 9.2 million shares traded. Livermore held his nerve and didn't buy back any of his position and instead sold another $50 million into the market but with a lot of difficulty. This was his most difficult and riskiest move of the whole campaign. The Dow closed at 230 points.

Newspaper reporters were dumbfounded at the record loss as it could find no reason for it. The New York Times said: "There was hardly a single item of news which might be construed as bearish."

Livermore's bravery paid dividends the following day as the market crashed again and the day was christened Black Tuesday. It was another record fall as the market dropped 15 per cent at its peak and 11.73 per cent by the close. A staggering 12.9 million shares were traded. Livermore could stand it no longer and bought back everything he had sold and made a reported $66 million profit to bring his total gain for the week at $93 million. Adding in the other smaller gains he had made in September and early October, his total profits exceeded $100 million. His profit on Black Tuesday was believed to be the second biggest single day profit of anyone in history.

As he sat at his desk that evening at five o'clock on his own, he could scarcely believe the figures on the page that Wendy Thomas had put in front of him. He already knew to the last cent what the figure was, but seeing it on paper was truly surreal.

He was emotionally and physically exhausted when he left his office at about nine o'clock. Instead of going home to his townhouse, he ordered his chauffeur to take him back to Great Neck. He had no intention of returning to his office for the rest of the week and being tempted to trade again. With that piece of paper firmly clasped in his hand, he simply wanted to enjoy the moment. He knew from experience that moments like this were few and far between.

When he got home, his wife Dorothy and the children greeted him at the door in tears and Dorothy's mother was wailing in the background. They had heard the news on the radio about the market crash and that many leading investors had been ruined. Dorothy assumed her husband had been one of them. She was getting ready to hear her husband say that they would have to leave their houses, sell the cars and yachts and return to living in a modest rented apartment in the city.

Livermore took a few seconds to understand what was happening and when he grasped it he quickly explained to a stunned Dorothy that, far from being ruined, they were now richer than anyone could believe. What he was saying took a few minutes for her to absorb and she said to him: "You mean we are not ruined?" He replied: "No darling, I have just had my best ever trading day – we are fabulously rich and can do whatever we like."

The relief suddenly became etched into his wife's face, and she turned round to her mother and told her to shut up. The children and even the family dogs seemed quickly to grasp the good news and the celebrations immediately began. Even Livermore's mother-in-law eventually caught on.

Livermore's instincts on the market proved right. The rot on Wall Street effectively was stopped the following day as the market enjoyed a modest rise. Not that he was really interested.

On Wednesday October 30th, Livermore observed it all happening from his bedroom in Great Neck as he slept for most of the day, literally drunk on his success and almost unable to absorb just how much money he had made in the previous seven days.

On Thursday, he caught up with all the newspapers for the week. It was hard, as it had been in 1907, to feel good when virtually the rest of Wall Street was in despair. Many of his old friends had been ruined. He was cheered only by the reports of the downfall of Arthur Cutten. Bullish to the end, Cutten had lost almost everything he had, a fortune that only a week earlier had been estimated at $250 million.

Livermore was also surprised by the number of so-called market sages who had been caught out and lost most of what they had. Irving Fisher, the top American economist and bull market cheer leader, was heavily invested in stocks and lost everything, including his family home. In England, his equivalent, John Maynard Keynes, regarded as Europe's leading economist, also lost heavily. Livermore observed: "A man can have great mathematical ability and an unusual power of accurate observation and yet fail in speculation unless he also possesses the experience and the memory."

Meanwhile, there was panic in Washington about what had happened. On Friday, at the urging of his cabinet, President Hoover made a positive speech and emphasized the excellent state of the economy and business in general. The words had some effect but the market's natural state was for shares to continue to fall; the drop was cushioned by bears buying back in their short positions.

The sheer number of shares being traded continued to rise and rise as the market underwent a fundamental readjustment. Nothing would ever be the same again.

Meanwhile, Livermore looked forward to the weekend to recharge his batteries and to ponder his next move. But the move he should have made never even came into his head. The best decision at that moment would have been to retire. He was 52 years old and one of the top ten richest men in the world. It could never get any better than that and that would have been the wisest decision, and deep inside he knew it.

But for the first time, he had tasted earning tens of millions on a deal instead of the few millions he used to make in the past. Instead of retiring, he would seek to repeat the feat many times in the future and thereby put in danger all he had achieved in October 1929.

The sheer amount of money he was now worth threatened his family life, although he completely failed to see the dangers at the time. He now had as much money as anyone could dream of and was one of the richest men in the world.

Livermore made no attempt to hide his good fortune from his family or friends. The publicity he received as a result led to a huge increase in threats to his family and the number of begging letters he received. He was forced to hire a permanent bodyguard called Frank Gorman, who, from that point on, shadowed him everywhere, even sleeping in a bunk outside his bedroom. The former Nassau County policeman merged himself as invisibly as he could into the Livermore family.

It would prove incredibly destructive, and the downward spiral began almost immediately.

From 1930 onwards, it seemed that Jesse Livermore single-handedly set out to prove the old adage "money does not buy happiness".

And so started 11 years of misery for the Livermore family that could, in the end, have only one outcome for a supremely complex man like Jesse Livermore.

CHAPTER 36

Personal Disaster
Home life falls apart
1932 - 1933

It was 1929, the year of the great crash, when Dorothy Livermore began to lose her battle with the bottle. She had always drunk a lot. Her response to prohibition had been to construct her own distillery and hire a full time employee to distill alcohol and brew beer. She liked to say that "Prohibition was a condition for people who did not have connections."

The trigger for her excessive drinking had seemingly come with the burglary at Great Neck in May 1927. That traumatic event had affected the whole family, and things were never quite the same again afterwards.

Despite being the victims after the robbery, the Livermore family had gained a certain notoriety across America. Stories of their great wealth and almost obscene and conspicuous consumption were splashed across America's newspapers for months. The Livermore lifestyle was not attractive to the average American, struggling to make ends meet, and now the entire family had to endure heavy security in their everyday lives as fear of being kidnapped and held to ransom pervaded their lives. There were plenty of unpleasant and unscrupulous characters roaming America in the twenties who would have been up for that. Lawlessness, fuelled by alcohol, abounded, which is why the somewhat desperate measure of prohibition had been introduced.

In her youth, Dorothy Livermore was a pleasant drunk; the life and soul of the party, she could handle it. But as she reached her mid-thirties, that changed. Suddenly she could no longer have just one, or two, or even three drinks. By the fourth glass, she got unpleasant: sometimes, very unpleasant.

Jesse Livermore had never met a woman that could drink like his wife. She started the evenings off with white wine and then moved on to whisky. One and a half bottles of white followed by half a bottle of whisky was the norm - she was incoherent by the time the servants put her to bed.

As she grew older, eventually drink and cigarettes removed her of her greatest asset, her clear skinned beauty. She gradually lost her effortless ability to charm the opposite sex. And when they started to be repelled by an increasingly unattractive middle-aged drunk, the downward spiral just gained speed. In the space of two years, she changed from being an extremely attractive, vivacious young woman into an overweight drunken frump who had completely let herself go and aged 15 years in the blink of an eye. It was all highlighted when a gossip columnist described her as "plump", causing consternation in the Livermore household.

Her husband was not blameless in her decline. He had lavished endless money on her so she could fulfill every dream she had. In the process, she became completely detached from the real world. Her downward spiral was also not helped by his increasingly frequent dalliances with other women, especially Ziegfeld showgirls of whom she used to be one. She could not help but get to hear of them. The situation at home became extremely tense and it started to spill over into his work life.

Sometimes she drove to his office on Fifth Avenue to confront him, and Harry Dache had to physically remove her from the building, but not before the inevitable scene had been created in front of his staff.

Dorothy still had friends who performed in the Ziegfeld Follies, and one day she challenged her husband with names and dates of a dalliance with a dancer in a hotel. Livermore vehemently denied the accusation, which was undoubtedly true. But Dorothy was only scratching the surface, which, underneath, would reveal a web of girlfriends (maybe as many as half a dozen) who her husband was financially supporting.

There was also seething tension under the surface caused by the fact that Dorothy's mother, Reena, who had moved into Evermore initially to help with the children and upgrading the house, was still there seven years later. Reena lived in a separate wing of the large house with her own retinue of servants. She never left, and Livermore increasingly resented her presence in their lives. Livermore, in common with many American males, had never liked his mother-in-law or her living in his house, constantly interfering and, as he believed, "putting strange ideas in his wife's head."

Eventually, fed up with her husband's affairs, Dorothy started her own in 1929 with a man called Walter Longcope. The 25-year-old Longcope was famous in his own right as a very successful federal prohibition agent. It was the age of the young detective. President Hoover had purged the police of its older and often corrupt detectives and replaced them with a cadre of extremely bright young men such as Eliot Ness and Longcope. A handful of them became celebrities in their own right as they led crack teams to come down hard on criminals. Reporters turned the often handsome young men into heroes, and Longcope was one of that elite breed. But his good looks eventually worked against him and he was starting to be written about in newspapers, which served to end his career as an undercover agent.

Livermore ignored the affair even though it was public knowledge. He believed that Longcope was on the make but chose to do nothing about it. In fact, the affair suited him, and it was the first step to a divorce that he realized was becoming inevitable. He was actually grateful for Longcope taking Dorothy and all her problems off his hands.

Longcope soon resigned from the police and began to spend all his time with Dorothy, soaking up the extraordinary lifestyle her husband provided for her. With his career over, Longcope became dependent on Dorothy for money, which she willingly provided. She encouraged him to emulate her husband and start speculating on Wall Street. To both their surprises, he was very successful in a rising market and soon had a million dollars in his bank account. In 1929, he went short on her advice and made another million.

As the rows between their parents grew more intense, the two boys Jesse Jr and Paul, were sent away to boarding schools, and in the holidays they went to camp to avoid the unpleasantness.

By 1931, life was no fun anymore. Jesse and Dorothy were leading separate lives, and when they were together, they were just making each other unhappy. By then, she wanted to marry Longcope and when her husband suggested a quickie divorce in Reno, Nevada, which specialized in such things, Dorothy was all ears and put up no resistance.

Livermore settled $10 million on his wife. It consisted of three trust funds she controlled of $1 million each. One was designed for her and the other two for Jesse Jr and Paul. But effectively the money was hers. She got the Evermore estate valued at $1.25 million. She also got the Fifth Avenue apartment. There was $2 million in cash and a separate portfolio of shares also worth $1 million at post-crash prices. Her jewels were worth $2 million. She was delighted to get the houses and naïvely believed she would be able to continue the same lifestyle, flicking between Evermore and Fifth Avenue.

To facilitate the divorce, Dorothy took up temporary residence in Reno, Nevada, where she had to be resident for 30 straight days to qualify for a quickie divorce. She arrived in Reno on August 16th 1932 and rented an apartment. Exactly a month later, on September 15th, she filed for divorce on the grounds of her husband's admitted desertion. On Friday September 16th 1932, Jesse Livermore flew in on a commercial long distance cross-country flight. Commercial aviation was exploding in America but only the wealthy could afford the fares.

Later that day, Jesse and Dorothy stood together in the courtroom in front of Justice Thomas Moran. It was necessary for Livermore to testify to his desertion and he gave the date of July 15th 1931 when the desertion took place. With that testimony, Justice Moran granted them a divorce.

As Moran spoke, Livermore looked over at Dorothy whose eyes were fixed straight ahead. Fourteen years of memories flashed through his mind, and he just shook his head at the waste of it all.

They walked out of the courtroom side by side to where Walter Longcope was waiting. When they reached the lobby, they turned to look at each other but Dorothy remained silent. Livermore shook his head again and headed for the airport and the long return trip.

He had no idea what his wife had planned until he read about it in the next day's newspapers. Twenty minutes later, she walked back into court arm in arm with Walter Longcope and back in front of Justice Moran. She had been single and divorced for less than an hour before she was married again and became Mrs Walter Longcope. And almost as quickly, her problems started.

Although Dorothy had received Evermore as part of her divorce settlement, she had really taken it only at the instigation and insistence of her mother, who wished to continue living there. Dorothy tried to tell her mother that the running costs were ruinous and they could not possibly afford it, but she would not listen. Seven years of extraordinary luxurious living at Evermore had dimmed her mother's senses along with old age. At the end of the summer, the realization hit Dorothy hard as a quarter of a million dollars disappeared into a black hole just to keep Evermore and her Fifth Avenue apartment running for six months.

Dorothy knew she would not be able to continue living there, and so she and Longcope started house hunting in Santa Barbara in California. The two children, Jesse Jr and Paul, went with her and their new stepfather, leaving Reena alone at Evermore.

The running costs of Evermore continued, and after three months and another $100,000, she had had enough. Dorothy and Reena had a huge row, and her mother prepared to move out. Dorothy paid off all the staff (other than a small security team) and left, never to return. She also stopped paying the bills that piled up in the hallway with no one to send them on to. Inevitably, lawsuits began accruing for small, unpaid household bills.

Her husband did not want to know and had also washed his hands of the estate, which was now in his wife's name and nothing to do with him. Without maintenance, the house began to deteriorate, and the garden became overgrown.

Eventually, the local authority intervened and, with Dorothy's agreement, it was settled that auctioneers would be appointed to sell off the house and its contents. Dorothy simply couldn't have cared less – she wanted rid of it. Jesse Livermore himself was powerless to intervene and, by then, struggling financially himself.

On June 28th 1933, Evermore, which had cost $250,000 to buy ten years earlier and had over $1.2 million lavished on it, sold for $168,000 which was the only bid received. Following the sale of the house, the auctioneers moved in to sell the contents. $24,000 was obtained for the furniture. The silverware was sold for $6,500 and the jade, which had cost $310,000, went for $12,000. Other valuable antiques that had cost more than $10,000 apiece were sold for under $1,000 each. The two-day sale brought in only $222,000 in all. The final ignominy was the sale of Dorothy's 1930 Rolls-Royce Phantom. The three-year-old car, with only 9,335 miles on the clock, sold for just $4,750.

The house, the refurbishment and the contents had cost Jesse Livermore $3.5 million but Dorothy appeared not to care. She was just glad to be rid of the place. But the $222,000 she had raised was not enough to cover the debts owed on the house. Her apartment at 825 Fifth Avenue was next to go. Debts had also been run up on that so she assigned all her east coast assets to her lawyer, Walter Kuhn, who arranged for the apartment to be sold and the remaining debts to be paid off. With that, Dorothy's connections with New Jersey ended and she remained on the west coast for the next five years. What became of her mother was never known.

Jesse Livermore himself sought a low profile and moved back into his house at West 66th Street and led a much simpler life as he sought to cut down his personal expenses. He also closed down his offices at the Heckscher Building and sold the lease, letting go all his staff except his office manager, his secretary and two of his best young assistants. He relocated to some spare offices at Pearl & Co., a stockbroker on the 13th floor at 120 Broadway.

He made an attempt to resume his old playboy lifestyle as a single man, unfettered by a wife. But he was now 53 and he found women were not as interested as they used to be. He had also lost his youthful looks. As much as he had always looked much younger than he was in his 30s and 40s, in his 50s the process reversed and he suddenly looked 10 years older than he actually was.

He quickly abandoned any thoughts of resuming his old life and started to look for a new wife, a woman he could spend his old age with in retirement, preferably someone with her own money, as he had very little left. He also stopped talking to the press and co-operating with reporters. He adopted a low profile on the way down just as he had on the way up, and he decided he had had enough publicity to last a lifetime.

In the summer of 1932, Livermore travelled to Europe on his own. He wanted to tour the great European capitals, many of which he had never seen. In Vienna, he attended a classical concert and found himself intrigued by one of the principal singers who appeared in the program as Miss Harriet Metz. He was intrigued enough to go backstage to meet Miss Metz, who he had realized was an American. He introduced himself as a fellow American alone in Vienna and asked her out for dinner after the concert. The rest was history.

38-year-old Harriet Noble, the former wife of Warren Noble, went by the name of Harriet Metz, her maiden name, and she hailed from Omaha. She was an accomplished concert singer of some repute in the state, but Harriet Metz had a very checkered and sad personal history. Her four previous husbands had all committed suicide after she married them. There was no common thread to the suicides, and she had been closely investigated by police in view of their numeracy. It appeared to be fate and bad luck.

As they talked over dinner, it emerged that Harriet had been in Vienna since 1930 and had sought to get away from America and all its bad memories after her fourth husband, Warren, had committed suicide. Livermore was intrigued by Harriet and quickly realized she was a very special woman who had been dealt an incredibly bad hand in life. Four times she had loved and lost in the most tragic of circumstances.

They had dinner every night that week and finally he realized he had met someone he believed fitted the bill to be the third Mrs Livermore. Importantly, she was a woman of independent means, and after inheriting four small but still substantial fortunes, was worth $7 million in her own right.

Livermore met Harriet at precisely the right time. She had no illusions about him and realized where he was in his life. After her fourth husband's deaths, she realized that she was no prize catch either.

And so, as Livermore prepared to leave Vienna, they made plans to meet again in New York.

As soon as she could, Harriet saw out her concert contract, gave up the lease of the apartment she had rented and returned to New York, where she moved in with Livermore and became his constant companion.

For all the right reasons, they both fell in love and could see no reason why they shouldn't marry as soon as possible. So when Livermore formally proposed, Harriet immediately accepted and told him it was "the happiest day of her life".

They decided to have a quiet wedding with no family present, and on Wednesday March 22nd, they travelled to Chicago, Illinois where Harriet had some very close friends, John and Susan Hutchins.

On Thursday March 23rd, they were married in Geneva, Illinois. The ceremony was performed in the Geneva Congressional Church by the Reverend Frazer Bell, the pastor. The Hutchins were the only guests, and they acted as witnesses to the union.

From Chicago, they travelled to Omaha for the 70th birthday party of Harriet's father, Frederick Metz. It became a double celebration after the newly married Livermores made their surprise announcement to the birthday guests. The *New York Times* picked up the story the following Wednesday. The headline read: "Livermore reveals marriage to singer."

After the marriage, Livermore sold his house on the west side and together they rented an apartment in the Sherry-Netherland Hotel until they found a new family home, a triplex apartment at 1100 Park Avenue. Finally, Livermore was happy again in his personal life – but his other life as a speculator and businessman remained deeply unfulfilled.

But just as personal happiness returned, there were another two blows from the past, the second of which devastated Livermore, who had just begun to pick up the pieces of his life.

The first was minor but rather annoying for a newly married man settling down with a new wife.

On October 27th, Nadia Krasnova, a Russian actress and Livermore's former mistress for much of his marriage to Dorothy, filed a breach of promise suit in the New York courts claiming $250,00 in damages. The affair was over, but Krasnova had become annoyed reading about his marriage to Harriet and believed that she was in line to be the next Mrs Livermore. She turned out to be something of a fantasist and the suit was mired in delays. The worse effects were the reassurances required by Harriet who at first had misread the situation and believed Krasnova was her husband's current mistress. The imbroglio quickly died down and together they laughed it off as the suit made its way through the courts.

Far worse was what happened next.

Dorothy Livermore, facing more unexpected debts from the Great Neck house, decided to have a sale of her jewelry. She resolved to dispose of everything that had been given to her by her husband to raise cash and pay off remaining debts.

Livermore was devastated when he saw the catalogue and the items in it. To him, each lot told the story of his 14-year marriage, its rise and its downfall. He was astonished that his ex-wife was selling every piece of jewelry he had given her. The auction attracted huge publicity and was extremely embarrassing for Livermore and his new wife.

There were 80 substantial items on offer and hundreds of smaller trinkets. The auctioneers made a big event of it, and it was scheduled for three days: Thursday December 14th through to Saturday December 16th. It was held at 664 Fifth Avenue under experienced auctioneer Harold Brand. None of the listed items had a reserve and were all there to be sold. Straightaway it was apparent that it would all be sold off very cheap. Bidders seemed put off by the story behind the sale, somehow ashamed to be associated with the items on offer.

An early item was the platinum, diamond and sapphire wristwatch that had featured in the 1927 burglary. It had cost over $6,000 and was appraised at $2,500. But it was knocked down for only $300 by an amazed Harold Brand, who told the audience it was worth much more. But despite his best efforts, bidding was listless. A platinum and gold lizard ring set with 33 small diamonds appraised at $700 sold for only $80. It had originally cost $4,500. Items that had cost $3,000, which the Livermores themselves regarded as trinkets, were sold for under $50.

During the second day of the sale, Harold Brand grew exasperated with the prices being fetched. He told the audience: "I can't understand you people at all." Brand was frustrated that the smaller virtually worthless trinkets were selling at relatively good prices whereas the good stuff was fetching a fraction of its real value. He scolded the buyers. After some Chalcedony cufflinks that were worth only a few dollars went for $22, he said: "You could go to any department store and buy them for $7.50."

One of the star items was a mesh handbag made of 2,900 oriental pearls strung on platinum wires and studded with diamonds and sapphires. It was appraised at $17,000 and sold for just $1,300, making it the bargain of the auction. Other bargains knocked down included a lingerie pin studded with thirteen emeralds and 26 rose diamonds that went for $40. A pair of platinum and gold cufflinks was knocked down for $45. Another pair of solid gold cufflinks went for $15.

The top price of the whole auction came when a 10-carat diamond ring was offered. It was appraised at $75,000. The bidding opened at $10,000 and progressed right the way up to $19,700. It was still only a quarter of its value and less than 15 per cent of what it had cost new from Harry Winston in 1920.

The saddest lot of all was the sale of Dorothy's gold wedding ring, inscribed with "Dotsie for ever and ever, J. L." The sale of that item reflected all that had gone wrong with the marriage and the sad wreckage left behind. Earlier in the week, Jesse Livermore had crept in and left an open bid for the ring and ordered the auctioneer to bid for it on behalf of his new wife. When it came up and Brand read out the inscription, there were groans from the audience, some of whom were old friends of the Livermores. Brand opened the bidding at $10 and quickly brought the hammer down to prevent any ghouls bidding for it.

All of this was reported in detail by the New York Times, further embarrassing Livermore, whose humiliation was by now complete. The auction, and its subsequent detailed reporting in the newspapers, made him severely depressed and he stayed in bed for much of the Sunday unable to face the outside world after the humiliation of the jewelry auction. It sent him into a funk that no one could get him out of.

Finally, after three days inside the apartment, at just after four o'clock in the afternoon, Livermore stepped outside on Tuesday December 19th, got into a taxi cab and promptly disappeared for 26 hours.

After a few hours, Harriet raised the alarm when he did not turn up at his office and she learned he had refused a ride in his chauffeur driven car which had been waiting at the curbside. At midnight, she went to the police station and reported her husband missing. At half past two in the morning, the Police issued a confidential message over its internal teletype alert system. The message read: "Jessie L. Livermore, the stock market operator, of 1100 Park Avenue missing and has not been seen since 3pm yesterday." Two minutes later, it spewed out a photo and detailed description of the missing financier. Two detectives were sent to his apartment to look for clues as to his whereabouts.

With that, a massive police search started on fears that Livermore had been abducted. The local police capital called in Federal investigators after it appeared Livermore could have been kidnapped.

Harriet told the Feds that her husband made a point of telephoning her every two hours when they were apart and it had now been ten hours since she had heard from him. She also told them he had failed to meet a friend at the Waldorf Hotel the previous evening without cancelling.

The following morning, as soon as news got out, photographers and journalists crowded around the private street entrance to 1100 Park Avenue waiting for news.

But as quickly as he was gone, he was back. At 20 minutes past six o'clock, he stepped out of a cab and fought his way through the 30 or so reporters and photographers on his doorstep. He shouted at them to "get out of the way" and refused to answer any questions, posing briefly for a photograph as he waited to be let in.

A team of detectives, led by Captain Louis Hyams, were waiting inside the apartment, together with his wife, to question him. He told them he remembered little but admitted he had been severely depressed after the jewelry auction and had sought solace by escaping to spend time on his own. He told them he had felt ill and spent the night at the Pennsylvania Hotel recovering and had never dreamed he would be reported as missing. Livermore said he returned home immediately after reading about his own disappearance in that day's newspapers.

After a brief conversation with Hyams, lasting five minutes, his wife put him to bed, where he slept for ten hours. But when detectives checked at the hotel, there was no sign of his ever being there. The taxi driver, whom he had hailed on Park Avenue, was named Abe Kamarick. Kamarick confirmed Livermore had felt nauseous during the journey and that he had dropped him off downtown. Livermore never revealed where he was or what he did in that 26 hours he was missing while the whole of New York was looking for him. He was thought to have been in touch throughout with James O'Gorman, his New York lawyer, although this was never admitted to the police. The best explanation was that he had spent the night with an old girlfriend as he sought solace outside the home to forget his sorrows. It later emerged that he had spent the night at the Pennsylvania Hotel in an apartment that he rented permanently for assignations with women under an assumed name.

Whatever it was, the absence seemed to jolt him out of his depression and he quickly re-joined normal life and went about his business again, and the whole affair was quickly forgotten.

CHAPTER 37

Official Bankruptcy No 2

$100 million seemingly disappears

1934

By 1934, Jesse Livermore was broke again for the fourth time in his life. It was an extraordinary state of affairs as he had started 1930 with a personal fortune of nearly $100 million, including his properties and yacht.

But then began an absolutely catastrophic series of market movements that went contrary to any logic and which Livermore was continually on the wrong side of. Four times he made the wrong decisions on major market movements.

In truth, it was a period of total inconsistency and illogicality during which, by his own rules, he should have been out of the market sitting on his money. But he wasn't. Having conquered the world, he wanted to climb the mountain again.

After sitting out the rest of 1929, he was long again in early 1930 and made modest profits as the market rallied. But he then piled into the market in a big way, sensing more gains for 1931. But he was bullish as the market slid all the way down to a low of 41 in mid-1932. All told, he lost nearly $40 million in 18 months. The stock market rally that began in mid-1932 had really hurt him as he had not seen it coming and was short millions of dollars' worth of shares, which he did not exit quickly enough. And then, inexplicably, he failed – as he had many times in the past – to switch to a long position as the market doubled from its low of 41 to almost 80. And he was on the wrong side again as it slid back to 50 at the beginning of 1933. By the end of 1933, he had lost all of the gains he had made in 1929. In the middle of that was his divorce from Dorothy, which cost him another $10 million.

Very quickly, he began to pile up debts.

He had a big decision to make. He had to borrow more money and try, as he put it to friends, to either "trade my way out of it or temporarily surrender and clear the decks."

Of the three times he had been broke, twice he had managed to survive and trade through with the help of friends. But this time, as in 1915, he knew that he would have to declare official bankruptcy if he had any chance of starting afresh with a clear mind. Livermore estimated that he owed around $5 million split between around 30 creditors; mostly stock brokers who had advanced him money to trade.

As in 1915, Livermore knew he was in a bad place psychologically and his judgement had gone. He began to analyze his situation and to compare it to 1915. This time, he had no worries about day to day living as he was supported by his wealthy wife who also owned the triplex on Park Avenue and every other asset of value they had.

As before, he believed the way out of his troubles was to resume his successful career in speculating, which had gone off the rails after his spectacular performance in 1929. It was hard to believe, but in the last five years he had lost every cent of the $100 million he had made in those few months.

He did not miss his physical possessions at all. Nor did he wallow in self-pity, and he believed that sooner or later the market would present opportunities for him to make money again. As he said: "As before, my trouble came from worrying over the money I owed, and I would never be free from the consciousness of my indebtedness." And sure enough, although the vast majority of his creditors were unworried about what he owed them, some of the smaller and less important creditors started filing suits for which he didn't even bother to try and put up a defense.

When this started happening, he knew he was in deep trouble. One of the two suits that worried him the most was the $13,130 he owed to the late John Williston, a stockbroker; his estate wanted the money back. The other was filed by his former friend and stockbroker Ben Block. Block had no faith that Livermore could make a fourth comeback and wanted the $90,840 he was owed repaid.

Once again, Livermore knew he couldn't carry on depending on the kindness of strangers in his professional life and that he had to make a new start free of debt. As in 1915, he made a personal visit to everyone to whom he owed money and told them what he planned. Once again, creditors to whom he owed $3 million said they did not want to be listed on his petition. They all trusted him to pay them back eventually.

So on March 6th 1934, he trod a vaguely familiar route down to the Federal Courthouse. He was due to meet with his appointed bankruptcy referee Oscar

Ehrhorn and to make a formal declaration that he could not pay his debts.

The petition, prepared by his accountant, listed liabilities of $2.259 million and assets of only $184,900, which included a life insurance policy worth $150,000. Other assets were seats on the Chicago Board of Trade and Commodity Exchange, valued at $10,500, and he owned $20,000 worth of jewelry, which was pledged as collateral for loans.

His liabilities included $561,000 for unpaid taxes for the years 1930 and 1931. $9,000 was listed as being "promised" to Lucille Ballantine a dancer for keeping him cheered and amused while getting his second divorce; a $250,000 claim was made by Nadia Krasnova, a Russian actress; a $125,000 balance owed to Dorothy from the divorce; $100,000 of loans from Harriet; and $142,525 was owed to Joseph Harriman's bank.

The following day, he was suspended from the Chicago Board of Trade under the rule that forbade members to be insolvent and to remain on the exchange.

In his press statement announcing his bankruptcy, his new lawyer Sam Gilman said: "Mr Livermore has made three very large fortunes... He has failed three times, on each occasion has paid 100 cents on the dollar with interest and hopes to do so again."

Livermore did not find bankruptcy so easy or accommodating the second time around. His first bankruptcy in 1915 had been relatively easy, and his only brush with officialdom had been the first meeting with his bankruptcy referee, which had also been his last. He had hardly noticed it was happening. But things had moved on in 20 years. This time, he was harried from all sides and by people who were very suspicious about where $100 million had gone.

Furthermore, this time, an outside receiver in bankruptcy, the Irving Trust Company, was appointed to manage his financial affairs whilst he was bankrupt. Irving conducted a thorough investigation of his financial transactions immediately prior to the bankruptcy. It found that just before he declared bankruptcy, he had assigned an annuity of $100,000 to his wife in return for a cash loan of $100,000. Although perfectly legitimate, it looked odd. And the transfer had been made after the two suits against him had been filed.

In a bankruptcy court hearing on April 17th, Livermore was questioned closely by George Levin, the counsel for Irving Trust, which effectively represented the interests of his creditors. He openly admitted that it had been the case but that agreement had been made prior to April 1933. He also revealed that he had borrowed $136,000 from his wife when they were married and that he had lost most of it on the stock market.

All through the hearing, Livermore gave off the quiet assurance that in due course he would repay all his creditors and that his indebtedness would be temporary. Sam Gilman, the lawyer representing him at the hearing, reiterated: "My client has owed more than this many times and paid it off in full."

During the hearing, Livermore also revealed three annuities worth $400,000 for the benefit of his first wife, three trust funds worth $450,000 for the benefit his second wife, and a $100,000 insurance policy held by his broker. Upon the deaths of those persons, they would all revert to him. He told the hearing his first wife's annuities paid an annual income of $22,340.

The final hearing of the bankruptcy was held on May 15th 1934 at the offices of his bankruptcy referee Oscar Ehrhorn. Again, he was questioned closely about his affairs by George Levin, counsel for the Irving Trust Company. Livermore revealed that many of his personal creditors were not listed in the bankruptcy as they did not wish to be. When Levin asked him to define a creditor, Livermore replied: "I don't know what you mean by creditors; suppose they don't want to be listed?" Levin also went through Livermore's bank paying in slips and check stubs. Livermore found this uncomfortable but batted off all questions, and Levin had no answers himself. With that, proceedings were closed.

On June 28th, less than four months after he declared bankruptcy, Livermore applied to be discharged. His discharge was duly granted by Federal Justice Woolsey. Livermore told Woolsey: "I have every intention of getting back to work in the hope I can restore my fortune and pay all my creditors in full as I have always done."

There is little doubt that Livermore had every intention of doing both. But this time it was not to be. The world had changed, and he was no longer the Boy Plunger he was in his 30s. He was now 55 but looked and acted like an old man of 70. Many of his creditors would not get paid, nor would his fortune be restored this time.

By the end of the year, Livermore was eager to get away from New York, and he and Harriet decided to take an extended trip to Europe to forget their troubles. On December 1st, he and his wife embarked on the Italian cruise liner *The Rex* and sailed away from New York for a vacation in the capital cities of Europe, beginning with Rome. They told reporters waiting on the quayside that they did not know when they would be back. Then, just as he was about to walk up the gangway, Livermore took aside a reporter from the

New York Times and told him that he would be undertaking a study of the European commodity markets as part of the groundwork for his comeback. He admitted he had made no progress in the five months since he was discharged from bankruptcy and said: "I have made comebacks before, but this one will take longer because conditions are worse."

The statement was ominous and was to prove so.

JESSE LIVERMORE - BOY PLUNGER

CHAPTER 38

Personal Tragedy

Ex-wife shoots eldest son

1935

Dorothy Livermore continued to drink heavily after her divorce from Jesse and remarriage to Walter Longcope. She had celebrated her 40th birthday very quietly; after all, there was little to celebrate. She had burned through two husbands and spent tens of millions of dollars with nothing to show for it in her first 40 years. Now she was down to her last two million and it hurt.

Even though she had received a $10 million settlement on her divorce, half if it was gone inside a year, and half of that at the end of the second year. Suddenly, after 10 years of unimaginable riches being able to afford anything and everything, she found herself a woman of moderate means and did not adapt particularly well.

All her hopes for a new start after the divorce had vanished. In less than a year, her new marriage was over as Walter Longcope, still not 30 and impossibly handsome, left her and returned to New York where, as the gossip columns avidly reported, he quickly found a new girlfriend called Lassie Honeyman. He filed for divorce in Mexico after agreeing a relatively modest financial settlement with his wife. But before the Mexican divorce was finalized, Dorothy filed in Santa Barbara, California, and was granted a divorce on July 26th, leaving Longcope whistling for his settlement.

Now the Livermore-Longcope household, with both husbands in the past, was not a happy one. She lived with her two sons who both attended the Laguna Blanca School at Hope Ranch, north of Santa Barbara. At 16, Jesse Jr was becoming a problem, which his mother, beset by her own woes, could not deal with it. His exceptional looks and muscular physique made it very easy for him to seduce women and he started sleeping with his mother's friends, causing terrible problems with their husbands, which Dorothy then had to deal with. He also occasionally drank heavily which she didn't like, and

Dorothy accused him of throwing his life away. Even at 16, he was a world-class yachtsman and had won many competitions. She begged him to focus on that.

But Dorothy herself was no model mother and a powder keg waiting to blow, and it finally exploded on Thanksgiving Day, November 29th 1935. That day, she had arranged a lunch for family and friends at her 14-room mansion house in the fashionable suburb of Montecito, near Santa Barbara. She had invited her new fiancée, Dennis Neville, and two friends of her sons, Catherine Hunky and Georgia Collins, to join them. She had met Neville when he came to the house as a private tutor for Paul. The six of them, including Jesse Jr and Paul, sat down for a Thanksgiving feast cooked by the chef and served by a maid.

It was a happy occasion, and Jesse Jr and 14-year-old Paul were charming company for their guests. Both were very self-assured for their age. But the bonhomie lasted for less than an hour. Jesse Jr watched his mother drink heavily over lunch, and when he objected, she rebuked him. As a consequence, as soon as lunch was over, he took his car and drove to a see his friend Josephine Frank who lived nearby. Mrs Frank was a lot older than Jesse Jr and divorced, and it was assumed they were having a relationship. She had cooked him another Thanksgiving meal, which he ate, and then they went to bed. At 11 o'clock, Jesse Jr said his goodbyes and drove home, apparently having drunk very little. At home, he found his mother and Dennis Neville enjoying late night drinks after the other guests had departed.

He and Dorothy got into a heated argument over her drinking. Jesse Jr grabbed a quart bottle of whiskey and downed a quarter of it in one slug, shouting: "I'll show you I can drink as much as a woman." Over the next hour, he finished it off ostensibly to show his mother how unattractive drunks could be. The young Paul Livermore, watching the argument unfold and sensing there might be trouble later, retired to his bedroom and locked the door. As Jesse Jr drunk more and more of the bottle, he grew more and more excited. Then it turned ugly, as Dorothy shouted: "I'd rather see you dead than drinking that way" as she knocked the bottle from his hands.

At just after one o'clock in the morning, suddenly, Jesse Jr, taking his mother at her word, ran up to his bedroom and grabbed a loaded shotgun. Rushing downstairs and handing it to her, he challenged her to make good on her threat, saying: "You haven't got the nerve to shoot me." Dennis Neville, still relatively sober, was horrified and quickly snatched the gun from Dorothy's hands and threw it through the open French windows, out of harm's way. That intervention by Neville effectively saved Jesse Jr's life.

But Jesse Jr's reaction was to immediately go back to his bedroom, chased by Neville, who remonstrated with him about bringing guns into the house. Neville then went to the lavatory. After he had gone, Jesse Jr grabbed a .22 caliber rifle he had under the bed and rushed downstairs and again challenged his mother to make good her threat.

Obliterated by alcohol, she took the rifle and almost randomly squeezed the trigger. A millisecond separated the bang and the bullet entering Jesse Jr's body. The bullet raced past the 16-year-old's chest, narrowly missing his heart, puncturing his kidney, and finally lodging in his back, near the spine. He seemed to freeze until the full force of the shock hit his body and he fell to the floor half unconscious, whispering almost inaudibly: "Mother, you did it." After that, he lost consciousness and his breathing grew labored. He was bleeding profusely as Dennis Neville re-entered the room and quickly took stock of what had happened. Neville grabbed some towels from the downstairs cloakroom and ordered Dorothy to press down on the wound to try and staunch the blood. He went to the hall to call an ambulance and phoned Dorothy's personal physician, Dr Ussher, who lived nearby.

Dr Ussher was asleep in bed with his wife and blearily grabbed the phone by his bed. When he grasped what had happened, he shot bolt upright, leapt from the bed, grabbing his trousers and car keys. He was the first to arrive at the scene, and he stopped the bleeding with a bandage and made the boy as comfortable as he could until the ambulance arrived. Dr Ussher was a very fine physician and as soon as the medics arrived, he got a line into him and stabilized his condition. Ussher undoubtedly saved the boy's life, which was quietly ebbing away. Meanwhile, alerted by the hospital, Deputy Sheriff Jack Ross had arrived, and Dorothy immediately admitted to him that she had shot her son. Ross noted the empty whiskey bottle and the .22 rifle on the floor.

As the medics slid him onto a stretcher, Jesse Jr regained consciousness and told his mother he forgave her as they rushed him out of the door into the ambulance. He told the medics: "I'm all right, it's nothing, don't blame mother."

But it wasn't nothing, and the wound, in normal circumstances, wasn't survivable. But these weren't normal circumstances. Jesse Jr was incredibly fit and the whiskey had temporarily anesthetized him. But no one thought he would still be alive by the time the ambulance arrived at the hospital – least of all the medics. Ross told Dorothy she could travel in the ambulance with her son in case he died during the journey. Ussher also jumped in but without any real hope that his patient would still be alive by the time they reached Cottage Hospital.

But, somehow, he did survive the journey and before he was sedated had the presence of mind to tell the police it had been an accident and they were not to arrest his mother. He was immediately wheeled into the operating theatre where an exploratory operation began to try and save his life. After an hour, the surgeons decided it was too risky to continue and they left the bullet in.

Meanwhile, the District Attorney Percy Heckendorf arrived at the Cottage Hospital, and he and Jack Ross took Dorothy to a private room to question her while her son was in the operating theatre. But she was intoxicated and in shock and made little sense. Her condition was giving cause for concern, so she was also admitted to hospital and sedated. Heckendorf placed an armed guard at her door.

Against all the odds, Jesse Jr was still alive in the morning. But the surgeons had not been able to remove the bullet as it was too close to his spine, and they reasoned that he was too weak for prolonged surgery. No visitors were allowed.

Amazingly, the next day's late edition of the *New York Times* had the full story on its front page. The headline stated that Jesse Jr was dying and left little room for hope of his survival. Reporters had spoken to the medics who had brought Jesse Jr in, and they said that his death was only a matter of hours away.

Overnight, Heckendorf had considered the situation with his staff and made some decisions. When Dorothy woke up, she was immediately arrested and taken to the County Jail for more questioning. She called for a lawyer, who advised her to say nothing and admit nothing when being questioned by Heckendorf.

Despite that, she was charged with assault with intent to kill. But if Jesse Jr were to die, Heckendorf left no one in any doubt that the charge would change to first-degree murder. And that meant that she would be imprisoned immediately with no possibility of bail.

At midday, Jesse Livermore was tracked down on the floor of the St Louis Merchants Exchange where he was trading. He had been staying in St Louis with his wife. He immediately hired an airplane to get them to Los Angeles by nightfall. On arrival at the airport, he was besieged by newspaper reporters and photographers. He told them: "If anything has happened to that boy, I will see that she pays." When he got to the hospital, he went straight in to see his son and broke down with emotion. He said to his sleeping son: "Fight boy, I'm standing by you." Later, he told reporters he would do everything he could to save his son's life.

With Dorothy in jail, Livermore camped down next to his son's room as pneumonia set in and his condition visibly worsened.

Meanwhile, Dorothy was taken into court for a preliminary hearing in handcuffs. She entered an initial plea of not guilty to the charge of assault with intent to kill. She was given bail on account of her own recognizance of $9,000.

When Dorothy arrived back at the hospital, the Livermores booked into the El Mirasol hotel in Santa Barbara. Dorothy was refused permission to see Jesse Jr by his doctors. They reasoned that the presence of the person who shot him might be counterproductive to his recovery.

The shooting was big news across America and literally hundreds of reporters were soon outside the hospital waiting for news. Lawyers were also limbering up. Sensing a high profile trial, Dorothy was contacted by most of the top criminal defense lawyers in America, confident of a big payday and many inches of newsprint.

Appointing a lawyer quickly to coordinate Dorothy's defense was essential. Livermore put personal differences aside and selected Harrison Ryon and agreed to meet his not insubstantial fees. Straightaway, Ryon decided they should run the 'unloaded gun defense.' He said it was crystal clear that Dorothy had not meant to shoot her son, and Ryon believed he would get her off. He told Livermore he doubted it would even get to trial.

By now, Livermore's initial anger had completely subsided and he put family first regardless of how he felt about them. He would get Dorothy off the charges and make sure his son had the best treatment so he could recover fully from the wounds. Both the legal and medical bills would be substantial at a time when he was very pressed for cash.

After a week, Jesse Jr was fully awake and could communicate with people. But he also declared that he wanted to think about things for a week before he saw his mother and father. He also declined to be questioned by the District Attorney who, surprisingly, acceded to his request.

Meanwhile, Livermore and Ryon found they worked well together. Livermore was enjoying the intellectual challenge of putting a defense together. At Ryon's suggestion, he hired America's pre-eminent gunshot wound expert, Dr Joseph D'Avignon. D'Avignon immediately flew in to examine the evidence whilst it was fresh.

The District Attorney was persuaded to put off the formal arraignment until after the Christmas and New Year holiday.

In the middle of December, the situation became more serious as Jesse Jr's condition deteriorated. Pneumonia had set in again and the bullet, which had split into three fragments, had become dislodged and was moving around. His temperature hovered between 103 and 104, and his pulse was continually racing. The hospital issued a press release on December 15th saying his condition was "extremely grave". It continued: "The youth took a turn for the worse yesterday."

Privately, doctors did not believe he would survive after the bullet had fragmented and became dislodged. They spent hours discussing a medical strategy and x-rays were taken every day. They were also worried about the risk of infection. Because of his age and his fitness, young Jesse pulled through. Eventually, when he was strong enough, the bullet pieces were safely removed and he slowly got better. On December 29th, Jesse Jr finally agreed to see his mother and they spoke briefly at his bedside. Dorothy was under strict orders by the doctors not to mention the shooting.

By the second week of January, the doctors announced Jesse Jr was officially off the danger list and it was clear he was not going to die, saving his mother the much more serious charge of first-degree murder.

On March 26th, three months after the shooting, Dorothy Livermore got the news she wanted when she was cleared on charges of shooting and wounding her son. All charges were dismissed at a special hearing in front of Ernest Wagner, a local justice. In the end, the dropping of the charges was no surprise since the District Attorney was in a very difficult position as his chief witness, Jesse Jr, would not testify against his mother and neither would the other people present at the shooting. The two doctors who had effectively saved Jesse Jr's life, Dr Ussher and Dr Wills, would also testify that Dorothy was drunk and incapable of anything when she arrived at the hospital on the night of the shooting. During the immediate aftermath, Dorothy had continually told people: "I shot my son." But rather conveniently, three months later, no one could remember her uttering those words, including the Deputy Sheriff Jack Ross. The DA finally realized it would be impossible to get a conviction.

Ironically, America was disappointed, denied its chance of a juicy celebrity trial. But Jesse Livermore was massively relieved, not least because it looked as though his son would make a full recovery with few side effects, and his ex-wife had been given the biggest warning possible about the dire consequences of her drinking. But she showed little remorse and was soon drinking again and being as vindictive as ever.

When he was released from hospital, Livermore settled all the medical bills as his son left for a long period of recuperation at Dorothy's home. He still needed plenty of specialist care, and there were substantial rehabilitation expenses. Jesse Livermore reasoned that he had done his bit and that his ex-wife should take care of those. When she sent him the bill, he did not pay and she was obliged to. But when she filed suit to recover the $12,000 from her ex-husband, Livermore was horrified and vowed to have nothing to do with her again.

The suit was initially heard in the Domestic Relations Court on July 30th 1936. But the magistrate, Stephen Jackson, refused to hear the case and referred it to the regular courts. Dorothy appealed against the decision. On August 1st, the appeal was heard and evidence was heard. Livermore's lawyer, Sam Gilman, argued that his client had made ample provision for his ex-wife and his two sons, that he had paid the hospital bills and should be liable for no more. On August 11th, the magistrate Charles Brandt gave his judgement and dismissed the appeal.

But it was not finished, and Dorothy encouraged one of her son's doctors, Dr Allen, to take the case to court. And so, on April 28th the following year, Livermore gave evidence in a suit filed by Dr Allen. Livermore maintained that his income was now provided by his new wife Harriet and that he had no funds of his own. His lawyers argued that his ex-wife was responsible for any post-hospital medical expenses.

The magistrate urged both sides to settle it privately and quickly threw the suit out in some disgust. And there, finally, ended yet another extraordinary saga in the life of the Livermore family.

CHAPTER 39

Partial Recovery

The good times are over

1935 - 1940

On June 28th 1934, Jesse Livermore walked away from the Federal Court, discharged from bankruptcy and free to resume his life on Wall Street. He had every intention of repaying the $2 million he owed to his creditors and the $3 million he owed to others. He genuinely believed, as he had done three times before, that he could come back from a minus millions position, repay it and also regain what he had lost. He had no reason in his mind to believe that he couldn't pull it off for a fourth time.

But this time it would not prove as easy as it had in the past. Coinciding with his bankruptcy came the passing into law of the Securities Exchange Act of 1934, the new regulation that led to the creation of the Securities & Exchange Commission (SEC). The SEC would enforce the Securities Act, which had been passed in 1933. The SEC was the brainchild of President Roosevelt, who pushed it through as soon as he acceded to office in March 1933. Roosevelt had beaten incumbent Republican President Herbert Hoover for the presidency in November 1932. Hoover had been undone by his handling of the 1929 crash and the aftermath. Roosevelt had pledged during the election campaign to reform Wall Street and the SEC was him delivering.

The coming of the SEC was an absolute disaster for speculators like Livermore, Billy Durant, Tommy Lawson and Arthur Cutten. Speculative shenanigans that were perfectly legal the year before were now punishable by prison and large fines. It was a nightmare for a man over 50 who suddenly had to play by some rules where none had existed before.

The SEC had been created as a direct result of what had happened in 1929 when the stock market went into meltdown, throwing America into a vicious depression. The Securities Act was aimed at preventing a repeat of the excesses of 1928, which had been fuelled by easy credit and unsustainable speculation in stocks and shares.

The framework of the 1933 Securities Act was shaped by Felix Frankfurter, one of President Roosevelt's closest associates. The detailed drafting work was done by Ben Cohen, Thomas Corcoran and James Landis. But the brilliant Frankfurter is generally seen as the father of the Act.

The curiously named Frankfurter was Austrian by birth and emigrated to the United States at the age of 12 with his parents. He was soon recognized as a child prodigy and graduated from New York's City College. He gained entrance into Harvard Law School and showed his early brilliance by being appointed editor of the *Harvard Law Review*. He graduated with high honors and was regarded as a model student, one of the best who ever attended Harvard. Unsurprisingly, he quickly rose through the ranks of the legal profession in New York and struck up a relationship with Franklin Roosevelt, then the Governor of New York. His relationship with Roosevelt eventually saw him appointed to the Supreme Court.

The Act was the first major Federal legislation to regulate the offer and sale of securities. It principally ensured that the offer or sale of securities must be registered with the SEC and comply with the new rules. The new agency had a three-part mission: 1) to protect investors; 2) to maintain a fair, orderly and efficient stock market; and 3) to facilitate capital formation. The main difference was that the new laws were Federal laws. Previously, the work of speculators had been regulated state by state, which gave investors limited protection against being defrauded.

After Frankfurter was lined up for the Supreme Court, there was a surprise when President Roosevelt appointed Joseph Kennedy to serve as the first chairman of the SEC. Most people thought he was part of the problem and undoubtedly Roosevelt sponsored his chairmanship, arguing that he would know how to enforce the new laws because he knew all the wrinkles and the seamy underside of the stock market. Aside from Kennedy, the commission was made up of James Landis, Ferdinand Pecora, William Douglas, Jerome Frank and William Casey.

At first, Jesse Livermore dismissed the new laws, and it was only when he read the statutes in detail that he realized that all the provisions in the new Securities Act seemed to be aimed straight at him. Stunts he had pulled off in the past were now illegal.

The Securities & Exchange Commission became like a monkey on Jesse Livermore's back. He felt like he was constantly looking over his shoulder at the Feds about to put their tanks on his lawn. In his heart, Livermore knew it was all over for people like him, but it didn't stop him trying to make a success of himself again whilst tip-toeing round the new laws.

His first attempt at a comeback was with Billy Durant. Durant, like Livermore, had lost his trading mojo and they decided to make their return as equal partners. There was some success trading commodities in the beginning but not enough to make the effort worthwhile. The partnership ended as quickly as it had started. Durant was now a dinosaur like Livermore.

Livermore moved back into stocks on his own again. He and his small staff traded out of the offices of Pearl & Co in Broadway, off Wall Street. There were only four of them and, despite the difficulties, they enjoyed their new circumstances.

Once again, at first there was some success as he found some of his old touch, but now it became what he couldn't do rather than what he could do. In the middle of 1935, he was trading commodities in Chicago with some success. So much so that in April 1937, he was able to pay the Internal Revenue Service the back taxes he owed from past years. This amounted to over $800,0000 and reports of it were carried in newspapers across America along with speculation about his current activities. His lawyer, Sam Gilman, professed ignorance of the current situation and just confirmed that Livermore's tax bill had been settled – $700,000 was for Federal tax and $100,000 for New York state taxes.

But the success petered out, and by 1936 Livermore had virtually given up on commodities and put his seat up for sale at the Chicago Board of Trade. It was bought by a member of the Los Angeles Stock Exchange called Clyde Vedder for $4,300.

In 1938, he wore out his welcome at Pearl & Co and took a small suite of offices at the Squibb Building at 745 Park Avenue. It was within walking distance of his apartment and the Sherry-Netherland Hotel, where he spent much of his leisure time.

The Art Deco office block sat in the southeast corner of Central Park and there were fine views from Livermore's suite, but unfortunately they did not give him much inspiration. He set up a trading room with chalkboards much as before, but with only six staff and his general manager Walter McNerney. Harry Dache was long gone. The performance was never better than mediocre.

In January 1939, Livermore made his last and final comeback attempt. The arena he chose was commodities, and he applied for a seat on the New York Commodities Exchange in January. A notice was published in the exchange on January 4th and stated that Livermore had applied for membership and that his sponsors were Allan Bond and Tim Brosnan. But it was more of the same, and Livermore did little better than break even.

All in all, he made seven fresh starts in those six years and there were very few sustained successful periods and certainly not of the kind that earned the huge profits he was used to.

He suddenly realized that he was older and times had changed, and things were never going back to how they were before. It was a salutary realization.

He also believed his performance was being affected by the financial cushion of his wife. After being married four times to wealthy men and being made a widow four times, Harriet was worth some $7 million and was keen to indulge her new husband. Whenever he was down on his luck, she came to the rescue. He knew it affected his trading, but he couldn't shake himself loose from it; nor did he really want to. He loved his third wife very much and she enjoyed helping her husband along and did it without rancor and with real enthusiasm. But every time she helped, a little bit of Livermore's soul went away.

Once he had realized what his future was, the now 60-year-old Livermore fell into a serious depression. He just couldn't face a future as a failure, and when he realized that he was not coming back for a fourth time, he decided it was time for him to check out permanently. Failure was a permanent future he just could not contemplate.

CHAPTER 40

Reflections in a Book

Understanding the good times

1940

After the shooting in 1935, Jesse Livermore Jr eventually made a full recovery from his wounds. He was reconciled with his mother but they gradually grew apart and he spent more and more time with his father in New York at Harriet's triplex apartment. His education had been effectively ended by the shooting, and he was now a young man of leisure. His father indulged him as much as he could and enjoyed the boy's company. Young Jesse, now 21, loved New York life, and father and son enjoyed a brief closeness they never had in his childhood.

In 1939, seeing his father at a low ebb after the continual attempts to rebuild his fortune failed, Jesse Jr suggested he write a book about his experiences on the stock market. Initially, Livermore rejected the idea but Jesse Jr persisted and persuaded his father to do it. He told him he would find him a publisher. His father gave his blessing.

But finding a publisher was not to prove as easy as Jesse Jr had imagined. First, he tried the George H. Doran Company, the publisher of *Reminiscences of a Stock Operator*. But Doran had merged with Doubleday, and the original founder had sold his shares and departed. Doubleday Doran, as the merged company was called, was now the largest book publisher in America and the new corporate managers were not impressed with the idea and did not think the book would sell in big enough quantities to be commercially successful. And it didn't help that none of them had heard of Jesse Livermore's stock market exploits of long ago. To them, he was just "another rich guy who wanted his memoirs published".

It was the first in a long line of rejections that Jesse Jr encountered. So he changed his strategy and started approaching newly set up publishers that he assumed would be hungrier to do business. With technical advances in printing and binding, and the American public's insatiable demand for books, there was a literary boom going on and a new publisher was opening up every day in New York. There was a glut of paper due to the war and it fuelled an unprecedented demand for the written word in the pre-television age.

After even more rejections, Jesse Jr at last found a publisher that had opened its doors the year before and needed material. Duell, Sloan and Pearce was founded in 1939 by Hal Duell, Sam Sloan and Charles Pearce. It published general fiction and non-fiction alike but avoided westerns, romance or children's books.

Although only a year old, it had already published books by many prominent authors, including such notables as Anaïs Nin, Conrad Aiken and Benjamin Spock. It specialized in photographic essays and launched the *U.S. Camera* annuals, which included groundbreaking photographs of nudes.

Two of the partners were keen stock market investors and liked to trade shares regularly. They had read *Reminiscences of a Stock Operator* and were intrigued to learn that Livermore was the fictional subject. As soon as they looked at the figures for *Reminiscences*, they became very interested in publishing Livermore's autobiography. They suggested he make it more like a manual for stock trading, and he enthusiastically took up the idea as he was not keen to write about the finer details of his own colorful life.

A contract was signed for a $1,000 advance and Livermore and his son were sent away to write the book. The writing came easy and Livermore decided to publish the mathematical formula he had sometimes used in recent years for working out what shares to trade. He named it the 'Livermore Market Key.' The book was announced to the book trade on March 7th 1940, and the *New York Times* covered it unenthusiastically with the headline: "J. L. Livermore Writes Book." The paper said the book would be published in early May. So, with a deadline to meet in a few months, Livermore got down to some serious work. Livermore had always had a keen writing style and was able to dictate almost perfect sentences to his secretary as he had done to Edwin Lefevre for *Reminiscences*.

A few days later, the *New York Times* published a lengthy preview of the book based on Livermore's speech at its launch. An analyst called Burton Crane, who attended the event, had been intrigued by Livermore's speech, particularly his comments about his Market Key which he hinted might be revealed in the book.

By the end, Livermore, helped by his son and wife, had written seven chapters that he believed covered the gamut of his stock trading methods.

When he got to 25,000 words, he suddenly stopped and declared to his wife: "That is enough." In truth, it was barely enough and the publishers had hoped for 50,000 words at least, and the 25,000 equated to only seven chapters.

To supplement it, after much thought, Livermore decided to add in his famous Market Key, his so-called trading formula. With an introduction and explanatory rules plus 14 pages of charts, it managed to add around 40 pages and significantly beefed up the book.

Very few people except Livermore really understood how his Market Key worked, but he assured skeptical readers that it did. When the book was finally printed, it was over 110 pages. It was published in hardback with an attractive dust cover and a photograph on the back showing Livermore in front of his chalkboards.

Chapter One was titled 'Challenges Of Speculation.' Livermore introduced himself and called his profession that of a speculator. He said being a stock market speculator was: "The most uniformly fascinating game in the world." But he warned: "It is not a game for the stupid, the mentally lazy, men of inferior emotional balance or the get-rich-quick adventurer." He warned that all those types of people would "die poor."

He also described how, because of who he was, he was continually asked for share tips at social events. And that his answer was always "I don't know". He told his readers that if he knew the profession of the enquirer, he would always fire back: "How can I make some quick money in law or surgery?"

Livermore told readers he had decided to write the book because he had finally come to the conclusion that people needed a "guide or signpost to point them in the right direction". He told them he had written the book for them. The first chapter contained all sorts of famous Livermore quotes that would be repeated for many years after his death, including "Markets are never wrong, opinions often are" and "Profits always take care of themselves but losses never do."

He also told his readers that impatience had been his biggest enemy throughout his career, writing: "I permitted impatience to outmaneuver good judgment."

Livermore also warned against human frailties, in particular being "hopeful and "fearful". He said that hope and fear were the most "formidable hazards" for stock traders. He lectured that it was necessary for any successful speculator to take his losses early and profits late. Not doing so, he warned, was a mistake that had cost him tens of millions of dollars in his career.

Chapter Two was entitled 'When Does A Stock Act Right?' It was basically a technical lesson in the art of timing and buying and selling. In it, he warned readers against being swayed by external opinion, which more often than not led to mistakes.

Chapter Three was entitled 'Follow The Leaders' and advised readers of the book to confine their trading to the major stocks and commodities and to specialize.

Chapter Four was called 'Money In The Hand' and reminded readers of the necessity to handle their own financial affairs. He also warned against what he called "averaging losses". He wrote: "Blunders by incompetent speculators cover a wide scale. I have warned against averaging losses. This is most common practice. Great numbers of people will buy a stock, let us say at 50 and two or three days later, if they can, buy it at 47 and they are seized with the urge to average down by buying another hundred shares, making an average of 48 on all." Livermore explained the sheer folly of "having bought at 50 and being concerned over a three point loss on a hundred and having the double worry when the price hits 44. At that point, there would be a $600 loss on the first hundred shares and a $300 loss on the second hundred shares."

He also warned of the danger of over ambition and advised speculators to look for plenty of small profits rather than one big one. He told readers that speculation was a business and advised would-be speculators not to be influenced by "excitement, flattery or temptation." He said it was a lesson he had learned painfully himself.

Chapter Five covered Livermore's theory of buying and selling on what he called 'The Pivotal Point', also the heading for the chapter. His pivotal points were when shares went through significant barriers up or down, usually the 100 or 200 mark. He said that the psychology of the market usually, in his opinion, led shares higher or lower after these points.

Chapter Six was entitled 'The Million Dollar Blunder'. The theme of the chapter was, in Livermore's words, to "lay down some general trading principles." It explained his system of probing before he made a big investment. He would first buy small stakes and buy more as each probe showed a profit. He explained he would never buy more shares if a probe showed a loss. He also described how he had had the cotton futures ticker removed from his office after he made substantial losses. Finally, he warned readers off soliciting and acting on so-called inside information. He wrote: "Beware of inside information…all inside information." He was speaking from experience and the many times he had been burnt by it.

Finally, he called Chapter Seven the 'Three Million Dollar Profit' and described his extraordinary coup in buying and selling wheat and rye in 1925 all the way up and down after they passed their pivotal points. He confirmed the resulting profit was $3 million.

He ended the book on a positive note with the advice: "The future is bright for the intelligent, patient speculator." It was, as always, good advice.

The book was not entirely satisfactory. It was a very quick run though his many trading principles and his successes and mistakes. The market key published at the back was very hard for anyone to understand, and it is not clear if anyone ever did.

For all those reasons and perhaps many more, the book was not an immediate bestseller and Livermore ended up disappointed with the way it was received. The reviews focused on his past rather than the book. And more than a few described him as a dinosaur and talked about his career with the emphasis on "past successes." The response to it depressed him further.

The market had also moved on from when the book was conceived and when it went on sale. By the time it was published, the bookselling boom had ended as a new age of austerity set in. The Second World War was underway and the stock market was also down in the dumps – interest in shares was at its lowest level for 50 years.

It was only after Livermore died that the book became a success. As the years rolled by, more and more editions were published and the book eventually became a best seller with its accumulated sales. But, by then, he was long gone and so was his son.

CHAPTER 41

Aftermath: Reflections On Life

Jesse Livermore's final reckoning

1940

When the death of Jesse Livermore was announced in the morning newspapers of Friday November 29th 1940, it shook Wall Street to its core. Although Livermore had effectively been out of the heat of Wall Street action for much of the previous five years and was considered a spent force, the publication of his book *How to Trade in Stocks* the previous May had revived interest in him.

There was talk of nothing else on Wall Street that morning and plenty of speculation as to why he had taken his own life. Many people considered him a delayed casualty of the 1929 crash when many bankrupted investors took their own lives. In many ways, they were right but for different reasons. Although Livermore was the big winner of 1929, his success was so colossal and so hard to handle, that its aftermath eventually caused him to end his life.

No man, it seemed, could really cope with having so much money so quickly and then losing it all almost as quickly again. And no man in history, before, then and since, had earned so much money so quickly and then lost it so quickly as Livermore had between 1929 and 1933.

And seemingly no man, throughout his life, had enjoyed his money so greatly.

His suicide was much discussed throughout New York, where he had many friends and associates from a near 40-year career on Wall Street. There is no doubt he had finally realized that his professional career was over and that he was not about to make a fourth comeback. He knew his financial future now depended on the largesse of his wife Harriet, which could not have been easy for him.

But they were not the only reasons. He had endured a terrible summer and had been very upset by the death of his close friend Walter Chrysler on August 18th at the age of only 65. He had been very close to Chrysler, whose death sharply reminded him of his own mortality.

He had also been devastated when his old house in Great Neck had been sold to real estate developers Johnson & Olsen. The developers promptly announced they were going to demolish the house and erect an upmarket housing estate on the site. The news was splashed all over the *New York Times*. The thought of his old home being torn down destroyed him inside. There were so many memories from his ten-year ownership of the house, and he felt a piece of his own body was being torn away when the demolition promptly got started as soon as the sale went through.

But most of this was lost on the 100 or so close friends and family that turned up for his funeral service at the Campbell Funeral Chapel at noon on the morning of Saturday November 30th 1940.

Mostly the mourners were the great and good of Wall Street past and present, as well as many of the characters who had partied with him throughout the twenties in Palm Beach at the Beach Club. There were also many old friends of the family from the social set in Long Island. Livermore's widow, Harriet, did not know many of the people who were there. They had mostly been friends of Dorothy, his second wife, who had accompanied him everywhere in his halcyon days. Dorothy herself was nowhere to be seen, doubtless made unwelcome by her replacement.

For them, Jesse Livermore's funeral was one that you didn't miss, and it was the memories and the nostalgia of an age gone by, never to be repeated, that drew those 100 people. They had all known about the stock market before the advent of the Securities & Exchange Commission changed investors' lives forever. It was that common bond that tied them all together, friend and foe alike, people like Arthur Cutten and Frank Bliss.

The brief service was conducted by the Reverend Edgar Crossland, the pastor of the Home Street Presbyterian Church in the Bronx. Crossland was the closest the Livermore family had to a family priest. After the service, the family travelled across town to Hartsdale, to the Ferncliff Crematorium. Ferncliff was the crematorium of choice for citizens of New York and many chose, if they could afford it, for their ashes to lay forever in the adjoining mausoleum. The cost of Livermore's funeral and interment was a staggering $4,700.

For that, one's ashes were laid to rest in some splendor in the Ferncliff Mausoleum, which had been built out of granite in 1927 and now totalled 200,000 square feet. The resting spaces were rented forever. Every type was available from plain and simple cut-outs in the marble walls to whole dedicated rooms.

The crematorium was situated in the Mausoleum and the building had stained glass windows throughout. The chapel was accessed via breathtaking marble corridors, and oriental rugs covered the floors to muffle noise. Only Harriet, Jesse Jr and Paul were there for the cremation, which was again presided over by the Reverend Crossland. After the casket was burnt, the ashes were delivered back to the widow who placed them in a niche in the wall, arranged the day before.

An hour after that, the family was back at the apartment at 1100 Park Avenue. Soon after they returned, Dorothy Livermore called to ask how it had gone. She was clearly very upset even though it had been seven years since the divorce. She asked Harriet if Paul could come and stay with her for a few days. The chauffeur took him over to Brooklyn where Dorothy now lived. When he arrived, the two burst into tears, sat down on the sofa and began to share their memories.

And that was that until Thursday of the following week, when Livermore's last will and testament was filed for probate in New York's Surrogates Court. When the contents were made known, the whole of New York was shocked to the core. According to the New York Times, the value of his estate was "under $10,000." New Yorkers had regarded Livermore as one of the city's richest citizens but that clearly was no longer true. It would be some weeks before the true figure was known, when the estate tax appraisal would be filed. In truth, he was worth much more although his debts were huge. The $10,000 figure turned out to be a mirage. Jesse Livermore's final net worth was more like minus $350,000.

The will had been drawn up by Livermore in early 1940 and signed by him on February 1st 1940.

His wife Harriet was the sole beneficiary and the executor. The New York Times wrote: "He bequeathed his estate outright to his wife after requesting that his 'just debts' be paid."

The will had been witnessed by his general manager, Walter McNerney, and two others, Herbert Meehan and Walter Randal. In the event that his wife had pre-deceased him, the whole estate would have gone to Paul Livermore. There was no mention of Jesse Jr.

A year later, on January 20th 1942, the estate appraisal document was published and it showed Livermore died with assets of $107,047 but had debts that totalled $463,517.

The assets mainly consisted of the Jesse Livermore Jr trust fund, valued at

$28,093, and the Paul A. Livermore trust fund, valued at $36,043. In addition, Harriet Livermore had his life insured for $70,000 of which $37,635 was included in the assets. The actual value of the assets left upon death was $5,276. Additionally, Harriet Livermore had received $40,000 separately from a life insurance payout.

The final act came on July 1st 1942 when the estate accounting was filed at the Surrogate's Court. The assets had dwindled to $3,795. But the debts had reduced down to $372,250. The reduction came as the courts ruled that the $93,000 that Harriet Livermore had claimed as a debt due to her from her husband should not be included since it could not be proved. What was included was $154,675 due in local state taxes, $39,128 to the Internal Revenue Service and a host of personal loans and debts, including $29,852 to Tom McKinnon, $35,140 to Irene Kelly, $34,144 to Charlotte Powell, and $10,573 to Renee Strakosch.

Shockingly, it was revealed that Livermore had a secret apartment at 550 Park Avenue that he rented, and the rent was overdue by $11,000 at his death. Harriet was not best pleased to learn of that, but perhaps not too surprised.

Even more shockingly, there had been severe losses on the value of his sons' trust funds. His eldest son's trust had been worth $119,300 when it was set up in 1919. By the time his father died, it was worth only $27,964. Although the trust had paid out an income for Jesse Jr of $65,987 for the period, trading in the trust's investments had lost $94,218 and only $4,402 profit had been made. The performance of Paul's trust was equally as poor.

It was clear that Livermore had died virtually a pauper, reliant on the kindness of friends for his lifestyle.

For various reasons, Harriet Livermore appeared to have done the best financially from his death. She didn't hang around for anyone to ask her questions and left New York for Los Angeles soon after the funeral.

Before she left New York, she wrote to the Ferncliff Mausoleum and told them she had changed her mind and wished her husband's ashes to be interred with his parents Hiram and Laura in Woodlawn Cemetery in Acton, Massachusetts. The urn was duly transferred, and Livermore's name and year of birth and death were carved on the reverse of his parents' own gravestone. No one knows why but it is thought that Harriet no longer wished to bear the not inconsiderable cost of Livermore's ashes being permanently interred at Ferncliff after she discovered the secret apartment he had rented until his death at 550 Park Avenue. She had no doubt what it had been used for and felt utterly betrayed.

Since his death, some commentators have since opined that much more of Livermore's legendary fortune remained intact than was thought. And there is some evidence to support this.

Many years later, in 2001, Livermore's modern day biographer, Richard Smitten, interviewed his last remaining close relative, youngest son Paul. Paul Livermore told Smitten a remarkable but scarcely believable story about the night his father died and the curious behavior of his stepmother.

Paul, by then 78 years old, who was to die a year later in 2002, recounted that on the night of his father's death, he had arrived at the apartment at 1100 Park Avenue at around 10 o'clock to be greeted by his stepmother, who was getting ready to go out barely four hours after her husband had shot himself.

Paul claimed that his stepmother greeted him at the front door of the apartment, beside which lay, on the carpet, three brown paper shopping bags stuffed with cash in high denomination notes. He said he estimated the three bags contained over $3 million in cash. He said there was also another brown paper shopping bag half filled with jewelry. He estimated the value of the jewelry at $1 million.

By way of explanation, Paul claimed his stepmother motioned him over to a sofa in the apartment's drawing room and sat him down and said: "Look Paul, I've just talked to a friend, a lawyer, who told me that the police often investigate suicides like they do homicides…I'm afraid they could come here and search the apartment and I could not explain certain things. Your father kept too much cash in the house. So I'm going for the evening. Besides, I'm very upset but I have to try and think straight. I must think straight, you understand. I'm in a hurry. They could arrive at any moment. I'm not going far. Just to a hotel. But you tell the police that I've gone to see a friend if they come."

With that, she went into the night and was driven somewhere by her chauffeur. According to Paul Livermore, the matter was never again discussed and the next morning his stepmother returned to the apartment early as if nothing had happened.

The story is feasible. In those days, the maximum denomination dollar bill was $10,000 and $1,000 bills were reasonably common. There could have easily been $1 million in a typical brown paper shopping bag common in the US.

The story, however, has never been written elsewhere except in Smitten's book. No one knows if it is true. Certainly the money, if it existed, never came to the Livermore boys. They had to rely on the values of their depleted trust funds.

Paul Livermore lived a very happy life. He flew US Air Force jets in the closing days of World War II and the Pacific War. After the war, he became a minor, but successful, actor in Hollywood and later retired to Hawaii, where he surfed every day. He met and married Margaret Seeley and had two children, Chad and Scott. Later, he divorced Margaret and bought the Embers Nightclub in Honolulu, where he met a talented singer called Ann McCormack. McCormack was a class act and had dueted with Frank Sinatra and Tony Bennett. She was considered a beauty of the age and they lived happily until his death in 2002. His wife was still performing professionally at the age of 90 and today lives quietly in Honolulu, alone with her memories aged 93.

Not so Jesse Livermore Jr. As happy as his brother's life was, his was unhappy and ultimately, like his father's, tragic. He married for the first time in 1937 to Toni Lanier, which ended weeks after the wedding. Almost immediately, he married for a second time to Evelyn Sullivan in 1940 and their son, Jesse Livermore III, was born on December 7th 1941. But he rarely saw him and soon moved out of the family apartment in Park Avenue into a suite at the Metropolitan Club.

His father had set him up in business and bought him the Pepsi-Cola franchise for Connecticut. But he mismanaged it and had to sell it to avoid bankruptcy. He then used his father's close friendship with Charles Revson, the founder of the Revlon Cosmetics empire, to get himself a job as sales promotion manager at Revlon. But he was no good at that either, and Revson soon sacked him.

Jesse Jr had no regard for money. He had been brought up as the eldest son of one of the world's richest men and had no reason to think that the seemingly endless supply of cash would ever run out. In 1963, he finally divorced Evelyn and she took the by now very valuable apartment in Park Avenue and the rest of his cash.

From then on, he lived more frugally, relying on handouts from his mother. His only real source of income, by then, was the original trust fund his father had set up for him in 1919. The income was around $3,000 a year, but his mother controlled the trust and thwarted his plans to get hold of it.

His divorce left him free to marry his long-time girlfriend, Patricia Schneider, the beautiful daughter of an Ohio real estate developer, in 1965. They bought a four-storey townhouse at 214 East 72nd Street in New York.

Eventually his mother, Dorothy, who was by then on her fourth husband and recently widowed, moved into the house, occupying the third floor. They installed a full time butler and both Jesse and Dorothy continued to drink heavily. Jesse turned the fourth floor into a bachelor floor and entertained women secretly whilst his wife was on a lower floor. According to Richard Smitten, he once told his wife: "It's no fun having an affair if you aren't married."

Drink began to destroy Jesse Jr as it had his mother. The beginning of the end came in 1975. By then, 35 years after his father's death, his drinking was out of control. It came to a head on the night of March 13th 1975 when Jesse Jr lost control of himself while in a drunken stupor. First he shot dead his beloved Doberman dog, Cesare, and then attempted to kill himself but was so drunk he couldn't manage it.

As things deteriorated in the house, Patricia called the police and fled next door. Ten officers from a special response team were dispatched and, when they arrived, they found Jesse seated in an easy chair, Cesare dead at his feet, two .32 caliber chrome-plated Colt revolvers in his lap. The officers spoke with Jesse for a while and then in a ruse asked if they could have a glass of wine. When Jesse rose to pour the wine, two officers, Lieutenant John Weeks and Officer Charles Brezny, rushed him. Jesse managed to retrieve one of the revolvers, pushed it against Officer Weeks's chest and pulled the trigger, but the gun failed to go off.

He was charged with the attempted murder of a police officer, a very serious crime, which would have probably attracted a prison term of eight years. But then it got much worse when the governor of New York, Nelson Rockefeller, enacted a new law making attempted murder of a police officer punishable by life imprisonment without any possibility of parole. It made a serious situation even more serious.

Jesse Jr was denied bail and taken to Rikers Island prison and placed in solitary confinement. But after 54 days in prison, he was finally given bail and released on the condition he did not visit New York and confined himself only to Palm Beach. A further condition of bail was that he consult a psychiatrist. The psychiatrist diagnosed him as a manic-depressive, paranoid, suicidal alcoholic. No one would disagree with that description. Inevitably, he resumed his drinking.

On the eve of his much delayed trial in New York, Jesse Jr decided he could not face it and decided to commit suicide just as his father had done

35 years before. But unable to summon up the courage, he went to a friend's unoccupied apartment in Palm Beach. He entered the kitchen and shut the door. He turned on the gas and opened the oven door. For good measure, he swallowed a whole bottle of barbiturates. The next day he was found gassed.

If he had not died, it was almost inevitable he would have been jailed for life.

In 1995, Dorothy Livermore, passed away at the age of 94. She asked that her cat, Caesar, be put to sleep and placed in her casket and cremated with her. Her wishes were carried out to the letter.

With that, one of the great stories of the 20th century came to an end. No one had enjoyed a life quite like Jesse and Dorothy Livermore. She and her husband were icons of the age: the paragons of a style of life certain never to be repeated again.

CHAPTER 42

Postscript

Third generation commits suicide

2006

In 2006, there was a terrible modern day postscript to the life of Jesse Livermore, when his grandson Jesse III reaped the terrible reward of his grandfather's and his father's legacies.

Jesse III never knew his grandfather, who had died the year before he was born in 1941. His mother was Jesse Jr's second wife Evelyn Sullivan, herself a divorcee, whom he married in 1940. Jesse III lived with his mother and had little contact with his father throughout his life although his parents did not finally divorce until 1963.

Jesse III, like his father and grandfather, was three times married. At the age of 23, he married for the first time to Marsha Hawkins in 1964. Together they had two children, David, born in 1969, and Tracey in 1973. He subsequently divorced Marsha and married his second wife, Karen. They divorced and he married for the third time to Carol. He was 34 when his own father, Jesse Jr, committed suicide in 1975.

His life was seemingly happy, and his son and daughter bore him five grandchildren. His son David had four children, three girls and a boy. The boy was the fifth generation Livermore male heir to be born in 137 years. Tracey had one child.

But on February 26th 2006, the unfathomable happened and Jesse Livermore III, at the age of 65, turned a room of his house into a gas chamber. He sealed the room and turned on the gas and lay down. The next day, the newspapers carried the news in a few words, seemingly not realizing who he was. It was the third suicide of the eldest male of the Livermore clan in a period spanning 66 years. Jesse Livermore, his son and his grandson all took their own lives in their 60s, seemingly unable to cope.

It was a terrible legacy for the man who, for a brief moment in 1929, had set Wall Street alight with his trading prowess, making him a $100 million profit in a few days: a feat, the scale of which, is likely never to be repeated again.

Principal Bibliography

Jess Livermore, Speculator King – Paul Sarnoff
Traders Press Inc – ISBN: 0-934380-10-4

Reminiscences of a Stock Operator – Edwin Lefevre
Wiley – ISBN: 978-0-470-48159-2

How to Trade in Stocks – Jesse Livermore
McGraw Hill – ISBN: 978-0-07-146979-1

The Day The Bubble Burst – Gordon Thomas, Max Morgan-Witts
Arrow Books – ISBN: 009 923 370 3

The Year Of The Great Crash 1929 – William K. Klingaman
Harper & Row – ISBN: 0-06-016081-0

Jesse Livermore's Methods in Trading Stocks – Ricard D. Wyckoff
Snowball Publishing – ISBN: 978 -1-60796-450-6

The Great Crash 1929 – John Kenneth Galbraith
Allen Lane – ISBN: 978-0-141-03630-4

The House of Morgan – Ron Chernow
Simon and Schuster – ISBN: 0-671-71031-1

Baruch – Bernard M Baruch
Henry Holt and Co

Carnegie – Peter Krass
Wiley – ISBN 0-471-38630 – 8

Andrew Carnegie – David Nasaw
The Penguin Press – ISBN: 1-59420-10408

Morgan, American Financier – Jean Strouse
Harvill – ISBN: 1- 86046-335-X

Mellon – David Cannadine
Knopf – ISBN: 0-679-45032-7

Timeline

Year	Event	Age	Description
1877	Birth	0	Born in Shrewsbury, West Acton, Massachusetts USA
1891	First job	14	Employed at Paine Webber Boston stockbroking offices
1892	First trade	15	Makes a $3.12 profit trading in Burlington stock
1893	Starts trading on his own	16	Makes $10,000 trading in Bucket Shops in Boston
1899	Moves to New York	22	Begins trading properly on NYSE
1900	First Marriage	23	Weds Nettie Jordan of Indianapolis
1900	Loses all his money	23	Loses everything as he misreads trading skills
1900	Returns to bucket shops	23	Makes $5,000 for new stake
1901	Returns to New York	24	Makes $50,000 and loses it again on cotton trades
1906	San Francisco earthquake	29	Makes $250,000 after earthquake causes slump
1907	Stock market crash	30	Makes $1 million shorting stocks on a random hunch
1907	Buys first yacht	30	Goes sailing in Palm Beach, Florida
1908	Makes and loses fortune	31	Makes then loses $5 million on cotton trades with Teddy Price
1908	Tangles with Charles Pugh	31	Pugh bankrolls return with limited success
1909	Start of lean years	32	Period of six years when he loses his touch
1915	First bankruptcy	38	Declares official bankruptcy with debts of $100,000
1915	Slow road to redemption	38	Makes $145,000 trading shares of Bethlehem Steel
1916	Return to form	39	Makes $5 million clear profit
1917	Consolidates progress	40	Makes another $1.5 million and establishes trust fund
1917	Pays off debts	40	Repays creditors $1.2 million
1918	First divorce	41	Finally divorces Nettie after 18 years of separation
1918	Second marriage	41	Marries 22-year-old showgirl, Dorothy Wendt in New York
1919	Birth of eldest son	42	Jesse Livermore II is born on September 19th

TIMELINE

Year	Event	Age	Description
1922	Moves into new house	45	Buys mansion in Great Neck
1923	Edwin Lefèvre book	46	Fictionalized biography is published
1923	Birth of youngest son	46	Paul Livermore is born on April 3rd
1923	Moves into Heckscher office	46	Moves into big office with 60 staff
1925	Huge grain profits	48	Makes $10 million trading corn and wheat
1927	Raid on Great Neck	50	Burglary in Long Island
1929	The crash	52	Goes short before October 1929 makes $100 million
1932	Second divorce	55	Dorothy gets settlement of $10 million
1933	Third marriage	56	Marries Harriett Metz Noble
1933	Long Island home sold	56	Great Neck house is auctioned off by ex wife to pay her debts
1934	Second bankruptcy	57	Liabilities listed at $2.29 million
1935	Ex-wife shoots eldest son	58	Dorothy shoots Jesse II on November 29th
1940	Own book published	63	Book is called How To Trade In Stocks
1940	Death	63	Commits suicide in New York on November 28th

Index

A

A. S. White & Company 266
Acton 9, 17, 18, 26, 38, 60
Aiken, Conrad 352
Aix-les-Bains 100, 101, 102
Aldrich-Vreeland Act 178
Allen, Dr 345
American Bankers Association 314
American Smelting Company 101
Anaconda Copper Mining Co. 98, 97
Anita 137, 138, 151, 161
Anita Venetian 213
Aquitania 223
Armour, Jonathan Ogden 134
Armstrong Laws 103
Aronhson, Harry 286, 287, 288
Aronhson, Sadie 286
Associated Automatic Machines Corp. 309
Associated Press Agency 114
Astor IV, John Jacob 213
Athero 281, 282
Athero II 232, 234, 280, 285, 286
Atterbury, John 117, 118, 120, 122, 124
Austin Friars Trust Ltd 309

B

Babson, Roger 310, 311, 312
Baker, George 109, 110
Baldwin Locomotive 268
Ballantine, Lucille 335
Baltimore & Ohio Telegraph Company 43
Baltimore Postal Telegraph Company 43
Bank of England 103, 313
Barney, Charles 105, 106, 111
Barry, Arthur 285, 286, 288, 291
Baruch, Bernard 188, 201, 202, 203, 255
Beach Club 139, 151, 190, 280
Bennett, Tony 362
Bethlehem Steel 182, 183
Billy the Kid 139
Blake, Anna 285, 288, 291
Blake, Teddy 253
Bliss, Frank 255, 256, 271, 273, 276, 358
Block, Ben 334
Boca Raton 265, 268
Boer War 89, 102
Bohne, Tom 141
Bologna, Pat 305
Bond, Allan 350

Boston Billy 285
Braccho, Gene 140
Bradley, E. W. 242
Bradley, Ed 139, 140, 142, 242, 280
Bradley, Jack 139
Brady, Jim 142
Brand, Harold 328, 329
Brandt, Charles 345
Breakers Hotel 139, 260, 265
Bretton Hall 173
Brezny, Charles 363
Brooklyn Rapid Transport Company 62
Brosnan, Tim 350
Burlington and Quincy Railroad 25, 26
Burnham, Tom 36
Burns Agency Detectives 290
Business Conduct Committee 241

C

C. C. Christie 59, 62, 64, 65
Cahn, David 219
Calahan, Edward 40
Campbell Funeral Chapel 358
Campbell, Sir William 103
Capone, Al 279
Carpenter, James 277
Carrère & Hastings 252
Carrère, John 252, 253
Casey, William 348
CBS 262
Chaplin, Charlie 278, 280
Chaplin, Lita 278
Chesapeake & Atlantic 168, 169, 170
Chicago Board of Trade (CBOT) 40, 42, 44,
132, 144, 155, 335, 349
Chicago Daily Tribune 131, 153
Chicago Exchange 43
Chrysler Corporation 278, 280
Chrysler, Della 278
Chrysler, Walter 230, 278, 357
City Equitable 309
Clancy, Carmel 18, 19
Clarence Hatry Group 308
Clark, Harold 285
Coe Commission Company 41, 59, 60
Coe, Louis 61, 63
Cohen, Ben 348
Collins, Georgia 340
Columbia University 42
Columbia Yacht Club 138, 145

Commerce & Finance Magazine 143
Commercial & Financial Chronicle 128, 130
Commercial Corporation of London 309
Committee of Inquiry, The 226
Commodity Exchange 335
Computing Tabulator Company 255, 271
Conan-Doyle, Arthur 246
Corcoran, Thomas 348
Cortelyou, George 112, 113, 115, 121
Crossland, Rev. Edgar 358, 359

D

D'Avignon, Dr Joseph 344
Dache, Harry 253, 254, 256, 257, 322, 349
Daily Globe, The 131
Davis, Jamie 62, 65
Davison, Henry 111, 112
Department of the Interior 224
Doran, George 246, 247, 248
Doubleday & Company 249, 351
Doubleday Doran 248, 351
Douglas, William 348
Dow Jones Industrial Average 295, 296, 303, 307
Drake, John 70
Drapery Trust 309
Duell, Hal 352
Dundee Trust 309
Durant, Clara 278
Durrant, William 230, 278, 280, 347, 349

E

E. F. Hutton & Co 49, 74, 75, 78, 80, 96, 101, 108, 111, 123, 144, 187, 188, 189
Earp, Wyatt 139
Eckardt, Heinrich von 193
École Nationale Supérieure des Beaux-Arts 252
Edison, Thomas 40
Edmondson, Richard 273
Edwards, Elvin 291
Ehrhorn, Oscar 3a34, 336
El Mirasol Hotel 343
Emery, Henry Crosby 42
Evermore 277, 278, 280, 322

F

F. A. Connolly & Co. 204

Fall, Albert 226
Federal Reserve Bank of New York 109, 297
Federal Reserve Bank of Washington 109, 297
Federal Trade Commission (FTC) 226
Ferncliff Crematorium 358
Ferncliff Mausoleum 358, 360
Financial America 273
Finlay Barrel 188
First National Bank 109, 110, 114, 203
Fischer, Carl 3
Fisher, Irving 312, 318
Fitzgerald, F. Scott 230
Flagler Memorial Bridge 139
Flagler, Henry 95, 138, 139
Flagler, John 137
Follette, Robert La 225
Ford Motor Company 278
Forrest and John Mars 5
Frank, Jerome 348
Frank, Josephine 340
Frankfurter, Felix 348
Freeport Sulphur Company 272
Freeport Texas 271, 272, 275
Frick, Henry 99, 127, 128

G

Galbraith, J. K. 308, 309
Galston, Robert 286, 288
Garfield, James 127
Gary, Judge 127, 128
Gates, John 70, 129
General Motors 278
General Securities Ltd 309
George H. Doran Company 246, 351
George S. Lawley & Sons 282
Gielow, Henry 280, 281, 282
Gilman, Sam 335, 336, 345, 349
Goldstein, Judith 229
Gomber, William 273
Gorman, Frank 319
Governing Committee 205
Grand Central Station 167
Grant, Ulysses 9
Great Gatsby, The 230
Great Neck 229, 232, 257, 277, 278, 280, 281, 285, 288, 316, 317, 321, 358
Great Northern 93
Green, Hetty 70

Green, Norvin 43
Grenfell, Morgan 115
Gridiron Club 103

H

Hadden, Briton 256
Haight & Freese 30, 31, 34, 35, 37, 41, 48
Harding, Warren 295, 296
Harriman, E. H. 99, 245, 259
Harriman, Joseph 335
Harris, Jim 49, 58, 63, 68
Harry Winston 329
Harvard Law Review 348
Harvard Law School 348
Hastings, Tom 252, 253
Hatry, Clarence 302, 308, 310, 313
Hawkins, Marsha 365
Hearst, William Randolph 209
Heckendorf, District Attorney Percy 342
Heckscher Building 251, 252, 257, 258, 259, 272, 325, 310, 325
Heckscher, August 251
Heinze, Augustus 105, 106
Heinze, Otto 105, 106
Held, Anna 209
Hemmings, Jack 17, 18, 19, 26, 29
Hennessy, Michael 17, 18, 20, 21, 23, 26, 29
Henriquez, Billy 174
Henry, Robert 202
Hill, James 93
Hine, Francis 203
Hollister, Dr 265
Home Street Presbyterian Church 358
Honeyman, Lassie 339
Hoover, President Herbert 296, 298, 301, 218, 322, 347
Hotchkiss School 5
Hotel Netherland 210
House of Representatives House Rules Committee 201, 202, 203
How to Trade in Stocks 261, 357
Howell, Cpt. 285
Hughes, Charles Evans 44
Hunky, Catherine 340
Hutchinson, Ben 42
Hutchinson, John 327
Hutchins, Susan 327
Hutton (née Horton), Blanche 51, 52
Hutton, Edward 49, 50, 51, 58, 63, 68, 74, 78, 80, 81, 82, 92, 94, 97, 108, 118, 122, 144,

167, 230
Hutton, Harris 53, 57, 63, 68
Hyams, Cpt. Louis 330

I

I. G. Wolf & Co 230
IBM 256
Ingersoll, William 262
Internal Revenue Service 360
International Herald Tribune 101
Irving Trust Company 335, 336

J

J. L. Livermore & Co. 215, 216, 252, 254
J. P. Morgan & Co 41, 108, 109, 115, 121
Jackson, Stephen 345
Janssen, August 231, 232
Jerome, William 212
Johnson & Olsen 358
Jordan, Chester 162, 208

K

Kamarick, Abe 330
Kane, Eddie 257, 285, 286, 288, 291, 292
Keene, James 274
Kelly, Irene 360
Kennedy, Joseph 95, 139, 304, 348
Kenny, Patrick 4, 7
Kent, Horace 61, 62
Kessler, George 124
Keynes, John Maynard 318
King, Cpt. Harold 288
King, Edward 128
Kiser, John 231
Knickerbocker Trust 105, 106, 108, 111, 112, 113
Krasnova, Nadia 327, 328, 335
Kuhn, Walter 325

L

Laguna Blanca School 339
Lamb & Blake 253
Lamb, William 252, 253
Landis, James 348
Lanier, Toni 362
Lawson, Tommy 202, 203, 255, 347
Lefévre, Edwin 71, 73, 160 245, 246, 247,

248, 249, 352
Lenox Hill 277
Levin, George 335, 336
Lewisohn Brothers 217
Lewisohn, Walter 217, 218, 219
Lincoln, Abraham 9
Lincoln Trust 128
Little Neck Bay 229
Livermore III, Jesse 362, 365
Livermore, Dorothy 211, 212, 229, 233, 234, 277, 287, 278, 279, 280, 317, 321, 322, 323, 324, 333, 335, 339, 340, 341, 342, 343, 344, 345, 358, 359, 363, 364
Livermore, Elliot 10, 11, 12, 173, 212
Livermore, (née Metz) Harriet (Nina) 1, 4, 326
Livermore, Hiram 10, 11, 12, 27, 52, 360
Livermore, Jesse Jr 4, 5, 213, 339, 340, 351, 363, 359
Livermore, Laura 10, 11, 12, 26, 52, 360
Livermore, Mabel 10, 11, 173
Livermore, (née Jordan) Nettie 51, 52, 57, 162, 207, 208, 211, 212
Livermore, Paul 5, 213, 283, 340, 359, 361
Liverpool Cotton Exchange 145
Livingston, Larry 246, 248
Lloyds of London 89
Long Island Railroad 232
Longcope, Walter 322, 323, 324, 339
Lonsdale, John 314
Los Angeles Times, The 153
Losey, George 293
Louis and Angelo Coe 60
Lowther, J. F. 273
Luce, Henry 5, 256
Luce, Teddy 262
Lusitania, RMS 184

M

M. J. Sage Company of New York 41
MacDonald, Joe 145, 281, 282
Making of a Stock Broker, The 248
Mammoth Oil Company 223, 224, 225
Manhasset Bay 229
Markman, Jon 274, 276
Markoe, Dr 113
Maugham, Somerset 246
Maxwell, Robert 308
McAdoo, William 178
McClellan, George 121

McConnell, Jack 288
McCormack, Ann 362
McDonald, Ramsey 301
McKinnon, Tom 360
McNerney, Walter 5, 6, 254, 349, 359
Meehan, Herbert 359
Meehan, Michael 296, 310
Mellon, Andrew 296, 297
Merrill, Elizabeth 230
Metropolitan Club 362
Metz, Frederick 327
Mexican Petroleum 220, 221, 222, 265
Miles, Raymond 6
Mineral Leasing Act 224
Mitchell, Charles 297, 301
Mizner Development Corp. 265, 268, 303
Mizner, Addison 265
Mizner, Elliot 265
Monaghan, James 285, 286, 287, 289, 291
Money Post, The 104, 117
Montgomery Ward 268
Moore & Schley 124, 126
Moran, Justice Thomas 324
Moore, Alex 142
Morgan, Pierpont 2, 95, 100, 108, 109, 111, 113, 115, 116, 117, 118, 119, 120, 121, 123, 126, 127, 128, 129, 137, 138, 159, 178, 216, 245
Morgan, Jack 216
Morse, Charles 105, 106, 251
Motor Boating Magazine 282
Murdock, Victor 226, 227
Murphy, Charles 273
Murphy, Vincent 4
Murray, Patrick 4

N

Nassau County Police 288, 290, 319
National City Bank 108, 109, 110, 114, 203, 297, 301, 315
National Financial News 206
Natrona County 223
NBC 262
Ness, Eliot 323
Neville, Dennis 340, 341
New York Coffee Exchange 197
New York Commodities Exchange 349
New York Cotton Exchange 153
New York Curb Exchange 216, 221, 265
New York Evening Mail 273

New York Evening Post 273
New York Herald Tribune 273
New York Hippodrome 222
New York Police Department 4, 42
New York Public Library 252
New York Stock Exchange (NYSE) 37, 41, 42, 44, 48, 104, 107, 115, 128, 205, 276
New York Sun 246
New York Times 40, 41, 42, 82, 94 147, 156, 177, 222, 223, 224, 240, 241, 247, 248, 256, 258, 273, 276, 288, 291, 303, 315, 316, 327, 329, 337, 342, 352, 358, 359
New York World 146, 147, 148
New York's City College 348
Nin, Anaïs 352
Norman, Monty 308, 309
Northern Pacific 93

O

O'Gorman, James 330
Oak Investment Corporation 309
Ochs, Adolph 247
Omaha Railway Company 61
Owens, George 290
Owens, James 141, 286, 290

P

Paine Webber 15, 16, 17, 18, 21, 23, 25, 26, 27, 29, 30, 47
Paine, Billy 15
Palm Beach Daily News 75
Palm Beach Inn 138
Patten, James 133, 134, 135
Pearce, Charles 352
Pearl & Co 325, 349
Pecora, Ferdinand 348
Pennsylvania Hotel 330, 331
Pennsylvania Railroad Company 168
Pepsi-Cola 362
Peter Pan 16
Peters, Jake 76, 90
Philadelphia & Reading Railroad 95
Photomaton Corporation 309
Pierson, John 175, 191
Piggly Wiggly Stores Inc 235, 236, 238, 239, 242, 271
Plant Railway Company 145
Plant, Morgan 145
Powell, Charlotte 360

Prentiss, John 248
Price Fixing Committee of the War Industries Board 196, 198
Price McCormick & Co. 143, 149
Price, Theodore (Teddy) 143, 148, 150, 156, 159, 160, 199, 219
Pugh, Charles 167, 168, 170, 179, 181, 182, 199, 219

R

Radio Corporation of America (RCA) 262, 268, 296, 310, 315
Randal, Walter 359
Redford, Robert 210
Reminiscences of a Stock Operator 160, 237, 238, 242, 247, 248, 249, 272, 273, 274, 351, 352
Republic Iron & Steel Company 125
Retail Trade Corporation 309
Revlon Cosmetics 362
Revson, Charles 362
Rikers Island prison 363
Rockefeller, John D. 95, 101, 114
Roesler, Walter 286
Rogers, H. H. 185
Rolls-Royce 212
Roosevelt, Franklin 1, 297, 347, 348
Roosevelt, Theodore 103, 127, 129
Root, Elihu 127
Ross, Jack 342
Rothstein, Abraham 24, 30
Rothstein, Arnold 24, 30, 31, 32, 34, 68
Royal Poinciana Hotel 95, 139
Russell, Lillian 142, 221
Rutter, Otto 292, 293
Ryon, Harrison 343

S

Sage, Russell 72
San Francisco Fire Department 77
Santvoord, George van 5
Saturday Evening Post, The 246
Saunders, Clarence 235, 236, 239, 240, 241 242
Scaffa, Noel 290, 291
Schiff, Jacob 99
Schley, Grant 124, 129
Schorton, William 162
Schwab, Charles 182

Securities & Exchange Commission 1, 348, 347, 358
Securities Exchange Act 347, 348
Seeley, Margaret 362
Seneca Copper 217, 219
Sherman Anti-Trust Act 127
Sherry-Netherland Hotel 2, 3, 4, 327, 349
Shreve, Rich 253
Simonson, William 203
Sinatra, Frank 362
Sinclair Pipeline Company 223
Sinclair, Harry 223, 224, 225, 226
Sloan and Pearce 352
Sloan, Alfred 230, 278
Sloan, Irene 278
Sloan, Sam 352
Smelters 101
Smith, Loyal 70
Smitten, Richard 70, 75, 283, 361
Snowden, Philip 314
Sobel, Robert 242
Spock, Benjamin 352
Squibb Building 349
St Louis Union Station 60
Standard Oil Company 95, 185
Stanley, Harold 5
Station Hotel 60
Stillman, James 108, 109, 116
Strakosch, Renee 360
Strong, Ben 111, 112
Sullivan, Dennis 77
Sullivan, Evelyn 362, 365

T

Teague, Merrill 43, 44
Teapot Dome 223, 224, 225, 261
Tennessee Coal & Iron (TC&I) 124, 126, 127, 128, 129
Thomas, Nancy 256, 257
Thomas, Ransom 115, 116
Thomas, Wendy 317
Thorne, Oakleigh 113
Time Magazine 256
Toomer, James 293
Townsend, Ralph 137
Triennial Episcopal Convention 109
Trust Company of America (TCA) 112, 113, 114, 115, 117, 128
Tuttle's 10

U

Union Pacific 75, 78, 79, 81, 90, 119
United Copper Company 105, 106, 129
United Press 311
United Steel Companies 309
US Congress 203
US Navy 223
US Steel 127, 128, 190, 228
US Treasury 121
Ussher, Dr 341, 342, 344

V

Van Emburgh & Atterbury 117
Vedder, Clyde 349
Venetia 145, 161, 173
Villeminia, Dr 4
Voit, Eugene 4
Volstead Act 279

W

W. W. Price 187
Wagner, Ernest 344
Waldorf Hotel 128, 330
Wall Street Journal 273, 305
Walmsley, W. F. 273
Walsh, Thomas 226
Warren & Wetmore 251
Washington Post 314, 315
Washington Star 187
Washington, George 9
Watts, Dickson G. 161
Webber, Wally 15
Weeks, John 363
Wendt, Dorothy 209, 210
Werner, Tom 5
West Indies 281
Western Union 40, 42, 43, 62
Wetmore, Charles 251, 252
Wheeling & Lake Erie Railroad 256, 271
Whipple, Sherman 201, 202
White House 127, 187, 201
White, William 273
Whitney, William 251
Williamson, Dan 168, 181
Wills, Dr 344
Wilson, Woodrow 188, 190, 193, 196, 201, 204, 246, 279, 296
Windsor Hotel 52

Wodehouse, P. G. 246
Woodlawn Cemetery 360
Woolf, Virginia 246
Woolsey, Federal Justice 336
World War I 193
World War II 362
Wright, Abner 43
Wyman, Dave 36

Y

Yale University 312

Z

Ziegfeld Follies 210, 211, 322
Ziegfeld Jr, Florenz 2, 208, 209, 210, 213
Zimmermann Telegram 193

JESSE LIVERMORE - BOY PLUNGER

JESSE LIVERMORE - BOY PLUNGER